Children and Youth on the Front Line

STUDIES IN FORCED MIGRATION

General Editors: Stephen Castles and Dawn Chatty

Children and Youth on the Front Line

ETHNOGRAPHY, ARMED CONFLICT AND DISPLACEMENT

Edited by

Jo Boyden and *Joanna de Berry*

Berghahn Books
New York • Oxford

First published in 2004 by

Berghahn Books

www.berghahnbooks.com

First paperback edition published in 2005.

Library of Congress Cataloging-in-Publication Data

Children and youth on the front line: ethnography, armed conflict, and displacement/
edited by Jo Boyden and Joanna de Berry.
p. cm. -- (Studies in forced migration ; v. 13)
ISBN 1-57181-883-9 (alk. paper) ISBN 1-84545-034-5 (pb: alk. paper)
1. Children and war. 2. Children--Relocation. 3. Children and
violence. 4. Child soldiers. 5. Child psychology. I. Boyden, Jo.
II. Berry, Joanna de. III. Series

HQ784.W3C535 2004
35.23--DC22   2004043378

British Library Cataloguing-in-Publication Data

A catalogue record for this book is available
from the British Library.

Printed in the United States on acid-free paper.
ISBN 1-57181-883-9 (hardback)
ISBN 1-84545-034-5 (paperback)

Contents

Acknowledgements

This book is the result of a collective process far beyond the editors and authors alone. Every chapter is based on and informed by personal conversations with children and young people, their parents and families, who know what it is to suffer the atrocities of war. Many of these remain nameless contributors in this volume, but every author would acknowledge the humbling privilege of meeting them. They have given freely of a lifetime of experience to affirm principles of strength in suffering and humanity in wartime. Deepest thanks are due to them.

Several of the chapters started as papers presented at the 'Children in Adversity' consultation, July 2000, which was hosted by the Refugee Studies Centre, University of Oxford and the Centre for Child-Focused Anthropological Research, Brunel University. The event was funded by The Department for International Development, The Canadian International Development Agency, UNICEF, The Bernard Van Leer Foundation, The Save the Children Alliance, The Andrew W. Mellon Foundation and the Queen Elizabeth House Oppenheimer Fund. Other chapters were presented initially at the 'Child Soldiers: An Anthropological Perspective' workshop June 2000, hosted by the Center for Child-Focused Anthropology Research, Brunel University and funded by the Diana, Princess of Wales Memorial Trust. In addition, the Andrew W. Mellon Foundation generously provided the funds that underpinned the work of compiling and editing the volume. We are very grateful to all of these organisations for the support and encouragement they have given us throughout.

Especial acknowledgements are due to Margaret Okole, Thomas Feeny, Jason Hart, Brian Pratt and Dawn Chatty for their comments on early drafts of the book, editorial advice and input. Margaret Okole in particular worked tirelessly to keep the editorial process going while several of the contributors were as far a field as Canada, Afghanistan, Sri Lanka, Mozambique, Sudan, East Timor and Tanzania.

Finally, we wish to thank Emmy Werner who has been a constant source of inspiration and guidance to us throughout the production of this volume and generously shared with us her wisdom and insight.

List of Acronyms

AFL	Armed Forces of Liberia
CDF	Congo Defence Force
CEH	Guatemalan Truth Commission
CRC	United Nations Convention on the Rights of the Child
DF	Female Detachment of FRELIMO (Destacamento Feminino)
FNLA	National Front for the Liberation of Angola
FRELIMO	Front for the Liberation of Mozambique
FRG	Guatemalan Republican Front
GUSCO	Gulu Support for Children Organisation
IDP	Internally displaced person
INGO	International Non-Governmental Organisation
INPFL	Independent National Patriotic Front of Liberia
IOM	International Organisation for Migration
KICWA	Kitgum Children's Welfare Association
KLA	Kosovo Liberation Army (also UCK)
LDF	Lofa Defence Force
LPC	Liberian Peace Council
LRA	Lord's Resistance Army
LTTW	Liberation Tigers of Tamil Eelam
LURD	Liberians United for Reconciliation and Democracy
MPLA	Popular Movement for the Liberation of Angola
NATO	North Atlantic Treaty Organisation
NGO	Non-Governmental Organisation
NPLF	National Patriotic Front of Liberia
NPP	National Patriotic Party
NRA	National Resistance Army
NRC	Norwegian Refugee Council
OAU	Organisation for African Unity
OCHA	Office for the Coordination of Humanitarian Affairs

OSCE	Organisation for Security and Cooperation in Europe
PEM	Protein energy malnutrition
PLO	Palestinian Liberation Organisation
PTSD	Post traumatic stress disorder
RENAMO	Mozambican National Resistance
SLORC	State Law and Order Restoration Council
TRC	Truth and Reconciliation Commission
ULIMO	United National Liberation Front of Liberia
ULIMO-J	ULIMO Johnson Branch
ULIMO-K	ULIMO Kromah Branch
UN	United Nations
UNDP	United Nations Development Programme
UNHCR	United Nations High Commissioner for Refugees
UNICEF	United Nations International Children's Emergency Fund
UNIFEM	United Nations Development Fund for Women
UNITA	National Union for the Total Independence of Angola
UNRWA	United Nations Relief and Works Agency
UPDA	Uganda People's Democratic Army
UPA	Uganda People's Army
WFP	World Food Programme

Introduction

Jo Boyden and Joanna de Berry

A Focus on War and Displacement

This book is about young people – children and adolescents – who have grown up with armed conflict, social upheaval and massive loss. As such, it bears testimony to the grim effects of warfare on the young. War leads not just to widespread death, but also to extensive displacement, overwhelming fear and economic devastation. It divides communities, destroys trust, weakens social ties, threatens household survival and undermines the family's capacity to care for its most vulnerable members. Every year it kills and maims countless numbers of young people, undermines thousands of others psychologically and deprives many of the economic, educational, health and social opportunities which most of us consider essential for children's effective growth and wellbeing.

During the course of the twentieth century there was a significant growth in the frequency of armed conflicts internationally. This has left a terrible legacy at the dawn of the twenty-first century, in which political hostilities have become firmly entrenched in many parts of the world. Most modern conflicts occur within states and are associated with extreme inequity in the distribution of resources; repressive and unjust governance; failed development; burgeoning black economies fuelled by the trade in arms and drugs; sectarian strife and other massively destabilising forces. One of the chief characteristics of this kind of warfare is that the elimination of civilians is the prime military objective, with civilian casualties rising sharply in recent conflicts as a proportion of the total (Machel 2000).

The fact that most modern hostilities are internal presents a special risk to young people. Fighting takes place in homes, fields and streets, and involves acts of extreme brutality and personal violence. The categories 'civilian' and 'combatant' are blurred, with children and youth, their families, neighbours and communities emerging as both victims and perpetrators. Because they are generally more agile, impressionable and expendable than adults, the young are actively recruited by many military units. Since they can carry, clean, reload and fire modern light arms with ease, the spread of small weapons in recent decades has exacerbated this trend. While many are engaged directly in combat, an even greater number are involved in ancillary functions, such as intelligence gathering, the delivery of food to the front line, road and bridge maintenance and repair, that are essential to the military endeavour. The distinction between civilian and combatant becomes especially confused with the prevalence of these kinds of quasi-military roles.

In such situations, children and adolescents are jeopardised not merely as random casualties but also because, as active agents of violence or members of military support teams, they are viewed as legitimate objects of attack. In addition, the political, criminal or military activities they engage in during war may bring them into conflict with the law, especially where emergency legislation is invoked. During flight or in post-conflict settings, involvement in such activities may result in denial of refugee status and exclusion from the benefits accruing to that status. Children are also vulnerable to atrocities because the mistreatment of the young undermines adult resistance: for example, children may be tortured, slaughtered or used as human shields to force parents to relinquish information. Finally, in the general climate of lawlessness and impunity that is so often associated with political conflict, many children are also exposed to raised levels of criminal violence. And as families come under increasing pressure from many different kinds of adversities, so children also become prone to greater domestic abuse.

Researching Young People in War

The War Literature

In recognition of the extent of civilian suffering globally and of the need to better understand the human consequences of severe adversity, there now exists a significant literature on young people affected by war and displacement (see, for example, Ayalon 1983; Djeddah and Shah 1996; Elbedour, et al. 1993; Gupta 2000; Hamilton and Man 1998; Hjern et al. 1991; Macksoud 1992; Magwaza et al. 1993; McHan 1985; Miller 1996; Sack et al. 1986; Ziv and Israeli 1973). Most of this literature is based on research conducted within the disciplines of medicine, psychiatry and psychology and adheres to a biomedical paradigm. Starting with the seminal work of Anne Freud and Dorothy Burlingham in the aftermath of the

Second World War, highlighting the catastrophic effects of war on the young has long been the central project of this research. The focus has been episodes of violence and loss – like shootings, torture, or forced migration – as such events are normally understood to be the defining feature of war. These events are conceptualised as antithetical to normal human experience, for their devastatingly destructive impact is felt not just at a personal and familial level but throughout society as a whole (Ager 1996: 16). Invoking the concept of trauma, assessing the prevalence of distressing psychological symptoms in affected populations and the diagnosis of disorders is the major objective of this enterprise. Many scholars confine themselves to assessment of prevalence of one particularly acute psychiatric condition, post-traumatic stress disorder (PTSD; see, for example, Kinzie et al. 1986; Magwaza et al. 1993; Nader and Pynoos 1993). PTSD was first distinguished as a syndrome in U.S. veterans of the Vietnam War and has subsequently been identified by the World Health Organisation as the most severe psychiatric disorder and primary stress resulting from a catastrophe.

In terms of how conflict affects the young, the accepted wisdom emerging from this kind of research is that the impact is resoundingly negative. Furthermore tenure this negative impact is seen as consistent; since it is generally thought that child development and wellbeing are based in biological and psychological structures that are fairly uniform across class and culture, children's responses are regarded as more or less the same everywhere. Much of the research also holds that the progression towards adulthood occurs in recognisable stages, early behaviours and experiences being causally related to subsequent developmental achievements. Therefore, it is posited that children exposed to stressful war events are prone not merely to traumatic reactions in both the shorter and longer term, but also to developmental impairment.

With regard to research methods, the notion that young people's responses are universally determined has justified the use of precoded research instruments, the majority of which have been developed in and imported from the minority industrialised world. These instruments are intended to quantify children's exposure to highly stressful incidents, whether as witnesses, victims, or perpetrators (see Garbarino and Kostelny 1996; Gupta 2000; Hjern et al. 1991; Willis and Gonzalez 1998), and gauge their psychological and emotional responses. Adverse effects on mental health are normally recorded through behaviour checklists or diagnostic questionnaires that list indicators of somatisation, behavioural and relationship problems, and/or psychological symptoms (Ahearn and Athey 1991; Gibbs and Boyden 1995). In most cases the informants are adults – parents, teachers or others presumed to be in close contact with children. The majority of studies are based on an extremely limited period of fieldwork; many rely solely on quantitative information, and often focus on children's responses to a single, acute episode of violence, separation or loss. Frequently, a single method is employed for assessing exposure to events and a second for measuring responses.

The war literature has produced an extremely consistent set of ideas, theories and results, many of which appear quite compelling. It chronicles the atrocities and physical, emotional and psychological effects of warfare. It provides important insights into young people's suffering and has raised awareness within academe, among aid and relief agencies and the general public as a whole, of some of their therapeutic, developmental and security needs. In many cases it has also had practical impact, having been employed in the planning and design of important interventions in health, education, psychosocial support and other areas.

Given the highly pernicious nature of conflict, it may seem self-evident that the dominant research focus on the psychopathological impacts on children is the most appropriate. Undoubtedly, some young people are overwhelmed emotionally and psychologically by such changes and by their exposure to highly stressful events: this is an important dimension of human experience that needs full exploration through research. Acknowledging this, the concept of trauma has become particularly pervasive in the literature. In some countries, the concept has even begun to influence public perception concerning not just major societal adversities but also random and far more minor incidents, like mass shootings or suicides, and major automobile or aircraft accidents. The power of the trauma model and other psychopathological paradigms is unquestionable. Nevertheless, fuller consideration of the assumptions that underlie such models brings into doubt the relevance and validity of some of the key findings.

An almost exclusive focus on intrapsychic functioning and impacts has certain adverse implications in terms of conceptualisation of the issues. It reflects the tendency of psychological and medical assessments to ignore the wider societal destruction that is associated with most conflicts. In this way, such studies have the effect of both pathologising the survivors of conflict and individualising a phenomenon that is in fact profoundly political. In most cases war is both causal in and consequent upon massive societal transformations; such transformations cannot be disregarded if research is to convey an effective understanding of the roots, nature and effects of armed conflict. War pervades all aspects of society, its institutions, political structures, culture, economy and communication systems. It does not just cause psychological and emotional harm, but also attacks the most fundamental conditions of sociality, endangering social allegiances and confidence, and drastically reducing social interaction and trust. To focus on individual reactions to highly stressful incidents is to lose sight of these important dimensions of conflict.

One can also take issue with prevalent research findings concerning the ways in which young people are affected by armed conflict. First, within the biomedical framework it is posited that a fairly mechanistic relationship exists between cause and effect: the young are exposed to and victims of a specific traumatic experience and suffer a disorder as a consequence of that experience. As indicated, such a framework generally omits important environmental and relational dimensions of people's lives, whereas in practice these are fundamental to the social integration, protection, care and development of the young. Even in the most stressful of situations, young people's psychological and emotional health, as much as their development, is heavily mediated by relationships with caregivers, peers and others, by access to services and availability of opportunities. In other words, the notion that a direct relation in mental health and development can be discerned between cause and effect is problematic. Different mediating factors come into play in different contexts and with different individuals, but the general point is that these factors can render the individual stronger or weaker, depending on the specific circumstances and context.

Second, medical investigations tend to yield an almost unitary representation of conflict that is bound neither by time nor context; a given percentage of children are exposed to a given range of experiences, with certain physical or mental consequences. In this way, children and adolescents are portrayed as the passive recipients of adult agency, the victims of wars waged by others and of brutality that is alien and imposed. Even when the young are researched in their role as combatants they are thought of as being divorced from the conditions and ideologies that produce and reproduce political violence. Personal volition is denied and emphasis given to their vulnerability and helplessness, to their abduction and forced conscription by brainwashing, treachery and deceit. The reality is more complex, in that some young people assume a voluntary role in combat even while others are abducted or otherwise cajoled into taking up arms. Moreover, children and adolescents can be very active in defining their own allegiances during conflict, as well as their own strategies for coping and survival. This implies that the prevailing dichotomy between adult as active perpetrator and child as passive victim needs challenging.

Third, psychiatric assessments that focus on traumatic reactions tend to overlook the broader range of attitudinal, emotional, developmental and behavioural effects in children and adolescents – the formation and maintenance of moral values, social competencies and a sense of self-efficacy, for example. Young people's experiences of war are far more diverse, subtle and complex than is implied by models that focus solely on individualised, traumatic responses to violent events.

A fourth concern is that a-historical analyses belie evidence that war is normally experienced as an ongoing, continuous phenomenon whose effects persist long after actual combat has ceased. The suffering of war is not contained in a single traumatic episode, or even a multiplicity of such episodes, but in a complex interplay of detrimental circumstances that endure and change over time (Cairns 1996; Ressler et al. 1992). Indeed, while it is true that certain experiences – such as rape, death and separation from family – have a high potential to overwhelm young people psychologically in any situation or context, it is not self-evident that isolated events of acute stress always have the greatest psychological impact (Garbarino and Kostelny 1996: 33). The culmination of stress in a long-term chronic situation can be most detrimental to psychological and emotional wellbeing.

A fifth issue has to do with the cultural specificity of biomedicine as an interpretative model and in particular with the notion of post-traumatic stress disorder, which originated in a specific country and set of historical circumstances. Several critics have questioned whether such a diagnostic tool, so firmly rooted in a specific psychiatric tradition, is appropriate for universal use, and many have argued for greater recognition of cultural understandings of misfortune, health and healing.

Sixth, due to the persistence of theories of child development that rely heavily on universal biological and psychological processes, differences of culture, social power and identity tend to be underplayed in much of the orthodox research on young people in war. Hence, paradoxically, mental health research that is designed to measure the impacts of conflict through individual responses has the effect of concealing major personal and social distinctions between individual children. The tendency to study children as an undifferentiated category disregards recent evidence from social science research that social status is a major determinant of childhood survival and wellbeing. It also ignores recent child development research that reaches beyond the commonalities of the human condition to highlight also major individual differences between the young. These differences arise from a combination of genetic heritage and personal agency and from the interaction of these two forces with and within a specific set of historical, social and cultural circumstances.

Shifting the Paradigm

There remain major gaps in understanding and knowledge and major methodological challenges in relation to young people's engagement with war. Despite some significant advances, scholarship has yet to capture the true magnitude, nature or effects of such experiences. There is a serious dearth of systematic empirical information, especially concerning long-term outcomes. There is immense scope for the development and refinement of research with war-affected and displaced children and adolescents. Further investigation is essential to balance the weight of research that has so far focused on the impact of war on mental health with work that looks at, for example, how political conflict affects adolescents' economic and social roles and integration, and its effect on gender relations, power within childhood and intergenerational relations. More research is essential also to understanding why children take up arms, what are their sources of emotional and social support and their strategies for survival and coping. Studies are needed to illuminate how children in different cultures perceive suffering, misfortune, healing and recovery, and the formation of their political and ideological commitments.

The present volume, which is driven mainly by anthropological theory and ethnographic methods, as opposed to medical or psychological paradigms, aims to complement the existing research with new findings and insights as well as to provide very different perspectives on many of the key issues. With an explicit focus on the narratives of young people, the chapters draw largely on the ethnographic literature and on first-hand accounts of conflict-affected populations in Guatemala, Liberia, Sri Lanka, Burma, Mozambique, Uganda, Jordan, Kosovo and Angola. Because the chapters in the collection are based mainly on detailed ethnographic research over extended periods, the events to which young people have been exposed are placed in a longer-term biographical context. This makes it possible to go beyond the immediate aftermath of a crisis and obtain a sense of its changing impact on and meaning for young people over time. Indeed, many of the research subjects whose stories form the heart of the book are young adults who have been asked to reflect on their past experiences as children living through war or displacement.

The collection warns us, first and foremost, against simplistic assumptions about children's reactions to conflict, suggesting that while it is difficult to exaggerate the horrors of war, it is quite possible to overuse concepts such as trauma. Young people's responses to war are revealed as multifaceted and nuanced; age is not necessarily the critical determinant of vulnerability, and even when profoundly distressed or troubled, the young frequently exercise remarkable resilience. In addition to the atrocities, the authors describe the aspirations and hopes, successes and achievements of young people and their ingenious survival strategies. Even when confronted by appalling adversities, it is revealed that many are able to influence positively their own fate and that of others who depend on them, such as younger siblings, sick parents, or their own children. The overwhelming lesson is that war does not inevitably destroy all that it touches, and that while war causes many to become extremely vulnerable, vulnerability does not in itself preclude ability.

At the same time, context is found to play a critical role in shaping personal responses to war and considerable space in the collection is given over to discussion of the material, social structural and ideational conditions that frame young people's experiences of adversity. Thus, reflection on children's condition, on their ideas, feelings and ways of coping with conflict, is closely juxtaposed with analysis of the broader ideological and structural transformations associated with war. Social constructs like child, youth and family, and practices in child rearing and childcare come to acquire new meanings and functions. As the circumstances and contributions of children and adults, girls and boys, and men and women are altered, so are the definitions and expectations of childhood, youth, adulthood, girlhood, boyhood and other social categories. Many young people assume proto-adult roles within the home and on the battlefield. Alterations in status, role and circumstance are found to have fundamental implications for survival and for self-perception, identity and adaptation during and following war.

By building the empirical evidence on the testimonies of young people who have lived through war and displacement, the volume favours an emic over an etic perspective. This entails a shift in research emphasis from the measurement of universal signs and symptoms of psychological and emotional distress towards reflection and analysis of subjective understandings and meanings. Populations exposed to war and displacement commonly have a heightened need to interpret, understand and explain the extraordinary events to which they have been exposed. In this volume, considerable weight is given to such cultural narratives of war, which are revealed as invoking culturally endorsed codes of conduct and powerful symbols of loyalty and belonging. These cultural narratives enable groups involved in conflict to define themselves as distinct from others, providing them with their own particular histories, and locating them in relation to key military and political processes and events. Often they assign individuals to the category of perpetrator or victim, thereby establishing culpability and innocence in relation to atrocities committed. In some cases they can even provide mechanisms for forgiveness and redemption that may promote social healing and reconciliation when conflict has ceased.

Researching young people's experiences of conflict and displacement requires considerable attention to methodological issues and some dexterity in the application of methods. And yet the literature in this field is rather deficient, for aside from occasional bland descriptions of research instruments and brief accounts of how statistics are compiled and analysed, very few scholars explore the methods used or obstacles encountered in the field. The emphasis on young people's narratives in this volume brings to the fore issues of research methodology, methods and ethics. Several authors point to the need for innovation in this area, since it is argued that precoded instruments such as questionnaires and symptom checklists cannot capture the true nature of war experiences or their meanings for affected populations. Attention is paid to the shifting, ambiguous and elusive nature of evidence in the context and aftermath of war, and to the special difficulties of conducting research with young people who are marginalised both socially and politically and whose views are overlooked by the powers that be.

Finally, as the collection questions accepted wisdom regarding family, children, childhood, adolescence and young people's involvement in war, so it highlights the implications for policy and practice. Clear indications are given of the need for review and change of objectives, approaches and strategies in humanitarian and other forms of provision for young people caught up in conflict. Perhaps the greatest of these suggestions raised in the volume is the acknowledgement that children and young people can and do reflect upon their own experiences of conflict. Too often programmes for war-affected children are dictated by adults' perceptions of the impact of war on young people. This volume is a powerful testimony to the ability of young people to analyse their past troubles and present concerns. Starting from children's and young people's definitions of constraints and opportunities is an important step in devising policy and programmes based upon a lived rather than theorised reality.

The Structure of the Volume

The collection has been divided into six sections with the intention of grouping the chapters according to the major issue(s) addressed by each one. The structure is as follows.

The Contexts of War

The book begins with contributions by Gillian Mann and Victor Igreja, both of whom challenge notions about the universality of human responses to adversity and emphasise how social and cultural context plays a critical role in framing the effects of war on children. Mann examines the literature on children separated from their families, decrying the tendency to research what she terms 'the generic child' and to ignore differences of status within childhood. In her view social distinctions such as gender, ethnicity and religious affiliation play a fundamental part in defining children's experiences of family separation and shaping the meanings they give to these experiences. She stresses the importance of social and cultural constructions of family and childhood, theories of child development and the nature of childcare practices in different communities in influencing children's understandings of and responses to events in their lives.

Writing about the Gorongosa region of Mozambique, Igreja's chapter has a similar focus in that it emphasises the cultural norms and social relations through which children experience armed conflict. He shows how prolonged exposure to civil war and drought in the region deprived the people of Gorongosa of vital social and cultural resources that had given meaning to their existence and allowed expression of their collective identity. The conflict created profound discontinuities within the family, with extremely serious consequences for the very young. In particular, key life-regulating rituals and cultural mechanisms of infant care were disrupted, threatening infant wellbeing and survival to a degree that could not be explained simply by poverty or food scarcity. By highlighting the devastating social and cultural consequences of conflict, Igreja intends to critique orthodox psychological research that confines itself to intrapsychic functioning and psychopathological outcomes.

In these chapters there are significant insights for aid policies and interventions, the most notable being the need to guard against unwarranted assumptions of children's needs based on globalised understanding of family and child. But they also diverge in certain important respects. Hence, Mann explores the ethnographic evidence from many different societies and finds that in communities where delegated parenting is the norm, child-rearing tasks are shared among a large family group. She challenges accepted views about the interdependence between parents and offspring and stresses the positive reinforcement – emotional and practical – which children gain from intimate relationships with siblings and peers. Igreja, on the other hand, is concerned with the exclusivity of the maternal–infant bond and pinpoints it as the key cultural resource in the care and survival of very young children. Similarly, while Mann calls for child protection measures to be built around local beliefs and practices, Igreja warns that these practices may be irretrievably disrupted and distorted in war and may therefore not serve children at all well.

Vulnerability and Resilience among Adolescent Girls

In the chapters by Joanna de Berry and Aisling Swaine with Thomas Feeny, the wartime experiences of adolescent girls are analysed. De Berry focuses on young girls who lived in government settlement camps during the 1987 to 1992 civil war in the Teso region of north-east Uganda. Exploring the social relationships, structures and strategies that operate during conflict, she highlights the girls' vulnerability to grave sexual violations, arguing that the investigation of sexual abuse requires a critical examination of the specific ways in which people become and are made vulnerable in the context in which they live. Vulnerability is not an inherent characteristic of adolescent girls, she maintains, but was in this case a direct consequence of the pattern of social life that evolved in the camps. Nor was the vulnerability of these young women all-encompassing and permanent, since their testimonies reveal that even while experiencing great sadness and pain they showed immense courage during the conflict and remarkable resilience in its aftermath.

Swaine and Feeny write about the wartime recollections of two groups of adolescent girls, both Albanian Kosovars. One group was based in a refugee camp in Albania and the second had also been displaced but by the time of the field research had returned to Kosovo. The authors argue that the wartime experiences of adolescent girls can only be understood by recognising their status as a specific social category circumscribed by gender, ethnicity and generation. The suggestion is that even though adolescents have certain developmental competencies that separate them from children, they lack the social and personal attributes that define adulthood. Moreover, in the patriarchal context of Albanian Kosovar society, unmarried adolescent girls have very particular susceptibilities and experience conflict in ways that are quite distinct from other social groups. Due to the war there was greater risk of sexual violence and fewer societal mechanisms for protecting girls against it. Yet at the same time in Kosovar society it is not thought appropriate for girls to provide for their own protection, and this constituted an additional source of risk for young girls during the conflict.

Both chapters argue that marriage is valued socially as a means of protecting adolescent girls against sexual violation, whilst also showing that the girls themselves perceive such matters rather differently. In their view, early and/or arranged marriages can lead to new difficulties and suffering and living independently may have greater advantages. This highlights how, despite their evident vulnerability and the tenuous support from the wider community these girls retain an ability to analyse their circumstances, activate their own definitions and choices, make meaning, define action and shape the environment in which they live. Indeed, the powerful stories told in the chapters disclose the complex way in which human frailty interacts with human courage and ingenuity during adversity. They also stress how some of the greatest threats to the wellbeing of the young are due not to enemy action but to the behaviour of kin, neighbours or other members of their own community who are driven by self-interest and/or complicity with adversaries.

What is a Child?

It is now a fairly well established axiom of sociology and anthropology that childhood and youth are social rather than biological constructs. The chapters by Jessica Schafer, Harry West and Andrew Mawson all demonstrate how readily and effectively such constructs may be manipulated during conflict to serve political or military ends, with important implications for post-conflict social reintegration and for aid policy and practice.

Writing about Mozambique – although concerning themselves with different historical periods, cultural regions and combatant groups – Schafer and West both explore the ideological basis for young people's engagement in warfare. They are critical of orthodox scholarship in this field and especially the premise that young combatants undergo a process of coercion, brutalisation and desocialisation to reach a state in which violence is normalised. West argues instead for the importance of revolutionary ideology in moulding the experience of female combatants, whereas Schafer speaks of patriarchal modelling. In fact, for the young fighters studied by Schafer violence was not even the most devastating aspect of war; many of them found separation from family far more painful. Appropriating Shona patriarchal imagery and casting the troops as children and leaders as fathers, the RENAMO forces filled this void and ensured filial loyalty and discipline through a system of 're-socialisation' using concepts of substitute kinship. West emphasises how the heroic images of the Front for the Liberation of Mozambique (FELIMO) Destacamento Feminino had a compelling influence on young girls, acting as a powerful incentive to their recruitment. With a clear view of their political role, the 'girls with guns' who feature in his chapter were not inducted into mindless violence but acted as central players in the historical drama that defined their times. The implication of West's chapter is that young people are not merely the passive receptors of adult ideas. In fact, in war children may be at the forefront of value formation and attitudinal change, while adults – less able to accommodate and overcome the many shocks and losses they have undergone – sometimes cling to idealised notions of the past.

Mawson's chapter on northern Uganda reflects on some of the dilemmas that can arise when societies and states try to resolve what to do about children who have committed atrocities during conflict. He contends that in this context different actors – local, national and international – had very different agendas and that these were negotiated in the development of a system of justice. These negotiations involved reconciling differing concepts of who is a child and differing ideas about what constitutes culpability and responsibility. Hence, Mawson's concern is less with how social constructions of childhood influence children's experiences of war, than with how this particular social construction was used in Uganda as a means of facilitating reconciliation and peace. He describes how in a conflict that involves abduction and conscription and brings people of the same ethnic group into confrontation with each other, the Acholi notion of childhood as a life phase free of moral responsibility is used to grant impunity to perpetrators of violence, both children and adults. A highly inclusive conceptualisation of the social category of child, in which many adult perpetrators are also incorporated, facilitates an extremely tolerant and liberal approach to justice. As such, the chapter emphasises the potential disjunction between international and local norms and standards in relation to both childhood and justice.

Children's Narratives

We have stated that in this volume the central empirical evidence is drawn from the narratives of children and young people who have experienced conflict and displacement. However, there are many difficulties associated with recording and interpreting the testimonies of young people affected by such adversities. One of the major challenges is the elusive nature of children's war testimonies. The chapters by Krisjon Rae Olson and Jason Hart explore the personal, social and political contexts in which children's narratives are not only constructed and represented but also modified and repressed. They describe situations in which the dominant cultural narrative of war provides an absolute truth that transcends all other versions of events, whilst also offering an overarching explanation of history. In this kind of context the voices and accounts of powerless groups generally become marginalised, the meta-narratives of war thereby undermining a real historical understanding of children. Hence, Olson argues that the settlement of thirty-six years of civil strife in Guatemala involved concealing children's experiences of violence within a master chronicle constructed by the Guatemalan Truth Commission. Similarly, Hart's chapter on Palestinian refugee children in Jordan deals with the suppression of young people's accounts by both nationalist and international interests that seek to promote a monolithic and seamless story of the Palestinian refugee experience.

Also emerging from these chapters is an important discussion of how children internalise, give meaning to and resist adult discourse and in particular how they reconcile their everyday experiences with adult interpretations of war events. Olson argues that taking children's voices seriously means acknowledging their active participation in social life, their engagement with the war and their suffering, which continues in the aftermath of conflict. Children in Santa María Nebaj, in the department of Quiché, are not only denied the refuge of social history, she suggests, but their consciousness of the atrocities and injustices of the past implies long term habituation to violence and loss. Hence her disturbing assertion about the necessary complicity of those who survive war in its violence.

Researching children who make up the third generation in a refugee population, Hart is not concerned with children's involvement in armed violence so much as their constructions of identity. He highlights how children negotiate the demands of parents and other adults who, as in many war-affected communities, are particularly insistent upon the conformity of the young to norms and values that are considered as defining their collective identity. Drawing upon the array of information and cultural material available, children demonstrate inherent creativity in fashioning identities which demonstrate their specificity as a generation. It is suggested that children and adults commonly reformulate identity and meaning in their lives in fundamentally different ways. This may be one of the abiding legacies of conflict and displacement, producing a serious generational divide and thereby the potential for intergenerational strife.

Research Methodology and Methods

The central contribution of the chapters by Mats Utas, Carola Eyber and Alastair Ager, and Jo Boyden has to do with methodology and methods, which they maintain play a fundamental role in shaping research findings. Eyber and Ager, whose chapter draws on research in Angola with former combatants in the town of Lubango and in centres for the internally displaced in Huila province, demonstrate this point graphically by comparing findings arrived at through use of a series of contrasting methodologies and methods. The application of psychometric instruments yielded a diagnosis in which a significant percentage of these young people appeared to be traumatised – indeed, they were found to be suffering from a severe psychiatric condition, post traumatic stress disorder. Information derived from observation, focus group discussions and other participatory methods, however, revealed that the youths were astute analysts of their situation, fully engaged in income generating activities, sustaining relationships and functioning quite effectively in many other ways besides. The disparity in these findings leads the authors to highlight the inadequacy of a methodology based in the trauma discourse and of methods built on predetermined ideas about the nature of risk and response in populations exposed to massive societal disruptions. It also leads them to call for the use of participatory methods as the best means of gaining insight not only into the issues young people define as difficulties but also into their coping strategies and strengths.

Utas writes about fieldwork conducted with a group of young former combatants living in an abandoned factory in Monrovia, Liberia's capital. He examines the art of relationship building, highlighting the delicate and changeable association between ethnographer and research subject. The particular focus is on issues of truth and trust, the argument being that truth is bound by context and relationship and that in the volatile world of homeless and socially ostracised youth, trust, which is hard earned, is easily lost. In his discussion of methods, research based on rapid assessments and interviews, and research which is reliant on aid agencies for access to its subjects is found wanting. The grounds are that this kind of research yields standardised responses in victim modes and masks nuances of lived experience that may in practice be extremely meaningful to respondents. With its attention to the question of how researchers work with highly sensitive information and how they manage personal safety and the safety of their subjects, the chapter also touches on a range of important ethical issues.

Drawing mainly on fieldwork in Burma and Sri Lanka, the chapter by Boyden highlights some of the major methodological, practical and ethical challenges and dilemmas associated with ethnographic research with war-affected populations. She questions the role of research in the reporting of human suffering, describing the difficulty scholars confront when access to respondents is mediated by security forces who have a vested interest in controlling civilians, and when research findings are a potential source of intelligence information. She argues that while the research process depends on trust, in communities that have been embroiled in conflict this can be an extremely rare commodity. Under such circumstances research may create a disjunction with reality. She maintains that legitimate protection concerns arising from children's involvement in research can override important considerations regarding their political consciousness, development and activism. Addressing children's responses to misfortune, she stresses the need for methodological innovation and the use of interpretive models that are sensitive to culture. The piece ends with a call for ethical codes that respect children's political and social competencies.

Agendas for the Future

On the basis of her extensive experience in this field, Pamela Reynolds sketches out a research agenda for the future in her concluding chapter to the volume and proposes some of the most critical questions for further investigation and analysis. She interprets the child soldier phenomenon largely in terms of an international model of exploitation and oppression and reminds us of the profound personal risks for young people that may be associated with their co-option into cultures of violence. It is her core contention that children are central to the whole business of warfare, for adults become deeply reliant on their many and varied contributions during times of political strife. Thus, the young black activists in South Africa that she refers to played a critical part in the struggle against a deeply unjust and harsh regime.

Reynolds urges us to remember that seeking to explore and understand the impact of war on the young is not the same as to condone. In delving into the effects of relationships, social structures and cultural mechanisms that operate in war, in looking for order, explanation and resilience during conflict, we should not ignore the fact that for all the children and young people mentioned in this volume, life will never be the same again and theirs is a life marred by the most terrible of suffering. Indeed, a fuller understanding of what it means to be born into and grow up in wartime should only serve to strengthen a resolve to protect children and young people in conflict. The seeds of protection appear in all the chapters in this volume: protection given by cultural norms, by creative narrative, self-protection, the protection of friends, family and community, rebuilding protection in the light of peace, ethical protection.

Often broken, often damaged, weakened and changed, the personal and social resources for the protection of children in conflict nonetheless remain. The challenge now is how to move from better understanding of such resources into practice: the practice of using, rebuilding and restoring what preserves and gives hope for the many hundreds of thousands of children living through war. Children who will today wake up and hear the sound of gunfire, run from a battlefield, cry for a lost friend, be separated from home and family and wonder how they will ever make sense of what they are living through.

References

Ager, A. 1996. 'Children, War and Psychological Intervention.' In S. Carr and J. Schumaker, eds, *Psychology and the Developing World*. Westport: Praeger.

Ahearn, F. and Athey, J. eds, 1991. *Refugee Children Theory, Research and Services*. Baltimore and London: Johns Hopkins University Press.

Allen, T. 1989. 'Violence and Moral Knowledge: Observing Social Trauma in Sudan and Uganda'. *Cambridge Anthropology* Vol. 13, No. 2, 45–66.

Ayalon, O. 1983. 'Coping with Terrorism.' In S. Breznitz. ed., *Stress in Israel*. New York: Van Nostrand Reinhold Co.

Bracken, P. 1998. 'Hidden Agendas: Deconstructing Post Traumatic Stress Disorder', in Bracken, P. and Petty, C. 1998. *Rethinking the Trauma of War*. London/New York: Save the Children, Free Association Books.

Cairns, E. 1996. *Children and Political Violence*. Oxford: Blackwell.

Colson, E. 1989. 'Overview'. *Annual Review of Anthropology* 18, 1–16.

Davis, J. 1992. 'The Anthropology of Suffering'. *Journal of Refugee Studies* 5 (2), 149–161.

Dawes, A. and Donald, D. 1994. 'Understanding the Psychological Consequences of Adversity'. In Dawes and Donald, eds, *Childhood and Adversity; Psychological Perspectives from South African Research*. Capetown and Johannesburg, David Philip, 1–27.

Djeddah, C. and Shah, P. 1996. 'The Impact of Armed Conflict on Children: a threat to Public Health.' Geneva: WHO, Family and Reproductive Health and the Division of Emergency and Humanitarian Action, June.

Elbedour, S., Bensel, R. and Bastien, D. 1993. 'Ecological Integrated Model of Children of War: Individual and Social Psychology.' *Child Abuse and Neglect* 17: 805–19.

Elwart, G. 'Conflict, anthropological perspectives' forthcoming IESBS p1—printout Smith 1951.

Garbarino, J. and Kostelny, K. 1996. 'What do we Need to Know to Understand Children in War and Community Violence?' In R. Apfel and B. Simon, eds, *Minefields in their Hearts: the Mental Health of Children in War and Communal Violence*. New Haven and London: Yale University Press.

Gibbs, S. and Boyden, J. 1995. *Children Affected by Organised Violence: An Annotated Bibliography*. Stockholm: Rädda Barnen.

Gorden, D. 1988. '2 Tenacious Assumptions of Western Medicine'. In Lock, M. and Gorden, D. eds, *Biomedicine Examined*, Kluwer Academic Publishers, 19–56.

Gupta, L. 2000. 'Psychological Assessment of Displaced Children Exposed to War Related Violence in Sierra Leone.' Freetown: Plan International, February.

Hamilton, C. and Man, N. 1998. 'The Impact of Armed Conflict on Children in Kosovo.' Report of the Children and Armed Conflict Unit, University of Essex, www2.essex.ac.uk/papersandreports/kosreport.htm.

Hjern, A., Angel, B. and Höjer, B. 1991. 'Persecution and Behavior: a Report of Refugee Children from Chile.' *Child Abuse and Neglect* 15: 239–48.

Kinzie, J., Sack, W., Angell, R., Manson, S. and Rath, B. 1986. 'The Psychiatric Effects of Massive Trauma on Cambodian Children: I. The Children. II. The Family, the Home and the School.' *Journal of the American Academy of Child Psychiatry* 25 (3): 370–85.

LeVine, P. 1999. 'Assessing "Detachment" Patterns and Contextual Trauma Across Cultures (Trauma Detachment Grid)'. Seminar, Refugee Studies Programme, University of Oxford, 3 June.

Machel, G. 2000. *The Machel Review 1996–2000: a Critical Analysis of Progress Made and Obstacles Encountered in Increasing Protection for War-Affected Children.* UNIFEM, UNICEF, NORAD, CIDA.

Macksoud, M.S. 1992. 'Assessing War Trauma in Children: a Case Study of Lebanese Children.' *Journal of Refugee Studies* 5 (1): 1–15.

Magwaza, A., Killian, B., Peterson, I. and Pillay, Y. 1993. 'The Effects of Chronic Violence on Pre-School Children Living in South African Townships.' *Child Abuse and Neglect* 17: 795–803.

McHan, E.J. 1985. 'Imitation of Aggression by Lebanese Children.' *Journal of Social Psychology* 125 (5): 613–17.

Miller, K.E. 1996. 'The Effects of State Terrorism and Exile on Indigenous Guatemalan Refugee Children: a Mental Health Assessment and Analysis of Children's Narratives.' *Child Development* 67: 89–106.

Mollica, R.D. et al. n.d. 'Repatriation and Disability: a community study of health, mental health and social functioning of the Khmer residents of site II. Vol I: Khmer adults. Vol II: Khmer Children (12–13 years of age).' Mimeo, Harvard Program in Refugee Trauma, Harvard School of Public Health and the World Federation of Mental Health.

Montgomery, E. 1992. 'Psychology Effects Torture on Adults, Children and family Relationships.' Paper presented at a course on mental health of children exposed to violent environments. Refugee Studies Programme, University of Oxford, 6–10 January.

Nader, K. and Pynoos, R. 1993. 'The Children of Kuwait after the Gulf Crisis.' In E. Leavitt and N. Fox, eds, *Psychological Effects of War and Violence on Children.* New Jersey: Erlbaum Associate Publishers.

Nir, Y. 1985. 'Children Traumatized by Central American Warfare.' In S. Eth and R. Pynoos, eds, *Traumatic Stress Disorder in Children.* Washington DC: American Psychiatric Press.

Ressler, E., Tortorici, J. and Marcelino, A. 1992. *Children in Situations of Armed Conflict: a Guide to the Provision of Services.* New York and Geneva: UNICEF.

Sack, W., Angell, R., Kinsie, D. and Rath, B. 1986. 'The Psyhiatric Effects of Massive Trauma on Cambodian Children II. The Family, the Home and the School.' *Journal of the American Academy of Child Psychiatry* 25 (3): 377–83.

Willis, G. and Gonzalez, A. 1998. 'Methodological Issues in the use of Survey Questionnaires to Assess the Health Effects of Torture.' *Journal of Nervous and Mental Disease* 1896 (5): 283–9.

Ziv, A. and Israeli, R. 1973. 'Effects of Bombardment on the Manifest Anxiety Level of Children living in Kibbutzim.' *Journal of Consultant Clinical Psychology* 40: 287–91.

Part I

The Contexts of War

1

Separated Children

CARE AND SUPPORT IN CONTEXT

Gillian Mann

Introduction

It is currently estimated that approximately one in every three-hundred children around the world is displaced by war and political violence (Machel 2000). This amounts to at least twenty million children, approximately one million of whom have been separated from their families (Djeddah n.d.). In Rwanda alone, by the end of 1994, more than 100,000 children had become orphaned or had lost contact with their parents as a direct result of the war (Machel 1996). The numbers in other countries are equally high: it is estimated that by 1992 the war in Mozambique had left nearly 200,000 separated children, and in 1995, a UNICEF study found that 20 percent of Angolan children had been separated from their parents and relatives as a result of the country's long-standing civil war (Garbarino et al. 1991). Moreover, recent UNHCR estimates indicate that at any one time, there may be up to 100,000 separated children in Western Europe alone (UNHCR 2001). Today large numbers of children around the world continue to be displaced from their families and communities as a result of armed conflict. Difficulties with definitions and with data collection have meant that the problem is probably larger than these statistics indicate.

In recent years these astonishing statistics have captured the attention of the international community. The plight of war-affected children, and separated children in particular, has become an issue of growing concern for governments and donor agencies worldwide. While the phenomenon of parent–child separation in times of crisis is not new (Ressler et al. 1988), in modern conflicts increasing numbers of children have become separated from their families (Petty and Jareg 1998; Rousseau et al. 1998). This situation may be due in part to the increasing impact of war on civilian populations and the heightening of associated risks, particularly for people in the developing world, where many communities have been terrorised by indiscriminate attacks, killing, abduction, rape, forced recruitment and other atrocities (Petty and Jareg 1998). Coupled with the devastation of subsistence agriculture and rural infrastructure, these threats have weakened the coping capacities of families and communities, thereby increasing the likelihood of parent–child separation.

Most people believe that family unity is essential for child survival in wartime. Without their parents or carers to protect them, children may be especially vulnerable to abuse, exploitation, abduction, hunger, malnutrition, disease and death. Recognition of these serious risks to children's physical and psychological wellbeing has led academics, practitioners and policymakers to consider those children who live without their families to be among the most vulnerable groups of war-affected populations. Efforts to protect separated children have thus become a priority for intervening agencies.

Despite a significant body of theoretical work on the subject, not enough is known about the impact of family separation on children. What is known about separation tends to be general in nature, referring mostly to the vulnerability of children of different ages while failing to account for the differences in experience between boys and girls, and children in different cultural and family contexts. The purpose of this chapter is to identify some of the shortcomings of the existing literature on family separation and to argue that these shortcomings arise from a failure to consider the role of context in shaping the meaning of family separation for children. Consideration of social and cultural constructions of family and childhood, theories of child development, and the nature of childcare practices in different communities can provide crucial information about the particular circumstances of children's lives and the cultural norms and values that have shaped their development. These contextual elements therefore play an important role in shaping the meaning children make of the various events in their life, including family separation.

Who are 'Separated Children'?

'Separated children' is a generic term used to describe children who have come to live apart from their parents, usually as a result of war or natural disaster (Tolfree 1995). The United Nations High Commissioner for Refugees (UNHCR) defines 'separated children' as those individuals 'under 18 years of age who are separated from both parents or from their previous legal or customary primary caregiver' (UNHCR 2000).

In the context of war, the economic, instrumental and emotional roles of children are often disrupted and children can become separated from their parents in a number of different ways. These include becoming lost while fleeing from attacks on villages, trying to escape forced recruitment into military service, or simply searching for food. Parents may die while travelling or fleeing, they may be killed, or they may abandon children because they or the child are too weak to continue. Some parents leave their children at a hospital or camp, believing their chances of survival are better if left in the care of others. Others send their children away, in the hope that they will escape danger and reach asylum in a neighbouring country. Some children choose to leave their families in order to gain employment, to fight in the war, to reduce the financial burden on their parents, to seek safety or to escape abuse. Many separated children have not chosen to be apart from their parents; rather, war has made it unavoidable for them. In many cases, separation can be a wrenching and difficult experience for both the parents and the child.

Boys and girls of all ages become separated as a result of war and other emergencies. However, the literature says that significantly more boys become separated than do girls (Ashabranner and Ashabranner 1987; Baker 1982; Ressler et al. 1988). The reasons for this disparity are not entirely understood. It is nevertheless argued that in many cultures, boys are believed to be best able to look after and protect themselves, particularly in wartime. This belief may lead parents to make a conscious decision to send their sons away, or boys themselves may decide to leave in order to escape to safety or to pursue new opportunities. The predominance of separated boys may also reflect the social construction of gender roles in most cultures, where girls are more likely to remain with their parents in order to support them in their domestic and child rearing tasks.

While these reasons may be true, they do not on their own provide a satisfactory explanation for why more boys become separated than do girls. Evidence from other sources suggests that in many societies, families accord a higher value to male offspring. The growing body of research on child labour, for example, suggests that large numbers of girls live apart from their families in order to work in the sex trade and in domestic service, among other types of employment. The fact that more boys have been found to be separated than girls may reflect the reality that most research with separated children has taken place in the public sphere, and in most places, girls are more likely to be found in the private, domestic sphere of the household. Their existence may therefore not be readily apparent to researchers, programme designers and policy makers. Furthermore, large numbers of girls 'disappear' through trafficking and may not be accounted for in statistics or research. It is therefore worth questioning the assumption or apparent truth that a large majority of separated children are boys.

Understanding the Impact of Separation

Academic interest in the wellbeing of separated children began during the Second World War, when large numbers of children were evacuated from England and other war-affected countries of Western Europe in the early 1940s. At the time, psychologists such as Anna Freud and Dorothy Burlingham (1943) began to study the behaviour of evacuated children in order to understand the psychological consequences of physical separation from their mothers. They found convincing evidence that separation from mothers was more traumatic for children than was exposure to bombings and the death, destruction and injury associated with air raids. These findings asserted the critical role of mothers (and other family members) in the maintenance of children's health and wellbeing and provided the basic framework within which parent–child separation has been understood by scholars to date, including the highly influential work of both John Bowlby (1973) and Mary Ainsworth (1967). Current understandings of the psychological needs of separated children, the consequences of separation for children and the factors for consideration in their care and placement have all been informed by these early studies.

Among both scholars and practitioners, it is widely believed that children who become separated from their families face profound physical and psychological risks. The literature argues that at all times, and particularly during situations of armed conflict and political violence, parental care provides children with an essential measure of physical protection and emotional security (Werner 1990). For children who are attempting to cope with chronic danger and stress, the love, care and affection parents provide is said to be integral to a child's sense of personal security and thus to the development of individual resiliency (Werner). It is argued that for those children who cannot access these relationships, separation can have a devastating social and psychological impact (Garbarino and Kostelny 1996).

This view of the impact of family separation on children is firmly rooted in dominant understandings of child development, which argue that secure attachment relationships with adults are central to a child's social and emotional development. The idea that the mother is the primary caregiver to her child is implicit in much of this research, as is the notion that the mother–child dyad is the most important relationship in a child's life. That these attachments are strongest within the nuclear family is a tacit, yet clear view expressed in the majority of the literature. These assumptions may be true in certain contexts, but in many societies childcare is a social enterprise in which children have multiple caretakers and experience exclusive maternal care only in the first few months of life (Harkness and Super 1992; Leiderman and Leiderman 1977; Nsamenang 1992b; Weisner 1984). In this context, parenting can be seen as an aggregate of services, sometimes provided by one or two parents, and other times provided by a series of different people at different times in a child's life. From this perspective, the term 'maternal behaviour' cannot be defined as 'that which is done by the mother' (Goldberg 1977).

Certainly no one would dispute the vital role that loving parents play in guaranteeing the survival and healthy development of their children. Parents who nurture their children, provide for them economically, and support them to develop into competent and confident individuals help to equip their children with the skills and attitudes needed to live happy and fulfilling lives. However, caring for children is a complex endeavour, and parenting goals and roles differ enormously across cultures and contexts. Parents protect and care for their children according to the norms and practices predominant in their specific communities and children rely on their parents for those things that they are accustomed to receiving from them.

Research into the risks and vulnerabilities of separated children of different ages has provided important insight into their needs and circumstances. However, there is a tendency in much of the literature to decontextualise the circumstances of children's lives, in which local context and cultural norms regarding child rearing are considered to be of secondary importance to understanding the psychological wellbeing of the child. While research often appears to consider culture, on closer examination it is clear that culture is seen to be an independent variable that affects child development, like gender or age, but not a system of meanings that creates alternative pathways for social, emotional and cognitive development. Studies may indicate the socio-economic level and ethnicity of a child, describe the physical environment in which he or she has been raised, and briefly outline the kinship structure particular to the community, yet in the end the child described is a generic child. Little attention is paid, for example, to a child's daily routine, childcare practices, child–child interaction, and the work that boys and girls are expected to do at different ages. Analysis of these and other measures is critical to understanding the immediate situational circumstances that provide the framework for how children learn to think, speak and behave (Weisner 1984).

The Role of Sibling Caregiving

Most separated children come from the developing countries of Africa, Asia and Latin America. For the majority of people in these regions, it is children who are responsible for performing the bulk of childcare tasks (Weisner 1987). The notion that children should have unlimited access to their mothers is often impossible, given the heavy domestic workloads and economic reality of most families in this context. The participation of older siblings and peers in the care of young children enables mothers to direct their energies elsewhere, either towards the family's subsistence needs, or towards the care of a newborn child. In this way, sibling care-giving is an essential contribution to household livelihood in many communities and a contextual feature which influences children's development.

For many families in this context, the care of infants and young children is an expected stage in the lives of most children and a daily activity (Harkness and Super 1992). From almost as early as they can remember, children begin to learn alongside their parents to care for their younger siblings and to provide them with emotional support and comfort. Usually the child caretaker is a young girl, but this varies according to culture and may also depend on the sibling composition of the family and the birth order of the child. As child caregivers come to understand the tasks that they are observing and practising, they are expected to take on increasing levels of responsibility for meeting the direct childcare needs of their younger siblings (Harkness and Super 1991; LeVine et al. 1994; Nsamenang 1992b; Watson-Gegeo and Gegeo 1991). From as early as 2 months of age, mothers may leave their infants in the care of an older child, first for a few moments and later for longer periods of time. This graduated process enables mothers to perform other domestic tasks. It also enables child caregivers to slowly develop a relationship, or 'unhur-ried attachment bond', with their infant sibling (Nsamenang 1992b). Mothers usually stop providing direct care at about the time of weaning, when responsibility is passed to the child caregiver and the multi-age sibling or peer group to which he or she belongs (Leiderman and Leiderman 1977). From this point on, mothers play a supervisory role, rather than an implementing role, in meeting their young child's needs for direct care (Goldberg 1977; Nsamenang 1992b). For example, among highland East African groups, by the time a girl (or a boy in those households which lack older daughters) has reached the age of 6 or 7, she or he will be entrusted with an infant of 4 months or older for two or three hours at a time. Once a child caregiver has reached the age of 9 or 10, she will be responsible for performing a series of household chores, including caring for an infant all day, with the help of younger siblings, while her mother is away from the homestead (Harkness and Super 1992).

In many cases, mothers may employ a deliberate strategy for training their children to cope effectively for periods of time with minimal or no adult involvement. This training appears in part to explain the successful coping of the sample of separated boys from the north of Somalia studied by Rousseau et al. (1998) in Montréal, Canada. Among the traditional pastoral nomadic peoples of northern Somalia, it is common for boys from approximately age 6 onward to become responsible for tending herds and to spend increasing periods of time away from their parents and homestead. By the time they have reached the age of 12, absences of up to several months are common. During these periods, boys live among their peers and rely upon one another for practical and emotional support. This period of family separation is traditionally associated with learning and initiation into manhood: in their own and others' eyes, the experience of adversity and the solidification of lasting, lifelong peer relationships enables boys to learn self-sufficiency and autonomy and to acquire adult status in their communities. Hence, in this particular context, Rousseau et al. (1998) found that for the separated boys in their study, exile and separation from family were viewed not as forms of deprivation or loss, but as having certain positive attributes. The boys' resilience could be in part attributed to the collective cultural understanding of travel and separation as a valuable life experience that brings with it knowledge and wisdom.

In those communities where parenting tasks are distributed among a large social network, childcare is not only seen as the 'proper' role for children, it is also seen as a predicted stage of life for children themselves. From an early age, boys and girls learn that the tasks they perform are important to the welfare of the family, and thus come to appreciate the social utility and legitimacy of their labour. Mothers inculcate in children a desire to participate as a means of feeling important and valued in their family and community by encouraging them to take on tasks that are congruent with their developing capacities. In fact, often a mother who does not expect her child to work is considered negligent in her child rearing role (Wenger 1989) because it is through childcare and other forms of work that children are expected to learn responsibility and the value of cooperation. For children in this context, being given responsibility for the care of a younger sibling or cousin is a way of being recognised as competent and signals to a growing child his or her acceptance and integration into family and community life.

This sense of competence and purpose derived from caring for others was apparent among the tens of thousands of Sudanese boys who became separated from their families by war in the early 1990s. Zutt argues that it was common for these boys to express a desire to assist others, as they had been assisted by their parents, friends, siblings and other adults. They saw 'themselves caring for others not only in the distant future, when their own children and their elderly parents will need help, but also in the immediate present, when younger children and other persons in their presence show demonstrable need' (Zutt 1994: 19). In this way, caring for other children provided these boys with an opportunity to contribute to the welfare of others and in so doing to feel valued among a large network of people previously unknown to them. Far from their families and other familiar cultural referents, they were able to develop a shared identity and a sense of belonging with other children and community members in the camp. These positive experiences of caring and community involvement have been shown to play a critical role in supporting children's resilience and coping, particularly in situations of armed conflict and political violence (Werner 1990).

Questioning Assumed Models of Care

Surprisingly, the role of delegated parenting is not discussed in the literature on separated children, despite the developmental implications for children reared in this way. Research with separated children has taken place almost exclusively in the context of refugee camps and children's homes. These environments have been accessible to researchers and have provided a window through which to learn how children cope with separation from parents. However, the majority of these studies have focused on the individual child, with little or no reference to his or her prior experiences of family life and domestic roles, responsibilities and relationships before separation. Without prior exposure to different models of childcare, such as delegated parenting, most psychologists have tended to rely on their disciplinary training (Göncü 1999) and to assume the universality and exclusivity of the mother–child bond. Furthermore, research with separated children has tended to use medical assessments, checklists of symptoms and events, and structured questionnaires. Rarely have children's perspectives on their own experience been solicited in an open-ended way.

There is ample evidence in the anthropological literature on child rearing to suggest that in sibling caregiving societies, children develop diffuse attachments with their mother and close bonds with their child caregivers (Harkness and Super 1992; Konner 1977; Leiderman and Leiderman 1977; LeVine 1994; Weisner 1997; Weisner and Gallimore 1977; Whiting and Edwards 1988). In fact, among the pastoral and tribal peoples of East Africa, where sibling caregiving is 'ubiquitous' (Harkness and Super 1992: 448), it is argued that some babies are fonder of their child caregiver than their mother. Whiting and Edwards (1988) also found that in many of the sub-Saharan communities that they studied, young children often approached older siblings for help and support rather than their mothers. Similarly, Nsamenang, writing about childcare patterns in Cameroon, comments that 'even a casual observer could not fail to remark how, in stressful situations like illness, some children preferred being handled by their sitters than by their mothers' (Nsamenang 1992a: 424). Some argue that this diffusion of early attachment may also increase a child's sense that others in the community will care for him or her (Weisner and Gallimore 1977).

These findings may be especially relevant to separated children affected by armed conflict in many parts of the world. Weisner (1987) argues that in places where there are significant threats to community safety, such as communal violence and warfare, sibling caregiving is more likely to occur. In these instances, adults (especially men) and adolescent boys may be involved in community protection away from home. The absence of these family members may intensify children's, and especially girls', responsibility for looking after one another. Research by Freud and Burlingham (1943) showed that in dangerous situations, children's feelings of trust and interdependence may take on increasing significance. In this way, war may encourage sibling caregiving and other mechanisms of delegated parenting, such as child fostering. It may also accentuate the practice in those communities where strong, caring relationships already exist between children. The young, and girls in particular, may play a more important role as buffers of stress than is commonly understood, offering emotional comfort and physical protection to their peers and siblings. Child–child relationships may be an essential protective factor for separated children.

These facts are important to consider in the design of psychosocial interventions for separated children because in certain cultures a child may feel that he or she needs to do specific tasks or have specific skills in order to become a respected member of the community. What does it mean for a child if he or she is unable to undertake these responsibilities? Research with teenage girls in a residential institution in Nepal highlighted the girls' concern that they were not given any opportunities to care for younger children, and as a result they were being denied the experience of traditional roles and relationships (Tolfree 1995). Furthermore, research with Eritrean orphans living in a large institution found that both younger and older children felt better cared for, protected and nurtured after the institution changed the dormitory groups to include children of different ages (Wolff et al. 1995). The authors of this study argue that enabling older children to care for younger ones resonated with the particular social worlds which these children had experienced and to which they would be introduced as adults. A sense of identity and personal coherence is tied not only to people and place, but also to the familiar and the predictable elements of life, including an understanding of one's place in the world and expected roles and responsibilities.

Children's Peer Relationships

That peers are crucial supports for separated children should not be underestimated: the majority of the separated children in the world today have been raised in societies where the management of childcare is shared, and in this context the sharing of domestic responsibilities and tasks promotes interdependence among siblings, parents, cousins, peers and neighbours. In these multi-age peer and sibling groups, children learn important survival skills, as well as how to relate to one another, to lead and follow others, to agree and disagree, to negotiate with one another and to support one another in the achievement of shared tasks. Membership in the multi-age peer and sibling group also enables children to set the terms of their relationships and collaboration themselves. Perhaps most importantly, it is widely argued that participation in this group eases the child's transition away from the mother (Konner 1977). Tietjen (1989: 47) states that 'it appears that in households with many children parents must spread themselves more thinly among the children, and the siblings, in turn, may come to rely on each other and on peers more than on adults'.

In her research among indigenous groups in the Pacific, Margaret Mead (1968) observed that in societies where child caregiving relied more on children than on parents, there was usually a 'fostering group' of peers (cited in Aptekar 1988: 185). In his exploration of what he determined to be strong, supportive relationships between street children in Cali, Colombia, Aptekar (1991) also found sibling caregiving to be the dominant mode of child rearing in the sample children's families. He argues that Mary Ainsworth's original research on attachment showed that separation from home was less stressful for children who had been reared in this way. This assertion is substantiated elsewhere in the literature, where it is generally believed that children who care for other children experience an acceleration of what are assumed to be universal stages of child development, especially in the development of pro-social, nurturing and responsible behaviour (Aptekar 1988; Harkness and Super 1992; Leiderman and Leiderman 1977; Nsamenang 1992a; Watson-Gegeo and Gegeo 1991; Weisner 1984, 1987, 1989; Whiting and Edwards 1988; Whiting and Whiting 1963). Aptekar (1991) argues that for most street children in Colombia, their developmental experiences are closer to those of adolescents or early adolescents than to 'childhood' as defined by traditional child development thinking. The same contention may apply to separated children in emergencies.

Many other researchers have explored the value of peer relationships to the psychological wellbeing of children who live apart from their families. The bulk of this literature has focused, like Aptekar, on the lives of street children and their moral development (see Aptekar 1988; Baker, Panter-Brick and Todd 1997; Connolly 1990; Ennew 1994; Felsman 1989; Patel 1990; Swart 1990; Verma 1999). It stresses the crucial nature of the emotional and material support that peers provide to one another. To date, these issues have not been a focus of the literature on children who are separated from their families in emergencies, despite the fact that street children and separated children share a common base of experience (both groups of children are, effectively, looking after themselves), and the fact that many street children come from war zones. The circumstances of these two groups of children are rarely examined alongside one another. Consequently, understandings of the needs of separated children in emergencies are rarely informed by those of other groups of children who live apart from families, and vice versa.

Research into the importance of peer and sibling groups as support mechanisms for separated children might provide important insight into the needs and functioning of child-headed households. Children in these domestic units may be relying on the 'training for interdependence and affiliation, not autonomous independence and achievement, among the peer group' (Weisner 1987: 248), which is associated with sibling care and delegated parenting systems. They may be accustomed to being the primary caregivers and socialising agents of their younger siblings. Again, insights from research with street children might be relevant to the experiences of separated children in this context: Verma (1999) argues that children who live apart from their families on the streets of Delhi, India, gained enough exposure as young children to the various roles that different family members occupy, so that they are able to replicate these roles through role playing the tasks of mother, father, etc. Similarly, Barker and Knaul (2000) suggest that street girls in Kenya and Bolivia often form common-law families with street boys through which they attempt to replicate their experiences of family life. These findings suggest that children on their own still know how the family functions and that they replicate these processes in their relationships with one another. This way of learning fits with the pattern of 'legitimate peripheral participation' (Rogoff et al. 1993) common in those societies where delegated parenting is the norm, and has important implications for understanding the care and protection needs of separated children.

While the role of peers and siblings as social supports has been underestimated in the literature on separated children, so too has an analysis of the role that parents play in the establishment and functioning of these supportive relationships. Children reared in delegated parenting societies are expected to perform many important domestic tasks, including childcare. However, children in this context are also expected to turn to adults and other, more experienced people in their immediate family and communal environment when they need help and support (Dembele n.d.; Harkness and Super 1992; Weisner 1997; Werner and Smith 1982). The close relationships between siblings who have been reared in this way does not render the role of mothers and fathers unnecessary or unimportant. On the contrary, it highlights for researchers and practitioners the fact that children and parents play different roles in different families and societies. To date, research with separated children has not adequately addressed these differences and as a result the nature of these roles and relationships has been poorly understood. Yet attention to these contextual variations in parent–child relationships might highlight other assumptions and misconceptions inherent in our understanding of the needs and experiences of separated children.

The reality is that a child's (just as an adult's) support network is a complex web of relationships with all kinds of different people, and the amount of time spent with each individual in this network does not necessarily reflect his or her meaning or importance to the child. It may be that the very existence of a particular adult is just as important to a child as is the direct involvement of that adult in his or her daily activities. Children heading households in Rwanda after the 1994 genocide reported feeling overwhelmed by the responsibility associated with caring for their younger siblings when they had no adults to turn to for support: not only were these boys and girls responsible for the day-to-day care of their younger brothers and sisters, but they also had to cultivate the land, and find money for food, school fees and clothing (Cohen and Hendler 1997). While these children may have been responsible for most of these tasks before their parents died, the implicit support and guidance their presence provided was no longer accessible to them. Children in these circumstances, like others who live without adults' support, may be especially vulnerable because they cannot decline to perform a task, or to manage the accumulation of tasks, that may be beyond their abilities.

The reality is that in those communities which have been devastated by conflict, HIV/AIDS, or both, the numbers of adults available to provide material and emotional support to children are rapidly decreasing. Female, elderly and child-headed households are increasingly prevalent in many communities and these demographic changes are dramatically altering the environment in which children are raised. In these circumstances, children no longer have access to a wide network of adults to structure and monitor their responsibilities and to assist them to take on tasks consistent with their growing abilities. They may therefore face increased risks to their health and wellbeing, particularly if they are forced to assume especially arduous and hazardous tasks. They may also have to restructure and develop new networks of support to meet their emotional and physical needs. How these changes will affect the capabilities and vulnerabilities of children is not yet well understood.

These questions are pertinent to the care and protection of war-affected separated children. In those communities devastated by conflict, where large numbers of adults may have been killed, surviving families may face pressures and challenges previously unknown to them. For example, the interethnic nature of the conflict in Rwanda has resulted in many places in the total elimination of trust at the community level. In these instances, neighbours no longer feel able to turn to one another for help and support in times of crisis. This lack of trust, coupled with conditions of often serious deprivation, can undermine the mutual ties and obligations of communities to care for children.

Effect of Age on Separation

The literature asserts that one of the most important determinants of the effect of family separation on children is the age of the child at separation (Baker 1982; Goyos 1997; Ressler et al. 1988; Tolfree 1995). Because children vary significantly in terms of their developmental needs, abilities and limitations, it is argued that separation at different ages and developmental stages will have different meanings and implications for every child (Ressler et al. 1988). A similar event of separation will evoke different reactions in children of different ages.

It is commonly understood by academics and practitioners that separated children under the age of 5 face serious risks because family separation at this age threatens to disrupt a child's socialisation process and growing sense of autonomy (Werner 1990). Without adult caregivers to help orient children to the world around them, it is believed that children are less likely to understand and adapt to the circumstances in which they find themselves. For children at this age, it is argued that family separation is very quickly felt as permanent loss and is accompanied by intense feelings of powerlessness and despair (Boothby 1984). These feelings often manifest themselves in the regression of previous developmental attainments, such as bedwetting and the re-commencement of baby-talk, and may also lead to significant increases in fear, both of imaginary and actual objects (Garbarino and Kostelny 1996; Ressler et al. 1988).

It is generally agreed that children aged 6 or 7 and older children, seem better able to cope with the stress of family separation than do their younger counterparts. Many believe this ability is due in part to a number of factors, including the growing sense of self-efficacy and independence experienced at these ages (Werner 1990). Moreover, children who attempt to establish positive relationships with adults and peers and actively engage with others are also considered to be more resilient (Boothby 1984; Eunson 1996; Garbarino et al. 1991; Garbarino and Kostelny 1996; Rousseau et al. 1998; Werner 1990). Furthermore, it is believed that older children may be better able to understand the nature and circumstances of separation because they have more life experience and possess more advanced language and cognitive skills (Tolfree 1995).

Research into the risks and vulnerabilities of separated children of different ages has provided important insight into their psychological and emotional needs and the behavioural manifestations of their separation from parents. However, it cannot be assumed that children of the same age range will experience separation in a similar manner in all contexts. Nevertheless, with a few notable exceptions,[1] understanding a particular culture or community's definition and goals for child development has not yet been the focus of research with separated children. Child development is assumed to take place in stages and these stages are seen to be natural and universal. Children are believed to understand and respond to the events in their lives according to their stage position, and the social and cultural construction of their responses is often not considered. For example, a widely-used UNHCR field guide for working with separated children states at the outset, 'Despite slight variations in timing owing to cultural and other influences, all children pass through the same stages of development from infancy, through childhood and adolescence. In normal circumstances, children of similar ages will be found to be very much alike' (UNHCR 1994: 3). Differential attainment of child development goals is attributed to factors individual to the child, such as temperament or ability, and rarely to population or culture-specific patterns that shape the way children interact with the world around them.

Considerations of Gender and Other Personal Characteristics

The majority of the literature on parent–child separation refers to 'separated children' as though they were a monolithic group. When the term 'separated child' is used, often it refers to boys rather than to both boys and girls. Rarely is any distinction made between the needs, interests and circumstances of these two groups. Yet throughout the world, boys and girls are treated differently from birth onwards and the gap tends to widen at puberty (Mensch et al. 1998). In times of war, the magnitude and nature of the risks they face may not be the same. For example, in certain contexts, girls may be more vulnerable to trafficking and sexual exploitation than boys. Similarly, boys may be at greater risk of forced recruitment in those societies where males make up the majority of combatants. However, the extent to which boys and girls may share these different risks is also not well understood. Moreover, the contextual nature of children's vulnerability is also important to consider in order to understand the different experiences of boys and girls. For instance, in Afghanistan, the greater mobility of boys puts them at increased risk of hazardous work such as landmine clearance. Girls' relative confinement to the domestic sphere means that they may be less vulnerable to these dangers, but more susceptible to nutritional deficiencies because their limited mobility means that they cannot access food for themselves (Joanna de Berry, personal communication).

These oversights in the differential experience of boys and girls arise in part from a lack of in-depth information about children's lives, and girls' lives in particular. Researchers and practitioners need to consult girls to learn more about their time use, their living arrangements, their health, mobility, productive work and other aspects of their lives (Mensch et al. 1998). More attention must be paid to local definitions of girlhood and womanhood. In many societies, boys pass through a stage of adolescence before acquiring the status of full adults within their society. But for many girls, the transition from child to woman takes place at menarche, often without an extended period of adolescence. Consequently, studies into the situation of separated children may miss the experience of girls after they reach the age of 12 or 13 years. At this point their needs and experiences may be understood as those of women and not of children. I found this to be the case in my research into the situation of separated Burmese children in Thailand in 2000, where it is widely argued that there are no separated girls. After speaking with members of an ethnic minority women's group, I learned that many of the 'women' who lived in the nearby shelter were between the ages of 14 and 18. I also learned that it was not uncommon for women to come to the border on their own. When I asked the age of these 'women' I learned that they were usually about 15 years or older. In this way, the invisibility of separated girls became ever more apparent to me. I suspect that there are many other ways in which the situation of certain populations of children remains unknown.

Gender is not the only social attribute that is overlooked in the literature on separated children. Little mention is made of the characteristics of those children who have become separated from their families; for example, birth order, physical abilities, or fitness. Yet within the general category of 'children', there are many structural and personal differences that distinguish individual children and groups of children. In conflict situations some may be more vulnerable to separation than others; for example, in the late 1970s in Cambodia, children of the urban elite were especially targeted by the military and forcibly separated from their parents. As well, during the civil war in Mozambique in the 1980s and early 1990s, the rebel army (RENAMO) deliberately targeted those individuals who were furthering the socialist project of the state. Teachers and nurses were at particular risk of abduction and murder. Consequently, their children were especially vulnerable to being orphaned or separated.

Within communities affected by war, children with social and economic power will experience conflict differently from those who have less power. The same applies to children's experience of family separation. A child's gender, class, ethnicity, religion and economic status will affect whether or not he or she becomes separated and if so, his or her experience of separation. Similarly, a child's personal attributes such as cognitive ability, temperament and physique, as well as sex and birth order may also influence his or her status and treatment within the family and the community (Boyden and Mann 2000). These factors may affect a family's or child's decision to remain together or to separate. They may also influence a child's experience of separation. For example, an intelligent and resourceful child may be more capable of arranging shelter and food for him or herself than another child who may not possess the same problem-solving abilities.

The literature on family separation does not explore the level of exposure of certain groups of children to adverse situations. It lacks a critical analysis of why it is that certain children experience more hardship, suffering, abuse and exploitation than others. However, even – and perhaps especially – in times of conflict, governments, communities, parents and sometimes children themselves, make considered, strategic decisions in order to maximise opportunities for survival as well as economic, political, social and spiritual gain. They make social choices and these choices are not made arbitrarily. Literature on the needs and circumstances of separated children rarely considers the nature and importance of these choices and the impact they may have on the determination of which children become separated and how they manage this separation. However, doing so is essential to understanding children's experience of war and separation.

Conclusion

The academic and agency literature on the care and protection of separated children in emergencies highlights some important issues for consideration in the design of policies and programmes to assist them. In particular, attention to the needs of children at different ages, the importance of at least one nurturing and reliable relationship, and the influence of children's individual characteristics on the way in which they experience separation are significant factors. These and other identified factors have to date provided a way of understanding the circumstances of separated children and a basis upon which to intervene on their behalf.

However, there are certain limitations to this research. Foremost among these is the lack of attention to the context in which children have been raised and the differential impacts contextual variations may have on child development. The assumption inherent in the vast majority of the literature is that children's experience of parental separation will have the same meaning in all contexts. Yet ethnographic evidence from many different societies suggests that this assumption may be mistaken: in communities where delegated parenting is the norm, child rearing tasks are distributed among a large sibling and family group, and exclusive parental care is extremely rare. In these circumstances, children may rely as much, or more, on their siblings for nurture and support as they do on their parents. Furthermore, they may be very mobile and accustomed to living in households that do not include their parents. In this context, concepts of family and parent–child relationships may be very different from what is generally assumed in the literature on separated children.

Interventions to assist separated children must understand and engage with local conceptions of child development and existing childcare arrangements. Supporting indigenous practices means recognising that they are often heavily prescribed and governed by specific social norms. Lack of recognition of the particularities of community childcare practices can have serious implications for the care and protection of separated children. By imposing systems of support that appear to outsiders to fit the local context, but which in reality may not recognise the specific content of existing practices, agencies can undermine traditional support mechanisms for children. Past ways of caring for children in crisis may be rejected in favour of new, externally imposed arrangements. These interventions may function well in the midst of an emergency, but may be difficult to sustain in the long term. In these circumstances, children may face risks from which they have been traditionally protected.

Much more research is required on the daily lives of children in different cultures and communities so that policies and programmes are appropriate to their needs and circumstances. Existing interventions for separated children should be monitored and evaluated in order to determine to what extent children's best interests are being met. This process should engage with all members of the community and, most especially, with children.

Notes

1. A few exceptions to this rule include the studies that have been conducted with separated boys from the north of Somalia (Rousseau et al. 1998) and south Sudan (Zutt 1994; Rädda Barnen 1994).

References

Ainsworth, M. 1967. *Infancy in Uganda: Infant Care and the Growth of Love.* Baltimore: Johns Hopkins University Press.

Aptekar, L. 1988. *Street Children of Cali.* Durham: Duke University Press.

——. 1991. 'Are Colombian Street Children Neglected? The Contributions of Ethnographic and Ethnohistorical Approaches to the Study of Children.' *Anthropology and Education Quarterly* 22: 326–49.

Ashabranner, B. and Ashabranner, M. 1987. *Into a Strange Land: Unaccompanied Refugee Youth in America.* New York: Dodd, Mead and Company.

Baker, N. 1982. 'Substitute Care for Unaccompanied Refugee Minors.' *Child Welfare* 61: 353–63.

Baker, R., Panter-Brick, C. and Todd, A. 1997. 'Homeless Street Boys in Nepal: Their Demography and Lifestyle.' *Journal of Comparative Family Studies* 28: 129–46.

Barker, G. and Knaul, F. 2000. *Urban Girls: Empowerment in Especially Difficult Circumstances.* London: Intermediate Technology Development Group.

Boothby, N. 1984. 'The Care and Placement of Unaccompanied Children in Emergencies.' Ed.D. thesis, Harvard Graduate School of Education.

Bowlby, J. 1973. *Separation, Anxiety and Anger in Attachment and Loss.* Vol. 2. New York: Basic Books.

Boyden, J. and Mann, G. 2000. 'Children's Risk, Resilience and Coping in Extreme

Situations.' Background paper to the Consultation on Children in Adversity, Oxford, 9–12 September.

Cohen, C. and Hendler, N. 1997. *Nta Nzu Itagira Inkigi: No Home Without Foundation: A Portrait of Child Headed Households in Rwanda.* New York: Women's Commission for Refugee Women and Children.

Connolly, M. 1990. 'Adrift in the City: A Comparative Study of Street Children in Bogota, Colombia and Guatemala City.' In N. Boxill. ed., *Homeless Children: the Watchers and the Waiters.* New York: The Haworth Press.

Dembele, N.U. (n.d.). 'Gender Differentiation: a Case Study of Bambara Children, Bugula, Southern Mali.' http://www.ecdgroup.com/cn/cn20case.htm.

Djeddah, C. (n.d.). 'Wars and Unaccompanied Children in Africa: Who They Are and Major Health Implications.'
http://www.ipafrance.net/pubs/inchines/inch8_2/djed.htm.

Ennew, J. 1994. 'Parentless Friends: a Cross-Cultural Examination of Networks Among Street Children and Street Youth.' In F. Nestmann and K. Hurelmann, eds, *Social Networks and Social Support in Childhood and Adolescence.* New York: Walter de Gruyter.

Eunson, P. 1996. 'Children in War: the Role of Child-to-Child Activities in the Therapy and Care of Displaced Unaccompanied Children.' Unpublished paper.

Felsman, J.K. 1989. 'Risk and Resiliency in Childhood: the Lives of Street Children.' In T. Dugan and R. Coles, eds, *The Child in Our Times: Studies in the Development of Resiliency.* New York: Bruner/Mazel.

Freud, A. and Burlingham, D. 1943. *War and Children.* New York: Ernst Willard.

Garbarino, J. and Kostelny, K. 1996. 'What Do We Need to Know to Understand Children in War and Community Violence?' In R. Apfel and B. Simon. eds, *Minefields in their Hearts: the Mental Health of Children in War and Community Violence.* New Haven, USA: Yale University Press.

Garbarino, J., Kostelny, K. and Dubrow, N. 1991. *No Place to be a Child: Growing Up in a War Zone.* Lexington, MA: Lexington Books.

Goldberg, S. 1977. 'Infant Development and Mother–Infant Interaction in Urban Zambia.' In P.H. Leiderman, S.R. Tulkin and A. Rosenfeld. eds, *Economic Change and Infant Care in an East African Agricultural Community.* New York: Academic Press.

Göncü, A. 1999. 'Children's and Researchers' Engagement in the World.' In A. Göncü. ed., *Children's Engagement in the World: Sociocultural Perspectives.* Cambridge, UK: Cambridge University Press.

Goyos, J.M. 1997. 'Identifying Resiliency Factors in Adult "Pedro Pan" Children: a Retrospective Study.' Ph.D. thesis, Barry University.

Harkness, S. and Super, C. 1991. 'East Africa.' In J. Hawes and N.R. Hiner, eds, *Children in Historical and Comparative Perspective.* New York: Greenwood Press.

———. 1992. 'Shared Care in East Africa: Sociocultural Origins and Developmental Consequences.' In M. Lamb, K. Sternberg, C. Hwang and A. Broberg, eds, *Childcare in Context: Cross-Cultural Perspectives.* Hillsdale, NJ: Lawrence Erlbaum Associates.

Konner, M. 1977. 'Infancy Among the Kalahari Desert San.' In P.H. Leiderman, S.R. Tulkin and A. Rosenfeld, eds, *Culture and Infancy: Variations in the Human Experience.* New York: Academic Press.

Leiderman, P.H. and Leiderman, G.F. 1977. 'Economic Change and Infant Care in an East African Agricultural Community.' In P.H. Leiderman, S.R. Tulkin and A. Rosenfeld, eds, *Culture and Infancy: Variations in the Human Experience.* New York: Academic Press.

LeVine, R.A., Levine, S., Dixon, S., Richman, A., Leiderman, P.H. and Keefer, C. 1994. *Child Care and Culture: Lessons From Africa*. New York: Cambridge University Press.

Machel, G. 1996. *The Impact of Armed Conflict on Children*. New York: UNICEF.

Machel, G. 2000. *The Machel Review: A Critical Analysis of Progress Made and Obstacles Encountered in Increasing Protection for War-Affected Children*. New York, NY: UNIFEM, Government of Norway, UNICEF and the Government of Canada.

Mead, M. 1968. *Growing up in New Guinea*. New York: Dell.

Mensch, B.S., Bruce, J. and Greene, M. 1998. *The Uncharted Passage: Girls' Adolescence in the Developing World*. New York: Population Council.

Nsamenang, B. 1992a. 'Early Childhood Care and Education in Cameroon.' In M. Lamb, K. Sternberg, C. Hwang and A. Broberg, eds, *Childcare in Context: Cross-Cultural Perspectives*. Hillsdale, NJ, USA: Lawrence Erlbaum Associates.

——. 1992b. 'Perceptions of Parenting Among the Nso of Cameroon.' In B. Hewlett, ed., *Father–Child Relations: Cultural and Biosocial Relations*. New York: Aldine de Gruyter.

Patel, S. 1990. 'Street Children, Hotel Boys and Children of Pavement Dwellers and Construction Workers in Bombay – How They Meet Their Daily Needs.' *Environment and Urbanization* 2: 9–26.

Petty, C. and Jareg, E. 1998. 'Conflict, Poverty and Family Separation: the Problem of Institutional Care.' In P. Bracken and C. Petty, eds, *Rethinking the Trauma of War*. London: Free Association Books.

Rädda Barnen. 1994. '*The Unaccompanied Minors of Southern Sudan: A Rädda Barnen Report*.' Stockholm: Rädda Barnen.

Ressler, E., Boothby, N. and Steinbock, D. 1988. *Unaccompanied Children: Care and Protection in Wars, Natural Disasters and Refugee Movements*. New York and Oxford: Oxford University Press.

Rogoff, B., Mistry, J., Göncü, A. and Mosier, C. 1993. *Guided Participation in Cultural Activity by Toddlers and Caregivers*. Monographs of the Society for Research in Child Development. Chicago, USA: University of Chicago Press.

Rousseau, C., Said, T.M., Gagné, M.-J. and Bibeau, G. 1998. 'Resilience in Unaccompanied Minors from the North of Somalia.' *Psychoanalytic Review* 85: 615–37.

Swart, J. 1990. *Malunde: the Street Children of Hillbrow*. Cape Town: Witwatersrand University Press.

Tietjen, A.M. 1989. 'The Ecology of Children's Social Support Networks.' In D. Belle, ed., *Children's Social Networks and Social Supports*. New York: John Wiley and Sons.

Tolfree, D. 1995. *Roofs and Roots: the Care of Separated Children in the Developing World*. London: Save the Children Fund UK and Arena.

UNHCR. 2000. *ARC Resource Pack on Separated Children*. Geneva: UNHCR.

——. 2001. *Refugees*. Geneva: UNHCR.

UNHCR (PTSS/Community Services). 1994. *Working with Unaccompanied Minors in the Community: A Family Based Approach*. Geneva: UNHCR.

Verma, S. 1999. 'Socialization for Survival: Developmental Issues Among Working Street Children in India.' In M. Raffaelli and R. Larson, eds, *Homeless and Working Youth Around the World: Exploring Developmental Issues*. New York: Jossey-Bass.

Watson-Gegeo, K.A. and Gegeo, D.W. 1991. 'The Role of Sibling Interaction in Child Socialization.' In P.G. Zukow, ed., *Sibling Interaction Across Cultures: Theoretical and Mental Health Issues*. New York: Springer-Verlag.

Weisner, T. 1987. 'Socialization for Parenthood in Sibling Caretaking Societies.' In J.B. Lancaster, J. Altmann, A. Rossi and L. Sherrod, eds, *Parenting Across the Lifespan: Biosocial Dimensions*. New York: Aldine de Gruyter.

——. 1989. 'Cultural and Universal Aspects of Social Support for Children: Evidence from the Abaluyia of Kenya.' In D. Belle, ed., *Children's Social Networks and Social Supports*. New York: John Wiley and Sons.

——. 1997. 'Support for Children and the African Family Crisis.' In T. Weisner, C. Bradley and P. Kilbride, eds, *African Families and the Crisis of Social Change*. Westport, USA: Bergin and Garvey.

Weisner, T. and Gallimore, R. 1977. 'My Brother's Keeper: Child and Sibling Caretaking.' *Current Anthropology* 18: 169–80.

Weisner, T.S. 1984. 'The Social Ecology of Childhood: a Cross-Cultural View.' In M. Lewis, ed., *Beyond the Dyad*. New York: Plenum Press.

Wenger, M. 1989. 'Work, Play and Social Relationships Among Children in a Giriama Community.' In D. Belle, ed., *Children's Social Networks and Social Supports*. New York: John Wiley and Sons.

Werner, E. 1990. 'Protective Factors and Individual Resilience.' In S.J. Meisels and J.P. Shonkoff, eds, *Handbook of Early Childhood Intervention*. Cambridge, UK: Cambridge University Press.

Werner, E. and Smith, R. 1982. *Vulnerable But Invincible: a Study of Resilient Children*. New York: McGraw Hill.

Whiting, B. and Edwards, C. 1988. *Children of Different Worlds: the Formation of Social Behaviour*. Cambridge, MA: Harvard University Press.

Whiting, B. and Whiting, J., eds, 1963. *Six Cultures: Studies of Child Rearing*. New York: John Wiley and Sons.

Wolff, P., Dawitt, Y. and Zere, B. 1995. 'The Solumna Orphanage: An Historical Survey.' *Social Science and Medicine* 40 (8): 1133–9.

Zutt, J. 1994. *Children of War: Wandering Alone in Southern Sudan*. New York: UNICEF.

2

Cultural Disruption and the Care of Infants in Post-war Mozambique

Victor Igreja

Introduction

This chapter aims to describe the ways in which prolonged and multiple exposure to civil war and drought in the Gorongosa district of Sofala Province, Central Mozambique, influenced not only the psychological wellbeing of affected populations but also the wider stability and integration of families and communities. Quite apart from the destitution and profound discontinuities within the social order created by such exposure, it became increasingly difficult to perform the ceremonies and rituals that had long regulated life from birth (*madzawde*) to death (*ntsanganiko*) (Igreja 2003). In this way, armed conflict deprived the people of Gorongosa of vital social and cultural resources that had previously marked out their collective identity and given meaning to their existence. The loss of such resources had particular consequences for the survival and wellbeing of infants, since historically it was through observation of the rite of *madzawde* that the physical, psychological and emotional development of the child in the first two years of life was regulated. Other trends observed through the research included an increase in domestic and community violence, marital instability, infant malnutrition and sexual abuse – all of which pose an added threat to infant survival.

According to annual surveys, rates of infant morbidity and mortality are generally very high in Mozambique. The national infant mortality rate is 145.7 per 1,000 live births, with infant protein energy malnutrition (PEM) as the main cause of death (UNDP 1999). However, while the national figures are themselves elevated, these averages tend to disguise

Table 2.1. *Infant Morbidity and Mortality in Gorongosa, January–June 2000*

	Mal-nutrition	Malaria	Diarrhoea	Pneu-monia	Anaemia	HIV/AIDS	Tuber-culosis
Cases	141	356	62	113	54	22	22
Deaths	20	12	7	2	5	7	7

Source: Gorongosa Health Centre. Vila Paiva – Gorongosa (08.08.2000)

serious regional disparities in which some areas are found to suffer even greater problems. Infant mortality rates are highest in the central region of the country, reaching 178.6 deaths per 1,000 live births in the province of Sofala. This compares with a figure of just 106.3 for Maputo Province in the south.

In the district of Gorongosa, the available figures for PEM among young children are based only on reported cases at the main health centre. There is very little information about the incidence of PEM cases in the more remote areas of the district. Yet the figures collected at the main health centre suggest that the problem is very serious. In the first six months of the year 2000, there were reported 141 cases of infant PEM. Of these infants twenty died. There were ninety-four additional cases of malnutrition in the second half of 2000. Every year the health centre treats a mean number of six hundred cases of different infant-related diseases in the paediatric ward, and PEM is the main cause of infant mortality in the district (see Table 2.1). The same infant mortality tendency was observed in 2001, where from the 196 reported cases of PEM 20 children died. What makes this trend particularly significant, though, is that since the end of the civil war in 1992, Gorongosa has not faced any food shortages of sufficient severity to threaten family or community integrity or survival. In other words, the high prevalence of PEM among infants cannot be attributed merely to problems of nutritional supplies, normally regarded as the most logical cause. Other explanations need to be sought. Empirical data suggest that changes in the care of babies and infants during the years of intensive war and drought may be causal in this case. This is the hypothesis that the research set out to test.

War and Drought in Gorongosa

Gorongosa is one of the districts of Sofala province in central Mozambique. It is located in the extreme west of Sofala, and borders on Maringue district in the north, Nhamatanda district in the south, Cheringoma and Muanza districts in the east and Manica province (Macossa and Gondola districts) in the west. Gorongosa is extremely poor and isolated from the country's main urban centres. There are only three shops in the entire district and the vast majority of the population is engaged in subsistence agriculture. Prior to the outbreak of war and drought, the population of the district was comparatively stable and dispersed. Gorongosa society is patrilineal and observes patrilocal rules of residence. The majority of families are extended and polygynous. Gender distinctions are marked and men make all the major decisions in both the domestic and public arenas.

For nearly thirty years the Gorongosa region of Mozambique experienced profound instability due to the combined effect of armed conflict, natural disasters and infectious diseases. The region was devastated both by the struggle for independence (from 1964 to 1974) and by the lengthy civil war (from 1976 to 1992), while severe droughts in the interim caused as much damage as both wars together. Cholera and malaria epidemics also took their toll, their impact greatly aggravated by the absence of adequate healthcare. These catastrophic events remain present in the memories of the inhabitants of the region and are reflected in their daily social interactions.

Mozambique's prolonged independence struggle against the former Portuguese colonisers had a significant impact on the Gorongosa region. The Portuguese authorities used their military power to force local populations to abandon their ancestral homesteads (*madembe*) and to take refuge in the settlements (*Aldeamentos*) built by Portuguese soldiers. While traditional family homesteads are separated from each other by quite long distances, the *Aldeamentos* were designed to keep the local population in compact groups to facilitate monitoring and control, while also preventing them from contact with FRELIMO (Front for the Liberation of Mozambique) soldiers. Meanwhile FRELIMO was using its influence, legitimated in terms of the 'fight against colonialism', to prevent people from going to the *Aldeamentos* by ordering civilians to take refuge in their military bases in the bush. Hence, for reasons of military strategy, both armies were fighting for control of the civilian population. Many civilians died as a result of these forced population movements, direct exposure to combat and through outbreaks of epidemics. Those who refused to comply with the demands of either of the military units were inevitably condemned to death.

Only a few months after Mozambique finally obtained independence, signs of a new war began to appear in mid-1976. The Gorongosa district was divided between Government and RENAMO (Mozambican National Resistance) controlled areas, and low-intensity, sporadic conflict quickly escalated into all-out civil war. Civilians were once again caught in the crossfire while the two armies fought to gain control of the area. Government troops forcibly moved the Gorongosa population into so-called 'Communal Villages' – a new version of the old Portuguese *Aldeamentos*. Many of those interviewed during my research expressed hatred for these institutions, comparing them to a 'pen for pigs'. One person recalled that, 'inside the communal villages people used to die like rats. It was like death, we were as if we were dead bodies.'

The RENAMO troops were meanwhile forcing people to remain in their *madembes* as part of a military strategy known as *Gandira*. Containment of civilians without their consent had two central purposes: to force them to produce and supply the soldiers with food; and to transport military armaments and food from one place to another. to travel long distances on foot carrying on their heads boxes of weapons and ammunition, bags of food and hippopotamus meat. At the same time, they were forced to apportion a sizeable part of their daily sustenance to support the war effort. As a result, the men were often far from home for two to three weeks at a time, leaving the women as easy targets for rape by the soldiers. Informants explained that the soldiers would arrive any time of the day or night for *Gandira*, and would sometimes force women to cook for them naked before raping them.

Nowhere and noone in Gorongosa was safe. Violence became the norm. According to one interviewee, 'war was our culture. We used to breakfast, lunch and dinner with war.' Civilians who tried to escape from one controlled area to another ran the risk of confrontation with soldiers and execution. The region was planted throughout with anti-personnel mines and many of those interviewed had been injured by these hidden devices, a high proportion experiencing permanent disability as a result. Some of the soldiers were ruthless and were even willing to kill their own relatives who had been labelled traitors (*capricornios*). One of the interviewees told how he had been shot by his own maternal uncle whilst living in his *madembe* under the control of RENAMO. Because of the drought and hunger that was sweeping across the region, he had gone out in search of food in the communal villages that were under government control. However, he was soon caught by a group of RENAMO soldiers (among whom was his uncle) and accused of being a *capricornio*. He was shot in the chest, but fortunately survived. Some days later he managed to return to his *madembe*, where he received the treatment that saved his life.

The consequences of drought were even more serious. For long periods of time there was neither food nor water in Gorongosa. The main rivers dried up completely. Both soldiers and civilians became severely malnourished. People were forced to eat roots of wild trees. Often, these roots were highly poisonous and consequently many people died. Others required extensive processing to reduce the level of toxins.

Thus, the daily life of civilians who were forced to remain within the war zones of Gorongosa was characterised by multiple and prolonged exposure to a range of highly detrimental experiences.

Factors Contributing to Infant Wellbeing

What happens to very young children in societies ravaged by war and drought when the sense of community ceases to exist? In physical terms, the people, huts, fields, schools, hospitals, traditional chiefs and healers, cemeteries and so on, remain. Certainly these are important symbols of community and provide meaning for local inhabitants. But following the devastation of war and famine, the loss of social consensus and trust brings value change and people no longer feel able to abide by cultural rules and prescriptions as they once did. Traditional practices may be observed but are transformed in vital ways. This raises the issue of the extent to which such practices guarantee the protection of children in the wake of catastrophic societal events. To what extent are these cultural prescriptions affected and disrupted by such events? And, what are the psychological, emotional and social effects of the deregulation of people's daily routine and the loss of important cultural resources to deal with adversity?

The wellbeing of babies and infants is heavily dependent on child-rearing beliefs and practices and the nature of mother-infant relations, which are highly variable across cultures and social groups. Among Hindus in Northern India, for example, both infant and mother are considered to be impure in the period following birth. They are massaged with oil and washed several times to enable them to return gradually to the 'normal' state (Khare 1977). Among the Balinese studied by Mead and Wolfenstein (1955), an infant is initially called 'caterpillar' or 'mouse' and only receives a human name if he or she survives beyond 3 months. Among the Wéménou people of the Ouémé valley in South-East Benin, the body of the newborn baby is considered to possess the spirit of a dead ancestor. Immediately following birth a ceremony is arranged to determine precisely which dead ancestor is present in the baby. The child is named after the ancestor that is revealed during the consultation. If this ancestor is still remembered by the parents they will often speak of him, telling the child about his habits and mannerisms so that the child will eventually come to resemble its ancestor completely (Brand 1989).

There is a lack of consensus regarding the aetiological factors affecting health and survival in the early years of life. Some scholars have tried to establish whether maternal depression threatens the socio-emotional development of infants (Field 1992; Gelfand and Teti 1990). In her literature review, Finerman (1995) found that failure to thrive among infants is generally attributed to: (1) parents' selective neglect or incompetence; (2) parenting ignorance or inefficiency in abandoning tradition; (3) poverty; (4) socio-economic inequalities; (5) lack of parental health education; and (6) lack of adequate health care assistance. However, Finerman notes that in most of these studies the interpretation of data is highly problematic, and poses far-reaching difficulties for research and application. She highlights in particular how many reports adopt a judgmental stance in the assessment of parental roles in child survival. Based on her fieldwork in Equador and Guatemala, she suggests that there is an overwhelming tendency to blame the parent in child mortality.

Significantly, the long-term effects of prolonged and multiple exposure to highly stressful experiences are not considered in these studies as an important aetiological factor affecting infant–mother relationships. Finerman, for example, does not mention the fact that thirty-six years of civil war in Guatemala may have played an important role in reframing parental perceptions and practices with regard to children's health and survival. Yet Foxen (2000) asserts that the armed conflict in Guatemala was a dirty war which penetrated Mayan communities to the core, putting families and communities against each other and instilling fear and distrust at every level.

In non-Western societies, in particular in Africa, there is a lack of ethnographic research on the long-term effects of traumatic experiences in post-war settings and the relationship with infant health. Studies exploring the links between trauma and child health are mainly conducted during armed conflict and in refugee camps, with no follow up. For instance, in Mozambique several of the health interventions implemented during the civil war involved assessments of the physical and psychological health status of children (Cliff and Noormahomed 1993; Richman et al. 1990; Shaw and Harris 1994). But no attempt has been made to develop systematic approaches to understand the prolonged effects of overwhelming societal experiences on individuals and their communities following war. Very few programmes, for example, make a link between psychosocial interventions provided during time spent in refugee camps with the same populations following their resettlement after war. It would seem that there is an implicit understanding among mental health professionals and researchers operating in refugee camps that after war 'everything gets better by itself'. In the worst cases, psychosocial intervention programmes in refugee camps are interrupted before completion and refugees are abandoned in the middle of the crisis (Richman 1993).

Some scholars, however, have attempted to understand the impact of rapid social change and population growth not only on populations as a whole, but also on individual children in particular. The studies of Super and Harkness (1989) in rural Kenya are useful examples of this kind of research. They have demonstrated that changes in traditional childbearing patterns can constitute a risk in terms of the treatment and survival of children. I suggest here that the prolonged and multiple exposure to war experiences has had dramatic and long-term psycho-socio-cultural effects (Richters 1994) on the populations in Gorongosa. War and natural disasters changed people's living patterns radically, bringing long-term consequences that put the health of the children and their mothers at permanent risk. Margaret Mead (quoted by Hauswald 1987: 145) observed that, 'difficulties multiply during periods of rapid social and cultural change, for then the old customary relationships and ways of doing things no longer are appropriated and yet are not replaced . . . And everywhere under new conditions parents are unprepared how to care for their children and the old support system has broken down'.

Madzawde

Here I argue that practices such as *madzawde* act as important regulating mechanisms, influencing the way in which different cultural groups organise family and social life. More importantly, they shape historical and cultural complexities surrounding the understanding of childbirth and child rearing. In societies such as that of Gorongosa, the birth of a baby is not a private event involving merely the closest kin of the parents. Ethnographic examples provided in the literature demonstrate that in many non-Western societies, the arrival of a new baby is also a very important community matter. The community mobilises itself to guarantee a protective social environment for the development and growth of its new members (Finerman 1995). Both the baby's parents and community members create the necessary conditions, often culturally prescribed, to safeguard the physical and psychological development of the child. Thus, there is a popular saying in Africa that 'to raise a child we need a whole village'.

In Gorongosa, before the war, the practice of *madzawde* ensured that a baby enjoyed a close relationship with the mother, family and the community more generally. *Madzawde* involved adherence to a set of strict rules. Breastfeeding lasted for two years, during which time the breast was used also to comfort the infant. Breastfeeding in this context afforded great intimacy between mother and infant. This symbiosis created the environment for the mother to socialise the child, and provide comfort, warmth (at nights when evenings are cool) and prevent diseases. Two years after the birth, the parents would perform a rite, also called *madzawde*, which ended the close proximity of mother and infant and heralded a new phase in the infant's development. Enactment of the *madzawde* rite also entailed the resumption of sexual intercourse by the parents. If the parents failed to perform the rite or respect the rules of *madzawde*, the child could fall ill, developing physical symptoms that are also known as *madzawde* or *piringaniço*. Without timely and appropriate treatment, the infant may die.

Thus, the term '*madzawde*' has several meanings and is used in different ways. First, it is used to signify birth itself; second, it is a state of being that determines both the place and role of the child during the first two years of life and the obligations of adults with regard to newborns; third, it is a ritual that is performed at a specified time after birth; and fourth, it refers to a range of physical symptoms that affect infants whose parents have failed to observe the practice correctly. The people of Gorongosa still observe *madzawde*, although there have been transformations in its structure and dynamics in recent decades.

The structure of *madzawde* includes nine elements and the child is at the core of this structure. The structure can be divided in four parts. (1) Human beings: the child, biological parents (mother and father), family in general, community, and midwife (*nhamuino*). (2) Nature: leaf of a tree (*muroro* and *dzade*) and maize flour (*ussembe*). (3) Place of reproduction and birth: hut. (4) Oral testimony (*ku pukuta*). (5) The *madzawde* repository (see Figure 2.1).

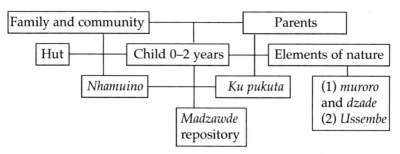

Figure 2.1. Structure of *Madzawde*

At one time, all these structural elements of *madzawde* were interrelated. The dynamic of this mechanism was based on the principle that every single element has a specific role to play and they interact with each other to fulfil the rules and expectations of *madzawde*. After the birth, the mother of the child would pass through a two-year period of sexual abstinence. During this period everyone within the family and the community in general was expected to follow a strict set of rules that preserved the integrity of *madzawde*.

After two years the *nhamuino* (midwife) and the parents of the child would prepare a ceremony to mark the end of the *madzawde* period. To perform the *madzawde* ceremony the parents and the child would enter the hut, while the *nhamuino* would kneel near the door. In this position she would perform *ku pukuta*, a narrative process of giving oral testimony of the most important events in the child's life since birth. For this, the *nhamuino* used some natural elements, in particular two leaves, one each from the *muroro* and *dzawde* trees, and a small amount of *ussembe* (maize). While touching the *ussembe* (which is placed in the two leaves) the *nhamuino* would recite the following words: 'I am the one who helped your baby in the day of birth . . . I was the one who used to touch this baby . . . Your baby is here, the maize is here, the leaves are here and I came to deliver the *madzawde* of your child . . .' When the *ku pukuta* was over the *nhamuino* would give the leaves and maize to the child's parents. They placed it under their mat and then brought the ceremony to a close by having sexual intercourse, following which they had to gather all the clothes and instruments that they used to nurse the child and throw them away somewhere in the bush. The location was then designated the child's *madzawde* repository and no family member could touch or pass near the spot. Otherwise contamination was believed to take place, putting the health of the child at risk.

This rite, which marks the termination of the period of *madzawde*, is an essential component of the process in that when all the prescribed steps have been performed, the child's development is considered to be in balance and he or she is protected from illness.

The Study

Ninety-four women, all war survivors, from various rural communities in the district of Gorongosa took part in the study. Contact was first made with the research subjects at the principal district health centre, to which each one had brought a child for treatment. The research combined quantitative and qualitative methods. Following the initial appointment and diagnosis, the women were invited to fill out a questionnaire. This provided data in ten broad thematic areas:

1. biographical and demographic details relating to the mother;
2. the child's health record;
3. health of the mother;
4. availability of food within the household;
5. birth spacing;
6. weaning schedule and reasons for early weaning;
7. practice and duration of *madzawde*;
8. domestic violence;
9. war and drought experiences;
10. health seeking behaviour.

Ten women, selected at random, were then asked if they would agree to take part in in-depth, semi-structured interviews. These interviews explored the women's lives and experiences during the years of war and drought. Other questions focused particularly on their domestic lives, exploring issues such as domestic violence, the use of cultural mechanisms to resolve domestic conflict, alcohol consumption among adult males (especially husbands) and marital disputes in regard to sexual intercourse and taboos during pregnancy. Special attention was given to the women's experiences of *madzawde*.

None of the ninety-four participants in the study had attended school. The great majority (ninety women) were married and their average age was 26. Just over half were involved in a monogamous union while the remainder came from polygynous households. Eighty-one women reported that food availability was not a problem in their households. Around half of the women had lost more than one child, the average number of live children being between two and three, and the average number of dead children, one or two (1.8). Approximately three-quarters reported they were in good health, while the rest said that they experienced a variety of health problems. Just under half of the women were found to have practised *madzawde*, the duration of which ranged from three to seven-and-a-half months. Compared with traditional practice, this represents a reduction in the period of *madzawde* of between seventeen and twenty-one months. Thus, the period of sexual abstinence following a birth has been greatly reduced, as has child spacing. Almost a third of the women who performed *madzawde* had become pregnant again three to seven months after a birth. A minority of the women reported domestic violence perpetrated by their husbands following the women's refusal to perform the *madzawde* ritual after a birth. One detailed case, which typifies the stories related by many of the women, will more clearly illustrate the effects of the disruption of *madzawde*.

Case Study

Mrs D. was born and grew up in Gorongosa district. She is a married woman of about 25 years of age who lives with her husband in a village called Mucodza. She was married in the traditional way, that is, her marriage was not registered by the official authorities. She is the only wife of her husband and both live from farming. She has three living children, one of whom is ill with PEM.

The War

At beginning of the war we were living in Casa Banana. We left there because of the intensity of the military raids. Then we went to Mucodza communal village. We did not stay long in Mucodza communal village. We just stayed one year. We suffered more in Mucodza than anywhere else. On the day that we were attacked I ran away together with my young brother and my elder sister. They burned all the houses and I was alone. In this day the rain began to fall until the following day. When we were living in Mucodza the suffering of *Gandira* did not stop. We used to do *Gandira* again and again. The longest distance I went was from Mucodza to the other side of Nhadare river, which took two days walking. I have relatives that were taken to the war and they have returned. I have one brother who was taken by RENAMO soldiers and he returned with only one arm. He was taken to be a soldier. He was taken while he was still a child. He was trained until he grew up. Then, they gave him a weapon to fight.

We suffered more with RENAMO soldiers. They used to come to the border to make ambushes. When the situation was worst at the border they used to run away from there to come here. When they kidnapped someone they did not use to take the person to their military base, they just killed him along the way. When we heard shots at the border we already knew that someone was being killed. When we walked in the direction where the shot had come from we used to find the person lying on the ground while already dead. This was their activity. When they found someone who was leaving their controlled area to go to the Government controlled area they just killed. If they found someone who was leaving the Government controlled area to go to their controlled area they just killed. There was no salvation. This is the suffering that they were causing to the people. They used to kill the person while there was no problem.

Drought and Hunger

We suffered a lot with hunger. There was no food and no water because of drought. We used to eat roots of banana trees. We used to eat things of the bush. *Nhamufo* [wild plant, creeper] – we used to eat the roots, and *nkó*. Sometimes when we were looking for food we used to reach the border and we used to walk in places where the soldiers had put landmines. One day we passed by a place that was full of landmines and the soldiers were amazed because we had escaped. If one of us had stepped on the landmine all the family would have died. In this day we were looking for food to eat. We stayed four years without food. We used to eat roots such as *maculi an figo* [banana roots], *nhamufo, dari, nkó, uliri wa ntsagaua* [crazy beans or wild beans]. These were very poisonous roots. They require a very careful and long preparation. Many people died because of eating these roots but there were no other alternatives available.

Living Conditions Following the War and Drought

I first got married during the war and I was still *nhamankunda* [a virgin of marriageable age]. I was married to this man, then he travelled and he did not manage to return home because the way was closed due to the war. My first husband went to Chimoio during the war and he could not return. Then, another man married me. The man with whom I am living now. He is causing me a lot of problems. We don't understand each other. When I was still pregnant I used to do the housework. When the time to cultivate arrived I went to the field, I used to cook, to pound, to look for wood, to clean the house, and to cover the walls of the house with mud. In the evening when I wanted to rest, my husband wanted to have sexual intercourse with me. I did not like to have sexual intercourse while I was pregnant but he used to force me. I used to say 'no, no' and he used to say, 'let's go'. I used to refuse. Sometimes I used to leave my hut to sleep outside in the cold. Sometimes he used to pull off my blankets and all my clothes and say, 'go to sleep outside . . . the husband that you love outside go to sleep with him'. On the following day I could no longer stand sleeping outside in the cold weather, so I went into the hut to sleep with him. This happened three times.

I went many times to present this problem to the elders but they got tired of trying to solve our problems. My husband drinks a lot of alcohol. He always drinks and many times he is drunk. Sometimes he beats me. Sometimes I don't do anything but he beats me. Other times when I refuse to have sexual intercourse with him he beats me. He beat me four times because of sexual intercourse. He used the belt that he tied his trousers to beat me. I cannot manage to fight against him because he is a man.

Infant–parents Relationship: *Madzawde*

When my first child was born, three months later my husband said that we had to perform *madzawde* ritual for the child. We did *madzawde* ritual for the child and then I got pregnant again. When I got pregnant, the elders told me that I should stop breastfeeding the child otherwise the child would get sick. The elders said that if I continued breastfeeding, the baby [i.e., the child at the breast] would be contaminated and would get sick. For this reason I no longer continued to provide the breastfeeding to my baby.

I had to make the sexual intercourse very early because my husband wanted me to. Sometimes I used to run away to the granary to sleep but he used to chase me. I used to run away from him because our child was still small and I wanted to wait much longer before we did *madzawde* ritual for the child. I wanted to wait for the child to grow older but he did not want to. Because he is the man I had to accept. I spoke many times with him but he does not take notice of what I say. My husband drinks a lot and when I refuse to have sexual contact with him he beats me. He says 'I am telling you to come to sleep together and you are refusing.' When I do not accept to do sexual intercourse with him he beats me. No matter if he is drunk or not, he just wants to have sexual intercourse.

Sickness of the Child: Cultural Explanations

Sometime later my child got sick. The elders said that it was because I breastfed the child while I was pregnant. My child was feeling pain in the body, then he had bubble in the face, and sometimes his body gets thin, other times the body increases the weight. Until today the child is still in the same condition – *tsakata tsakata* [exaggerated long-term weight loss]. That's why we came here to the hospital.

Now that I am here at the hospital with our child that is ill, my husband does not stay at home. I received a message saying that he has another wife. He is playing with other women. I don't know what he does with these women but every time he comes here to the hospital to touch our baby, when he leaves, in the evening our baby does not sleep. The baby begins to cry, to cough, and gets diarrhoea. Sometimes he stays a week without coming here and the child gets better but when he comes and touches the baby, the baby gets sick again. I am not enjoying this. That's why we are in conflict all the time. These are the problems that I am going through. I don't know why the child gets ill when he touches him. I only know that when he comes here he has already slept with another woman. When he stays one week without coming here the child gets better, the child no longer coughs. But as long as he comes here to the hospital, when he touches the baby, the baby begins to get ill: cough, vomiting and diarrhoea. My husband likes to have sexual intercourse with other women. When he has sexual intercourse with other women, when he arrives here and touches the baby, the baby gets ill. If he does not confess what he has been doing our child will not survive. Our child will die.

Discussion

This case study illustrates the effects of prolonged exposure to war and drought on the social, cultural and psychological worlds of women in Gorongosa. Mrs D's testimony mirrors the experiences of many of the mothers who sought treatment at the local health centre and took part in the study. It shows that the impact of war and starvation lingers on long after peace has been established and food supplies restored and may be expressed in a multitude of ways, through domestic violence and related alcohol abuse, through reduced protection to infants and so on. The testimony emphasises that while the war experiences were extremely distressing for the inhabitants of Gorongosa, the post-war period remains very difficult and full of paradoxes. Richters (2001: 70) notes that 'history shows that if the percentage of seriously traumatised people reaches a critical point, the balance in that society becomes disturbed'. It would seem that this critical point may have been reached in Gorongosa, where the upheavals of armed violence and starvation had a tremendous effect not merely on the inner psychological state of the population but on their entire way of life (Summerfield 1995). Several of the traditional healers and leaders I spoke to emphasised this point, their explanations of the effects of war and drought being couched in terms not of psychopathological consequences but of the destabilisation of fundamental sociocultural processes. Not only were the people of Gorongosa no longer able to perform their rituals and ceremonies but also the process of transmission of cultural knowledge and practice from the older to the younger generations was interrupted. In the words of one traditional healer:

> We had no house to do *madzawde* … we had no time to think about our traditions … We were running away all the time from one place to another in the middle of the bush … We could not teach our children how to live and grow up properly, they were growing like animals … We were living like animals that's why there is a lot of confusion nowadays because of *madzawde* … in the past, before the war, I had never heard that a family was fighting because of *madzawde* but nowadays there is a lot of fighting, people are changed … *Tsanganiko, madzawde, ku banhira, ma kutchafia*, all these important traditions were changed and people are fighting because of it … children are suffering and dying because of their parents not respecting tradition … (interview with Fernando Faera Mculuzado, Nharoi-Vunduzi, Gorongosa, 16 October 1999).

Today in Gorongosa there is no consensus regarding the best way to deal with the challenges of the post-war period or over the norms, values and practices of child rearing. Many no longer engage in *madzawde* and those who do no longer respect many of the features of the system that were once regarded as crucial. Many believe that the war polluted the environment in such a way that they cannot trust even close relatives. Above all, raising children is no longer a community affair. As I shall explain, this has particular implications for children's survival and well-being in light of local theories of causality in illness and recent demographic trends.

In regard to explanations of illness, it is believed that people have 'hot blood' after sexual intercourse and that this is a source of pollution, extremely dangerous in particular for babies who have not passed through the rite of *madzawde*. It is held that if a person touches a baby in this polluted state, the child will become ill. If this sickness, also termed *madzawde*, is not treated in time the child can die. Hence, children who have not undergone all the steps of *madzawde* are highly susceptible to disease. On the other hand, as *madzawde* ends, so the infant is protected from ill health and a new phase in its life begins. In the past, there was no need to be concerned with other people's sexual practices because in principle everyone knew and respected the rules attached to *madzawde*. Parents could wait two years before completing *madzawde* without fearing that someone with 'hot blood' would touch their baby in the intervening period. However, since the years of war and drought there has been a growth in the local population and a marked increase in social differentiation, resulting in overcrowding in some areas. Such trends are perceived by many as a grave threat to infants. The concern is that with the overcrowding and the lack of community involvement in child rearing there is a serious risk that adults who have just had sexual intercourse may touch babies who have yet to undergo *madzawde*, thereby threatening their health and survival.

High levels of social heterogeneity have also made it difficult for traditional healers to identify the author of a child's misfortune, that is, the person who touched the baby with 'hot blood'. This makes reparation difficult, forcing parents to become engaged in the troublesome and at times painful process of trying to discover the reason for an infant's ill health. In an environment in which there is a loss of a sense of community and trust, this commonly leads to accusations against neighbours and other community members. Usually the accused person will present their case before the traditional court, the *Matako Wa Ukulo* (the Buttock of the Old Men). In this way, personal conflicts acquire a community dimension.

Because parents cannot be confident that other adults will observe social taboos surrounding sexual intercourse, many perform the *madzawde* ritual early, at around three months after the birth, in order to prevent possible contamination of a baby and to release it from *madzawde*. But this adaptation creates problems of its own, for a reduction in the duration of *madzawde* is associated with early weaning and a decrease in the period

between births, which in turn increases the likelihood of obstetric compli-
cations and infant morbidity and mortality. Beliefs about weaning are
enshrined in the *ku wa muira* custom, which dictates that as soon as a
mother becomes pregnant she must cease breastfeeding. The justification
for weaning in this situation is that the milk no longer belongs to the newborn baby but to the developing foetus. This explanatory model, regarding the quality of the milk of a pregnant woman, differs from the one
identified, for example, by Marie Creyghton (1992) in her study among
the Baraka people in Northern Tunisia. Among the Baraka, 'bad milk' or
'milk illness' is one of the causes of child sickness. In the case of
Gorongosa people, the question is not related to the quality of the milk
but to its ownership. If the baby sucks the milk of the pregnant mother,
the baby gets sick because the milk belongs to the foetus. Whether she
wants to or not, the mother has to detach from the baby. This early detachment of the mother from the infant has very adverse implications for the
health of the child. One of the main reasons for this is that in Gorongosa
there are no foods or nutritional fluids that are suitable as a replacement
for breast milk. However, when a child becomes ill under such circumstances, it is not attributed to the abrupt interruption of breastfeeding but
to a violation of *madzawde*. The following diagnosis of *madzawde* by a
healer illustrates this belief:

> Do you think that someone bewitched your child? This child was not
> bewitched. This child has *piringaniço*. Her mother is pregnant. She stole the
> pregnancy from this child. She spent one month while the child is breast-
> feeding. She did *ku wa muira*. She breastfed this child during one month
> while she was already pregnant. Can this child get better? The baby will
> not live well. That's why every day I say 'the mothers of today, they rush
> to get inside the hut to have sexual intercourse while she does not have
> knowledge about these problems. Will these children live well? No', unless
> the parents change their behaviour. (observation of a healing session in the
> hut of the traditional healer Nhamita Benjamin, Nhataca 2, Gorongosa, 30
> April 2002)

One of the women described her experience of weaning in the following
way:

> Three months after the birth of my child my husband told me that we
> should do *madzawde* to the child. I told him that the child was still very
> small. He disagreed and he forced me to do it. Some time later I discovered
> that I was pregnant. The elders told me that I could no longer continue to
> breastfeed this other child. They said that if I continued breastfeeding the
> baby would be contaminated and would get sick and I would be responsi-
> ble for that. They said that I should not do *ku wa muira* because the milk
> belongs to the child that is in the belly.

In the modern era when there is so much uncertainty about customary
practice there is the additional problem, alluded to by this woman, that

parents may not agree about breaking with the traditional regime of *madzawde*. The research showed that most often it was the father who sought an early closure to *madzawde*, while the mothers wished to have it run its full course. In such cases there is an increased likelihood that performance of the ritual may be associated with marital discord and violence. One of the women described her experience:

> One day my husband told me that he was already tired of sleeping inside sacks and alone. But I told him that he could not sleep with me yet because the three months after the birth of our child had not yet been completed to perform *madzawde*. Then, he went out to drink and came back home drunk. When he arrived at home he wanted to sleep with me but I did not accept again. Then, he took his cutlass and lunged at me. I tried to defend myself with one arm while I was carrying the baby with another arm. He launched his cutlass again and I defended myself with the other arm and I let the baby fall on the ground. When I turned to get the baby my husband struck me in the neck with the cutlass. I began to bleed and to scream. The neighbours who heard my screams ran to my hut, but he had already run away. I was immediately taken to the hospital otherwise I could have died.

Violence of this nature surrounding the practice of *madzawde* is, as far as I have been able to establish, fairly common in Gorongosa. Frequently it is exacerbated by high levels of alcohol consumption among men, as in the case of Mrs D. Resort to psychoactive substances has been a widespread coping strategy in the post-war period in Gorongosa. Alcohol in particular provides short-term relief from pain or distress, sleep disturbance, nightmares and other intrusive symptoms (Keane et al. 1988; Saxe et al. 1993). But the social costs are high. I recorded several cases of community violence in which alcohol consumption had played a major role. The dramatic effects of *Nipa*, a local beer, are well recognised in Gorongosa among war survivors. People often say, 'when someone drinks Nipa the person becomes two … he is no longer the person we know but someone else comes in his place'. Dissociation through the rapid stimulation obtained from *Nipa* allows many disruptive behaviours to be placed in a normative context because the person involved cannot consciously remember the damage caused to others.

Conclusion

The study showed that because of the changes brought about by the war and drought, parents, in particular men, seek to perform the *madzawde* ritual early to protect the newborn baby and reinstate intercourse as soon as possible. But by performing the ritual early they are inviting new problems. If women refuse to comply with this, there is a risk of domestic violence and marital insecurity. In the event that the ritual is performed early and the woman becomes pregnant again, she is confronted with the proscription associated with *ku wa muira* which requires her to stop breastfeeding. Given the lack of foodstuffs appropriate as a replacement for breast milk, this greatly increases the likelihood that the child will fall sick. When the child becomes ill, the problem is transferred from the domestic to the community domain.

The disruption of cultural structures and systems of support leads to a complex situation where solutions are difficult to find. The case of *ku wa muira* law illustrates this observation. The whole structure and dynamic of *madzawde* has been disrupted: the *nhamuino*, who is the gatekeeper of the structure, is often no longer invited by the parents to play her part in the ceremony and consequently the elements of nature are not used; the duration of *madzawde* is different; but *ku wa muira* has remained intact. If the mother manages to solve the conflict with the cultural rules by obeying *ku wa muira*, she fails to care for her child effectively. The practice of *madzawde* and *ku wa muira* are permanently clashing with each other and the result of this cultural paradox is that both the infants and mothers live under permanent health risk, including the risk of death.

Understanding the disruption of this cultural mechanism and its effects on the child and on the society is very important in order to develop effective and culturally sensitive responses. We still have to learn about the explanatory models provided by local healers and the nature and type of their intervention in such cases. From the perspective of Western medicine, a campaign to educate the parents on the importance of breastfeeding, together with the practice of contraception to ensure a sufficient interval between births, might seem to be what is required. In fact, the local health centre in Gorongosa created a team to travel from one community to the other to explain to both parents not only the importance of breastfeeding but also the advantages of modern contraception. Yet, from the cultural perspective it seems that this was not an appropriate way of addressing the many complexities and paradoxes associated with modern approaches to childcare and weaning.

Addressing the long-term effects of destructive experiences in non-Western societies, as in the case of Gorongosa, requires integrated approaches. Cultural factors which determine conjugal or kinship roles must be carefully understood and addressed (Maher 1992). There is a need to acquire more insight into the ways in which domestic violence and abuse against women covered by cultural tenets is putting at risk their psychosocial health and their ability to properly nurse their children. This study has demonstrated that the disruption of *madzawde* practice and the degree of violence it involves are compromising the future of the postwar children in Gorongosa.

Acknowledgements

I wish to thank all the women in this study, the local team of AEPATO and the health professionals at the health centre in Gorongosa. I extend my acknowledgements to Jo Boyden and Tom Feeny for the extensive revision of this chapter. And I also thank professor Peter Riedesser (Hamburg) and the Volkswagen Stiftung (Hannover) for their support.

References

Brand, R. 1989. 'Fertility and Anthropological Significance of Coitus in the Wéménou Society (Benin).' In K. Peltzer and P. Ebigbo, eds, *Clinical Psychology in Africa South of the Sahara, the Caribbean and Afro-Latin America*. Chuka: Nigeria.

Cliff, J. and Noormahomed, A.R. 1993. 'The Impact of War on Children's Health in Mozambique.' *Social Science and Medicine* 36 (7): 843–8.

Creyghton, M.-L. 1992. 'Breast-feeding and Baraka in Northern Tunisia.' In V. Maher, ed., *The Anthropology of Breast-feeding: Natural Law or Social Construct. Cross-cultural Perspectives on Women*. Oxford: Berg.

Field, T. 1992. 'Infants of Depressed Mothers.' *Development and Psychopathology* 4: 49–66.

Finerman, R. 1995. '"Parental Incompetence" and Selective Neglect: Blaming the Victim in Child Survival.' *Social Science and Medicine* 40 (1): 5–13.

Foxen, P. 2000. 'Cacophony of Voices: A K'iche' Mayan Narrative of Remembrance and Forgetting.' *Transcultural Psychiatry* 37 (3): 355–81.

Gelfand, D. and Teti, D. 1990. 'The Effects of Maternal Depression on Children.' *Clinical Psychology Review* 10: 329–53.

Hauswald, L. 1987. 'External Pressure/Internal Change: Child Neglect on the Navajo Reservation.' In N. Scheper-Hughes, ed., *Child Survival: anthropological perspectives*. Dordrecht: D. Reidel.

Igreja, V. 2003. The effects of traumatic experiences on the infant-mother relationship in the former war-zones of Central Mozambique: the case of *Madzawde* in Gorongosa. *Infant Mental Health Journal* 24 (5), September.

Keane, T., Gerardi, R., Lyons J. and Wolfe, J. 1988. 'The Interrelationship of Substance Abuse and Posttraumatic Stress Disorder: Epidemiological and Clinical Considerations.' In M. Galanter, ed., *Recent Developments in Alcoholism*. Vol. 6, New York: Plenum Press.

Khare, R.S. 1977. 'Ritual Purity and Pollution in Relation to Domestic Sanitation.' In D. Landy ed., *Culture, Disease, and Healing. Studies in Medical Anthropology*. New York: Macmillan.

Maher, V. 1992. 'Breast-feeding and Maternal Depletion: Natural Law or Cultural Arrangements?' In V. Maher, ed., *The Anthropology of Breast-feeding: Natural Law or Social Construct. Cross-cultural Perspectives on Women*. Berg: Oxford.

Mead, M. and Wolfenstein, M. 1955. *Childhood in Contemporary Cultures*. Chicago: University of Chicago Press.

Richman, N. 1993. 'Annotation: Children in Situations of Political Violence.' *Journal of Child Psychology and Psychiatry* 34 (8): 1286–302.

Richman, N., Ratilal, A. and Aly, A. 1990. *The Effects of War on Mozambican Children: Preliminary Findings*. Maputo: Ministry of Education.

Richters, A. 1994. *Women, Culture and Violence: A Development, Health and Human Rights Issue*. Leiden: Women and Autonomy Centre (VENA), Leiden University.

——. 2001. 'Trauma as a Permanent Indictment of Injustice: A Socio-cultural Critique of DSM-III and DSM-IV.' In M. Verwey, ed., *Trauma and Empowerment*. Berlin: VWB.

Saxe, G., van der Kolk, B., Hall, K., Schwartz, J., Chinman, G., Hall, M., Lieberg, G., and Berkowitz, R. 1993. 'Dissociative Disorders in Psychiatric Inpatients.' *American Journal of Psychiatry* 150 (7): 1037–42.

Shaw, J.A. and Harris, J.J. 1994. 'Children of War and Children at War: Child Victims of Terrorism in Mozambique.' In R. Ursano, B.G. McCaughey and C.S. Fullerton, eds, *Individual and Community Responses to Trauma and Disaster: The Structure of Human Chaos*. Cambridge: Cambridge University Press.

Summerfield, D. 1995. 'Addressing Human Response to War and Atrocity: Major Challenges in Research and Practices and the Limitations of Western Psychiatric Models.' In R. Kleber, C. Figley and B. Gersons, eds, *Beyond Trauma: Cultural and Societal Dynamics*. New York: Plenum Press.

Super, M. and Harkness, S. 1989. 'The Developmental Niche: A Conceptualization at the Interface of Child and Culture.' *International Journal of Behavioral Development* 9: 545–69.

UNDP. 1999. *Mozambique. Economic Growth and Human Development: Progress, Obstacles and Challenges*. National Human Report. Maputo, Mozambique.

Part II

Vulnerability and Resilience among Adolescent Girls

3

The Sexual Vulnerability of Adolescent Girls during Civil War in Teso, Uganda[1]

Joanna de Berry

Introduction

Between 1987 and 1992 the Teso region of north-east Uganda was in the grips of civil war. An insurgent group called the Uganda People's Army (UPA) fought against the forces of the newly established government of Uganda, the National Resistance Army (NRA). The UPA had widespread support amongst the civilian population in Teso, and in seeking to curb the insurgency the NRA tried to cut off links between the militants and the local people. They did this by moving rural communities out of their homes and placing them in settlement camps, which were guarded by barracks of army soldiers. Land outside the camps was considered a free-fire zone and anyone found there was assumed to be hostile to the government and killed. Government troops scoured the area looking for UPA bush camps to attack.

Whilst the NRA heralded the camps as 'safe havens' so that the conflict could be fought in the bush without involving the local population, the adversities of the period also extended to the conditions in the camps. Lack of adequate sanitation and food security, starvation and the rapid spread of disease, restriction of movement and curfews all characterised the years the Iteso people lived in the settlements. The camp inhabitants were sometimes killed in the fighting; either by the army as they tried to escape back to their homes to recover food stores, or on suspicion of being a rebel sympathiser, or during attacks by the UPA militants on the army barracks. Ostensibly for the 'protection' of the civilian population, these camps saw as many casualties of the war as the conflict between the UPA and NRA itself (Amnesty International 1992).

For adolescent girls in the camps there was a particular threat: rape and sexual abuse at the hands of government soldiers.[2] An unknown but significant number of young girls experienced the humiliation, terror and suffering of sexual violation at the hands of army personnel (Turshen 1998: 15; WILDAF 1994: 18). Some were taken directly by the soldiers; others became victims of organised networks of traffickers amongst the Iteso in the camps who provided sexual companions for the military. During my anthropological fieldwork in Teso, between 1996 and 1998, I met with young women for whom the rape and sexual abuse they had suffered during the conflict tortured their memories, shadowed their present and had consequences for their future. This chapter uses their words and experiences to explore how and why their sexual abuse came about, how they responded to it and what it means for their life in the present.

Armed Conflict and Sexual Vulnerability: A Framework

In recent years growing attention has been paid to the incidence of rape and sexual abuse as a war crime. The recent conviction of Serbian soldiers for repeated and horrific sexual violence against Bosnian women, at the International War Crimes tribunal at the Hague, represents international condemnation of sexual violations against civilian women during wartime. As awareness of war-related sexual abuse has grown, so too has concern to understand the phenomenon better. Enough investigation has been done to show that it cannot simply be explained as just a terrible but natural occurrence in the upheaval of war. In her seminal piece on children in armed conflict Graça Machel writes:

> Rape poses a continual threat to women and girls during armed conflict, as do other forms of gender-based violence including prostitution, sexual humiliation and mutilation, trafficking and domestic violence. While abuses such as murder and torture have long been denounced as war crimes, rape has been downplayed as an unfortunate but inevitable side effect of war … . [but] rape is not incidental to war. (1996: 22)

She goes on to suggest that sexual violence may become a part of war as a deliberate form of torture, a tactic to humiliate and terrorise a perceived enemy. It can be used with the intent of ethnic cleansing through forced pregnancy. In Rwanda, for example, Tutsi women were raped and made pregnant by Hutu men who constructed their sexuality and fertility as a demographic and political threat (Bennet et al. 1995: 8). Anthropological work confirms this perception of sexual violence in conflict as being related to social and symbolic meanings (Littlewood 1997: 11). From Bosnia comes evidence that organised mass rape can be used as a systematic weapon of war. Mass rape was used in the former Yugoslavia as a strategy to destroy community identity in the name of ethnic and religious purity. Bosnian women were forced to bear the children of their Serbian captors, to reproduce and thus embody their intended servility (Bringa 1995). By subjecting women, undermining the honour of family and marriage relationships, Serb forces also hit at the ethnic pride and integrity of the male population. Defiling women was a way of violating and demoralising Bosnian men – rape was often committed in front of family and community.

Here is an understanding that if people (for it is not always women) are vulnerable to sexual abuse during times of war, it is due to the social relationships, structures and strategies in operation. The investigation of sexual abuse thus requires a critical examination of the way in which people become and are made vulnerable in the context in which they live.

This perspective counts for children and young people as much as it does for adults. Since it was young adolescent girls in Teso who were the particular subjects of sexual abuse, they must have occupied an especially vulnerable place, a place defined by relationships and circumstances in the camps. When it comes to the young, however, it is easy to assume that their suffering is a result of their inherently vulnerable nature. There is no doubt that children have a special status in any society, a status often closely aligned with their physical fragility and dependence. Yet the notion of children's vulnerability is often conceptually weak. First, it can be forgotten that whatever vulnerability is imputed to children is as much a result of social and cultural perceptions as it is due to their physical nature. As Mann's work in this volume shows, there can be complex social relationships and cultural understandings that define what children are perceived to need and how this is delivered (see also Scheper-Hughes 1992). These understandings are not immutable but can change in time according to circumstances. Children might indeed be vulnerable, have certain special requirements and face particular risks but this is a structural position, a product of the interrelation of biological features and social constructions (Kirby and Fraser 1997: 10). It is not an inherent value.

Second, the different status-related vulnerabilities of children may be overlooked. This trend has been exaggerated by the move to international age-based definitions of childhood. Activists for child protection have tended to equate the international definition of children – all those under the age of 18 – with characteristics that might accrue only to a fraction of children within that range. Often features such as physical immaturity, the need for physiological nurture, attachment to mothers, physical and emotional vulnerability, which might well be relevant to the very young are ascribed to all those below 18. Yet the differences of social status, gender and familial roles within the bracket of eighteen and under, are often far more salient in framing children's experiences of adversity and determining their relative vulnerabilities (de Berry and Boyden 2000).

There is a strong case then for using a perspective which takes into account the social, structural and cultural aspects of vulnerability to understand children's experiences of adversity. This is the framework used in this chapter. It is applied to the testimonies of young women from Teso to ask how it was that sexual violence became part of their experiences in the camp and why young adolescents girls rather than anyone else faced this ordeal. Their particular vulnerability stems from the nature of being a young unmarried, adolescent girl in times when Teso social life was lived under military occupation.

Yet that is only half the story. During my time with young women in Teso, the ethnography of their histories, feelings and choices, brought out not only stories of their suffering but also evidence of their strength and coping. Indeed, a growing body of literature suggests that even when people do find themselves vulnerable and exposed to harmful events, they do not lose the ability to contest and negotiate, to use their social and emotional resources to make things better for themselves and to cope with even the most horrific of circumstances (de Smedt 1998; Frankenberg et al. 2000). Studying child victims of sexual abuse in the U.K., for example, Kitzinger (1997) found that the children employed a variety of resistance tactics to refute complete submission. People can actively respond within a situation of adversity to ease the pain and once it is over they may have ways and means of healing the suffering. One of the main criticisms of studies of people's experiences of war is that they focus upon victimisation rather than the capacity of people to confront and recover from the hardships that face them (Allen 1989: 47; Boyden 1994: 257; de Waal 1997: 82). Increasingly credit is given to people's creative and resilient ability to rebuild their lives, even after the cruellest of circumstances (Gibbs 1994: 270; Honwana 1999; Malkki 1995). This chapter adds to such work.

Armed Conflict and Sexual Vulnerability: Narratives from Teso

Schola was 14 when she and her family were moved into the camp. I recorded her story during a group discussion with several young women, all members of a church prayer group:

> For me I get too much thinking when I get memories of the war. I used to get too much thinking also, those days when people were gathered in the camps. I got so many troubles being a girl. You found that soldiers gathered and came into the camp looking for girls. Now you would find that for someone like me who was unmarried at that time, people really used

me badly. They could use you for eating from soldiers. They would go to the barracks looking for a way of eating and they would say to the soldiers 'I can find you an unmarried girl'. Then they would move with soldiers showing them girls who were not married. Then one by one the soldiers would come and say 'I want you' and what could I do? So many soldiers were asking me and I could not know which was good and which was bad. Then they took you by force because they had already given out money to someone to find them a girl and that person had eaten the money. They would say to me, 'Don't play with us, because we can kill you,' and they would put their guns by the door when they came into the house.

One day soldiers came to kill me. Some men from the camp had got money from the soldiers in return for telling the soldiers that I was an unmarried girl. The soldiers came to me and I tried to refuse and they started shouting at me telling me that I was proud because I was a schoolgirl. They started following me and abusing me but I just kept quiet and kept on refusing. I tried to deceive them and said that I was married. This was an idea that I had been given by a friend of mine. He said to me that I should say that I was married to him. However, the soldiers went and beat up this man until he admitted that I was not his wife. The soldiers came back and started shouting at me: 'Who do you think you are? You are so proud. Do you think that we don't have wives ourselves? Do you think that our wives are like stones? Yet we have been taken away from our wives to come and protect your village.' Then they brought their grenades and started following me. My neighbour's wife started crying saying to me, 'If you don't go with them then they will kill us all. Just go with them and get their money because I don't even have a shilling for feeding my children'. So I agreed to go with the soldiers. Then I got advice from my friends that it is better to choose one soldier and accept to stay with him so that the other ones will not disturb you.

Then I got another problem when the soldiers were transferred and new ones came. I had to get another soldier to protect me. Some men brought a soldier to me; that was their work, to organise girls for the soldiers. The soldier they brought was very short and blind in one eye and I got very annoyed. I thought, 'I have accepted everyone, every soldier that was brought to me I have accepted, because there is no way out. But I don't even know which soldiers are good and which are bad'. So I decided that I would escape. I got one of my friends, an Itesot, who was a bodyguard to the soldiers and I asked him to help me escape. He was one of the people to organise girls for the soldiers and he told me that if the soldiers found that I had escaped then they would come and kill me. But he helped me and showed me a secret route to Soroti [regional capital] and he organised with the L.C. [Local Councillor, lowest level of the administration] to get me a letter, which would allow me to pass to Soroti, and I escaped there, walking all the way at night.

When I reached to Soroti I was not like a normal person in any way. I would meet soldiers on the street and I would walk slowly like a person who does not have control in the body. I would dream at night that more and more soldiers were coming into my hut. I had too much thinking, too much thinking. Until my heart was full of thoughts and I became thin, thin. I got ulcers in my heart and there was no sleep in my mind. I produced my child from there and I thought that I did not know which was her father.

Slowly, slowly I got advice from my friends in Soroti. We would share eating together and after eating we would start joking. They taught me good ideas until I got some peace and began forgetting those bad thoughts. When I was quiet they would make me talk and when I didn't want to talk they would talk themselves. I would laugh when I saw my daughter playing. However, even now I get too much thinking. I see my daughter and I think that I don't even have money to feed her, I have too many problems. I think that if it were not for the war I would not have to bring up a child in such conditions. And what of AIDS? Too much thinking … .

Florence was 13 at the time she was moved into a camp. I heard this story when I went to visit her home and found that three of her children, who I had never met before, had recently moved to be with her. She explained how she had come by these children:

My story is a story of suffering, real suffering. We really suffered during those days of war and we suffered because we were unmarried girls. You know many of us suffered during those days, Apio, the girl who works in that hotel, Agouti who is always in the village, Akello, the one with the sick child, Emuge, the brown girl who is always talking at the borehole, well these things happened to all of us. We suffered together.

There was a day when people had been moved into the camp. We had been staying in the camp for about four weeks and were getting used to the conditions. We were wondering what was going to happen to us, when we would be allowed out of the camp to go and grow our food, where we were going to buy salt and sugar from. In those days the soldiers were strangers to us, we saw them at a distance, sitting in their barracks, but people did not talk with them very much. We young people feared the soldiers because they had guns and wore uniforms so we avoided them as if they were strangers. But we were also interested in watching them, watching in case they did any harm to anyone and getting to know the different ones and their characters.

One day a new lot of soldiers were brought to the camp and things began to change. Early one morning the soldiers called all the people out of the camp and made us line up in front of the borehole. It was a hot day and they made us stand there for a long time. There were old people standing there, old people, young people and all people. Some women were carrying babies. It was a very hot day and there was no shade where we were standing, we were not allowed to go and get drinking water. We just stood there. After some time one of the old women collapsed. She fell down right where she was. The soldiers just carried on walking by not noticing that anything had happened. Then after about an hour they shot the old woman. They just shot her like that, they left her body there and then told the rest of us to go back to our houses. Then we knew that things were really bad and we became very frightened.

One day a big lorry drove into the camp, the soldiers who were driving it were different again. We had not seen them before. They drove the lorry straight into the middle of the camp, where the market used to be, and they jumped out carrying their guns on their backs. Some of us were standing around and we wondered what was happening. Then suddenly the chief of the soldiers started to point at girls like myself. He said 'That one!' and

'That one!' He said 'You, you and you!' He pointed at me and soldiers came towards me. I tried to run into the house but the soldiers caught me and they lifted me up and put me into the lorry. They went round in that way pointing out girls and catching them. Some of the girls tried to run but they were caught and the soldiers beat them so it was bad for them. The chief kept on shouting 'That one, that brown one!' 'Yes that one is very beautiful take that one!' Soon the lorry was full of girls, full I mean completely full. We were squeezed in and then the soldiers got in with their guns and we drove off. We drove a long way, through the night and through the bush. We were not going on the normal roads. We went through bushy places and we were tired and hungry. They gave us no food. After a long time we reached a place in the jungle. There was an army barracks there. I now know that the place is called Busia but at that time I knew nothing.

Then the awful thing happened. The soldiers came out from their barracks and each one took one girl. They dragged off each girl. A man took me and because it was dark I couldn't even see his face. He put me inside a hut and he closed the door. We stayed like that for a very long time, for years even. The men just used us for sex. They didn't even use us for cooking. We were just inside the huts all the time, day and night. They had other women to do the cooking. These other women used to bring us food and water for bathing but for us we just sat inside the huts all day every day, never going out, even urinating we did in the huts. Just kept there. We really suffered, we really suffered … all of us we were like that. Myself, Apio, Agouti, Emuge. We were all there and we began to get children from there. That is how I got these children. Their father is a soldier and they speak Swahili. When the children were born the other women came and took them and looked after them but for us we just remained inside. That is the suffering that war brings, that is my story of suffering. All of us were like that and we really suffered.

Factors in Vulnerability

Schola and Florence's narratives reveal in graphic and painful detail the ways in which adolescent girls in the camps became the subjects of repeated sexual abuse at the hands of NRA soldiers: by being abducted to far-off army barracks, by being singled out for soldiers by fellow members of the camp who were rewarded for their services, and by offering sexual services in return for payment. Their narratives also allude to the circumstances and social relationships through which such events could happen.

Militarisation

For the three years that they were in the camps the people of Teso lived under the watch of a heavy military presence. The army dictated the terms under which they ate, travelled, slept and worked. The soldiers had guns, the residents of the camps did not: there was little leeway for escape or resistance. What the soldiers wanted they got and evidently they wanted sex. They wanted sex because, in their own words, they were away from their own wives, and they wanted sex because they could have it. Their power over the camp population was unchecked and unaccounted. The fact that they could come in and drive off with a lorryload of girls exposed, as so often in conflict, the defencelessness of the entire community and the lack of deference of the army hierarchy to international laws for protection of civilian populations. The soldiers here acted not so much as defenders of a civilian people but as an occupying force who equated the people in the camp with their enemies the UPA, placing them all in the bracket of people whose rights and liberties were disposable.

Not just in Teso, but all too often, the incidence of sexual violence is closely linked to the militarisation of society during times of conflict (Machel 1996). In the ill-defined battlegrounds of many modern day conflicts, civilians are often placed under military control, or continue to live in their homes where combatants demand to be accommodated. Soldiers, even peacekeeping forces, have commonly abused the power they can exert over a civilian population by demanding sexual services in a systematic, rather than random, way (Nordstrom 1997b: 15).

The Commoditisation of Sex

The power of the NRA soldiers to acquire sexual services in the camps in Teso was due not only to their ability to demand or force it, but also to their willingness to pay for it. Indeed, through all the years lived in the camps, the soldiers represented the main significant market and economy. Although links to the UPA militants were also a source of income, members of the camp who showed any real financial success at this time were those who ingratiated themselves with the soldiers; either getting permission to attend to crops, which they could then sell, to travel to town to bring back stocks to be sold in the camp, or by supplying the soldiers with alcohol or sexual services.

In Teso, as is often the case in conditions of conflict-related impoverishment, women forwent their own sexual protection in return for economic survival. Economic gain was an incentive to do as Schola later did and agree to live with one soldier, so that he would 'keep' her: protect her from the advances of other men and offer financial support. Even if a young girl herself might not willingly trade her sexual services, the pressure on her to do so by friends and family – as Schola also experienced – might be irresistible, especially if she then knew that she would be able to provide for them.

Sexual exploitation may occur on the initiative of women and children themselves: 'poverty, hunger and desperation may force women and girls into prostitution, obliging them to offer sex for food or shelter, for safe conduct through the war zone or to obtain papers or other privileges for themselves and their families' (Machel 1996: 23). Under severe economic duress parents may give their children up to sexual sale. In other words, women may become vulnerable to sexual exploitation as part of the social, economic and material pressures of war, in which peacetime relations and access to resources are undermined or even destroyed. This is particularly the case amongst refugee populations. The commoditisation of sex may represent the only coping strategy left to women, children and families in times of conflict and impoverishment.

Interpersonal Violence

Yet in Teso another dynamic was also evident – the organisation of girls for the soldiers by fellow Itesot men in the camps. A series of middlemen, taking advantage of the soldiers' willingness to pay for sex and their own connections within the camp, got money in advance for pointing out young unmarried girls. They hijacked the commoditisation of the sex provided by others for their own ends. Once the soldiers had paid them money there was little escape for the girls.

Well hidden in accounts of war that focus solely upon two opposing sides, these middlemen are actually common features of conflict. In Mozambique, Nordstrom found them identified by the local population as 'jackals', 'becoming rich on the pain of others. Selling information to one side, and to the other, selling people out for money' (1997a: 57). They take on roles of informers, traders and even pimps.

Certainly in Teso these agents were in it for the money, but they also had more insidious purposes. Notably they did not put forward their own daughters, sisters, cousins and friends for sexual services. They pointed out the daughters, sisters, cousins and friends of others. Furthermore it is the opinion of those in Teso today, that the middlemen deliberately singled out girls connected to those they had a grudge against.

In Teso social life is marked by interpersonal grievances over disparities and inequities that are manifest in witchcraft and spiritual violence, commonly against adolescent girls of a rival family (Lawrence 1957). The idea of community, with overtones of harmony and collective common interest over and above family life, does not apply to Teso (de Berry 2000; cf. Guijt and Shah 1998). Yet under peacetime conditions these tensions are managed and controlled by the physical distance between homes and families. People can generally avoid their enemies and thus protect themselves from the dangers of witchcraft. In the camps, in contrast, thousands of people who depend upon physical and social distance for the management of conflict, were packed together in squalid and overcrowded conditions. The lack of social space is the most frequent adversity Iteso refer to about the camps. As the idiom used by a friend in Teso suggests: 'We call the days that we were in the camp "the days when there was no salt".

Salt is a good thing; it makes food taste sweet. Salt is the one thing that you can share between families. But in the camp there was no sharing. Everyone was divided.'

The camp population was not a united community; the interpersonal and interfamilial grievances and jealousies that mark so much of social life in Teso, were intensified in the cramped conditions. Interestingly, however, the use of witchcraft to act upon these grievances appears to have decreased as people turned to physical rather than spiritual violence to effect their disputes.[3] Indeed the whole course of the conflict in Teso was marked by people using the license granted by the conditions of war to act on interpersonal grievances with violence. Those who had a dispute with others – disputes over land, women, cattle or witchcraft – often informed UPA fighters that those with whom they were in contention were supporters of the government. UPA fighters could in this way be hired or persuaded to attack personal enemies (Henriques 2000). Likewise people might inform the NRA troops that their adversary was a UPA informer and subject them to NRA attack, detention or torture. For many in Teso, the war was not so much about the NRA against the UPA but about the mire and violence of micro-level relationships, with which they had to contend.

The men who singled out girls to provide sexual services to soldiers appear to have been acting on the same lines. They used and even arranged the sexual abuse of other men's daughters, sisters and cousins as a tactic to humiliate and terrorise a perceived enemy. There are echoes here of Bosnia: the rape and sexual violation of women being used to cause men suffering. Yet whilst in Bosnia this strategy occurred through intercommunal hatred and violence, in Teso it occurred through intra-communal violence.

Paradoxically, this phenomenon put the men who arranged the girls for the soldiers in an ambiguous position: whilst they might arrange the suffering of one girl, they could act to protect another. Schola approached her friend, one of the men who singled out girls in the camp, to arrange her escape and safe passage out of the camp to the local town. The contacts that this man had with the soldiers through the sexual exploitation of girls, gave him the ability to help Schola. The very same system and relationships that contributed to girls' vulnerability could also provide their refuge.

Young Girl: Youth, Beauty and Social Status

The conditions of militarisation, the commoditisation of sex and the fragmentation of social relationships all contributed to the vulnerability of girls in the camps to sexual abuse at the hands of government soldiers. But how was it that young girls were especially targeted?

First, the soldiers themselves seem to have wanted young girls. Virginity may have been a factor here. Certainly in the context of the HIV/AIDS pandemic across Africa, virgin girls are increasingly desired as sexual partners and may be placed under considerable pressure by older men, conflict or no conflict. What is clearer from Florence's account, however, is that the soldiers wanted beautiful girls. In Teso, as in so many cultures, youth is equated with beauty. Florence describes how important the notion of beauty was to the soldiers since they went even further and singled out 'brown' girls, those with the light complexion seen as so attractive in Iteso women, to be herded into the lorry. This is not the only case where this has happened: in abductions of young girls in the north of Uganda by the Lord's Resistance Army, those with dark skin are often sent home, those with 'brown' skin retained. In Teso the soldiers had the power to pick and choose who to provide them with sexual services, and so attractiveness, equated with both youth and skin complexion, became not an asset but a liability.

Second, both accounts lay stress on the fact that the soldiers sought unmarried girls. The Iteso middlemen who looked out girls for the soldiers made sure they were unmarried. It was girls' youth hand in hand with their social status that was important and made them vulnerable. This phenomenon exists alongside an extraordinary protection of the institution of marriage in the camps. Soldiers and the middlemen were not prepared to break into a marriage relationship, yet exerted power over the unmarried.

In Teso, control over a woman's sexuality changes with her social status. As an unmarried daughter her father should ideally restrict and protect her sexuality. This protection is related to the bridewealth a father will acquire on the marriage of his daughter. By protecting her from sexual relations a father guarantees that his daughter remains marriageable and that he retains control over the potential bridewealth.

At the same time, the Iteso do accord considerable sexual freedom to unmarried women (Vincent 1988). Sexual relations are the basis for marriage, not vice versa, but a woman is not obliged to marry the first person she has sexual relations with. Even if an unmarried woman gets pregnant this does not discount the possibility of her father acquiring bridewealth. Indeed, the bridewealth is often increased through the imposition of an additional 'fine' paid by a man to a father for the premarital pregnancy of his daughter. The control a young woman has over her own sexuality is evidenced in the knowledge that all young men in Teso have, that to 'woo' a woman for sex takes skill. Women will only be won over by material presents from their potential lover. Relations between lovers, known as *apapero* relationships, are relatively egalitarian amongst the Iteso. They are marked by the provision of gifts from the man to his lover (Nyanger 1995: 117). Women retain an amount of freedom in these relationships. Not only do they have license to refuse the advances of men who wish to become their *apapero*, they can also exercise the choice not to marry but to remain as a man's friend if he asks them to marry him.[4]

A daughter who is post-pubescent but not yet a wife is, for her father, in a vulnerable position. In her rest his hopes for bridewealth cattle, cattle that he will often need in order to marry his sons. At the same time she is in possession of a sexuality that is hers to bestow. The sexual abuse directed at young girls in the camps seems to have targeted this social and structural liminality. By handing over girls to soldiers, the middlemen destroyed the claim of their fathers for bridewealth, whilst also commoditising and curtailing the autonomy a girl had over her sexual partners.[5] Indeed, in the case of Florence and the many girls like her who were kept confined in barracks, the soldiers appear to have tried to keep them in a liminal status, denying them the role of mother and wife, household chores and responsibilities.

The sexuality of a married woman was not targeted in this way. In Teso, authority over the sexuality of a married woman belongs to her husband. Adultery is treated severely both by a woman's husband, who may choose to divorce her and leave her with dependant children, and by her father, who stands to lose the bridewealth cattle. Soldiers and middlemen alike appear to have respected and refrained from undermining the social status of a wife. Married women were, in this instance, less vulnerable than their unmarried sisters and friends.

Coping with the Consequences of Sexual Abuse

There were, then, a number of factors at work in the sexual vulnerability of young adolescent girls in the camps in Teso. Their youth, their liminal social status combined with the conditions of militarisation, the commoditisation of sex and the tensions of social relationships made them especially prone to exploitation. Yet despite their ordeal, the girls never appear to have completely lost the ability to respond to events. Throughout her time in the camp Schola, for example, sought to make things better for herself; she agreed to become the regular partner of one soldier, earning his protection and provision and finally she escaped. Even in this appalling situation she still seems to have retained a small grain of the sexual autonomy accorded to unmarried women in Teso; deciding that a short and blind sexual partner was beyond her endurance. How Florence coped I did not dare to ask but one of her friends with her in the camp alluded to a solidarity, an unspoken support that might have produced courage: 'When we [she and Florence] meet these days we don't have to do any talking about those times. We just know, because we all saw what it was to suffer like that. When something is in your heart it cannot be destroyed, not like a book that can be burnt.' Even in the most narrow of confines, through long and unrelenting suffering, the young women found means to modify the impact of the abuse. Some, like Schola, who at one time used complicity with events to her advantage, managed to retain a sense of control. For others like Florence, knowledge of common suffering was a source of resilience and strength.

Yet the emotional and social consequences of the girls' experiences have stayed with them. Many of these young women are bound to be HIV positive, for it is estimated that 80 percent of the NRA army who so systematically abused them were HIV positive at the time. Although, as yet, few of the women that I met who underwent abuse have developed AIDS, it is a worry and fear that they carry with them, as so poignantly expressed by Schola. These young women struggle daily with conditions of depression and anxiety, known in Teso as 'too much thinking'.[6] They also live with the ambiguity of their social position. Now, in the post-war environment, they are unmarried mothers caring for children from relationships they were forced into. Their status does not conform with the patriarchal ideals of Iteso society in which resources for keeping and bringing up children should come from a woman's relationship with her husband and access to his land and resources.

The social and emotional costs of the war have been high for the women. Surprisingly, however, now that the war is over in Teso, these women, far from being socially ostracised and in a position of further vulnerability, have actually taken up positions of comparative social and economic advantage. During my time in Teso both Schola and Florence were well known and liked in the community, and both were more economically successful than married women of their age, having more access to cash and more spending power. Indeed one young woman, who as a girl in the camps had been given over to the soldiers, was five years later reported to be amongst the richest residents of the village in which I lived for fieldwork. She had used her wealth to marry brides for two of her brothers, a role traditionally undertaken by a man's father.

This achievement is directly related to the end of the fighting and the new social relations and circumstances of peace. Here again, there is benefit in using an analysis of the women's social relationships and position in the post-war history. The following factors underlie such standing amongst the former victims of sexual abuse in Teso.

The Solitary Woman

There is nothing new in the phenomenon of single women enjoying comparative social advantage in Iteso society. Whilst it goes against the grain of patriarchal ideals, it accords with the relative autonomy a young woman has over her sexuality. Vincent, who did research in Teso in the early 1970s, remarked on the occurrence of women choosing to live alone who were financially independent of a husband (Vincent 1988: 217). The precedent thus exists for women like Florence and Schola to live as unmarried mothers, continuing to have relationships with men, to gain from them financially, to bear children but not to marry.

Relationship with Natal Family

The young unmarried mothers in Teso use the resources of their parents. Some still live in their natal home, work on the gardens of their parents and thereby lay claim to the granaries of the household in order to feed their children. The young women also use the land of their fathers to establish their own gardens of food for sale, to raise the cash needed for their children's clothes, school fees and medical requirements. The links between a young woman and the members of her natal home were often strong and cooperative. Mothers enjoyed having an older daughter around to assist in cooking for their household; married brothers living on their father's land often helped their unmarried sister with the heavier agricultural tasks and developed close relationships with her children. The affective ties between a woman and her family were at the heart of her coping with her post-war situation.

Again this situation appears contrary to patriarchal ideals, where an unmarried daughter with children of her own represents a loss of potential bridewealth for her father and brothers. At the same time, as discussed above, it was not an uncommon position for women in Teso to take, even before the war. Now, after the war, fathers and brothers are inclined to be even more lenient. They empathise with the plight of their sisters and have gone out of their way to accommodate them and stand by them in their suffering. In addition, an unmarried but economically active woman in the household can be a welcome and significant resource. The men have reached practical and caring solutions for the situation their daughters and sisters are now in.

Business Opportunities

The young women have made full use of the opportunities presented to them through the business of brewing millet beer and cassava gin. The commoditisation of alcohol, traditionally used throughout Africa as a means of paying work parties and consolidating men's political control in a rural environment, is a common trend throughout the continent (Cheater 1986: 103; Obbo 1991: 126). This commoditisation has occurred hand in hand with women selling alcohol as a moneymaking strategy. In Teso women put surprising amounts of time and energy into brewing beer; the reward they reap is a cash income with which they can independently pay for soap, salt, paraffin, cooking oil, medical treatment and schooling for their children. For married women, brewing beer and selling it is a way of achieving some degree of financial self-reliance within the household, where it is often extremely difficult for them to get access to their husband's cash (Edaku 1995: 45; Nyanger 1995: 112; Pottier and Orone 1994: 17). For the unmarried mothers of the war, brewing beer is a resource by which they can manage the financial difficulties of catering for children.

New Social Spaces

With the end of the conflict the majority of families returned to their homelands. Those who have remained in the camps have contributed to their transformation into economic and community centres, with markets, hotels, bars and small shops. Many of the families that stayed behind consisted of single war-mothers and their offspring. In the camp where I lived, for example, 37 percent of the households were headed by women, most of whom had been victims of sustained sexual abuse during the insurgency. The camps represent a marginal social space in which women who embody ambiguity in terms of social and historical status can live and flourish. Within the camps, they may buy land, build their own houses and lead their lives by a new set of social codes away from the patriarchal norms of married life.

Conclusion

This chapter has applied an anthropological perspective – with a reliance on ethnography, narrative, longitudinal analysis and the investigation of social relationships and structures – to the phenomenon of the sexual abuse of adolescent girls during civil war in Teso. Clear patterns have emerged that indicate how and why it was that these girls were vulnerable to sexual violation at the hands of government soldiers. Such patterns also suggest how and why the girls have been able to cope with the consequences of these events in ways that are constructive and which have even brought social and economic advantage. Their vulnerability was not an inherent quality that came to the fore in the war setting, but a consequence of the way of life that existed in the camps. As such this vulnerability was not all-encompassing and permanent.

The evidence from Teso demonstrates that caution is needed in making assumptions about young people's experiences of armed conflict. Through adopting a holistic and contextualised approach, common beliefs about the natural or inevitable vulnerability of the young, especially girls, are made questionable. Furthermore, this case shows the fragility of many categories that abound in times of war. The adolescent girls in Teso were both the victims of extreme adversity as well as active and resilient survivors. Their social relations and family status were sources of both suffering and salvation: just as the same man who organised girls for the soldiers could also be Schola's protector, so too the structural position of liminality that contributed to the girls' vulnerability in the camp, has provided the basis of their strength in the post-war period. Having become marginalised due to their imposed, wartime role as providers of sexual services, women have been able to use this marginality to their advantage, enriching themselves and achieving independence through involvement in the socially-dubious but lucrative beer brewing industry. Victims were also perpetrators: Teso men in the camp were as threatening to the girls as the NRA soldiers themselves. Victims could also negotiate, in some sense, the scale of their suffering.

Even in the chaos of war, people, including the young, are not divorced from the relations and structure of their society. Indeed, the experience and conditions of conflict are strongly influenced by these factors. In the words of one social anthropologist who has studied the experience of war in Guatemala, 'not only do violence and warfare produce suffering and alienation, but they may also give rise to human and humane possibilities' (Green 1999: 113). In the quest to better understand the human dimensions of war, the holistic, ethnographic approach commonly adopted by anthropologists may offer an invaluable tool.

Notes

1. An earlier version of this paper was given at the conference 'Dimensions of Vulnerability', held in Coventry, U.K., in 2001. The fieldwork on which the paper is based was funded by the Economic and Social Research Council of the U.K. and by the Diana, Princess of Wales Memorial Fund, via the Royal Anthropological Institute and Brunel University Centre for Child-Focused Anthropological Research where the author was a research fellow.
2. This article only considers the sexual abuse perpetrated amongst the Iteso by government soldiers; it does not consider the less systematic rape of Iteso women by UPA combatants. This did occur, especially if the UPA suspected a woman of being a government informer or supporter (Brett n.d.).
3. I have explored elsewhere (de Berry 2000) the complex relationship between the war and growth of physical violence and the decrease in spiritual violence in Teso. This formula differs from other societies where witchcraft has been seen to increase in direct proportion to incidences of armed conflict (Allen 1989).
4. I knew of a number of cases where women had borne their lovers' children and had refused to marry them. The women's rationale was that they did not want their lovers' meagre resources being wasted in bridewealth when it could be used to support their children. Whilst in other situations women might fear to decline an offer of marriage from their children's father for fear of not having another chance at marriage in the future, this does not seem to be a considera-

tion for women in Teso. For there is little stigma in Teso attached to marrying a women who has already had children with another man. Men often bring up their wives' children from another relationship although these children can also be left with the women's parents. Women argued that a man was more likely to give them material provision as a friend rather than as a husband. Where women have less volition is in the circumstance when the lover is already married and, either for fear of antagonising his wife, or because he does not want to set up a polygamous household, or because he is a student and does not want to use the resources he will need for paying his education costs on bridewealth, he does not ask his lover to marry him even though she might want to.

5. Interestingly, years after the conflict when the girls were living back with their fathers there was some attempt to legitimise the sexual relations of these days by their male kinsmen. In 1997 Florence's clan, for example, managed to trace the soldiers she had been taken by during the war. They made a trip to Busia to demand bridewealth, arguing that some support was needed for the clan as they were now having to cater for Florence's three children from this relationship.

6. There is not space here to elaborate understandings of 'too much thinking' in Teso. Needless to say it was an extremely common emotional reaction attributed to the experience of war. There were well defined and strong mechanisms for coping with and healing it, many of which centre on the use of laughter and joking.

References

Allen, T. 1989. 'Violence and Moral Knowledge: Observing Social Trauma in Sudan and Uganda.' *Cambridge Journal of Anthropology* 13 (1): 45.

Amnesty International. 1992. *Uganda: The Failure to Safeguard Human Rights.* London: Amnesty International.

Bennet, O., Bexley, J. and Wanock, K. 1995. *Arms to Fight, Arms to Protect.* London: Panos.

Boyden, J. 1994. 'Children's Experience of Conflict Related Emergencies: Some Implications for Relief Policy and Practice.' *Disasters* 18 (3): 265–72.

Brett, A. n.d. 'Post Traumatic Stress Disorder in War Affected Regions of Uganda: A Preliminary Study.' Mimeo, London: London School of Hygiene and Tropical Medicine.

Bringa, T. 1995. *Being Muslim the Bosnian Way: Identity and Community in a Central Bosnian Village.* Princeton: Princeton University Press.

Cheater, A. 1986. *Social Anthropology: An Alternative Introduction.* London: Unwin Hyman.

de Berry, J. 2000. 'Life After Loss: An Anthropological Study of Post-war Recovery, Teso, Uganda with special reference to Young People.' Ph.D. thesis, London: University of London.

—— and Boyden, J. 2000. 'Children in Adversity.' *Forced Migration Review* 9: 33–6.

de Smedt, J. 1998. 'Child Marriages in Rwandan Refugee Camps.' *Africa* 68 (2): 211.

de Waal, A. 1997. *Famine Crimes: Politics and the Disaster Relief Industry in Africa.* Oxford: James Currey.

Edaku, C. 1995. 'Strategies of Household Food Security Among Farmers in Orungo Sub County, Soroti District.' BA dissertation. Makerere University, Kampala, Uganda.

Frankenberg, R., Robinson, I. and Delahooke, A. 2000. *Countering Essentialism in*

Behavioural Science: The Example of the 'Vulnerable Child' Ethnographically Examined. London: Centre for the Study of Health, Sickness and Disablement, Brunel University.

Gibbs, S. 1994. 'Post War Reconstruction in Mozambique: Re-framing Children's Experience of Trauma and Healing.' *Disasters* 18 (3): 268–76.

Green, L. 1999. *Fear As A Way of Life: Mayan Widows in Rural Guatemala*. New York: Colombia University Press.

Guijt, I. and Shah, M. 1998. *The Myth of Community*. London: Intermediate Technology Publications.

Honwana, A. 1999. 'Negotiating Post-War Identities: Child Soldiers in Mozambique and Angola.' Codesria Bulletin.

Henriques, P. 2000. 'Peace Without Reconciliation: War, Peace and Experience among the Iteso of E. Uganda.' Ph.D. thesis, Denmark: University of Copenhagen.

Kirby, L. and Fraser, M. 1997. 'Risk and Resilience in Childhood.' In M. Fraser, ed., *Risk and Resilience in Childhood: An Ecological Perspective*. Washington DC: NASW.

Kitzinger, J. 1997. 'Who Are You Kidding? Children, Power and the Struggle against Sexual Abuse.' In A. James and A. Prout, eds, *Constructing and Reconstructing Childhood*. London and Washington DC: Falmer Press.

Lawrence, J.C.D. 1957. *The Iteso: Fifty Years of Change in a Nilo-Hamitic Tribe of Uganda*. London: Oxford University Press.

Littlewood, R. 1997. 'Military Rape.' *Anthropology Today* 13 (2): 7.

Machel, G. 1996. *Children Affected by Armed Conflict*. UNICEF.

Malkki, L.H. 1995. *Purity and Exile: Violence, Memory and National Cosmology Among Hutu Refugees in Tanzania*. Chicago: Chicago University Press.

Nordstrom, C. 1997a. *A Different Kind of War Story*. Philadelphia: University of Pennsylvania Press.

——. 1997b. *Girls and Warzones: Troubling Questions*. Uppsala: Life and Peace Institute.

Nyanger, J. 1995. 'The Psychological and Socio-economic effects of War on Rural Women and the Coping Strategies Adopted. A Study of Bukedea County, Kumi District.' MA dissertation, Makerere University, Kampala, Uganda.

Obbo, C. 1991. 'Women, Children and a Living Wage.' In A.B. Hansen and M. Twaddle, eds, *Changing Uganda*. London/Kampala/Nairobi/Athens: James Currey/Fountain Press/Heinemann Kenya/Ohio University Press.

Pottier, J. and Orone, P. 1994. 'Report of Proceedings of FSUV/PRA Workshop, Wera, Soroti District, 15–18 August 1993.' In J. Pottier, ed., *African Food Systems Under Stress*. Proceedings of the Second International Conference, Gaborone: April.

Scheper-Hughes, N. 1992. *Death Without Weeping: The Violence of Everyday Life in Brazil*. Berkeley: University of California Press.

Turshen, M. 1998. 'Women's War Stories.' In M. Turshen and C. Twagiramariya, eds, *What Women Do In War Time*. London: Zed Books.

Vincent, J. 1988. 'Abiding Women: Sexuality and Control in Modern Teso.' In M. Diaz, R. Randolph and D. Schneider, eds, *Dialectics and Gender: Anthropological Approaches*. London: Westview.

WILDAF (Women in Law and Development in Africa). 1994. *Women's Human Rights Abuses in Conflict Situations in Uganda*. A report prepared for the activities of the NGO forum at the Africa regional preparatory meeting of the Fourth World Conference of women in Dakar.

4

A Neglected Perspective

<small>ADOLESCENT GIRLS' EXPERIENCES OF THE KOSOVO CONFLICT OF 1999</small>

Aisling Swaine with *Thomas Feeny*

Introduction

After nearly a decade of non-violent opposition to repression by the Serbian administration, an armed wing of the Albanian Kosovar liberation movement was formed. With both ethnic groups claimharging right to Kosovo's territory and administration, Kosovo was plunged into violence. Severe clashes and a summer-long offensive in 1998 between the two factions resulted in the deaths of over 2,000 people from both communities, prompting intervention by international actors. In March 1999, after negotiations for peace broke down, NATO intervened and began strategic bombing raids on Serbian targets. Serbian offensives in Kosovo subsequently intensified, leading eventually to thousands of Albanian Kosovars fleeing into Albania, Montenegro and Macedonia as refugees. This chapter focuses on the experiences of adolescent girls who lived through this conflict both as civilians within Kosovo and as refugees in Albania.

Humanitarian agencies and scholars often give priority to 'children' in the context of conflict, on the assumption that they are a particularly vulnerable group. In most cases their understandings of who is a child are in accordance with the UN Convention on the Rights of the Child, which defines this life phase in terms of chronological age, 18 years being the official upper limit. Individuals under this age are believed to have specific needs due to their immaturity and particular susceptibility and are accorded special rights in relation to societal protection and provision. However, at the same time, in many cultures puberty is taken to be the upper age limit of childhood and children (especially girls) who reach this threshold are regarded and treated as adults, receiving no special attention. In this way restrictive legal and cultural definitions of childhood and adulthood serve to isolate the group of adolescents or youth who cannot be classified or labelled as children in the Western sense, much less adults.

Thus consideration and analysis of the situations and needs of the adolescent/youth group especially are often overlooked or forgotten in provision and research with war-affected communities. Priority may be given to children, but such priority is seldom conferred on adolescents, who tend to be ignored as a specific social group and absorbed within the broader category of adulthood. As a consequence the specific experiences, circumstances and needs of adolescents generally remain hidden, and humanitarian programmes ignore their plight. Added to this, the subordination and invisibility of female adolescents in many societies and the likelihood of their being targeted for a range of violations during conflict (Almquist et al. 1996: 5) means that investigation into their experiences is especially neglected. Inspired by this observation, I chose to focus my research on adolescent girls, to investigate their particular experiences of conflict in relation to both their age and gender. In my research and here, 'adolescent' refers to young people aged from 13 to 19 years inclusive.

In this chapter I argue that the wartime experiences of adolescents can only be understood and validated by recognising their status as a specific social category. Whereas adolescents may have developed certain abilities and capacities that differentiate them from children, this does not mean that they have acquired all the social and personal attributes normally associated with adulthood. For example, in most societies they do not enjoy the same social power as adults. Hence, it is inappropriate to subsume adolescents uncritically within the category of adult. In fact, this chapter shows that by virtue of their age and gender, adolescent girls experienced the conflict and its effects in ways that were quite distinct from other social groups. Indeed, they turned out to have very particular susceptibilities and capabilities. This chapter offers a descriptive summary of the narratives related by adolescent girls who lived through the crisis in Kosovo in 1999. Such was the quality of the articulation of their experiences that their voices alone are sufficient in offering a profound insight into how adolescent girls live through and survive conflict. The piece therefore focuses solely on their perceptions of and reactions to their experiences, their coping mechanisms and a general analysis of these first-hand accounts which this research brought together.

Insecurity had long been a reality of life for all ethnic Albanians living in Kosovo, but the crisis had a major detrimental effect on family and community networks, which left adolescent girls highly vulnerable to exploitation and abuse. In the absence of male family members and other traditional sources of protection, these girls found themselves confronted with new difficulties and dangers including sexual violence, trafficking, psychological persecution and early marriage. Circumstances often demanded that they surpass or abandon the traditional roles expected of them in times of peace, and at times this invited animosity and criticism from within their own community. However, despite the very difficult situation, as their testimonies show, many of the girls were anything but the passive 'victims' that children are so often assumed to be in times of conflict. Thus, it is suggested that vulnerability does not exclude ability, and while these girls undoubtedly continue to suffer long-term hardships arising from the conflict, they have nevertheless provided an exceptional insight into just how competent, articulate and mature adolescents can be in situations of adversity.

Research Methods[1]

With the help of an interpreter, interviews were conducted with seventeen adolescent female refugees in Albania and twenty-three adolescent female returnees who had gone back to Kosovo during June and July, 1999. Many of the girls that I interviewed mentioned how sitting down and talking to me was the first time that they had been given the opportunity to explain how they were feeling. It was also the first chance they had had to take time out from their heavy workload and responsibilities to analyse their experiences of war. On some occasions, the fact that I was a stranger unattached to their families allowed them to let down their defences and explore their feelings in relation to the many issues they now faced. A number of girls even commented that they could not speak about these things with their families, and without close friends around our interviews were an outlet for their emotions.

In the context of armed conflict and displacement, parents, carers and other adults often discourage discussion of stressful events in front of young people. This may be due to their own distress, their inability to deal with the fact that their children have witnessed such events, or environmental influences such as cultural taboos. However, based on prior experience and on the research with Kosovar Albanian girls that is reported here, I would suggest that in order to adjust to adverse experiences young people need to be able to process them to a point at which they can be reconciled and laid to rest. Thus, the exploration of adolescents' interpretations of the violence and displacement that they are confronted with during times of war can be an important factor in contributing to their healing and recovery. One way of helping them to move forward is simply to give them the opportunity to articulate their experiences, inner thoughts and feelings.

Events beyond normal human experience cause great stress, felt as much by the young as by adults; of course, talking about what they had undergone sometimes brought considerable mental anguish to the girls. Almost all of those interviewed had found the whole experience of displacement and return extremely distressing. Many were frequently tearful and upset during interviews, displaying obvious signs of shock at what had happened to them. It was critical, therefore, that no pressure was put on the interviewees to describe their experiences, and they were free to express as much or as little as they liked. If a girl did become upset during an interview, the conversation was immediately brought to an end, and encouragement and support were always given in helping her to regain her composure. If so desired by the interviewee, a friend or family member would also be invited to be present during or immediately following the interview, and I found it of utmost importance to allow a significant amount of time to be given to the girl following the interview if needed. Interviews were often undertaken in conjunction with a member of staff from a non-governmental organisation (NGO) that was working in the area. This ensured a continuing relationship with respondents, making it possible also to offer longer term support and monitoring for those girls who were particularly distressed.

Conducting the research itself was a difficult task on many levels. The language barrier and reliance on an interpreter were obvious problems. A female interpreter was essential but difficult to find, due to the limited number of girls sufficiently fluent in English. At times the interpreters themselves became upset, having been vicariously reminded of their own experiences of conflict. Moments like this really brought home how deeply the war had affected these young women.

In selecting candidates for interview, receiving introductions and establishing trust, it was essential to forge links with NGO staff or other personnel working in the camps or villages. Upon entering the refugee camps we were often approached by the male members of the community, who would demand to know our reasons for being there. It was always important to explain fully the purpose of the research at this point. Among other things, it was essential to avoid the misconception that we were conducting an assessment in order to provide additional aid. Having understood this, the men were often very helpful in introducing us to possible interviewees. As word of our presence spread through the camp, many girls also approached us as volunteers, offering to have their stories recorded. Young girls in particular would come on their own or with friends, eager to sit and talk about all that they had been through.

My age and sex appeared to help considerably in establishing a rapport with the girls. Often the interviews would turn into chatty conversations, with boyfriends and fantasies about the future the prime topic of conversation. 'Girl talk' would allow interviews to end on a light-hearted and often fun note, with girls inviting me back for tea on a social basis. Invitations such as these were always accepted in order to show my appreciation of the important contribution the girls had made and to ensure that they did not feel in any way misused by the research. The fact that I was not a great deal older than the girls appeared to reassure them that they would not be disapproved of or criticised for their attitudes or opinions, as they may have been with someone older.

Effects of the Conflict

Disruption of Family and Community Support Networks

Attempting to come to terms with and give meaning to extraordinary events is a slow yet necessary process for anyone caught up in conflict. It requires help and support from close friends and family who can provide a solid, trustworthy base upon which to rely. During their interviews, the girls placed great emphasis on the need for these kinds of intimate relationships, which for them provided a protective layer of comfort and assistance in dealing with new feelings of fear, anxiety and grief. As has been seen in many conflicts around the world, the absence of these support systems undermines a young person's ability to make sense of all that has occurred. It was evident in this case in the fact that, from the very outset of their interviews, many of the girls spoke powerfully of missing loved ones. Those who had lost family members during the conflict also seemed more despondent, and displayed profound sadness throughout the interviews. Separation from or loss of family members seemed to be the most difficult thing for many of the girls to cope with, as their own feelings of personal security and confidence in survival were deeply embedded in the stability of their familial and communal structures. Despite their grief and feelings of insecurity, the girls also portrayed a deep understanding of the need to cope with what had happened and mitigate further loss and hurt.

Matila,[2] 17, now lives with her uncle in Albania after she fled harassment at the hands of Serbian soldiers in Kosovo. Her father was already dead, but she was forced to leave her sick mother and paralysed brother behind because they had neither the physical nor financial means to escape. 'I am separated from my family ... the Serbs separated us when we were in Peje [Serb, Pec]. I miss relationships especially. We were very close and connected to each other and it is very hard to be without each other, to be without my friends.'

Thirteen-year-old Bessa was very close to her family, and in her interview she expressed deep remorse for her uncle and grandmother: "All I thought about was my uncle and grandma here. Serb neighbours told us they would be safe and they would mind them. All the time I had hopes I would find them.' When Bessa returned to Kosovo, she found her home burned and the bodies of her uncle and grandmother inside. She later discovered that they had been killed by the very same neighbours who had reassured her of their safety. Unsurprisingly, she explained how she has found it very difficult to trust anyone again, and feels very insecure at losing two such important figures in her life.

Vjosa, 16, also lamented that: 'Relationships are what I miss the most because I need to discuss with my friends about the things that happened to us, about how the Serbian military maltreated us, about the things we've lost and all the other things that have happened.' For these girls, coming to terms with the effects of the conflict meant the inclusion of close friends in the exploration of feelings and emotions, and the sharing of stories and events. Speaking with an intimate and trusted friend of their own age meant that together they could gain a sense of closure on the extraordinary events they had been through. The loss of friends may be more acute for adolescents than younger children because their friendships have had more time to develop and grow stronger. Younger children tend to be more dependent upon and influenced by family, whereas adolescents are likely to seek support and guidance from peers.

When 15-year-old Meqa became a refugee in Albania, she missed her friends badly. 'I had older friends than me [in the camp] that I liked. I talked with them all the time. We talked about what happened in Peje, about my feelings of what happened. But they weren't the same as my own friends from home. I missed them so much.' Like most of the other girls, Meqa had looked forward to rejoining her friends upon returning home, only to find when she got there that most had dispersed: 'Now only four of my eleven friends are left, they have gone abroad. I miss them now too.' A number of the returnee girls interviewed in Kosovo echoed her sadness and reported that they had not seen or heard from their friends since their return, even though they had been back for some time. Some families had decided to go abroad to live and would not be returning; others had been forced to take shelter with relatives who lived elsewhere in Kosovo, because their homes had been destroyed. One 13-year-old respondent was living in an apartment in Peje, as her home in an outlying village had been reduced to rubble. She thus had no contact with her friends or original community and still felt as though she was displaced, revealing how a sense of homelessness and feelings of 'belonging' are as much psychological as they are geographic.

Absence of Males

One of the most serious consequences of the widespread disruption to social networks was the loss of male family and community members.

Through their Muslim upbringing, the girls had come to rely both economically and emotionally on the presence of a male figure. Traditionally, male family or community members would have been looked upon as the protectors of girls and women. Hence, separation from or the slaughter of male relatives was a terrifying prospect.

The girls fully understood the implications of Serb soldiers finding the male members of their family and saw this as a very serious threat to their own happiness and safety. Despite their own feelings of insecurity and fear, they would almost instinctively prioritise the survival of male relatives above their own. For girls like Pramveera, 17, helping her younger brother stay alive was one way of confronting her own fears and overcoming these to do what she could to prevent further tragedy in her family – although this led to her being subjected to significant physical abuse:

> I was frightened when the war started. There was fighting and bombing and we could hear it. I was frightened for my brother, he is 15 years old, as the men are always separated from the women and we were frightened for him ... Everyone was ordered to leave. I was sick and very afraid. I got some courage together and some energy and we started to prepare to leave. We tried to hide my brother ... we were taken by the police and beaten ... they used police batons. Twice they used the butt of a gun on my neck and shoulder area. They used the baton on my back. I have aches and pains in my back now.

Blerta, 14, also focused all her efforts on the safety of her brother. 'I was so scared as I have one brother and I only cared about his life, not mine, because he is the only boy in this family. He is 10 years old. If anything happened to my brother I would kill myself.'

Trafficking in the Refugee Camps

Even in the refugee camps, the absence of male family members continued to pose serious threats to the girls' personal security as there they were vulnerable to trafficking rings that most people (refugees and NGO personnel alike) believed were being operated by the Albanian mafia. The girls' fears of being trafficked were very valid and received endorsement from the International Organisation for Migration (IOM) in Albania (IOM 2001). In the previous decade alone more than 7,000 women and girls had been trafficked from Albania to other countries. This number increased in the late 1990s during the Kosovo crisis with the arrival of attractive young Kosovar girls, as they became a prime target for markets abroad. It was reported by the IOM that girls who had previously been raped or sexually abused in Kosovo were especially vulnerable to being trafficked, largely because taboos surrounding the issue of rape had made it impossible for them to talk to others about their experiences and come to terms with them. Without the proper support they needed to recover, such girls were easy targets for the traffickers. Their raw emotions and resulting vulnerability meant that they were more likely to succumb to false promises of freedom and happiness abroad.

Meqa's story highlights the exact nature of the threats facing girls in camps. She felt that her time in Albania was one of increased risk and fear. One day, she and several other girls in the camp were approached by Albanian men who told them that they would be taken away to America or Italy as they were suitable for prostitution. Following this incident the girls were told by the camp community that they must not leave the camp or even go near the gates. One of the Albanian guards told Meqa that he knew of a group of Albanian men who had plans to enter the camp one night and kidnap her. She was subsequently advised to remain close to her family at all times to avoid abduction. Terrified, she related the story to her family. In response, the Kosovar Albanian men in the camp decided to tackle the problem themselves by confronting the gang that was known to be involved in this illegal trade. Meanwhile, Meqa felt terrible, that her time in Albania was 'dreadful' and that all she wanted was to return to Kosovo. As she put it, 'better to be killed in Kosovo than to live in Albania'.

Other girls who had not been targeted as directly as Meqa had nevertheless felt similarly threatened during their stay in the camps. Inadequate security meant that movement in and out of the camps was poorly monitored and the girls could never be sure of their safety, even when carrying out daily tasks such as going to wash or collect water. This fear prevented them from meeting friends or leaving the camp area without being accompanied by a family member. As 16-year-old Floria recalled: 'I did not feel safe to go alone at night to the bathroom. The road was very near and so was the city, too many people were coming and going. I did not feel safe. A light was put up for us, but I don't think a light can make me safe. Even when I went out with my brother I was afraid.'

Violza, 18, was equally terrified of being alone and always ensured that she was with a family member when outside. However, one of her friends, a 19-year-old girl, had been less vigilant and at the time of the interview had recently disappeared from the camp. At this stage, the girl's family had no idea of her whereabouts or what had actually happened to her. She had made friends with some Albanian men who entered the camp, and on the night before her family was due to return to Kosovo she disappeared, along with many of their possessions. Violza suspected that her friend had been tricked by these men into going abroad and, like many others interviewed, blamed the girl for associating with such men in the first place.

Psychological Abuse

The girls stated that ridicule, insults and verbal threats were commonly used by Serbian soldiers to both humiliate and intimidate the Kosovo Albanians. Moreover, the girls were themselves often targeted specifically on such occasions, for they were regarded by the Serbian forces not merely as the future mothers of the enemy, but also as the bearers of the Kosovo Albanian cultural identity. The constant denigration of their status, religion and tradition took a heavy toll on these girls, who were appalled that their very existence could be debased in so hostile and crude a manner. As 19-year-old Norzmie recalled, Serbian soldiers would often arrive at a house, force the family outside and then loot and mistreat their belongings in the street: 'They took Albanian flags and put them on their tanks, they were insulting us and making jokes of our flag. They even took our traditional wedding dresses and did the same with them – using them as flags over their tanks, jeering at us. Our wedding dress is a very symbolic thing for us.' That such important symbols of their future could be sullied with so little respect was a great shock, but the girls were too afraid of the soldiers to do anything but watch in terror.

Arita, 16, related how Serbian soldiers had burst into her home one day and given her family just fifteen minutes to pack and leave. She fled with her family to a factory in town where they all took shelter. But the Serbs continued to persecute and threaten them: 'They drank a lot and then started making comments like "we will massacre you, just as we did the other Albanians. You should see how a child can be massacred".'

This kind of unrelenting intimidation had a deep effect on the girls, particularly the younger ones, who were haunted by a pervasive fear of becoming targets. As 15-year-old Giyilde described, this fear penetrated and permeated all aspects of her experience while in Kosovo: 'Every night we didn't sleep as Serbs robbed everything from shops. We were afraid. We were afraid of the darkness. We waited for the sun and the light. I was afraid at night because of what the Serbs were doing.' Having fled with her family to Albania during the NATO bombing raids, she eventually returned to Kosovo and found that her house had been looted, burnt and destroyed. 'When I saw my house was burnt I felt so bad. I suffered. Sometimes I go and visit my house even though it is burned, it is my street.'

Rape and Sexual Harassment

Rape – and indeed any form of sexual assault – is a taboo subject in Kosovar society. Very few women are prepared to speak about it, those who have undergone such experiences being terrified that they may be blamed for what has happened to them. According to a report by the

Organisation for Security and Cooperation in Europe (OSCE), 'The stigma of rape is so deep that it is often stated that a "good" woman would rather kill herself than continue to live after having been raped'. For girls who had been raped or abused by Serbian soldiers, silence was more often than not employed as a means of preventing further misfortune. This is why Human Rights Watch maintain that the number of rapes committed by Serbs during the NATO bombing was in practice far higher than the ninety-six cases documented officially. According to their report, 'Rapes were not rare and isolated acts committed by individual Serbian or Yugoslav forces, but rather were used deliberately as an instrument to terrorise the civilian population, extort money from families and push people to flee from their homes' (Human Rights Watch 2001).

Given the levels of shame and terror associated with sexual assault, it is hardly surprising that very few of the girls interviewed were prepared to discuss their own experiences in relation to this issue. Respondents often mentioned 'abuse' and described Serb soldiers as 'disturbing girls'. But usually such remarks were made with reference not to themselves but to other girls they knew of; stories of rape and abuse were always told in the third person and never directly linked to the interviewee. When giving an account of their past lives, some girls simply opted to omit certain incidents or periods. By saying 'Suddenly I lost my consciousness', they would skip over events that they did not wish to talk about whilst at the same time conveying the strong impression that they had been raped. In this way respondents were able to avoid discussing a topic that was deeply sensitive both for them as girls and for their culture as a whole. Often the interpreter chose to inform me of her understanding of what had gone on in the interview only after it was over. She felt strongly that whilst interviewees were intending to communicate the message that they had been violated by soldiers, she could not relay this information to me during the interview due to the girls' obvious discomfort and their attempts to skip quickly past this part of the interview.

A typical example of this is 17-year-old Valentina, who was separated from her family during their attempted escape from Kosovo. A troop of Serbian soldiers confronted the group of family and neighbours she was travelling with before they could get across the border into Albania. They took Valentina to a large building where she was held for a long time in a room with other girls of her age. Valentina explained how the soldiers insulted and abused the girls, making pejorative remarks about the Albanian people and their origins, and being offensive about the girls themselves, although Valentina declined to state explicitly what had been said. She also indicated that the girls had been abused physically and while sexual abuse or rape were not mentioned specifically, the interpreter understood that this had occurred. Valentina's mother, present in the background, tried consistently throughout to divert the interview away from this topic. Family members often requested to be present during the interviews. Their presence was understood as a means by which interviewees could be protected from questions that were too sensitive and in many cases was intended to prevent the articulation and thus recognition of events such as rape.

Rape – or at least the threat of rape – was a pervasive anxiety among all Kosovo Albanian girls during the conflict, and many took to disguising themselves as a protective strategy. Serbian soldiers would target young girls, not only because this dishonoured them but also because it was believed that the younger the woman the lower the risk of her having a sexually transmitted disease. While the prospect of rape seemed an inevitable risk in some girls' terrified imaginations, they nonetheless were sharp enough to develop strategies in their own defence. Many of the girls reported that they would dress up as older women, covering their faces with dirt and walking and acting as if they were elderly. Sixteen-year-old Arita was one such girl. She described fleeing to the mountains where:

> All the young girls dressed up like old women because of the Serbians. We heard that the soldiers took away twenty young girls and then put them in their military camp. I had to dress up like an old woman when I was living in the mountains. All the men had left because if they had stayed they would have been assassinated. When the Serbs came I was extremely frustrated, I totally lost control, lost my mind. They had tattoos all over their bodies and a napkin over their faces. I went behind all the women and I had to dress up as an old woman.

Arita felt that by hiding her youth and beauty and assuming the attire of an older woman she had taken positive action to avert the possibility of being raped.

While the most immediate danger was to the young girls who were the direct targets of sexual violence, rape also had implications for the entire female Albanian population. Particularly in rural areas, the strict regulation of female sexuality and reproduction has long been a major feature of Albanian Muslim society. The girls indicated that as a matter of custom they would be allowed only one boyfriend, their betrothed. As befits a strong patriarchal tradition, the father would in most cases decide – or at least heavily influence – the choice of partners for his offspring. In choosing a wife it was critical in most communities that she be a virgin. Those girls who were not 'pure' in this sense – even if through no fault of their own – stood very little chance of ever being married, and would face a life alone.

Before the conflict there had been a gradual shift away from such traditions as girls moved into higher levels of education. But with the crisis ethnic pride began to assume new significance, and these cultural practices once more became powerful social directives. Albana, a member of the national staff at Concern Worldwide, argued that the Serbs were fully aware of this, and would rape adolescent girls specifically in order to render them unsuitable for marriage. As Adelina, 14, observed, they would even discriminate between married and single girls for this reason:

> They separated young girls and people who were married. They took away some young girls, told us they just needed them to prepare some food for them. We heard later that they abused them. I had a friend from Peje, the police had come into her house and abused her. She told me about it on the way to Albania. She was 17 years old.

A rape victim who has been deprived of her honour is unlikely to marry and add to the Albanian population. Rape was thus seen and used as a form of ethnic cleansing. But rape also had the potential of undermining political aspirations for ethnic purity among the Kosovar Albanians, since many of the affected women bore children by the perpetrators.

Early Marriage

In an attempt to protect their daughters from these kinds of experiences, parents began to resort to early marriage as a protection strategy. Girls were betrothed at a very young age in order to avoid the suffering of rape and the dishonour of being deemed 'impure'. A typical example is the story of 17-year-old Matila. When the Serbs attacked Peje at the beginning of the NATO strikes, she and her family joined hundreds of Kosovar Albanians who were ordered onto the streets of Peje. Matila described how during this time the soldiers taunted her – telling her she was beautiful, that 'you were made for us, we will do what we want with you'. Terrified of being harmed she managed to return with her family to the safety of her home. But the family had neither the means nor the funds to travel to Albania.

The house was then entered again, by a different group of soldiers. They made Matila collect the identity cards of all those present in the house. This included not only her own family but also that of her uncle, for they had just journeyed to her home from their village near Peje. All the identity cards except Matila's were returned and she was told that hers would be kept so that her picture could be shown to other soldiers. Although the two families were allowed to remain in their home, the soldiers told her: 'You can stay in your home but you must keep all the doors and windows open so we can come in when we want to. You must stay here day and night, you are not allowed to leave.' When they left, Matila became hysterical knowing what they were planning to do to her. She recounted that when her uncle 'saw me like this, crying and screaming' he determined that the only option was for her to be married immediately, since if she was raped she would never be able to marry. He took her to the house of a man he knew, and by simply giving her to him this meant that in that instant Matila became a married woman. Her uncle returned alone to the family home, as she was required to remain with her new husband and his family.

During her time in the marital home, Arkan (a notorious leader of the Serb forces who was at this time being pursued for war crimes) entered their home and beat her husband in front of her. Following this incident she fled to Albania with her husband and his family, but was forced to leave her own family behind. Consequently, Matila spent most of her time in Albania worrying about her sick mother and brother. Her husband was beaten and tortured again several times at checkpoints along the way.

The girls reported numerous problems with early marriage and made it clear that, unlike their parents, they did not believe this was an effective strategy for their protection from rape or sexual assault. One of the difficulties they cited concerned the contrast between the celebratory traditions of marriage and the terrible context in which they were living. For example, tradition demanded that in order to please their husbands and to be presentable to their in-laws, young brides should wear a significant amount of make-up and dress elegantly for the first few months of marriage. Many of the girls expressed their discomfort at this practice, believing it to be inappropriate when all they felt inside was a great sadness. As Matila observed: 'I must make up my face as I am a bride, but I don't want to. I am too upset … I don't know how to describe it. I am forced to do this for the family of my husband. Even though I like this sometimes, I do not feel like it now. But it is a custom and I must do it now. I liked to do it before, but not now.' She blamed the Serbs rather than her uncle for her early marriage, and highlighted her regret at being forced to sacrifice her youth in this way: 'I am too young. I can't describe how I feel. I was forced to marry him because of the war.'

For Matila, the bond she formed with her husband is forever rooted in the violence she experienced during the crisis in Kosovo. The basis of her marriage was not love, as she had hoped, but a perceived need for her protection stimulated by the threat of dishonour. Her distress was further compounded by separation from her family and the strong supportive familial relationships they provided, since she felt a great need for their support at such a time.

Yet such measures were not always sufficient to prevent assaults by Serbian soldiers, as 17-year-old Elvana, who saw the slaughter of two such young brides, recalled.

> The Serbs told us to go to Montenegro or Albania. It was night and some people were turned back because (the soldier said) the war had ended. He lied to us. There, two young brides were massacred. They were covered in

blankets but were discovered. I went insane when I saw that ... We were very frightened. Many people told us that many young girls were kidnapped from their families. I was very scared.

During their interviews, the girls reflected on the circumstances of others they knew, friends, neighbours and relatives. They noted how instances of early marriage among girls had increased markedly during the crisis throughout the Kosovar Albanian community. The reasons for these increases were threefold: as already mentioned, early marriage was used as a strategy by parents to protect their daughters; second, girls who found themselves alone or heads of households saw marriage as one option for coping with the huge task of providing for their own and their siblings' futures; third, it was also a way to hold on to betrothed boyfriends who were likely to emigrate abroad. In contrast to the attitude that marriage was not an effective or welcome protective strategy, those girls who had taken on proto-adult roles as household heads were observed to take the initiative to marry themselves off as quickly as they could to men they had already been betrothed to. They felt they were in intolerable circumstances as a result of the political condition of their country, and in the face of their anguish they resorted to getting married so that some semblance of a future could be assured. Their futures were terribly insecure, and many girls feared that they would never again see the men that they had originally been betrothed to. Some girls travelled to other countries where their boyfriends had been working in order to marry and find safety. Others left their own families and fled from Kosovo with the prospective in-laws to ensure they did not become separated. According to Albana, some families were so desperate that they even encouraged daughters to 'marry' (by leaving their family and going with a man as his wife) during flight from their homes.

Feelings of despair were very prevalent among the unmarried girls who were trapped in refugee camps. One 17-year-old described how she saw no hope for the future and no end to the desperate situation in Kosovo. She did not think she would be able to finish school due to her displacement in Albania, and had resigned herself to the fact that marriage was the only remaining option. She demonstrated great strength in coping with her situation as she saw fit by taking her future in her hands and hurriedly marrying in the camp.

Feelings of Revenge and Active Resistance

Some of the girls argued that there was another option: giving expression to their feelings of anger and revenge by becoming an active part of the resistance. Many described how their older sisters had joined the KLA (Kosovo Liberation Army) movement and envied them the opportunity to actively support the struggle – whether by taking up arms, or providing traditional support in health and domestic realms within the guerrilla camps. The dangers of this choice were self-evident, and yet for the some of the girls it seemed to offer several important benefits. Among the gains most frequently mentioned as a consequence of these resistance activities were a sense of personal achievement and reinforcement of pride in their ethnic identity. Some simply felt glad that they were able to contribute something to their people's struggle. That adolescents, especially girls, could possibly *want* to play an active role in a context of conflict has not generally been considered either by academics or practitioners. However, adolescents are just as likely as adults to be aggrieved by an injustice or to desire revenge and these feelings prompt many to become involved in active resistance. Thus, a 13-year-old declared during an interview that one of her greatest wishes was to have a Kalashnikov so that she could use it to shoot Serbs. Her desire for revenge was stimulated by her return to Kosovo, finding her home burned and looted and the bodies of family members inside. Such feelings of anger and hate towards the aggressors were common in girls, both as refugees and returnees. The shock precipitated by the devastation that awaited them in Kosovo upon their return was very new at the time of research, and their emotions were very raw.

Fatima, 19, seemed to take great pride and fulfilment in telling me about her experiences in Kosovo prior to expulsion. She explained that, as her sister was away fighting with the KLA, she had been obliged to find a job in order to support her family. She eventually managed to secure a position in a shoe factory near her home, and worked there for seven days a week. What she had not told her parents, however, was that the job actually consisted of only five days of paid work a week. She had in fact joined a small group of people in the factory who were involved in manufacturing weapon holders, belts and shoes for the KLA, returning voluntarily to work at the factory at weekends. She described to me how proud she felt to have been able to provide some support for the rebel forces; that it was something she held dear and that she felt good about making her own contribution to the freedom of her country. However, her parents knew nothing of her activities and she had only told me this story because I was a stranger, unknown to them. 'My parents didn't know what was going on. I wasn't really afraid, I made an oath. If I had told my parents they would have been afraid and wouldn't have allowed me to work. I am very proud of this. My parents still don't know.'

Fatima's story demonstrated her ability to turn an extremely difficult and bleak situation into one in which she felt able to make a positive contribution. Taking control of one's life in this way is not by any standards an easy task, and yet in conflicts all over the world adolescents have proved themselves capable of doing just that. Fatima's experience emphasises the ability of adolescents to use their own initiative to survive and overcome great difficulties, to turn a negative and upsetting experience into actions which they feel illustrate their own wishes and needs, rather than having these imposed upon them by adults.

Ongoing Insecurities

Even though the conflict was over at the time of interviewing the returnees, the majority of girls stated that they felt far from safe. Abnora found that while the end of the conflict brought a sense of release from Serbian oppression, it did not allay her fears about the future for she was anxious that they could attack again at any time. Other girls expressed similar concerns. Indeed, fear had permeated 15-year-old Valentina's life to such an extent that she was finding it difficult to feel secure anywhere. The translators, who knew her personally, lamented how she had been transformed by the conflict from a bright bubbly girl to one who would rarely venture outside her home. As Valentina described:

> I am afraid. In Albania we were scared to go out because they take girls there. Now I am afraid that the same will happen here. Some girls disappeared two days ago. I am afraid a lot about times during the war, when I was in Albania and seeing my house like that. [Valentina's house was looted and burnt to the ground] I think about all the sufferings. I am so afraid. Everything is mixed up. My life is upside down. I am afraid the same will happen again. I can't believe I am free.

Matila is similarly haunted by memories of what she had seen during the crisis: 'I suffer during the night, I keep seeing all the terrible things that I saw … Sometimes I sleep, not always. I remember all the things that happened during the war. Seeing all these destroyed homes brings it back to me. It will take a long time.'

Individual Struggle in a Collective Social Context

Part of the reason why the girls remained so insecure after the conflict had ceased was because of the broader social context in which they located their struggle. Threats to personal security were only one of the anxieties they experienced. Their worries extended to the wider impact of the crisis on their country, its infrastructure and political and economic future. They understood that many families were now incomplete and that in many areas social relations had completely broken down. The girls expressed a deep pity for those who were suffering so badly, and they were preoccupied with the pains and horrors experienced by others, especially mothers who had lost sons. Due to their reliance on and powerful links with their own families, the girls were able to empathise with women who had suffered such losses.

Arta's fears did not centre on herself, but on the problems faced by others in the Kosovo Albanian community:

> Mostly I worry about these destroyed houses. All of the mothers without their sons, too many orphans, this all worries me very much … Even though there is freedom here I can't feel the freedom because they lost their sons. I feel like these mothers myself, as if I have kids too. I feel frightened so I take medicines to make me feel OK.

At this point in the interview both of the translators broke down and were unable to continue translating for some minutes. They said that in their view Arta had captured the essence of how the people of Kosovo were feeling.

This sense of despair was echoed by Matila, who displayed deep distress throughout the interview and proclaimed: 'I can't stand this situation, when I see all of this around me. For my neighbours, for all the children without fathers, for mothers without sons. I am traumatised.' Fifteen-year-old Floria also felt burdened by the widespread devastation she witnessed around her: 'It's a good thing to be free now, but there are too many families who are missing members of the family, whose house has been burned down. I think that's the part that I cannot feel good or happy about.' For many of these girls, happiness and hope for their own future did not seem possible given the widespread destruction and deterioration of all around them.

The Post-conflict Future

When asked what their three wishes would be following the end of conflict, the girls highlighted their three main goals as being: to achieve a free Kosovo (which equated with 'to be happy'); to go to school; and to find a job or a missing family member (these latter two objectives were mentioned with equal frequency).

Achieving these ambitions would be a difficult and for some, impossible, task. The crisis had not only destroyed much of the physical infrastructure in Kosovo and changed the political and economic climate, but it had also transformed the roles and responsibilities of its inhabitants. With huge numbers of men dead or missing, presumed dead, girls were often required to work or take on leadership roles within the household.

Rebuilding broken homes and lives involves a heavy emotional and financial investment. Meeting their families' economic needs forced many girls to look for paid work outside the home in addition to fulfilling domestic duties within it. The majority of those interviewed expressed a keen desire to secure some kind of employment, not merely for the economic benefit, but also because keeping busy allowed them to forget to some extent the atrocities they had experienced. However, despite their willingness to work, few returnee girls had actually found a job at the time of interview. The conflict had destroyed most of the businesses in Kosovo, both physically and financially, and opportunities for income generation remained scarce. Some of the girls' families had relied previously on subsistence agriculture, but were forced to abandon their fields due to the widespread dissemination of landmines. Given the patriarchal norms that had long prevailed among the Kosovo Albanians, many disapproved of girls assuming such responsibilities and the girls themselves had to overcome much prejudice.

Learning to live with and work around the abnormal events they had undergone also radically affected the girls' perceptions of the future. To the surprise of the girls themselves, the conflict had brought out new strengths and resources in some of them and several emerged from the crisis with a clearer understanding of their identity and a clearer sense of direction. For example, the misery of the conflict and the ensuing sense of injustice helped Fatmira focus her ambition and made her determined to overcome the disadvantages of her social status: 'I have never been happy, and I would like to be as happy as everyone else in the world ... I would like the rights that all other girls have. It is not right that we are girls and cannot go to school ...'

That said, close to half of the girls interviewed, particularly those who had lost family members, revealed a complete despondency and helplessness when talking of the future. Of the twenty-three girls interviewed in Kosovo, ten explained that they had no hope whatsoever of ever enjoying a happier or more secure existence. Some were simply too scared to let themselves hope for a better life, fearful of the disappointment that would follow if their aspirations failed to be realised. Blerta, disconsolate after finding her home destroyed and loved ones missing, summed it all up by saying 'I don't want to have false hope so I don't plan anything for the future. Whenever I plan something it never comes true.'

These feelings of resignation were quite common, and yet the girls also showed a strong sense of determination to make the most of what they could salvage from their lives. Even Blerta admitted that 'When we first came here [returned to Kosovo] I found it difficult to take. Then I figured out that my life will go on so I feel okay now.' Despite her losses, she was determined to try and rebuild her life in whatever way possible.

The girls expressed strong sentiments of loss, hopelessness and despair both in relation to their own personal experiences of the conflict and its impact on the wider social context in which they lived. However, they simultaneously voiced an acute awareness of the fact that their current and future realities would be determined solely by the actions they took at this time. These girls dealt with the enormous psychological and emotional turmoil they had encountered by striving to cope and make decisions based on their own individual interpretations of the events and the meanings they placed on these.

Case Study

During the crisis the girls confronted multiple issues and difficulties. At any one time a girl may have had to cope simultaneously with the pressures of separation from her family, being a refugee, a survivor of rape, despair from within and without, being a household head, and so on. Therefore, it is appropriate to conclude this chapter by relating the story of Jurisali, whose experiences of conflict demonstrate both the range of vulnerabilities that young girls commonly display in such situations and the coping strategies they may employ.

Jurisali, 19, and her family lived outside the village of Lubiniq. Their house was situated on a main road, and with so many Serb military convoys passing by they feared for their safety. So, just before the NATO air strikes began, they decided it would be safer to leave their home and move in with relatives in the village. After three days of bombing by the NATO forces they received word that a peace deal had been signed and all was well, so they returned to their home.

Since their house was in such a prominent position overlooking the valley, Jurisali's father was designated as the lookout for the village on the first night following their return. Jurisali awoke the next morning to her father's shouts. He told them that the whole area was surrounded by Serbian Police, and ran off to warn the village. This was the last she ever saw or heard of him. Her mother, who was tending the family's livestock, was then attacked by the police. Without being given time to dress properly, Jurisali was pushed out of the house with her brothers and sisters. Her mother was then beaten in front of the children before finally being told by the police that they were leaving. The soldiers then indicated their intention of taking Jurisali and her sister with them. 'The police put their guns in our backs. There were two policemen in the road. They pointed at me and my sister and said "both of you are going to stay with us, to make us dinner and lunch. We will stop you along the road to Decan and take you then"'. Terrified, Jurisali began leading her family to Decan, as ordered. Her younger brother thought it dangerous for her to continue as she was sure to be abused by the soldiers, so they escaped down an alleyway to another, remote village. They stayed with others in a cellar of one of the houses in the village. Since her mother was not only physically injured but also deeply distraught from her ordeal, Jurisali realised at this point that she was going to have to assume charge of the family.

Despite her mother's protestations due to the danger of venturing out, Jurisali sought information about her father from the villagers. Pretending that she was not from Lubiniq she eventually found out that a large number of men had been killed there. She returned to the cellar amidst shelling and gunfire, and had to deal with the fears of her younger siblings and the family's inquiries about her father's whereabouts.

Following the arrival in the village of a group of Serb soldiers, the family was forced to leave once again. Her exhausted brothers and sisters became hysterical as they had no transport and were sure that they would be killed. Even though she shared their anxieties, Jurisali tried to placate them and encouraged them to continue the journey. Many others, also without transport, were attempting to escape along the same road. Some were walking very slowly, especially the elderly. Before long Jurisali was leading the entire group in a long straggling column. When they arrived at the next village, they were able to join a convoy of buses and trucks that had been sent to transport people to Albania. Her mother was so ill she feared she would not survive the journey.

When they finally crossed the border, Jurisali and her family took shelter with another family in Fier. But Jurisali remained fearful even there because of warnings she had been given about the trafficking of girls for prostitution.

Some months later, Jurisali and her family were able to return to their house in Lubiniq which had been burnt down and was by then no more than a ruin. Over 75 percent of the men in that community had disappeared and there was still no sign of her father. The village was littered with bodies, bones and human ashes (witnessed by the author). The survivors began to bury the dead in the large front garden of Jurisali's home. Jurisali asked why they were doing this, and attempted to stop them, but noone listened. The local men failed to acknowledge her new status as head of the family, referring to her as 'only a woman', and told her that if she did not stop complaining they would return with a gun and shoot her. Her brothers and sisters became hysterical at this threat and at the sight of so many bodies in their homestead, and kept pressing Jurisali to do something about the situation.

Jurisali began to feel that it was inadvisable to remain in the family home. She was frightened of the local men, and was concerned about the lack of security due to the destruction of the property. She worried that remaining under these circumstances may worsen the already serious condition of her physically and mentally distraught mother. She was also concerned about the children, who were scared at night by the bodies in the garden. She wished that they could move into a tent, anywhere. But they had nowhere else to go.

Every day she works at preparing the one intact room that is left in the house for the coming winter. She has no time to see her friends, many of whom are either married or departed. She rises at 5 or 6 a.m., goes to town to look for a job, returns to do domestic chores and work on the reconstruction of the house. She finds it very difficult to manage without an adult male to help with the physical jobs since her brothers and sisters are too young to help. According to her mother, whose condition has since improved slightly, 'she is like a boy now'. Her life has become entirely focused on looking after the family. She shows no consideration for herself, and does not know how long she will be able to cope. She still harbours intense hatred for the Serb people, and feels Kosovo can never be truly happy with so many now dead. As she concluded: 'The heart of Kosovo has been destroyed. I don't have any plans for the future, I just want to kill myself.'

Conclusion

All the girls who were interviewed for this research had stories of violence, bereavement and loss to relate. They had lived through a terrible conflict and had each absorbed and responded to it in their own individual way. Their distress was apparent during the interviews and the harrowing accounts of their experiences provide a permanent record of the terrible suffering they endured during the 1999 conflict.

Yet, even whilst highlighting their vulnerabilities and suffering, it is also important to emphasise the resourcefulness and resilience demonstrated by these girls. Their understanding of the turmoil that disrupted their lives was startlingly mature and their accounts of survival and resistance showed how they were able often to act directly on and ameliorate their situation. They have proved to be not merely victims of war, but rather competent individuals capable of developing their own analysis of the situation and their own responses and survival strategies. Some were found to have assumed responsibility not only for themselves but also for younger siblings and/or incapacitated adults.

Nevertheless, resilience in the context of war often carries a high price. Young people may find themselves disagreeing or even in conflict with parents and other adults in their community. In the face of opposition from within their own community, some of the girls had assumed roles that challenged traditional hierarchies based on gender and generation. In devising their self-protection approaches, some found their views to be at odds with those of adults. Girls were forthright in expressing ideas on what was best for them. They often faced cultural and social resistance to their refusal to conform to social behaviour expected of them, and they proved to possess a greater understanding of their own needs and experiences than adult carers and peers claimed to have. For example, they argued that certain strategies – such as early marriage – that were thought by adults to enhance their protection, in practice exacerbated their pain and anguish. Such divisions in approach and attitude were found to create difficulties for their social reintegration and sense of self-efficacy following the cessation of fighting.

Added to this, that girls may be forced to assume the roles of income earner, household head, political activist and fighter in the context of war and displacement is not always a consideration in humanitarian assistance programmes or indeed in the formulation of research hypotheses. If war-affected populations are not to be further debilitated by inappropriate assistance programmes and through outsiders' ignorance of their self-perceived needs, it is vital that interventions to support and protect them be built on and reinforce, rather than attempt to replace, their resources and coping mechanisms. In order to do this the opportunity needs to be created whereby the voices of different age groups and genders can be listened to, recorded and then acted upon. Research into the particular vulnerabilities and capacities of the adolescent age group, particularly girls, would help to create awareness of gender- and age-specific needs, and influence a move away from the application of current generic social and legal definitions of 'children' and 'adults'. It would also ensure that their lack of status in the current unfixed position, somewhere in between that of child and adult, is no longer neglected but formally recognised and addressed. While some of the girls in Kosovo remain despondent about prospects for the future, all were united in the understanding that their future protection and survival would be ensured through their own capacities and instincts rather than those of others. Thus, given the opportunity, the chances are that these girls would choose employment over marriage as a post-conflict survival strategy and would seek full involvement in family and community decisions rather than a return to the submissive role normally assigned to girls and women. These are important considerations for future programmes and policy in this area.

Notes

1. The fieldwork that provides the basis for this chapter was conducted by the principal author, Aisling Swaine. In this section, Swaine reflects on a range of methodological and ethical issues that arose during her field research.
2. The names of all interviewees have been changed in order to protect their anonymity.

References

Almquist, K., Muhumuza, R. and Westwood, D. 1996. *The Effects of Armed Conflict on Girls*. Ireland: World Vision.

Human Rights Watch. 2001. 'Under Orders – War Crimes in Kosovo: March–June 1999 – An Overview.' http://www.hrw.org/reports

IOM. 2001. 'Kosovo Anti-trafficking Report.' http://www.iom.int

Part III

What is a Child?

5

The Use of Patriarchal Imagery in the Civil War in Mozambique and its Implications for the Reintegration of Child Soldiers[1]

Jessica Schafer

An Ethnographically-based Concept of 'Child'

Definitions and understandings of childhood in the West, which inform the concepts used by development agencies, are essentially age based. They assume that a child is someone under the age of 18, and is vulnerable, dependant and innocent. Implicit in this definition is the assumption that all those below 18 share these characteristics. Hence, the label 'child soldier' is applied to anyone under the age of 18 who bears arms.

In the rural and urban areas of Manica province, Mozambique, where this research was carried out, the study sample indicated that almost half of both the RENAMO and FRELIMO fighters were younger than eighteen at the time of recruitment, and therefore were technically child soldiers (Schafer 1999: 123). But the research also suggests that the concept of 'child' soldier in the sense in which it is commonly understood, with the implications of childhood vulnerability and innocence, is not useful or accurate in this particular context. Amongst the Shona, the main ethnic group of Manica province, a distinction is made between the activities of a child and the activities of an adolescent. In Manica, labour migration was considered part of the process of entering manhood,[2] beginning as early as age 12. The majority of the young RENAMO rural recruits had already spent some time living away from their family. (They generally went to nearby Zimbabwe for work at this age, and further afield to South Africa once they had more experience.) Thus, they were not really considered children by their communities in the sense in which the term is understood in the West.[3] The fact that young men are involved in economic processes makes them, in the eyes of that society, potentially legitimate perpetrators of violence even though they are not yet 18 years of age.[4]

We need to take account, therefore, of the way in which the concept of 'child' is malleable and constructed within the bounds of particular times and places. In the context of this research, the actual concept of childhood that was effective and meaningful for young fighters during the war concerned being a *child of someone*, of a family, rather than being a child per se. This concept was free from age-based distinctions, but linked more to understandings of structural relations of power and hierarchy, patriarchy and kinship, and the content of those social relationships. The concept of childhood that results from these constructions does not necessarily imply that children are vulnerable, but more centrally that there are a set of parental and patriarchal responsibilities towards children. It was the ideology of the child-to-father relationship which framed the experiences of the young people in military service, rather than that of a 'child' as opposed to an 'adult'. My arguments and findings, therefore, apply to excombatants as a group, rather than simply to excombatants who had been recruited at any age below 18.

In this chapter I maintain that, as part of their mobilisation strategy, the military leadership of both government and RENAMO forces took advantage of the recruits' psychological need for a substitute family. I start by sketching the background to current understandings of the war in Mozambique, and present the ways in which my research challenges the popular view, particularly in respect of the participation of young men in the armed conflict. This is followed by an examination of the myriad uses of patriarchal imagery by the military leadership during the civil war in Mozambique. The final part of the chapter argues that this use of moral beliefs embedded in the combatants' social codes was effective during the war, but has left a particular legacy in the post-war period. In contemplating the reintegration of excombatants, therefore, the use of patriarchal imagery and the father–child relationship are more significant than many of the ideas about violence, desocialisation and childhood which have formed the basis of academic, governmental and international agencies' work with demobilised soldiers.

Background to the War in Mozambique

Analysis of the post-independence war in Mozambique can be divided into two main phases.[5] In the first decade after independence, most academic writing on Mozambique was done by analysts generally sympathetic to the FRELIMO party-state because of its anti-colonial credentials and revolutionary claims. The consensus at this stage was that RENAMO was a proxy guerrilla army set up by Ian Smith's Rhodesian regime and later supported by the South African apartheid state as part of the destabilisation campaign against southern African frontline states.

Consequently, explanations of the participation of young people in RENAMO's army focused on the forcible nature of recruitment of men (and to a lesser extent, women) (Geffray 1990; Minter 1988; Nordstrom 1994). The view favoured by the Mozambican government and advanced by some academics was that RENAMO's unwitting recruits were then kept in the army by a mixture of physical coercion and psychological brutalisation and dehumanisation (Finnegan 1992: 68; Nilsson 1993: 36–7; Nordstrom 1994: 10; Roesch 1992a; Vines 1991: 73; Wilson 1992: 534). RENAMO's use of child soldiers was highlighted as part of an attempt to discredit the guerrilla army and put pressure on South Africa to cease its support for this force. The presence of child soldiers was also cited by analysts as an explanation for much of the aberrant violence and terror tactics reported by civilians (Finnegan 1992; Nordstrom 1994; Roesch 1992a).

By the mid-1980s, however, a new wave of research and analysis began to challenge the previously accepted explanations. Initiated by French anthropologist Christian Geffray's research in northern Mozambique, and spurred on by the spread of RENAMO into most parts of the centre and north of the country, this research began to reclassify the war as a civil struggle rather than an externally motivated campaign of destabilisation. Researchers identified a broader and more diverse section of the population as having motivations for rebellion against the FRELIMO government, and argued that the guerrilla army had tapped into deeply rooted social conflicts that reached across classes and back into history.

This line of analysis did not deny that incidents of physical coercion and psychological brutalisation occurred during the war in Mozambique, a war internationally reputed for its savagery and atrocities against civilians. But the new research did reveal that the story of the civil war was more nuanced than this stark picture would have us believe. More recent research, particularly local case studies after the end of the war, has demonstrated that interaction between guerrilla forces and civilians varied considerably from place to place, for historical, social, economic and purely contingent reasons (Alexander 1995; Finnegan 1992; Geffray 1990; Legrand 1993; McGregor 1998; Nuñes 1992; Roesch 1992a; Roesch 1992b; White 1985). In areas where the population supported the guerrillas politically, coercion and brutalisation were less common, and a wide range of motives brought people into RENAMO in different capacities.

It is not surprising that this evidence surfaced after the war ended, because previous accounts were primarily based on research done in areas sympathetic to the government. Thus, any earlier reports by civilians or even former RENAMO combatants were influenced strongly by the government's political position, and informants had powerful incentives to support the government line that RENAMO was merely a puppet of the South African destabilisation campaign (Finnegan 1992: 69; Geffray 1990: 94).

Despite the recent wave of revisionist history, however, there has been little reexamination of the motives and experiences of the fighters themselves. The original analysis that perceived only brutalisation and desocialisation became the basis for post-war predictions of social marginalisation and the consequent need for efforts at reintegration (Barron 1996: 15; Harrison 1994: 431). The idea that most fighters were unwilling, coerced and often uncomprehending children persisted and was implicit in the design of reintegration programmes for the former combatants.

My own research, done four years after the signing of the General Peace Accord, in areas sympathetic to both government and RENAMO, revealed a much broader range of motives on the part of the guerrillas. Their descriptions of their participation and experiences revealed a very different emphasis from that of violence for its own sake. Nor did they see themselves overwhelmingly as innocent children, co-opted into a war without knowledge or understanding. The former combatants' views were generally backed up by civilian accounts from the same areas. However, we must also accept that present interests have influenced both guerrilla and civilian stories of their participation in the war to a certain extent, just as they did during the period of conflict itself.

Elsewhere, I have presented oral accounts suggesting that psychological brutalisation, atrocities, ritualisation of violence and social promotion were not the main features that guerrillas recalled of their war experience in the post-war period (Schafer 1999). What they spoke of amounted to a process of resocialisation in the context of civil war, rather than the internationally accepted image of desocialisation into a world in which violence was pursued for its own sake. Although guerrillas suffered serious deprivation, eating badly, sleeping rough and facing exhausting physical demands, the suffering that the young men (and even more so the women) emphasised most was being separated from their families and taken away from their homes, having to suspend normal life and their plans for the future. Interestingly, this applied to the young men taken into the government army (*Forças Armadas de Moçambique*: FAM, later *Forças Armadas de Defesa de Moçambique*: FADM) as well as those taken into the RENAMO guerrilla forces, as both groups were moved away from their home areas and often lost contact with families for long years. Thus, in my study sample, only three percent of RENAMO excombatants had been able to visit their families during the war. Half of the FRELIMO soldiers had gone home to visit, but even so, they spent on average eight years without seeing their families.

In the following section, I focus on the ways in which the military leadership drew upon local conceptions of 'family' to meet the young recruits' psychological need for a substitute family during the war period.

The Use of Patriarchal Imagery during the War

Rather than losing all stake in society, as the catch-phrase about combatants in African civil wars suggests (Kaplan 1994), during the war the young recruits clung defiantly to practices and beliefs which maintained their links with home and family, attempting to counteract the radical transformations foisted upon them by military life. They did this through various means, including contracting marriages with local women, setting up second homes outside the base within the community, learning the local customs of the areas in which they were posted and intervening in community affairs, taking on war 'godmothers' and 'godfathers', exchanging valuable items obtained externally for those needed locally, and generally socialising with local people where possible.

RENAMO excombatant (male)

> I got married while I was still in the army, because I saw that I didn't have any family, and I married to have family. Also a man when he grows up, he has to get married.[6]

FRELIMO excombatant (male)

> Since I was far from home, we would adopt a 'mother' and 'father' in the population. Sometimes when I was homesick, I would go there and we would eat manioc [cassava] to remind me of my family at home.

Not only did guerrillas and soldiers struggle to establish some kind of normality and semblance of their former lives in the midst of the chaos of war, but the military leadership also made gestures in this respect when it suited their purposes. When Zimbabwe gained independence and RENAMO backing was taken up by South Africa, RENAMO strategy moved from destabilisation to a 'hearts and minds' style campaign requiring more civilian support (Legrand 1993; Venâncio and Chan 1998: 16). As their forces became more dependent on civilian support, commanders moved to promote officially what had been taking place unofficially on the initiative of the young guerrillas themselves – namely, more cooperative and less coercive interactions between fighters and rural populations.

From the late 1970s the RENAMO forces grew in size, and changed in composition from a small group happy to act out their disaffection with FRELIMO in violent opposition, to a large group of less-than-willing recruits (Hall and Young 1997: 128). As a result, the leadership's iron grip was loosened and they needed to find ways of securing and maintaining the loyalty of large numbers of fighters scattered across a very large territory. One attempt to achieve this was by appealing to social forms and structures already ingrained in the young men's moral code, and stepping in to fill the breach created when they were removed from their families and communities.

Thus, former combatants recalled being instructed by Afonso Dhlakama, president of RENAMO, to respect local elders and traditions. Strong emphasis was put on the return of former chiefs and holders of traditional titles to the posts from which they had been removed by FRELIMO in the immediate post-independence period.[7] Commanders recruited the help of local spiritual advisors to assist in their campaigns, in an attempt to bolster fighters' morale as well as to integrate local civilians into the military effort. All of this made sense in that it helped not to alienate local populations by maintaining a moral universe with which they were all familiar, and it also reinforced the young combatants' need to feel links with their former lives, and to feel morally justified in what they were doing. Further, it answered a grievance felt by local communities against FRELIMO's post-independence policies.

But the needs of the leadership and those of the young fighters did not always coincide exactly. The RENAMO leadership also issued instructions to fighters themselves to keep a distance from local populations, in order to create a powerful mystique around the forces and to keep tight control (Geffray 1990; Wilson 1992). RENAMO then attempted to fulfil the young men's psychological needs for a replacement family with figures from the military movement rather than local civilians. Military bases were physically separate from local residential areas, and the boundaries were strictly policed. The guerrillas were forbidden to marry local women, and punishments were meted out to those caught disobeying. In contrast to other, previous, accounts that emphasised the use of women as a reward for young recruits (Geffray 1990: 111; Wilson 1992: 536) this practice appears to have been limited in my research area to those in positions of high command rather than the rank-and-file soldiers. Punishment also followed attempts by soldiers to intervene in local social life, although in some cases commanders took part in conflicts within the community if they were seen to affect the guerrilla army. Spiritual ceremonies were generally conducted without the participation of the rank-and-file soldiers.[8]

Instead, military leadership set itself up as a substitute family for the young recruits, playing on the image of the leader as 'father', soldiers as kin and the war as a dispute between brothers. Although this usage of patriarchal imagery in the military is not unique to the RENAMO guerrilla movement, it was particularly powerful in this context because of the cultural background of the recruits. In this research area in Manica province, the dominant cultural group was the Shona, so I will explore the concept with reference to Shona cultural precepts. However, informants from other cultural groups found the patriarchal imagery equally compelling, which suggests that it is possible to generalise this finding elsewhere in Mozambique (Dolan and Schafer 1997). The widespread nature of these beliefs also explains the power of patriarchal imagery for government soldiers as well as for RENAMO guerrillas, as the government used similar images in both its military and political mobilisation.

Shona cultural historian Michael Bourdillon (1987: 30) argues that within Shona culture, the most important relationship is between a father and his child. The father has absolute authority over his children and complete responsibility. The child 'fears' his father and displays deference and respect. In return for this obedience, the father is responsible for feeding and clothing his children. He is also responsible for all their actions, represents them in disputes and may even pay their debts and fines.

This patriarchal framework became the basis of the relationship between guerrilla fighters and their father figure, Afonso Dhlakama (see also Cahen 1995) – or in the case of government soldiers, the president of Mozambique, first Samora Machel and later Joaquim Chissano. Interestingly, soldiers sometimes spoke of this relationship in terms reminiscent of a cultural analyst, with distance and awareness of the metaphorical aspect of the military propaganda.

FRELIMO excombatant (male)

> People think of the government as a father because he does everything. He protects, gives orders, forbids certain things, and many other things. For these reasons they think of the government as a father.

Author

> There is no father without a mother – so who is the mother in this case?

FRELIMO excombatant (male)

> When people talk of a father, they mean it in the sense of someone with responsibility who is put in charge of all the work. The word father is used in the sense of a responsible person who is in charge.

This definition of childhood – as being part of structural relations of power, hierarchy, kinship and patriarchy – was heavily invested in during the war. In the middle of the confusion, loss and destruction of the war period, the use of this concept created a moral space for fighters to understand their world, and organise their relations. The ideas about relations between children, parents and families were harnessed to create a set of loyalties and affinities in the war. The moral space built up in the war around definitions of childhood makes no reference to age distinctions. It counted for those over eighteen and those under 18. A high proportion of the soldiers were under eighteen but their experiences within this moral space did not differ substantially from those over eighteen. In other words, it was important that all fighters were seen as children of someone.

The portrayal of the military leadership as a father figure worked in many different ways in the lives of the young soldiers and guerrillas. Perhaps its most significant role was to meet a psychological need to fill the gap left when the young men were taken away from their families. As mentioned above, former combatants interviewed most commonly identified the pain they felt at being taken from their home environment as the greatest single source of suffering. They also cited family as their first priority upon being demobilised.

As substitute for the young men's biological families, the leaders of both RENAMO and FRELIMO promoted the image of themselves as father – of the nation in general and more specifically of the soldiers and guerrillas under their command. As in other war situations, comrades in the fight became brothers in arms (Garton 1996: 20), although interestingly, in Mozambique's civil war, the enemy was also portrayed as a brother and the war as a fight within a family.

Former combatants of both sides emphasised their brotherhood after the war. During the war, however, only RENAMO had been keen to present its fighters as 'sons of Mozambique'. FRELIMO portrayed RENAMO guerrillas as external agents, marginals and bandits because of RENAMO's Rhodesian and South African connections, and because of their opposition to FRELIMO (Hall and Young 1997: 165).

RENAMO excombatant (male)

> Our old man [Dhlakama] didn't tell us anything when we left [home], just to tell us why we were fighting, that we weren't fighting to kill anyone, or to destroy, but to kill the law of Racism with Samora [Machel, first President of Mozambique],[9] kill the system which is bad in order for us to live well, since we are all in the same family. And up to now [in the years after the war] we are greeting each other, even shaking hands.

Author

> How did you feel when you first met a soldier from FRELIMO [after the war]?

RENAMO excombatant (male)

> We just looked at each other, what could we do, when these were things which were in the past. We just waited for our fathers to organise something [for us to do after the war]. . . . Now when we meet, we are amongst family, since these were things which happened at that time, and it's over, and now we're family, we shouldn't insult each other and say bad words to each other. Just live well.

Another use to which the patriarchal imagery was put in the war was to prevent relationships between male and female soldiers within REN-

AMO. Such liaisons were portrayed as being akin to incest, since Dhlakama was presented as the father of all the combatants, male and female. Female combatants were particularly emphatic about the taboos on relationships during the war, something which reflects their greater difficulties in reintegrating after their wartime experiences (Barron 1996). The number of children born to female combatants belies their attempts to deny such relationships, but nonetheless they maintain the patriarchal imagery as a framework for their experiences. Some also portrayed Dhlakama as acting *in loco parentis*:

RENAMO excombatant (female)

[Sexual relationships were] controlled, because he [Dhlakama] said that these DFs [*destacamento femenino*: female soldiers] were someone's children. Now if she is someone's child, and she becomes pregnant, and then dies during the birth, tomorrow how will he answer to the father of that woman?

Author

But your father was far away . . .

RENAMO excombatant (female)

He was far away, true, but when the war is over, didn't I receive money?[10] And didn't I go back home? So if I had died in the war, who would answer for it to my father?

RENAMO even took the role of father in the crucial ceremony for the dead, so as to comfort combatants and prevent them from worrying about ill consequences of improper burial. In Shona culture, treatment of the dead is crucial, as the spirits of the dead are believed to influence the living, both directly, for example, affecting their health and wellbeing, and indirectly, affecting the climate and agricultural yields.

RENAMO excombatant (male)

Here in our land, if someone dies it is his father who must explain to the spirits that this person died, and ask them to open the path for him to go. If you don't do this, when you begin to dig the grave you will hit big rocks.

Author

So you never had any problems if you didn't want to do this burial for people who died in the middle of a big battle and you couldn't do the proper ceremony?

RENAMO excombatant (male)

There was none of that suffering because our leader, who was our father already, took all the responsibility for each of us.

Hence, this excombatant suggests that the RENAMO military leadership created ways of convincing the soldiers that he would take care of the funereal responsibilities of the family patriarch, in order to ease their worries about death on the battlefield. The leadership clearly recognised the importance of these crucial practices.

The Repercussions of Patriarchal Imagery in the Post-war Period

Perhaps the most positive effect of the use of patriarchal imagery by the military in Mozambique's civil war is the way in which it set up a framework through which excombatants of both sides can view the past, allowing them to be reconciled with their former opponents. Although in many areas, political allegiances were quite clearly geographically split, such that former combatants from opposing sides did not have to live next to each other (Cahen 1995: 129), this was not the case in urban areas. The reintegration support schemes run by the international community also brought former opponents together perforce, such that some kind of reconciliation was necessary.

One aspect of this strategy was to disavow responsibility for their actions during war, claiming ignorance. This was not, however, the ignorance of the naive and innocent child, but the unquestioning and loyal obedience of a son to his father's dictates.

RENAMO excombatant (male)

> [In the post-war training courses, do we try] to see whether this one is from FRELIMO or not? No, but to know that we were fighting each other in vain, yes. Because he is my brother, and we made the war because we were possessed by bad ideas to kill each other, without knowing what we were doing, to exterminate each other between brothers.

FRELIMO excombatant (male)

> Hunh! In this war, we were the goats who were being pastured,[11] and as such we didn't even know why we were fighting between brothers for some little thing, and then the big men[12] sat down and talked and decided they had to get it together in our country.

If the soldiers themselves were to be portrayed as ignorant, then blame had to be passed onto their 'fathers', the military leaders.

RENAMO excombatant (male)

> After the war? I met lots of soldiers from FRELIMO. There was friendship, everyone was friends, no one really cared that I was from RENAMO, the other from FRELIMO. We knew who was from what side, but we would go drink together, be friends. Because this wasn't the bad thing. The ones who know what was bad are the presidents, we were just the sons.

In some cases, the issue of who won the war even became secondary; because of the sense soldiers had that it was an inter-familial dispute, there was no need to win. As one FRELIMO excombatant put it: 'Who could win the war, since we were cousins[13] fighting against each other?'

As the cultural precept dictated, the father was seen to be responsible for his sons' actions. Another way in which this was used by excombatants during the process of reintegration was in order to set things right with the spiritual world. The former combatants, from both RENAMO and FRELIMO forces, admitted to appealing to their household spirits[14] during the war to help them survive. But spirits cannot be invoked to assist automatically, without social negotiation. Thus, in many cases a show of appeasement or gratitude was necessary after the war to set the spirit world in equilibrium. A ritual of thanks to the household spirits was often one of the first things which the former combatants did upon return to their home areas, something that also brought members of the family together to reconnect or reaffirm their connections after long absences (Dolan and Schafer 1997).

Author

Didn't your spirits get angry when you went to war?

RENAMO excombatant (male)

Oh yes, they got angry, but when my father explained to them, because on the day that I went, my father prayed to the spirits and explained to them that their son has gone to war, and asked them to take care of me, because I was the son but I had nothing in my head yet.

For former government soldiers, it was a fairly straightforward matter to expect the government which acted as their father to fulfil its obligations to its children after the war.

FRELIMO excombatant (male)

I would not like it if the demobilised soldiers were forgotten by the government, since we are the sons of the government. For example, there are many people who are marginalised.

They used the image of the soldier as a child also in order to claim support, and maintain dependence on government in the post-war period.

FRELIMO excombatant (male)

We need support, because a soldier, the person who left home, and went all that way, when he comes back he is just like a child. Here we are just like a child. We are really begging for a company [to give us work] to reduce our poverty.

This request is also rooted both in promises made during the war, and in the actual experience of excombatants from the war for independence from Portugal, some of whom acceded to important positions in government, while others were given land – although this group of former combatants also sees itself as having been poorly compensated for its efforts in the war.

We should not forget that these claims were flexible, though. In other contexts, the former soldiers portrayed themselves as superior to the civilian population, more politically aware and therefore more entitled to a voice in national politics (Schafer 1999: 232).

It was somewhat trickier for former RENAMO guerrillas in the postwar period to negotiate for themselves based on the idea of the military leadership as a father figure, since it was Afonso Dhlakama who had been their father during the war. However, Joaquim Chissano of FRELIMO won the first national elections in 1994, two years after the end of the war. Chissano was therefore in control of the governmental purse strings.

Dhlakama himself encouraged his excombatants to transfer their filial allegiance to the FRELIMO-led government after the war, in order to avoid having to take responsibility for the promises made during the war and the high expectations of the former guerrillas. He made statements to the effect that since he was not in government, he was not in a position to look after his former charges. The excombatants accepted this stance to a certain extent, but managed to present their position cleverly to maintain claims on both RENAMO for which they had fought, and the new government under which they had to live.

Author

Whom do you consider your personal leader at the moment?

RENAMO excombatant (male)

It's this one who is governing now, it's him, because he's the President of Mozambique. Now it would be difficult for me to say that I don't need this father, when he is the one who is governing now.

Perhaps less cynically, we could also say that the former RENAMO combatants had imbibed the idea of a democratically elected government being responsible for all its citizens, not simply the ones who voted for it, in the same way as a father is expected to look after all his children and not simply his favourites. RENAMO propaganda urged the guerrillas to present themselves as the winners of the war and the election, because they claimed that their aim in fighting was not to seize power, but to institute a democratic system (Cahen 1995: 143–4).

Thus, the government's decision to treat FRELIMO and RENAMO excombatants differently was perceived by RENAMO excombatants as hugely unfair. This created the potential for divisions and conflict – perhaps deliberately on the part of government in order to 'divide and conquer', and prevent a unified excombatants' movement (Schafer 1998). But this was quite a dangerous approach, given that one important aspect of FRELIMO's loss of popularity and the social support garnered by REN-AMO was FRELIMO's urban bias and perceived neglect of peripheral rural areas (Cravinho 1995; Finnegan 1992; Geffray and Pedersen 1988; O'Laughlin 1996).

RENAMO excombatant (male)

> We are seeing that we of RENAMO suffered many years without shoes, without any help or food, clothing, we walked naked just because we knew our objective. But the FRELIMO government, we see things are not going well, even in the districts we haven't seen anyone working yet, only those who were here [i.e. FRELIMO] and they are doing more exploitation. They say to us, your father died, Samora won, where is Dhlakama?

Governmental assistance programmes not only created divisions between former RENAMO and FRELIMO combatants, but also within the FRELIMO forces themselves, owing to the structure of the assistance programme. Only those soldiers demobilised in 1994 with the United Nations programme were entitled to assistance, thus leaving former comrades in distinctly different positions with no clear justification which they could accept.

FRELIMO excombatant (male)

> I talk with those who suffered with me and we were demobilised together, we have talked about the lack of assistance, the benefits which were given only to those who were demobilised with ONUMOZ [Operação das Nações Unidas em Moçambique (United Nations Operation in Mozambique)] . . . I don't understand why we weren't given benefits if we are from the same mother and the same father.

As a result of the perception that the fathers had failed to discharge their responsibilities after the war, a number of protests and strikes have taken place across the country since demobilisation (Diario 21 March 1996: 1; Noticias 23 March 1996: 1). The former combatants argue that the government has not fulfilled its promises and therefore its obligations towards them, despite the fact that they behaved as obedient sons during the war, fighting for a cause that many did not even understand or accept.

RENAMO excombatant (male)

> In my opinion, the demobilised soldiers were right to hold the strike, because it was a promise, the [leaders] promised and they didn't fulfil their promise. Whoever makes a promise must keep it.

It was very rare, therefore, to hear admissions such as the following, that the promises were made purely for morale, and that soldiers did not really believe what their 'father' was telling them during the war.

FRELIMO excombatant (male)

> I would say that [the promises] are like a father saying to his son, 'do this and afterwards I'll give you that', but as time goes on, the child realises there is nothing, it's just talk, just the way parents will talk. But we know that a father always talks so that the son will have morale.

Thus, what was perhaps an innocent tool of military mobilisation has been transformed in Mozambique into a platform for the former combatants of both armies to demand compensation. The failure of the military leaders to do their duties by their 'sons' has left a residue of great frustration with the government, and a high degree of political disaffection. It is possible that this will present long-term problems for government, as was the case in Zimbabwe, where the former independence guerrillas burst into activity a full fifteen years after the end of the war (Kriger 1995).

FRELIMO excombatant (male)

> Truly at the moment I still can't say who is the government. I used to think it was the one which put me into the army, I thought I had a government. But really, when I look at the way things are now, I'm not at all sure I have a government. Because a father can never forget his son. Even if the son died five centuries earlier, there will come a day when he [the father] will prepare something in remembrance of his son who died . . . Well, our government is not doing that. My very own government . . . I can say that it doesn't think that the person I took into the war was a living being, perhaps they were stones . . .

Conclusion

From the evidence of this research in Mozambique, it is clear that wartime mobilisation strategies have a strong influence on post-war reintegration processes. It is also clear that we must look at what happened during the war from the perspective of the combatants themselves if we are to understand their behaviour in the post-war period. The way in which the former combatants in Mozambique interpret their participation in the war differs markedly from previous academic portrayals, and hence their predictions for the post-war period.

Where previous writing on the war focused on physical coercion and psychological brutalisation tactics by the RENAMO guerrilla army to create desocialised killing machines, oral accounts by former guerrillas revealed instead a process of resocialisation in which they attempted to maintain links with their former lives and hold on to their moral beliefs as much as possible. In particular, the young recruits' attachment to family and belief in the patriarchal structures were maintained through both their own actions and the manipulation of the leadership. The portrayal of the military leaders as father figures answered a psychological need for the recruits, as well as becoming a tool of military mobilisation. RENAMO used the patriarchal framework to draw parallels with local moral codes and avoid alienating fighters and civilians, to keep control of fighters and inculcate obedience, to justify its struggle politically to the recruits, and to prevent relationships between male and female combatants. FRELIMO also promoted the image of its leaders as father figures, to garner the same kind of obedience and devotion from its recruits, who were unwilling and unconvinced of the justification for the war.

In the post-war period, however, excombatants are finding that the moral space created by the military leadership by deploying a patriarchal frame of reference no longer holds the same relevance for all parties. Whilst expanded during the war, the post-war period has seen that moral space contract and remain unfilled. This has caused tension, resentment and a sense of betrayal by the political leadership, amongst those who invested and believed in it. Former combatants of both sides have there-fore chosen to use patriarchal imagery for their own purposes.

With respect to community reintegration, this symbolism can be seen as having a positive effect. Portraying themselves as obedient 'sons' of the fatherly military leadership allows excombatants to disavow responsibil-ity for what happened during the war, and thereby be reconciled with their former opponents. For political reintegration, however, the patriar-chal framework is more problematic. The failure of the military leadership to fulfil wartime promises to the combatants has become a symbol of the betrayal of patriarchal responsibilities. Differential treatment of former combatants with different status exacerbates tensions, and creates griev-ances reminiscent of those that were at the root of conflict in the first place. The superimposition of the patriarchal framework onto the current system of democratically elected government by former combatants of both sides may discredit the ideal of democracy, because of the way in which they hold the government responsible for fulfilling wartime prom-ises. RENAMO excombatants, in particular, are in danger of revolting against the current situation, which they perceive as discriminatory. If they are looking for models to imitate, they need look no further than neighbouring Zimbabwe to see how it is possible for veterans to create serious political pressure even decades after the end of war.

The evidence presented also provides an argument against the rele-vance of age-based definitions of children and child soldiers for an under-standing of the experiences of the young people in the research. Instead, contextualised definitions of childhood are much more revealing, as ideas about what activities are appropriate for children at what ages and stages vary greatly between cultures and traditions.[15] Indeed, taking an ethno-graphic perspective in the case of the Mozambican civil war shows that all fighters were considered as 'children' to some degree, whether under or over the age of 18. They were children in relation to a father figure, rather than in relation to a developmental paradigm of childhood marked by age distinctions.

Notes

1. This paper is based on field work done in Mozambique from November 1995 to November 1996, principally in Manica province, central Mozambique, and a supplementary period of three months from September 1999, also in Manica province. The research has been written up in a report for USAID, and in my doctoral thesis at Oxford, completed in 1999. I would like to acknowledge my colleague, Chris Dolan, for his contribution to the ideas and research presented in this paper. I am also grateful to the participants at the Brunel conference, 'Child Soldiers: An Anthropological Perspective', 2 June 2000, for their comments, and also to the editors and referees of this volume.
2. Throughout the chapter, the majority of references are to the experiences of the young men who entered the guerrilla and government armies, rather than to the women who participated in the war. In general, girls' and women's experiences differed significantly from those of their male counterparts, and therefore we should be cautious about generalizing from the male experience to that of the female. However, there are some similarities and overlaps and these are noted explicitly in the chapter. Unfortunately, it was not possible to explore the experiences of female combatants more fully in this chapter.
3. It was only a small minority in this area who were recruited at ages below 13. This group may conform more closely to the Western understanding of 'child' soldiers because they were considered locally as naive children rather than boys in the process of becoming men.
4. Note also that Portuguese labour laws dating from 1899 required all Mozambican men and women over the age of fourteen to work, and this legislation remained in effect until 1961 (Newitt 1981: 107).
5. The post-independence conflict in Mozambique began in the late 1970s in Manica province, in close connection with the Rhodesian counter-insurgency campaign against the Zimbabwean guerrillas fighting for independence. After Zimbabwean independence in 1980, South Africa became more involved with the conflict and encouraged the transformation of the small terrorist band into a fully-fledged guerrilla army with local bases: the Mozambican National Resistance (RENAMO). For more detail on the war, see among others Geffray 1990; Vines 1991; Hall and Young 1997; Chan and Venâncio 1998.
6. All quotations are translated by the author and research assistants from either the Portuguese or ChiNdau original.
7. Although the reality was often quite different from the rhetoric. See West and Kloeck-Jenson 1999.
8. Wilson (1992: 544) also argues that much of the ritual was done only on behalf of leaders, to emphasise the difference between them and simple soldiers and create a hierarchical 'cult of military prowess'.
9. This is probably a reference to the RENAMO accusation that the FRELIMO government favoured people from southern ethnic groups or from their own ethnic groups.
10. Referring to demobilisation pay, given monthly for approximately twenty-four months after demobilisation.

11. Metaphor suggesting that the fighters were being led unknowingly into military action.
12. Referring to military leaders and politicians.
13. In Shona culture, 'cousin' and 'brother' are used interchangeably, and are virtually equivalent in social meaning.
14. In Shona, as in many other African cultures, deceased family members are believed to continue to play a role in the lives of following generations, both to good and bad effect. Ancestors become the 'spirits' of the house, or 'household spirits', for whom rituals are performed and who behave accordingly in respect of their family.
15. See Boyden (2000) for an exposition of the arguments in favour of socially and culturally differentiated understandings of childhood, rather than the traditional paradigm of child development accepted in the West. She places particular emphasis on the wide variation in ethno-theories of middle childhood and adolescence, (as opposed to ethno-theories of early childhood that are more universal) which rings true with the Shona paradigm and practices.

References

Alexander, J. 1995. *Political Change in Manica Province, Mozambique: Implications for the Decentralisation of Power.* Maputo: Friedrich Ebert Stiftung.
Barron, M. 1996. 'When the Soldiers Come Home: A Gender Analysis of the Reintegration of Demobilised Soldiers, Mozambique 1994–1996.' MA thesis, University of East Anglia.
Bourdillon, M.F.C. 1987. *The Shona Peoples: An Ethnography of the Contemporary Shona, with Special Reference to their Religion.* Gweru: Mambo Press, 3rd edn.
Boyden, J. 2000. 'Children and Social Healing.' In L. Carlson, M. Mackeson-Sandbach and T. Allen, eds, *Children in Extreme Situations.* Proceedings from the 1998 Alistair Berkeley Memorial Lecture, DESTIN Working Paper No. 00–05, London School of Economics and Political Science. March. www.lse.ac.uk/depts/destin.
Cahen, M. 1995. '"Dhlakama é Maningue Nice". Une ex-guérilla atypique dans la campagne électorale au Mozambique.' In *L'Afrique politique*, 'Le meilleur, le pire et l'incertain'. Paris: Karthala. 119-61.
Cravinho, J. 1995. 'Modernising Mozambique: FRELIMO Ideology and the FRELIMO State.' D.Phil. thesis, University of Oxford.
Diário Newspaper, Beira, Mozambique.
Dolan, C. and Schafer, J. 1997. *The Reintegration of Excombatants in Mozambique: Manica and Zambezia Provinces.* Oxford: Refugee Studies Programme.
Finnegan, W. 1992. *A Complicated War: The Harrowing of Mozambique.* Berkeley: University of California Press.
Garton, S. 1996. *The Cost of War: Australians Return.* Melbourne: Oxford University Press.
Geffray, C. 1990. *La Cause des armes au Mozambique. Anthropologie d'une guerre civile.* Paris: Karthala.
Geffray, C. and Pedersen, M. 1988. 'Nampula en guerre.' *Politique africaine* 29: 18–40.
Hall, M. and Young, T. 1997. *Confronting Leviathan: Mozambique since Independence.* London: Hurst and Co.
Harrison, G. 1994. 'Mozambique: An Unsustainable Democracy.' *Review of African Political Economy* 61: 429–40.

Kaplan, R.D. 1994. 'The Coming Anarchy: How Scarcity, Crime, Overpopulation and Disease are Rapidly Destroying the Social Fabric of Our Planet.' *Atlantic Monthly* February: 44–76.

Kriger, N. 1995. 'The Politics of Creating National Heroes: The Search for Political Legitimacy and National Identity.' In N. Bhebe and T.O. Ranger, eds, *Soldiers in Zimbabwe's Liberation War*. London: James Currey: 139-62.

Legrand, J.-C. 1993. 'Logique de guerre et dynamique de la violence en Zambézia, 1976–1991.' *Politique africaine* 50, June: 88–104.

McGregor, J. 1998. 'Violence and Social Change in a Border Economy: War in the Maputo Hinterland, 1984–1992.' *Journal of Southern African Studies* 24 (1): 37–60.

Minter, W. 1988. 'The Mozambican National Resistance (RENAMO) as Described by Ex-participants.' Research report to the Ford Foundation and the Swedish International Development Agency. Washington DC.

Newitt, M. 1981. *Portugal in Africa: The Last Hundred Years*. London: C. Hurst and Co.

Nilsson, A. 1993. 'From Pseudo-Terrorists to Pseudo-Guerrillas: The MNR in Mozambique.' *Review of African Political Economy* 58: 35–42.

Nordstrom, C. 1994. 'Rituals and Realities of Terror/Warfare.' In S.P. Reyna and R.E. Downs, eds, *Studying War: Anthropological Perspectives*. Langhorne, PA: Gordon and Breach.

Notícias. Maputo, Mozambique.

Nuñes, J. (1992). 'Peasants and Survival: The Social Consequences of Displacement – Mocuba, Zambezia.' Ms.

O'Laughlin, B. 1996. 'Through a Divided Glass: Dualism, Class and the Agrarian Question in Mozambique.' *Journal of Peasant Studies* 23 (4): 1–39.

Roesch, O. 1992a. 'RENAMO and the Peasantry in Southern Mozambique: A View from Gaza Province.' *Canadian Journal of African Studies* 26, March: 462–84.

——. 1992b. 'Mozambique Unravels? The Retreat to Tradition.' *Southern Africa Report* May: 27–30.

Schafer, J. 1998. '"A Baby Who Doesn't Cry Will Not be Suckled": AMODEG and the Reintegration of Demobilised Soldiers.' *Journal of Southern African Studies* 24 (1): 207–22.

——. 1999. 'Soldiers at Peace: The Post-War Politics of Demobilised Soldiers in Mozambique, 1964–1996.' D.Phil. thesis, University of Oxford.

Venâncio, M. and Chan, S. 1998. 'War and Gropings Towards Peace.' In S. Chan and M. Venâncio, eds, *War and Peace in Mozambique*. London: Macmillan.

Vines, A. 1991. *RENAMO: Terrorism in Mozambique*. York: Centre for Southern African Studies; London: James Currey; Bloomington: Indiana University Press.

West, H. and Kloeck-Jenson, S. 1999. 'Betwixt and Between: "Traditional Authority" and Democratic Decentralisation in Post-War Mozambique.' *African Affairs* 98 (393): 455–84.

White, L. 1985. 'Review Article: The Revolution Ten Years On.' *Journal of Southern African Studies* 11 (2): 320–32.

Wilson, K. 1992. 'Cults of Violence and Counter-Violence in Mozambique.' *Journal of Southern African Studies* 18 (3): 527–82.

6

Girls with Guns: Narrating the Experience of War of FRELIMO's 'Female Detachment'[1]

Harry G. West

Introduction

Just as Africa is a continent on which youth constitute a demographic category of tremendous and increasing importance, because of the troubling number of military conflicts in Africa today it is also a continent on which a large percentage of the world's 'children at war' are to be found.[2] Children at war and, particularly, 'child soldiers', feature prominently in international media coverage of Africa, especially when journalists wish to portray a chaotic continent plunging headlong into anarchy. Even if such media accounts and images often sensationalise and exoticise Africa, they not only play on the anxieties and suspicions of their readership, but also echo the ambivalence of many Africans toward the liminal category of youth. If we are to deepen our understanding of the broader issue of youth in Africa, we must better understand the place of Africa's youth in war.

Since the early 1990s, many of those contributing to the literature on children and war in Africa, and elsewhere, have argued that children are particularly vulnerable to violent conflict (Garbarino et al. 1991; Machel 1996; Save the Children 1992; Walker 1993). The atrocities children witness, the argument goes, disrupt them developmentally in their most important formative years. As their families are broken up and larger social institutions cease to function, children are denied lasting relationships of affection as well as stable ground upon which to develop in physical, intellectual and moral terms. Under such conditions, Garbarino et al.

(1991: 16) tell us, 'children may be socialised into a model of fear, violence and hatred'. Because the scars of 'trauma' are borne by these children for the rest of their lives, it is argued that they come to constitute a 'lost generation'.

Increasingly, the literature also focuses on how children are drawn into violent conflict as combatants and perpetrators of the violence. The roles of victim and perpetrator, this literature seeks to demonstrate, are not necessarily mutually exclusive.[3] In the stereotypical scenario, portrayed in the literature on children and war in locations around the globe, the young are conscripted to serve guerrilla insurgencies and, sometimes, state militaries well below the age of eighteen. After a brief training period, the loyalty of new conscripts is often tested through compelling them to commit atrocities, sometimes against former neighbours, and even members of their own family. Having done this, these children are overtaken by a sense that they no longer have a home and a family to which they might some day return.[4] Whereas state militaries and guerrilla armies are often successful in driving a wedge between new conscripts and their communities of origin, producing for societal consumption an image of these young people as insensate killing machines, many who have worked with ex-child-soldiers in a post-war context have reported that they suffer long-term remorse and guilt for such deeds, even when carried out under compulsion (Fleischman 1994). In any case, the general assumption in the literature is that war, and young people's participation in it, gives rise to a future generation of adults for whom violence is a part of everyday life. Today's victims reproduce the 'trauma' they have experienced, giving rise tomorrow to cycles of recurring violence.[5] If this is true, it does not bode well for Africa, a continent in which so many of today's population are young people who have experienced violence at first hand.

Recently, however, the assumption that young people are irrevocably scarred by violence has been challenged. Sara Gibbs (1994), for example, has suggested that the application of Western notions of 'innocent' and 'vulnerable' youth to contexts of violence elsewhere can be misleading; among the Mozambicans of Milange, Zambesia, with whom she conducted research after the end of the Mozambican civil war (1977–1992), youth were seen, and saw themselves, not as more vulnerable but, rather, as more resilient than other social groups in coping with the impact of war. Jo Boyden has pointed out that within the context of violence in Uganda, for example, children's participation in conflict can, unfortunately, be seen as an appropriate adaptive strategy – 'an extremely practical survival mechanism' given that the armies they join provide them with 'food, shelter, companionship, clothing and security, with some protection from actual combat for the youngest recruits' (1994: 263).[6]

Whereas Gibbs argues that Western notions of 'youth' can limit our understanding of young people in the context of violence elsewhere,

Boyden suggests that Western notions of 'trauma' can be just as misleading, prompting journalists, academics and aid workers to assume that the
experience of war will produce similar effects in young people everywhere – effects that can be diagnosed and treated as a form of 'Post
Traumatic Stress Disorder' (PTSD). Boyden contributes to an emerging
critique of PTSD in the psychiatric literature.[7] Patrick Bracken (1998: 40–1)
asserts that the PTSD model assumes that 'trauma' is experienced at the
level of the individual; that it produces similar results in individuals anywhere and everywhere; and that individual 'victims' of violence everywhere can thus be treated similarly.[8] Arguing against these assumptions,
he writes:

> What clearly emerges from work in a number of areas is the importance of
> contextual factors in shaping the experience of and response to trauma.
> Issues of context are not secondary factors that merely impinge on the
> progress of a universal psychological or biological process. Rather, issues
> of context in terms of social, political and cultural reality should be seen as
> central to this experience and response ... These realities structure the indi-
> vidual's response to violence by determining the practical context in which
> violence occurs and in which the individual recovers. They also structure
> and determine the meaning of the event for the individual and the com-
> munity involved. In turn these factors will determine what therapeutic
> efforts will be relevant, will be available and will be successful. (1998: 55)

Arguing against the idea that violence is similarly experienced everywhere, Derek Summerfield (1998: 22) has written, 'It is a fundamental
premise that what victims of terror and the upheavals of war experience
is a function of what these events mean to them, or come to mean'. Both
Bracken and Summerfield therefore assert that meaning, and thus experience of violence is in significant measure culturally determined, and that
non-Western cultures may not similarly frame the experience of violence
in terms that produce 'trauma' at the level of individual 'victims'.

There is, of course, a fine line between challenging the Western origins
and biases of universalistic perspectives on young people's experience of
violence and war, and implying that non-Western cultures have inherent
tendencies toward violence and/or produce individuals with greater
immunity to its effects. The call to take social, political and cultural contexts into account might too easily degenerate into the claim that 'life is
worth less to Africans' and other non-Westerners. Jo de Berry (2000), however, has suggested that analysts of the child soldier phenomenon in
Africa and elsewhere can and, indeed, must forgo the false dilemma of
choice between universalistic and relativistic paradigms. The key, she
suggests, lies in avoiding the 'essentialisation' of culture while taking culture into account as a factor in young people's experience of violence.

'De-essentialising' culture requires situating cultural norms and practices within the flow of historical events and processes as well as within

the fields of power relations that define these.[9] In this vein, several recent analyses of young people's experience of violence have focused on the role of ideology. Andy Dawes (1992), for example, has posited that the generalised experience of violent conflict in South Africa was accompanied by the production of social discourses that gave structure and meaning to violent action, even for youth. Elsewhere, Baker (1991) has argued that a strong sense of political identity has allowed Palestinian youth to cope with the complex psychological consequences of their participation in the Intifada.[10]

Jo Boyden (1994: 262) has suggested that 'ideology may be one of the most important factors mediating children's responses to violence'. Bracken et al. (1995: 1076–7; 1081) further suggest that ideological involvement may in part determine why some people exposed to violence suffer traumatic effects while others do not, and they argue that addressing the ideological commitments of victims of violence may be essential in healing trauma when and where it *is* experienced. Others, however, warn that the ideological interpretations of violence to which children are exposed may not always serve them well. Where Krijn Peters and Paul Richards (1998) assert that youth in Sierra Leone 'chose to fight with their eyes open', Garbarino et al. (1991: 26) argue otherwise: 'Children can participate in ideology directly, but with the limitations imposed by their concrete intellectual orientation and their concern for first hand relationships.' Cohn and Goodwin-Gill (1994) warn that children may lack the capacity to sift through competing ideologies to make fully informed 'choices' and that, years after the violence has subsided, they may pay unforeseen costs of their decisions.

What emerges from my reading of the literature is the conclusion that an anthropological approach has much to contribute to our understanding of young people and their experience of violence in Africa. Such an approach allows for a focus on the complex social processes wherein the meaning of individual experiences of violence is constructed.[11] In what follows, I present an anthropologically-informed account of the experiences of a group of girls and young women[12] who served as combatants in the guerrilla army of the *Frente de Libertação de Moçambique* (Front for the Liberation of Mozambique, or FRELIMO) in its campaign for Mozambican independence from Portuguese colonial rule between 1964 and 1974. My account constitutes a particular contribution to the literature on child soldiers not only because it focuses on female combatants, but also because it approaches their experience through the narratives of now-mature adults who served as combatants more than twenty years ago.

The narratives I gathered suggest the need to refine our understanding of how ideology frames the experience of young people at war. To begin with, I will argue, young female guerrillas were not merely indoctrinated by FRELIMO – for better or for worse – but also themselves contributed substantially to the narratives that would frame their experience as combatants. Because FRELIMO ideology was dialogically constructed in the discursive spaces between the guerrilla command and its rank-and-file members, it both mediated and reflected the experience of violence of young female combatants.[13] This is not to suggest that the girls and young women who served as guerrillas in the FRELIMO army were as well positioned to contribute to the ideological constructs that framed their participation in the war as were their elder, male commanders. Rather, it is to suggest that these ideological constructs powerfully influenced how young female combatants experienced the war precisely because they also 'empowered' these young people through the creation of discursive space for their contribution to the social construction of new roles and identities.

Beyond this, the longitudinal perspective afforded by work with excombatants more than twenty years after war's end leads me to propose a further revision to our understanding of the role of ideology in framing the experience of war for young people. Where Derek Summerfield (1998) has argued the need to examine 'social memory' in order to appreciate whether the experience of war has or has not been traumatic, I wish to call attention to the fact that social memory is sustained in the medium of ever-changing social contexts. Where trauma is held at bay in the moment of the experience of violence by the force of narrative accounts that frame the violence as purposive and meaningful, these narratives may shift and disintegrate when present-day realities undermine their ideological claims. Such has been the case, I will argue, for many Mozambican women who served as guerrilla combatants but later became frustrated with the failures of the post-independence government to 'fulfill promises' made to them during the war. For these women, the war experience has become more troubling with the passage of time and with the loss of conviction provoked by the destabilisation of the narrative through which their experience of war was mediated.

Before my presentation and analysis of the narratives of and about young female Mozambicans at war, however, I offer a brief synopsis of the war for Mozambican independence and of the participation in it of girls and young women.

'The Liberation of Women is a Fundamental Necessity for the Revolution'

In the late 1950s and early 1960s, as other European colonial powers prepared to grant independence to their colonies, Portugal remained committed to the preservation of its colonial empire. FRELIMO – formed in 1962 of three protonationalist movements in exile – sent guerrillas to

Algeria for training in 1963, and initiated its *luta armada* (armed campaign) in September 1964. Operating out of rear bases in the newly-independent Tanzania, FRELIMO quickly came to control most of the countryside surrounding colonial towns and military installations in large portions of the northernmost Mozambican provinces of Cabo Delgado and Niassa. Sympathy for the insurgency was widespread in these areas, but fear of and respect for FRELIMO guerrillas were inseparable: those who refused to aid FRELIMO were considered to be collaborators with the colonial regime, and were threatened and sometimes executed (West 1997).

The insurgency, already comprising large numbers of young men from these areas, recruited new guerrilla trainees from among the population living in what it came to call *zonas libertadas* (liberated zones), and it called upon 'civilians' in these areas to assist guerrilla detachments through the provision of food, porterage and information about enemy movements. In the first months of the campaign, FRELIMO printed the following story in Mozambique Revolution, its English-language newsletter:[14]

23 Mozambican Girls Participate in the Armed Struggle
Niassa Province

As a result of the political activity of our militants – each FRELIMO militant is an active agent of revolutionary propaganda among the people – 23 young girls from different villages, 18 to 24 years old, declared they were ready to participate in the struggle and to join our forces. We constructed a special base for them, where they received military training. Since then they have participated in the attacks and ambushes, as true militants, revealing a courage and consciousness of their duties and responsibilities in no way inferior to that of FRELIMO men.

Last August, for example, a group of 6 FRELIMO militants was intercepted by a troop of 30 Portuguese soldiers. Our militants fanned out, and shooting, they gradually drove the Portuguese soldiers back to near the girls' base. Hearing the shots, the girls dispersed and encircled the Portuguese soldiers, killing 5 and forcing the others to run away. (*Mozambique Revolution* 21: 7)

Whereas this account portrays these events as a unique occurrence, and suggests that the female recruits involved were 18 years of age and older, the oral histories that I gathered suggest that from quite early on in the war, FRELIMO guerrilla commanders systematically recruited (and sometimes armed) girls as young as 10 years of age to assist the guerrillas, although the training given such recruits was, at first, often minimal.[15] Many accounts attribute this general phenomenon to the exigencies of a nascent guerrilla campaign in which commanders sought to make whatever use possible of every person within their reach. By 1966, however, the practice of recruiting and arming girls and young women was sufficiently widespread to prompt male elders and authority figures among liberated zone civilians to complain that girls with guns slung over their shoulders presented an unacceptable challenge to 'traditional' social relations (Munslow 1983: 106). FRELIMO military leaders – most of whom were themselves much younger than the chiefs and elders who exercised 'traditional authority' within Mozambican rural society – recognised truth in these claims, but this truth did not disturb them. Instead, they celebrated the ways in which the insurgency was overturning 'traditional' age- and gender-based hierarchies even as it challenged the institutions of colonialism.[16] The issue of the participation of girls and young women in the war effort remained a point of contention in the early years of the war as young guerrilla leaders and the elders who had joined FRELIMO and who exercised power as 'civilian' leaders in the liberated zones vied for control of the movement. Between 1966 and 1970, however, FRELIMO military leaders consolidated their power in the organisation and in the liberated zones, subordinating 'traditional authorities' to the military command structure and institutionalising the participation of girls and young women in the armed campaign.[17] Essential to this consolidation of power was the formation, in 1967, of the *Destacamento Feminino* (Female Detachment),[18] composed of girls and young women who had been sent to FRELIMO's rear base in Nachingwea, Tanzania for politico-military training similar to that given male guerrilla recruits.[19]

Once trained, members of the *Destacamento Feminino* (the detachment was referred to as the 'DF' and its individual members as 'DFs') served FRELIMO in a variety of capacities. In limited instances, they participated in armed combat missions.[20] FRELIMO commanders found DFs particularly effective in gathering intelligence and mobilising support in areas not yet controlled by FRELIMO as they could move among local populations without attracting the attention that unfamiliar men might (Isaacman and Isaacman 1984: 156). Most DFs, however, were given less dangerous assignments, often being deployed in and around population concentrations in the liberated zones to protect civilians in case of Portuguese attack. At the same time, they were instrumental in organising and managing the social and economic institutions established by FRELIMO in the liberated zones, including elementary schools and adult literacy classes, health posts and collective agricultural fields.

The role DFs played in the Mozambican war for Independence made legends of them not only in southern Africa but, more broadly, among leftist and feminist militants worldwide.[21] What distinguished DFs from other girls and young women in the liberated zones, however, was not the extent to which they participated in military operations – for many girls and young women who were never trained as DFs also did this, while many DFs never, or rarely, saw combat – but, rather, the degree to which their experiences were framed by a heroic FRELIMO narrative. DFs were not merely taught guerrilla strategy at Nachingwea, they also studied the socialist ideology that animated the FRELIMO anti-colonial campaign. According to FRELIMO rhetoric, the 'emancipation of women' was both a means and an end in the war for Mozambican independence, and DFs both studied and embodied FRELIMO's ideal of the 'new socialist woman'.

The practical interests of the FRELIMO guerrilla command gave foundation to the discourse on the 'emancipation of women'. To exclude girls and women from the war effort, FRELIMO leaders realised, would be to leave more than half the population unutilised, a luxury the insurgency could not afford. Samora Machel proclaimed in a 1973 speech that: 'The emancipation of women is not an act of charity, the result of a humanitarian or compassionate attitude. The liberation of women is a fundamental necessity for the Revolution, the guarantee of its continuity and the precondition for its victory' (in Isaacman and Isaacman 1984: 174). At the same time, the leadership argued, it was within the interests of girls and women to contribute to the struggle, as their freedom from the shackles of 'traditional' forms of age and gender hierarchy would be inextricably bound up with the FRELIMO campaign to liberate all Mozambicans from 'oppression and exploitation'. As trained guerrillas, DFs were expected to 'raise the revolutionary consciousness' of the populations with which they came into contact – especially women and girls – wherever they were deployed. Because many female inhabitants of the liberated zones were unsuited for military training, FRELIMO took the decision in 1972 to form a broader 'Organisation of Mozambican Women' that would mobilise civilian girls and women to support the revolutionary struggle in other ways. DFs, however, played a central role in the organisation, educating their comrade sisters in FRELIMO revolutionary ideology. The report published by *Mozambique Revolution* on the First Conference of Mozambican Women, staged in 1973 (a year before the end of the war), is worth quoting at length for the way in which it encapsulates the discourse to which DFs both were exposed and contributed:

> The situation of women being exploited and oppressed beings is not a phenomenon limited to Mozambique. In most countries and on every continent women are to differing degrees deprived of their most fundamental rights, prevented from taking part in political life, confined to the tasks of procreation and looking after the home, and subject to tyrannical authority.
>
> Yet it is in countries such as ours, where traditional concepts on women's submission and colonialist concepts have been combined or juxtaposed, that this oppression and exploitation take the most extreme forms ...
>
> Throughout their lives, at different phases of their growth, girls are subject to what is [sic] known as 'initiation rites' which, although varying in form from region to region, all have in common the fact that they instil in girls a submissive attitude towards men and teach them that their place in society is a secondary one. During the puberty ceremony, specifically, girls are told that their role henceforth is to produce children and to look after

their husband and home, all other tasks being forbidden to them. These initiation rites, which are surrounded by an aura of mystery and religious solemnity, have a very powerful psychological impact and make girls blindly accept what they are taught, traumatising them for the rest of their lives ...[22]

The colonial system further worsened this situation. Itself also instigated by the idea that women are 'the second sex', it subjected Mozambican women to double oppression and exploitation: first the general oppression and exploitation inflicted indiscriminately on men and women alike in the form of forced labour, compulsory crops, arbitrary imprisonment, racial discrimination, etc. And then the other more specific form directed only against women. By separating women from their husbands through forced labour and denying them the means to support their homes and children, colonialism created the conditions whereby women were forced to resort to selling their bodies, to prostituting themselves, in order to be able to survive. Women debased themselves, degraded themselves and were subjected to the most extreme humiliation by the colonialists, who not only made of them a labour force and machines for reproduction, but also made them into instruments of pleasure. (*Mozambique Revolution* 54: 22–23)

After thus attributing women's suffering to the dual causes of racially-based colonial hierarchy and gender-based 'traditional' African hierarchy, the conference report suggests that inside FRELIMO's liberated zones, 'a new life is being built, inspired by an ideology which puts the interests of the masses of the people before all else, which rejects all forms of oppression and exploitation by any individual, group, class or sex over another, and which aims at establishing healthy and harmonious human relations'. The piece then goes on to detail 'the means to be used by Mozambican women to achieve their liberation':

Considering that the liberation of women cannot be separated from that of men, and that the enemy and its objectives are common, the 1st conference of Mozambican Women pointed out that the only road for women to take was to engage in the tasks of the struggle, in the revolutionary process ...

In this way, they will contribute directly to the victory of the revolution, that is, hastening the day of their liberation. What is more, by joining the struggle at all levels, they are opening up new prospects for their future, destroying in practice the concepts which relegated them to a passive and voiceless role in society. In short, they are creating the conditions for participating in the exercise of power, taking their destiny into their hands. (*Mozambique Revolution* 54: 23).

It is difficult to know to what extent FRELIMO rhetoric initially resonated with the experiences of the girls and young women it sought to recruit. As stated above, respect for and fear of FRELIMO were inseparable, and the measure of each component impossible to gauge. At the most basic level, FRELIMO portrayed DFs and young female civilian supporters alike not as conscripts but, rather, as volunteers committing 'acts of heroism' on behalf of the revolution, even if these young people might have felt that they had no option but to comply with FRELIMO 'requests' of them.[23] What is clear is that, to varying degrees, these recruits themselves eventually contributed to the production of FRELIMO discourse on their participation in the *luta armada*, as we see in the above quoted report of the First Conference of Mozambican Women, and as we will see also in the life story narratives of DFs presented in the following section. For DFs, the experience of the war was, in many instances, saturated with a FRELIMO narrative that made of them heroic youth – harbingers of a new era. When DFs themselves spoke of the war, then and when I met with them decades later, they most often told not of traumatic events that *happened to them* but, rather, of purposive acts and of epic events to *which they contributed* in defining ways. Where young people in the context of war are often conceived of and portrayed as innocent witnesses and victims of violence perpetrated by 'men with guns' who present a threat no matter which 'side' they are on,[24] DFs presented and present themselves as 'girls with guns' – central players in the historical drama that defined their times.

The Stories of Girls with Guns

In the eleven months that I spent conducting dissertation research on the Mueda plateau in the north of Cabo Delgado province between August 1993 and February 1995, I collected several dozen life histories.[24] My research focused on how Muedans of various social groups (distributed along lines of generation, gender, religious conviction, educational background, and wealth) had experienced the dramatic social changes occurring in the plateau region as a consequence of colonial conquest and rule and of anti-colonial insurgency and post-independence governance.[25] Among the most memorable interview sessions were many of those I spent collecting the life histories of DFs. Then mostly in their late thirties and early forties, most of these women spoke with an intensity that distinguished them from other Mozambican women whom I interviewed, whether older or younger. DFs had led lives profoundly different from those of their mothers and grandmothers. While participating in armed combat side-by-side with young Mozambican men, while orchestrating the movements and activities of vulnerable populations living in FRELIMO's liberated zones, most DFs gained locally unprecedented self-assurance and assertiveness.

My very first interview with DFs was conducted on a humid March evening in 1994 in the yard of Basalisa Musa's house in Pemba, the coastal capital of Cabo Delgado province. Basalisa asked three compatriot DFs to join us in order to, as she put it, 'animate our conversation'. Once all had arrived, I turned on my cassette recorder and asked the first of my prepared questions. I would not have a chance to ask another. Teresa Casiano, the youngest of the group, began with her story, needing no prompting to tell it to completion. The others followed suit, knowing exactly what they wanted to say.[26]

Even twenty years after independence, the stories DFs tell of their participation in the campaign for independence bear witness to the ways in which they absorbed, contributed to and embodied the FRELIMO narrative of heroic youth fighting valiantly for the cause of independence and the elimination of exploitation of all kinds. Teresa's grandfather, Jacob Kaindi, was a legendary mobiliser for the FRELIMO nationalist movement before being captured by the Portuguese secret police and tortured until he cut his own tongue out so as to eliminate the possibility that he could inform on his comrades. Teresa told me that FRELIMO had no trouble recruiting the sons and daughters of such casualties of colonial oppression to aid in its war of national liberation, even if her story, and those of her comrades, betrayed complex sentiments and reactions to the FRELIMO insurgency.

Basalisa, for example, was around 12 years of age when, prior to the outbreak of the war, FRELIMO mobilisers started to recruit adherents in her region and to instruct them in how to support the FRELIMO operatives then laying the groundwork for the coming campaign. She told me:

> My brother arrived in the settlement at night and said, 'Sister, the men who are going to liberate us are living in the bush now. They need food. I want you to come with me to take them food. But I must tell you, there you will like it so much you will want to stay.' So we went to the bush. There in the lowlands, I saw them. They were many! And they all had beards, and very big hair that had not been cut or combed. This was the first time I had seen them. They were strange looking with their big hair! But they greeted me well and gave me biscuits from a plastic wrapper. I thought to myself, 'despite being so strange, hidden away here in the bush, they eat such wonderful things!' And there were four women among them. Then they told us, 'Look, it's better if you stay here with us. We, here, are going to bid farewell to the Portuguese.' They said that if I returned to the settlement, I would no longer be their friend. So, I stayed. The men would leave from time to time. One day, we heard gun shots, and then they returned. I realised, then, what they meant by 'bidding the Portuguese farewell'.

Basalisa took up residence in the guerrilla camp, where she performed tasks not unlike those she had done for her mother back in her settlement. Soon after the commencement of hostilities, however, Basalisa, like so many children and youth who had gathered in the guerrilla camps, was given a weapon and shown how to fire it. At first, she was told that she might need to use her weapon if the camp was attacked. Within a short time, however, she was asked to help transport war material and supplies to and from the camp. Wherever she went, Basalisa carried her gun to protect herself and her cargo; 'We were told that if we were attacked, we should flee, but we could not drop our arms or, even, our cargo. We were told, 'Never let the enemy capture war material so long as you live.' Porters who arrived at their destination without their weapon or without their cargo were executed.' Eventually, the inevitable happened. Basalisa's caravan encountered a Portuguese patrol and a skirmish broke out. Over the coming months, she was involved in five fire fights, and was wounded in the fifth encounter.

After receiving treatment for her wounds in one of FRELIMO's bush hospitals, Basalisa was not returned to camp. Instead, she was sent to Nachingwea, the principal FRELIMO rear base located across the Rovuma river border in Tanzania. There, she underwent an intensive six-month politico-military training course with the second unit of the *Destacamento Feminino*. At the time of her integration into the DF, Basalisa was – like most members recruited on the Mueda plateau – considered a *mwaali* back home. This meant that she had recently undergone female rites of initiation and had been adorned with elaborate scarification on her face and body, but she had not yet had sexual relations. Because *vaali* (plural) – generally between the ages of 10 and 15 – were energetic, but free from the responsibilities of motherhood, FRELIMO militants considered them ideal candidates for involvement in the armed struggle for independence, Basilisa and her fellow DFs often told me (see also Artur et al. 1992: 5, 26).

Once inducted into the Female Detachment at Nachingwea, DFs like Basalisa were dispatched to the interior where they were placed under the charge of FRELIMO base commanders. Although they were used by these commanders in diverse tasks, many of which made of them camp 'little sisters' (Artur et al. 1992: 27), DFs spoke of these activities proudly, reminding me constantly that these too were contributions to the revolutionary cause. For example, DFs staffed the FRELIMO bush schools where children and adults alike were taught reading, writing and arithmetic (skills necessary to the prosecution of guerrilla war, they explained). They cared for war casualties in FRELIMO bush hospitals and staffed FRELIMO orphanages, caring for children whose parents had been killed in the war or who had been separated from their families in the midst of wartime chaos. DFs told me how they were deployed to organise collective work teams on agricultural plots intended to feed both guerrillas and the civilian populations upon which the guerrillas depended for support. They also organised and accompanied caravans to carry agricultural surpluses out of the Mozambican interior and war materials back in.

Many DFs told me that they also participated in covert operations of one sort or another. Even before the war began, many of these young women had aided nationalist mobilisers by gathering information on potential supporters and/or potential enemies. As a woman I will call Elisa tells it: 'My task was to spend time at the water source listening to what people were saying about FRELIMO. I also listened in on conversations at the mission after mass, as people talked quietly in small groups. People would talk openly in front of me because they considered me a child. I reported what I heard.' With conviction, Elisa told me, 'I was told never to lie because people would be executed based on what I said'.

Once the war began, DFs continued with similar covert activities. In the 'advanced zones' where FRELIMO was struggling to win popular support, several DFs recounted to me, they worked effectively as mobilisers and spies because, as unfamiliar outsiders, they attracted less attention than men. DFs often told me that they were effective in encouraging women to prod their husbands into joining the cause, and boasted that, simply by their example as women who had taken up the struggle, they often shamed men into joining FRELIMO (see also Isaacman and Isaacman 1984: 153).

In addition to all of these activities, DFs told me, they sometimes participated in combat missions. Jacinta Bakar had participated in several combat missions prior to her official training at Nachingwea, where she was selected as commander of the third unit of the *Destacamento Feminino*. Her pretraining action involved the sabotage of enemy installations and the mining of roads. After training, Jacinta was dispatched to the third sector, an advanced zone where FRELIMO was having difficulties securing the support of the local population. In the company of four detachments of male guerrilla fighters, Jacinta's unit attacked a settlement under government control near the town of Macomia: 'We freed 140 people and took them back to the liberated zones. Later, we captured a Portuguese soldier named Gomez. He, too, was liberated from Portuguese colonialism by FRELIMO!'

According to Jacinta, midway through the war orders came down through the FRELIMO command structure that women were no longer to participate in combat missions.[27] Upset by this, Jacinta requested transfer to the fourth sector, a zone situated even more deeply behind enemy lines. There, still in the company of her unit, she participated in the capture of a cache of arms and a large group of African soldiers fighting within the ranks of the colonial army. In her own words:

> After that mission, I wrote a note to [FRELIMO commander] Samora Machel. I said to him, 'Look what we did! Why should we let our brothers die and not fight ourselves.' Samora never answered me, but he seemed to have the attitude that if we wanted to continue fighting, that was okay, but it couldn't be official policy. I went on participating in combat missions. For a while, I was at Manica [a base in the farthest advanced zone in Cabo Delgado province]. Male guerrillas never gave me, or my group, any problems. They never left us behind, and they never excluded us or resented us. They appreciated having us along.

Notwithstanding the limits to women's involvement in combat, most former DFs today look back upon their experiences in the *Destacamento*

Feminino with nostalgia, and they celebrate their contributions to freeing Mozambicans from colonial rule and themselves from both colonial and 'traditional' forms of oppression and exploitation. As Basalisa Musa expressed it to me:

> Our mothers led a limited life. Outside the house and, even, inside it they could not speak freely. During the *luta armada*, we lived a different life. We rose to meet the needs of our whole society, not just of husbands and our own children. In this way, we were just like men and we had to be treated just like men.

To this, Teresa Casiano added: 'During the luta, when we spoke, people listened. Not just other young people, and not just women. Everyone listened to what we said because we were equal to the tasks that were given to us.'

These remarks are telling. Participation in the armed struggle broadened horizons for these young women, just as it did for young men. Upon joining the *Destacamento Feminino*, many told me, they delighted in the fact that their lives would not be limited to tending agricultural fields, carrying water, cooking and caring for children. Life as a DF would give them greater range of movement across both social and geographical landscapes. They would experience fears and triumphs unknown to the generation of their parents. They would have tales to tell evenings around the fire, just as their brothers did.[28] Through participation in the war as combatants, they could expand and extend the autonomy from family elders they enjoyed as *vaali* without moving directly into new relations of dependence upon husbands.[29] Even as these young women fought for the cause, they often reminisced, their participation in the war armed them as youth vis-à-vis their elders and as women vis-à-vis men. Basalisa once reminded me that where her mother had carried children on her back when she fetched water for her household and had been required to carry her father on her back from the bath to the bed, so that he might sleep with clean feet, the 'babies' that DFs slung over their backs were AK47s.

While the accounts of DFs betray that they faced very real dangers – dangers sometimes posed by the disciplinary practices of the FRELIMO organisation itself – and that they witnessed, and sometimes participated in acts of violence, these accounts also bear testimony to the power of ideological conviction that gave meaning to these events and protected the wellbeing of these young people in extremely difficult circumstances.

The Wages of Waging War

Even if the narratives above give evidence that the FRELIMO ideological framework in which the *Destacamento Feminino* was suspended helped to define the experience of war for many DFs and helped to arm them against war's potentially traumatic effects, we must, nonetheless, assess the consequences wrought by ascription to this ideology with greater ethnographic rigour, paying heed to the variable experiences of DFs as well as to the subtle changes in consequence over time.

For some DFs, the complexities of the war and of their involvement in it eventually overpowered FRELIMO's vision of heroic youth fighting to create a better world for themselves and their neighbours and kin. Not all DFs whom I interviewed were as confident and assertive as Teresa Casiano. Some hesitated to speak with me, and consented to an interview only so long as I allowed them to be accompanied by a relative who, in some cases, spoke for them.[30] After years of work in advanced zones, where they lived in constant fear of discovery and ate only erratically, many DFs told me they suffered from 'illness' and/or 'exhaustion' that did not subside. Many of these DFs were 'retired' by FRELIMO before the end of the war. Other DFs, who worked as operatives in FRELIMO's internal security apparatus ferreting out traitors, collaborators and saboteurs, struggled to come to terms with the roles they played in the deaths of people they had known well enough to condemn.

Time and again, as I collected the life histories of these DFs, I realised that we sat together conversing in a yard where the work of traditional healing was taking place. A sizable proportion of DFs, it turns out, sought treatment from traditional healers during and after the war, and many married such specialists once the war ended. Where FRELIMO had actively campaigned against the practices and practitioners of traditional healing in the liberated zones (West 2001), some of these ex-DFs had abandoned the FRELIMO campaign and, with it, FRELIMO ideology and had turned to other narratives in their quest to make sense of wartime experiences. These narratives often framed the events of the war in the language of sorcery, and healing in the language of counter-sorcery and rituals to appease the avenging spirits of the dead. The life stories of these DFs parallel those of young Zimbabweans, studied by Pamela Reynolds (1996: 41–68), who suffered from guilt produced by having (rightly or wrongly) accused members of their community of 'selling-out' the guerrillas and having witnessed their consequent execution. Reynolds argues that the traditional healers who treated these young people 'refashioned moments of stress in the lives of their patients' (xxxvii); in other words, where the revolutionary narrative was inadequate in rendering wartime experiences meaningful, traditional healers provided an alternative narrative framework that many found more cogent.[31]

Cases of 'burnout' within the ranks of the *Destacamento Feminino*, while by no means unusual, were not, however, the norm. Many DFs not only 'empowered themselves' during the war, but also harvested benefits that continue to the present day. Many of the women who today occupy influential positions in the FRELIMO party hierarchy at national, provincial, district and local levels owe their power to their wartime careers as DFs. Included among ex-DFs are Marcelina Chissano, wife of the current Mozambican President Joaquim Chissano, and many other spouses of party leaders. The life trajectories of most DFs, however, fall somewhere between these extremes, and require even closer scrutiny if we are to appreciate sufficiently what these stories have to tell us about the experience of young people in war.

In the above discussion of the literature, I cited the critique by Cohn and Goodwin-Gill (1994), who suggest that children lack the capacity to sift through competing ideologies and make informed 'choices'. To this, I juxtaposed Jo Boyden's (1994: 263) assertion that, *given the circumstances*, children's 'choice' to participate in war often constitutes a sensible adaptive strategy. What is most difficult for children to ascertain, I suggest, is the consequences of their 'choices' in the long term, when the circumstances that made their strategy of fighting sensible no longer pertain. If carrying an AK-47 'empowers' young women in the moment of war, what becomes of this power when the war is over, and are 12- or 15-year-old girls able to envision this?

Lila Abu-Lughod (1990: 42) has written that 'where there is resistance, there is power', meaning not only the power that is resisted but, also, the forms of power made use of and produced in the act of resistance. She warns, 'If the systems of power are multiple, then resisting at one level may catch people up at other levels' (53). The case she uses to illustrate her point is revealing. She describes how young Bedouin women resist forms of gender and age hierarchy similar to those encountered within kin-based institutions by young Mozambican women in the prerevolutionary period. Abu-Lughod tells us that young Bedouin women challenge the mores and codes of conduct through which elders control their sexuality through the purchase of Western-style goods such as lingerie and satin wedding dresses. However, in doing so, she points out, they entangle themselves with the power of the marketplace, cultivating their own dependence on forces ultimately beyond their control.

The same might be said of the girls and young women who subscribed to the FRELIMO notion that their emancipation from traditional hierarchies was bound up with the FRELIMO campaign for national independence. During the war, FRELIMO leaders argued that the participation of women in the exercise of power could not be 'arbitrary or casual' but that it had to come 'within the framework of FRELIMO, the revolutionary political organisation which upholds all the interests of the exploited people and which is capable of giving a correct orientation to women and defining their tasks' (*Mozambique Revolution* 54: 23). In accepting and contributing to this ideological perspective, DFs both allowed FRELIMO to use them in the campaign to achieve independence *and* used FRELIMO in their more personal struggles to carve out new gendered and generational roles. In doing so, they cast their lot with the FRELIMO revolution, committing themselves to its agenda as well as subordinating themselves to its institutional hierarchies and cultivating their own dependence upon the fulfillment of its promises for an independent Mozambique. In a very tangible sense, DFs achieved autonomy from the authority of lineage elders only by taking on the mantle of 'heroic youth' – *junior* members of the nascent FRELIMO party. Their status as FRELIMO *dependents* would continue long after the war had ended, making of them youth in perpetuity. This persistent paternal relationship between elder, male FRELIMO leaders and DFs in the postindependence period was symbolically enacted at the 1994 FRELIMO presidential elections campaign rally in Mueda that I attended, where an ensemble of DFs sang the praises of 'Papa Chissano'.[32]

For most DFs, the period of the *luta armada* was a 'golden age' in which they felt the surge of power afforded by their centrality to what Samora Machel called the 'principal task' – the collective social project of socialist revolution. Hence, they now look back upon the period of the liberation struggle with persistent nostalgia. However, they often speak of the postindependence period with bitter cynicism and resentment, suggesting that FRELIMO failed to fulfill the promises made to DFs during the war – failed to lay a solid foundation beneath the social transformations that would empower DFs as mature women in the postindependence period. DF recriminations reflect a flagging FRELIMO commitment to the project of gender equity outside of the exigencies of a war that made such a project urgent. The leadership roles reserved for women after the war were increasingly limited to positions in the Organisation of Mozambican Women, which largely served as a vehicle for dissemination of party directives and not as a means of 'participation in the exercise of power'. Jobs for DFs – many of whom had forgone formal education to join the *Destacamento Feminino* – diminished over time as a better educated generation of students – generally male, and often family members of ranking FRELIMO officials – displaced DFs in schools, hospitals and state farms. A DF I will call Matilda told me: 'After the war, I worked for a while in education but, in time, I was 'retired'. Younger cadres, who had been educated and trained after the war, were better prepared to teach. We were not given training to improve our skills ... FRELIMO failed to meet our needs for improvement, for progress. ' Another DF punctuated Matilda's observations, saying simply, 'FRELIMO abandoned us'. At a FRELIMO presidential election campaign dinner that I attended in 1999, DFs were given prominent seats, but by night's end, a somewhat intoxicated Basalisa was hurling abuse and recriminations at President Chissano, for all to hear. When Chissano called for her to approach him and told her, 'I remember you,' she asked, caustically, 'Really?'

Vesting faith in the continuity of the FRELIMO revolution as youngsters, DFs distanced themselves from the types of social relations that had
sustained their mothers and grandmothers. Most DFs were *vaali* (initiated
girls who were still virgins but who were considered 'eligible for marriage') when they joined the *Destacamento Feminino*, although a core of the
initial group trained as DFs were actually prostitutes who had worked in
the environs of the Portuguese military base on the Mueda plateau
(referred to locally as *vaali va matalopa*, or, 'soldiers' *vaali*'), and who subsequently fled to join FRELIMO in the bush, bringing with them valauble
intelligence on Portuguese personnel, bases and movement patterns.
FRELIMO found *vaali*, in general, well suited to serve the insurgency precisely because they had not yet established cumbersome social networks
and commitments. In particular, guerrilla commanders found *vaali va matalopa* more independent, assertive and engaging than most young women
from the region. It was often said of them, with double entendre, that they
had 'no shame', a valuable trait in guerrilla insurgency.

In any case, FRELIMO strictly controlled the sexuality of both male and
female guerrillas during the war. To some extent, FRELIMO measures
were intended to protect girls and young women, whether civilians or
guerrillas, from the predation of 'men with guns'. The FRELIMO leadership remained constantly concerned with insuring that its guerrillas not
be perceived as a threat to the civilian populations upon whom they
depended.[33] Commanders recruiting girls to assist in the base camps had
to overcome fears among their parents that they would be used as prostitutes (Artur et al. 1992: 7), a fear that the presence of *vaali va matalopa* in
FRELIMO camps must have agitated. Even consensual sexual relations
between guerrillas and civilians, or among guerrillas, were strictly prohibited.[34] FRELIMO leaders feared personal bonds that might take prece-
dence over loyalty to the guerrilla campaign. In practical terms, they
feared pregnancies that would demobilise female guerrillas.[35] To police
the sexuality of its guerrillas, FRELIMO depended upon an ad - hoc mixture of preaching and scare tactics. Commanders fuelled popular suspicions that sexual activity before battle rendered one more vulnerable
(Artur et al. 1992: 23–5). Punishments for those caught in sexual liaisons
were severe (Artur et al. 1992: 20). All of this sheds new light on the statements often made by former DFs that they were 'considered men' and
'treated as men' within the ranks of FRELIMO (Artur et al. 1992: 3–4, 16).
In a sense, these statements reflect not so much the profession of gender
equity within the ranks of the guerrilla army as the desexualisation of
guerrillas, particularly female.

In any case, with such stringent controls on their sexuality, DFs rarely
developed relationships that would produce marriages and families in
the post-war period, despite the fact that by war's end most were mature
women of child-bearing age. This meant that, in comparison with their

mothers and grandmothers, DFs lacked the strong family networks produced and consolidated – even with cognatic kin – by marriage and childbirth. After independence they were faced with difficult choices between
navigating the bleak employment market in towns and cities or returning
home to insecure places among families they had left years before, and
within which their rights and privileges were tenuous because their
bridewealth had never been paid. Many chose to remain in the urban
milieu but found it difficult to create new homes and family and social
networks. Following the war, the FRELIMO leadership encouraged marriages between exguerrillas. With the end of FRELIMO measures to
desexualise guerrillas, however, came the erosion of all aspects of women
being 'treated as men'. 'During the war,' Teresa told me, 'we were equal
with men, and we were friends. That's no longer true.' Many former DFs
today lament that men, even former guerrillas, did not want equal partners in their marriages after the war. Despite the rhetoric, several DFs told
me, FRELIMO men remained sexist and patriarchal, and complained that
former DFs were too feisty and independent to be married. Many of the
DFs I interviewed had taken lovers (often in relationships of short duration) and had had children, but had never married. Some emphasised that
they saw no reason to marry; the war had taught them to 'act as men' and,
even if the war had ended, they still did not need a man to order them
about. The attitudes and practices of these women towards sexuality and
reproduction did not differ tremendously from women of their generation
who had not been DFs, but what distinguished these women was their
greater isolation from extended family networks that might have assisted
them in the raising of their children.

As I came to know DFs living in the city of Pemba better, it became
apparent that they were frustrated and overwhelmed by the task of raising children. 'They have no respect', a DF I will call Amelia told me.
Ironically, Amelia's eldest daughter gave her the most difficult time. Like
Amelia, she rebelled against her mother and sought adventures of her
own. Without a father to discipline her, without other family members to
look after her when Amelia worked, I was told, this girl did whatever she
pleased: skipping school; stealing items from the market and from neighbours' houses; and watching Kung Fu movies at the town cinema. Her
struggle for independence, devoid of the ideologically-articulated purpose of Amelia's, seemed to mock all that Amelia had sacrificed so much
for.[36] Once, as I sat talking with Amelia, a boy of a few years old carried a
crying infant from the house and gave her to Amelia to nurse. The boy
was her son, she told me. 'And the girl?' I asked. 'My daughter's', she
replied. Still young enough to bear children herself, Amelia nursed her
own grandchild while the child's mother, barely a teenager, passed her
nights in Pemba's dance halls and beer stalls. Leaning back and addressing herself to the warm night air, she asked, 'Is this what we fought for?'

Women without Guns

Many contributors to the literature on child soldiers focus on the issue of the reintegration of excombatants into post-war society. The re-establishment of social networks, they often assert, is fundamental to healing the trauma of war. The testimonies of exmembers of FRELIMO's *Destacamento Feminino* provide a slightly different angle on this issue, for it is precisely in the moment of post-war reintegration that these women have been most troubled by their wartime experiences. In many ways, most of the DFs I interviewed shared the dilemma of the former Sandanista guerrillas described by Derek Summerfield (1998: 24), who were 'sufficiently disappointed by the electoral defeat of the Sandanista government to lose the sense of having suffered in a good cause', and who 'now feared that it had all been in vain and for a second time were having to come to terms, different terms, with physical disability and the other losses'. Many DFs, it seems, were less traumatised by their wartime experience than they were by the post-war unravelling of the narrative that had made sense of that experience at the time. Because post-war political realities undermined the project to which DFs had dedicated themselves, they also undermined the very identities of these women – identities that had been forged in the precarious spaces of youth and war.

In speaking of the world that FRELIMO and members of its Female Detachment had made in the wartime bush camps of Cabo Delgado, Teresa Casiano told me, 'We were convinced that this was FRELIMO's culture; we believed that it would persist'. For young women like Teresa, the 'emancipation of women' and the victory of FRELIMO socialism truly were bound together. The project DFs shared with the FRELIMO leadership could only endure, however, as long as new chapters were added to the narrative that animated their collective struggle. Yet with the post-war transformation of FRELIMO politics came the dissipation of discursive space in which young women could participate in the 'exercise of power' and the attribution of meaning to historical events. FRELIMO's narrative ceased to make sense to many ex-DFs. Now, as they cope with the unforeseen consequences of choices made as children and as youth, as they seek to continue the stories that are their lives, DFs' narratives lead them ever further from the world of shared purpose that once animated them in dangerous times. As much as ever, FRELIMO's battle cry remains salient for these women: *A Luta Continua!* (The Struggle Continues!). Now, however, they fight in relative isolation, as women, and without guns.

Notes

1. Reprinted from *Anthropological Quarterly* 73 (4): 180–94. Copyright 2000 The Catholic University Press. Preliminary versions of this article were presented at the 'Youth and the Social Imagination in Africa' panel of the 1998 Meetings of the American Anthropological Association on 3 December 1998 in Philadelphia, and at the International Workshop 'Child Soldiers: An Anthropological Perspective' held 2 June 2000 at the Centre for Child-Focused Anthropological Research at Brunel University, U.K. Jo de Berry provided valuable references throughout the writing of this article. Insightful commentary was also provided on draft versions by Debbie Durham, Eric Gable, Simon Ottenberg and anonymous reviewers for *Anthropological Quarterly*.
2. In the literature on children and war, 'children' are generally defined as those under the age of 18. In this chapter, I focus on a group whose members straddle this age divide. I generally refer to those under 18 as 'children' (or 'girls' when the gender specific term is appropriate) and those over 18 as 'youth' or 'young women'. Because I often refer to groups encompassing these two categories, I adopt the terms 'young people' and 'youngsters' in these cases for lack of more precise terminology.
3. See Cairns (1996: 107–37) for a general discussion of debates over children as passive victims versus children as active agents of violence.
4. For renderings of this scenario in the case of the Mozambican civil war, see Dodge and Raundalen (1991: 57–8); Finnegan (1992: 68); Hall (1990: 53–4); and Vines (1991: 90); on Liberia, see Fleishman (1994); on Uganda, see Ehrenreich (1997). See also Machel (1996) for a general discussion of this phenomenon.
5. For critical commentary on this perspective, see Boyden (1994: 261).
6. See also Cairns (1996: 28–69) regarding debates on the resilience of children in violent contexts and Apfel and Simon (1996) for a discussion of the 'factors' that may contribute to resilience in individual children in a violent context.
7. See de Berry (1999) for a summary discussion of this literature.
8. Bracken first made this argument in an article published with Joan Giller and Derek Summerfield (Bracken et al. 1995).
9. This point was underscored by Christina Toren, Director of the Centre for Child-Focused Anthropological Research, in her remarks at the International Workshop, 'Child Soldiers: An Anthropological Response', 2 June 2000, Brunel University, U.K.
10. This perspective is shared by Punamäki and Suleiman (1990).
11. My conclusions emerge from stimulating discussions with Jo de Berry and Jo Boyden.
12. The group I examine is delineated by shared experiences that began when they were best categorised by the local Shimakonde language term, *vaali*, meaning girls who have passed through initiation rites but not yet married or had sexual relations. As some Makonde girls are initiated as young as 10, and as some remain unmarried well into their twenties, this category straddles the conventional divide in the literature on war (18 years of age) between 'children' and 'youth'. What is more, the experiences shared by the group under consideration lasted for as long as a decade, making most of them mature women by the time of the period's conclusion.
13. I am grateful to Ian Robinson, Director of the Centre for the Study of Health, Sickness and Disease at Brunel University, for stimulating comments on this point.

14. *Mozambique Revolution* was produced at FRELIMO headquarters in Dar es Salaam, Tanzania, and was used to inform existing and potential supporters abroad of the events of the war. The publication, however, mirrored literature produced in Portuguese and African languages for consumption within the community of FRELIMO militants.

15. FRELIMO cadres writing for *Mozambique Revolution* most likely recognised the potentially controversial nature of FRELIMO's use of women in its guerrilla campaign – not to mention girls under the age of majority – and may have modified their accounts of this phenomenon to render it more broadly acceptable to the publication's audience.

16. Isaacman and Isaacman (1984: 156–8) provide a summary of the political debates revolving around this issue.

17. For detailed description of the shift in power in the liberated zones of northern Cabo Delgado away from heads of kin-based authority structures towards younger FRELIMO militants, see West (1997).

18. *Destacamento Feminino* is generally translated in the literature as 'Women's Detachment'. However, as my research indicated that many of its members were not in fact above the age of majority, I have chose to translate the term as 'Female Detachment'.

19. Isaacman and Isaacman (1984: 161) describe training for members of the *Destacamento Feminino* in detail.

20. Officially, units of the DF were never to have engaged in combat without the accompaniment of male guerrillas (Artur et al. 1992: 12), but there are scattered accounts of this taking place (e.g. Artur et al. 1992: 14).

21. Only recently, I conversed with the daughter of a woman from Oakland, California who, as a member of the Black Panther Party, had followed the exploits of the FRELIMO Female Detachment with keen interest. The PAIGC forces that fought against the Portuguese to achieve independence in Guinea Bissau also included among their ranks formalised units of female guerrillas whose story runs parallel to that of FRELIMO's *Destacamento Feminino* in many regards (see Urdang 1979 for a detailed account).

22. Arnfred (1988) has argued that this FRELIMO position constituted a gross oversimplification and misrepresentation of initiation rites as they were perceived by those who underwent them. In fact, Arnfred suggests, these rites allowed for the maintenance of a gendered space for critique of male-dominated social institutions.

23. In her account of the Zimbabwean guerrilla insurgency that took place only a few years later just across Mozambique's western border, Norma Kriger (1992) calls attention to the importance of coercion and subtler forms of pressure in the recruitment by guerrillas of young men and women.

24. This motif is expressed in the John Sayles film entitled 'Men with Guns', set in an unspecified Latin American country defined by guerrilla warfare and military anti-insurgency operations, as well as in David Stoll's (1993) book on the civil war in Guatemala.

25. My research was funded by the Fulbright-Hays programme, the United States Institute of Peace and the Wenner-Gren Foundation. Assistance was provided in the field by Marcos Agostinho Mandumbwe, Felista Elías Mkaima and Eusebio Tissa Kairo.

26. This was, most likely, not the first time any of these women had told their stories. Since independence, DFs have figured among those regularly identified by FRELIMO officials as appropriate subjects for interview by journalists and academics alike.

27. It is difficult to find confirmation of this shift of policy in the written record.

As late as 1969, Josina Machel (Machel 1969: 24), political commissar in the Female Detachment, wrote in FRELIMO's English-language news circular: 'In Mozambique the women's military activities are usually concentrated in the defense of the liberated areas, thus freeing the men for the offensive actions in the zones of advance. However, many of the women prefer the more active combats in the advance zones and choose to fight alongside the men in ambushes, and mining operations, where they have proved themselves as capable and courageous as any of their male comrades'.

28. According to Christian Geffray's (1990) ethnography of the Mozambican civil war, a similar hope of escaping the drudgery of rural life and the authority of their elders motivated many youth who embraced involvement with REN-AMO.

29. Formerly in northern Cabo Delgado, young women were granted land to cultivate by their husbands and depended upon them for other essential household inputs. If divorced, a women would generally lose her rights to that land and be required to return home to farm land provided her by male family elders.

30. In most cases, these were DFs to whom I was not referred by FRELIMO party officials but, rather, whom I discovered after gaining familiarity with the communities in which I worked.

31. Murray Last (2 June 2000, personal communication) suggests that many of the women who fought in the war in Eritrea also sought 'traditional healing' and made of the healer's compound a new home.

32. I am grateful to Debbie Durham for stimulating comments on this point.

33. This is not to suggest that FRELIMO was entirely successful in this regard, even if reports of rape in the liberated zones are quite limited.

34. FRELIMO commander Samora Machel granted himself an exception to this rule. In 1969, he married Josina Abiatar, a founding member and political commissar of the *Destacamento Feminino*. It was said among those I interviewed that Josina's first lover had been Filipe Samuel Magaia, the first commander of the FRELIMO guerrilla army who was assassinated in 1966. Many suggested that Machel had arranged Magaia's death, usurping his position and taking his lover at the same time. By war's end, life in FRELIMO-held zones had calmed considerably and the ban on relationships between FRELIMO comrades had been lifted (Artur et al. 1992: 22). In the final years of the war, ordinary guerrillas were permitted to marry, but they could not be stationed at the same base.

35. Abortion was prohibited, partly on the grounds that it polluted the guerrilla camp. As a result, most women who became pregnant either left guerrilla service until after giving birth or underwent dangerous clandestine abortions (Artur et al. 1992: 17, 20–1).

36. I am grateful to Debbie Durham for stimulating comments on this point.

References

Abu-Lughod, L. 1990. 'The Romance of Resistance: Tracing Transformations of Power through Bedouin Women.' *American Ethnologist* 17 (1): 41–55.

Apfel, R.J. and Simon, B. 1996. *Minefields in Their Hearts: The Mental Health of Children in War and Communal Violence*. New Haven: Yale University Press.

Arnfred, S. 1988. 'Women in Mozambique: Gender Struggle and Gender Politics.' *Review of African Political Economy* 41: 5–16.

Artur, M.J., Mpalume, E., Aquimo, J. and Labés, V. 1992. *O Estatuto da Mulher na Luta Armada: Relatório.* Maputo: Arquivos do Património Cultural.

Baker, A.M. 1992. 'Psychological Response of Palestinian Children to Environmental Stress Associated With Military Occupation.' *Journal of Refugee Studies* 4 (3): 237–47.

Boyden, J. 1994. 'Children's Experience of Conflict Related Emergencies: Some Implications for Relief Policy and Practice.' *Disasters* 18 (3): 254–67.

Bracken, P.J. 1998. 'Hidden Agendas: Deconstructing Post Traumatic Stress Disorder.' In P. Bracken and C. Petty, eds, *Rethinking the Trauma of War.* London: Free Association Books.

——, Geller, J.E. and Summerfield, D. 1995. 'Psychological Responses to War and Atrocity: The Limitations of Current Concepts.' *Social Science and Medicine* 40 (8): 1073–82.

Cairns, E. 1996. *Children and Political Violence.* Oxford: Blackwell.

Cohn, I. and Goodwin-Gill, G.S. 1994. *Child Soldiers: The Role of Children in Armed Conflict.* Oxford: Oxford University Press.

Dawes, A. 1992. 'Psychological Discourse about Political Violence and its Effects on Children.' Paper presented at the meeting on The Mental Health of Refugee Children Exposed to Violent Environments. University of Oxford: Refugee Studies Programme.

De Berry, J. 1999. 'Post-Conflict Reconstruction in Teso, East Uganda'. Ph.D. thesis, London School of Economics and Political Science.

——. 2000. Opening Remarks to the International Workshop 'Child Soldiers: An Anthropological Perspective'. U.K.: Brunel University.

Dodge, C.P. and Raundalen, M. 1991. *Reaching Children at War: Sudan, Uganda, and Mozambique.* Bergen, Norway: Sigma Forlag.

Ehrenreich, R. 1997. *The Scars of Death: Children Abducted by the Lord's Resistance Army in Uganda.* New York: Human Rights Watch.

Finnegan, W. 1992. *A Complicated War: The Harrowing of Mozambique.* Berkeley: University of California Press.

Fleischman, J. 1994. *Easy Prey: Child Soldiers in Liberia.* New York: Human Rights Watch.

Garbarino, J., Kostelny, K. and Dubrow, N. 1991. *No Place to Be a Child: Growing Up in a War Zone.* Lexington: Lexington Books.

Geffray, C. 1990. *La Cause des armes au Mozambique. Anthropologie d'une guerre civile.* Paris: Karthala.

Gibbs, S. 1994. 'Post-War Social Reconstruction in Mozambique: Re-Framing Children's Experience of Trauma and Healing.' *Disasters* 18 (3): 268–76.

Hall, M. 1990. 'The Mozambican National Resistance Movement (RENAMO): A Study in the Destruction of an African Country.' *Africa* 60 (1): 39–68.

Isaacman, A. and Isaacman, B. 1984. 'The Role of Women in the Liberation of Mozambique.' *Ufahamu* 13 (2–3): 128–85.

Kriger, N. 1992. *Zimbabwe's Guerrilla War: Peasant Voices.* Cambridge: Cambridge University Press.

Machel, G. 1996. *Impact of Armed Conflict on Children: Report of the Expert of the Secretary-General Submitted Pursuant to General Assembly Resolution 48/157.* New York: United Nations.

Machel, J. 1969. 'The Role of Women in the Revolution.' *Mozambique Revolution* 41: 24.

Munslow, B. 1983. *Mozambique: The Revolution and Its Origins.* London: Longman.

Peters, K. and Richards, P. 1998. '"Why We Fight": Voices of Youth Combatants in Sierra Leone.' *Africa* 68 (2): 183–210.

Punamäki, R.-L. and Suleiman, R. 1990. 'Predictors and Effectiveness of Coping with Political Violence among Palestinian Children.' *British Journal of Social Psychology* 29: 67–77.

Reynolds, P. 1996. *Traditional Healers and Childhood in Zimbabwe*. Athens: Ohio University Press.

Save the Children Fund. 1992. *Growing Up with Conflict: Children and Development in the Occupied Territories*. London: Save the Children Fund.

Sayles, J. 1998. *Men with Guns*. Sony Pictures Classic Films, Lexington Road Productions and Clear Blue Sky Productions in association with Independent Film Channel and Anarchist Convention.

Stoll, D. 1993. *Between Two Armies in the Ixil Towns of Guatemala*. New York: Columbia University Press.

Summerfield, D. 1998. 'The Social Experience of War and Some Issues for the Humanitarian Field.' In P. Bracken and C. Petty, eds, *Rethinking the Trauma of War*. London: Free Association Books.

Urdang, S. 1979. *Fighting Two Colonialisms: Women in Guinea Bissau*. New York: Monthly Review Press.

Vines, A. 1991. *RENAMO: Terrorism in Mozambique*. London: James Currey.

Walker, J.R. 1993. *Orphans of the Storm: Peacebuilding for Children of War*. Toronto: Between the Lines.

West, H.G. 1997. 'Sorcery of Construction and Sorcery of Ruin: Power and Ambivalence on the Mueda Plateau, Mozambique (1882–1994).' Ph.D. dissertation, University of Wisconsin-Madison.

——. 1998. '"This Neighbour is Not My Uncle!": Changing Relations of Power and Authority on the Mueda Plateau.' *Journal of Southern African Studies* 24 (1): 141–60.

——. 2001. 'Sorcery of Construction and Socialist Modernisation: Ways of Understanding Power in Post-Colonial Mozambique.' *American Ethnologist* 28 (1).

7

Children, Impunity and Justice: Some Dilemmas from Northern Uganda[1]

Andrew Mawson

Introduction

The use of children as soldiers is a growing phenomenon that has become a focus of advocacy and programme intervention by both human rights and humanitarian non-governmental organisations. Such interventions fall broadly into two strands. The first involves efforts to keep children out of conflict. This is exemplified by campaigning for an optional protocol to the UN Convention on the Rights of the Child to raise the minimum age of recruitment or participation in hostilities to 18 years. The second involves direct intervention to provide assistance to former child soldiers. Many of these programmes emphasise the psychosocial needs of children perceived to be victims of war. The aim is commonly to help children deal with the experience of being soldiers and to reunite them with their families or reintegrate them with the communities they are perceived to have been separated from by becoming fighters.

The increasing use of child soldiers is an aspect of the growing numbers of internationalised internal wars involving weak states confronting weak armed opposition groups sometimes receiving support from other states. Ideologies of race and ethnicity are common, and such wars are also generally characterised by the mobilisation of civilians to fight, large scale violence against civilians and massive levels of forced displacement. It has been estimated that around 75 percent of deaths in many contemporary wars are of civilians (compared to approximately 90 percent of war deaths being of soldiers in conflicts at the beginning of the twentieth century). A proportion of these deaths is the result of acts of genocide, murder and other human rights abuses by combatants – some of whom are children.

This chapter reflects on the dilemmas that can arise when society and the state try to confront atrocities committed by children. In general little attention has been paid to this; the main focus of child rights organisations and child protection organisations has been on the children themselves, who are seen as victims. It is based on information collected in four periods of human rights fieldwork in northern Uganda on behalf of Amnesty International (May 1997, July 1997 and May 1998) and the International Council on Human Rights Policy (May 1999).

When confronting human rights abuses, different actors – for example, the civil authorities, the army, non-governmental organisations, elders, parents and family members, victims of atrocities and young people themselves – usually have different agendas. In the conflict in northern Uganda which has been going on since 1986, the armed opposition group the Lord's Resistance Army (LRA) has abducted approximately 18,000 children to become soldiers. The issue of how to deal with children who have committed atrocities is a pressing concern highly relevant to the political process of trying to build peace. It involves negotiating a path through different agendas, through differing concepts of who is a child and differing concepts of what constitutes justice. The path taken has significant consequences for the wider administration of justice in the legal sense.

This chapter explores conceptualisations of justice and peace among the Acholi in the late 1990s, one of the groups most profoundly affected by the war. It argues that in the context of northern Uganda, where the population has experienced numerous atrocities and many combatants were recruited by force, legal punishment-orientated approaches to justice have little likelihood of resolving conflict and bringing stability or peace. It explores the Acholi definition of a child and suggests that this has been augmented and adapted to the circumstances of war to enable the adoption of a non-punitive approach to justice and allow for widespread social reconciliation.

War in Northern Uganda

Since August 1986 there has been an extremely violent but relatively localised war in northern Uganda, centred on Gulu, Pader and Kitgum Districts inhabited by the Acholi, and fringing areas of Apac and Lira, inhabited by the Langi. The forces opposed to the Ugandan Government in the Acholi parts of Uganda have existed in a variety of forms. Initially they were largely made up of former government soldiers and politicians who reorganised in Sudan after the overthrow of the military government of Basilio Okello and Tito Okello by the National Resistance Army (NRA) of Yoweri Museveni in early 1986. Armed by the Sudanese Government, this movement was known as the Uganda People's Democratic Army (UPDA).

In parallel, a spirit medium called Alice Auma, also known as Lakwena (which can be loosely translated from Luo as 'messenger'), mobilised a group that became known as the Holy Spirit Mobile Forces. Her powers left her in November 1987 and the group was shattered in a series of battles. The UPDA, which failed to create a united leadership, did not last much longer as a fighting force. In 1988 key factions signed a peace accord with the government and most UPDA troops gave themselves up.

Meanwhile, in early 1988 another spirit medium, Joseph Kony, emerged as the main focus of military organisation against the government. In April 1987, Kony joined a UPDA unit which he then rapidly took over. Since then his group has gone through various guises. Initially known as the Lord's Army, Holy Spirit Part Two or Lakwena Part Two, by early 1990 it had been renamed the United Democratic Christian Army. In late 1993, by now receiving military support from the Sudanese Government, the group became known as the Lord's Resistance Army (LRA). Until 2002, the Sudanese Government supplied the LRA with arms and bases in Sudan, where it fought alongside the Sudanese army against the Sudan People's Liberation Army (SPLA), the Sudanese rebel group that exerts loose control over large parts of southern Sudan, including the border with Uganda.[2]

Apart from action in Sudan, military activity is largely limited to just a handful of districts in Uganda. It does not directly affect the south, west or central parts of Uganda, the economic heartland of the state and the political heartland of the government. In Gulu, Pader and Kitgum, however, it has been extraordinarily destructive. Families and communities have been dislocated and destroyed. Between 1996 and early 1999, approximately 400,000 persons, were internally displaced. Many moved into approximately thirty ill-prepared camps, but large numbers sought refuge in Gulu and Kitgum towns and other parts of Uganda. After a period of relative tranquillity fighting intensified again in March 2002 leading to the internal displacement of approximately 800,000 people. The Acholi were once cattle agro-pastoralists but now both Kitgum and Gulu are largely devoid of cattle – looted by Karamojong cattle raiders from the east and, claim many Acholi, by NRA soldiers occupying the area in 1986 and 1987. Trade has diminished and the already limited manufacturing and agricultural processing sector is curtailed; in times of insecurity agricultural activity itself is severely restricted. Control of the civilian population is a key objective for both government and rebel forces (Amnesty International 1999a).

To understand the situation of children in this armed conflict, one must realise that Acholi in all sectors of society have a deepseated mistrust of government objectives in relation to the north. This is a product of many decades of Uganda's history. Particularly between 1980 and 1986, security forces, including many northern troops, among them Acholi, committed grave human rights violations in other parts of Uganda. In the context of the war since 1986, mistrust has been inflamed by government human rights violations against civilians in the north – particularly between late 1986 and late 1988 and in the summer of 1991 – and the periodic use of mass displacement as a counter-insurgency tactic. Killings and other forms of human rights violation by government forces continue to take place but not on the same scale as in the period from 1986 to 1988.

At the same time, Kony's forces have visited extreme violence on their fellow Acholi civilians in villages all over Gulu and Kitgum districts to a degree that has overshadowed and obscured government human rights violations. Thousands of villagers have been murdered, raped and tortured, often in the most staggeringly cruel ways. This violence is not random; the LRA controls few resources and no territory and has sought to impose its will through terror. Violence has been used to move people away from roads, to extort food, to drive people out of camps and to punish those suspected of informing.

Above all, since 1994 in particular, the LRA has needed troops. In 1994 the Sudanese Government increased its supply of small arms, mortars and landmines. The LRA had more weapons than soldiers and needed new recruits quickly. It is from this date that the mass abduction of young people began. Although some people undoubtedly join voluntarily – many more than would ever be prepared to admit it if and when they return from the LRA – since 1994 possibly as many as 80 percent of fighters have been abducted. Most of these are under the age of eighteen; nearly 50 percent are aged between eleven and sixteen. Both girls and boys are taken. The uses to which girls are put by the LRA (domestic and sexual servitude, as well as being soldiers) means it is often more difficult for them to escape; however, approximately 30 percent of escapees are girls.

UNICEF has estimated that between 1988 and 1998 approximately 10,000 children were abducted (AFP, 12 February 1998). Since March 2002 another 8,000 have been taken. Basing a fighting force on abducted recruits means that the internal composition of the fighting units tends to be fluid. It is difficult to know how many children run away. Non-governmental organisations in Gulu working on the recovery and reintegration of child soldiers have seen over 5,000 since 1995. In the mid to late 1990s it was relatively common for LRA units that crossed into Uganda from Sudan to lose as many as 50 percent of their soldiers through desertion. Many others were killed in combat, and so taking people, particularly children, to replenish the ranks was a daily practice. In addition, the LRA deals with recaptured escapees with extreme violence, often using new captives to execute in almost ritual ways friends or people from the same village who have tried to escape but failed (Amnesty International 1997).

For many villagers in the north of Uganda, day to day survival involves steering a careful passage between what to them are two broadly unacceptable alternatives. The government is distrusted for historical reasons, compounded by its creation of camps of internally displaced persons, its perceived failure to protect people from the LRA and the violence of government soldiers against civilians. Common questions asked in the north are: Why has the government failed to end the war? Does it suit the authorities or the army for the war to continue? At the same time, there is almost no support for military solutions to the conflict; those LRA members killed in the fighting are family members.

On the other hand, the LRA is deeply feared. Even the most bitter of government opponents denounce LRA methods. Few families are untouched by LRA violence. In the words of a man from Kony's home area of Odek, who in April 1998 was ordered back to his fields by the LRA and then rounded up at gunpoint by the UPDA and sent back to a camp: 'People are torn between two deadly orders. The LRA does not want people in the protected camps, while the UPDF does not want anyone in the countryside. We don't know what to do' (*The Monitor*, 29 April 1998).

My impression from interviews with villagers, priests, elders, local councillors and other community leaders – and with some civilian government officials – is that, among the Acholi at least, there are very few people who wish to see this war continue. For a wide cross section of society, a current priority is how to create peace. A key issue in this is the relationship between peace and justice. Some people want revenge for what LRA soldiers have done to them or their families. However, others, including almost all educated people, want to bury the past as the price of peace.

This is the context of the collective response on the part of the Acholi to children – and adults – who have committed atrocities.

Childhood and Responsibility

It is a basic tenet of legal approaches to justice that the failure to punish serious crimes increases the likelihood that similar crimes will be committed in the future. This is perhaps especially true in a war situation where social constraints are reduced and there may be significant pressures – and opportunities – to commit serious crimes. If perpetrators believe they can get away with atrocities, there is little incentive not to commit them. If everyone around me is killing and looting and getting away with it, there is little to stop me doing the same – especially if I am also under pressure to commit atrocities from my peers and/or commanders. What is likely to follow, especially in a war situation, is a spiral of violence and brutalisation.

Although confronting impunity is an article of faith underlying international human rights law and legal systems around the world, it is clear that in northern Uganda (and probably many other complex internal wars involving non-state actors where there is little likelihood of one side or the other winning an outright military victory) a narrow, punishment-orientated definition of justice is deeply problematic. It does not take into account the political and social dynamics of the conflict or of building peace. Who is dispensing justice and who is receiving it? It seems to ignore the pattern of abduction and the use of extreme violence within the LRA to enforce the will of commanders. It does not take into account a fairly widely held Acholi view that their society as a whole is the collective victim of monstrous injustice: longstanding injustice on the part of government and now the additional injustice of LRA terror.

While it would be theoretically possible for the state to charge and try alleged killers and rapists, in northern Uganda it would strengthen the widely shared view among Acholi that the government is somehow 'out to get them'. From the state's point of view, it would undermine key elements of its stated counter-insurgency strategy: the effort to lure people out of the LRA and to build positive relations with the civilian population. Since the war began there have been periodic presidential amnesties for persons who give themselves up to the authorities or are captured by them. These have covered waging war against the state, but have not formally extended to serious crimes against the person. A parliamentary amnesty came into force in 2000.

However, pretending atrocities have not been committed is also not an option. It is not too far-fetched to suggest that the very existence of the LRA is in part a response to (and cause of) the long-term brutalising effects of violence and warfare on Acholi society. This might seem somewhat circular; but this is a war in which the motivations of those voluntarily fighting the government have evolved and changed very considerably over time.

While most civilians appear to want peace, the degree to which people are prepared to subsume their own familial or individual desire for revenge or compensation in order to achieve it is a moot point. There are examples of communal revenge on returnees from the LRA (although not many). However, individuals – including children – who return are often feared. They may be violent and unpredictable. They may bring with them spiritual contamination, including possession by those they have killed. According to some Acholi, usual methods of dealing with spirit possession are often overwhelmed by the sheer scale of the violence that has taken place.

At another level, ignoring atrocities could undermine the wider administration of justice. It could become difficult for judicial decisions in relation to other crimes to retain much credibility if far worse situations are just ignored.

In northern Uganda the use of concepts such as 'child' – and, to a degree, the 'child's best interests' – appear to have created some space at the level of officialdom, educated Acholi and the wider Acholi community to negotiate a way forward. In national law in Uganda a child is anyone under 18 years of age. This is enshrined in the Children's Statute of 1996 that incorporates into Ugandan law aspects of the Convention on the Rights of the Child (CRC) and the Organisation for African Unity (OAU) Charter on the Rights and Welfare of the Child. However, for rural Acholi the definition of who is a child is not so much based on achieving a certain chronological age but more on factors such as physical maturity, social expectations, peer group seniority and position within the family. Defining who is a child is to a degree a process of negotiation between individuals, family members, peer groups and the wider community in the context of real events, marked by rites of passage.

In the specific context of returnees from the LRA, the authorities and the Acholi community appear to have come to the collective agreement that virtually anyone who has been with the LRA and who gives themselves up or is captured in combat has characteristics that enable them to be defined as a child. Firstly, under the state's legal definition most (but not all) are children in terms of chronological age. Secondly, many are children under Acholi notions of what constitutes a child (or at least they were before they became part of the LRA). Thirdly, most (but not all) were abducted. In combination this allows a collective presumption of a degree of lack of responsibility for their actions.

It also means that both wider Acholi society and the authorities are prepared to pretend that the proportion of LRA returnees who are much older than 18 (and who were already older than 18 when they became part of the LRA) are also, effectively, children. This proportion is not negligible: between 15 and 20 percent of returnees are over 18. Six percent of the 3,000 seen by World Vision between 1995 and 1997 were aged above 29. In other words, they would already have been over 18 in 1986 when the war began.

Having ascribed to LRA returnees the characteristics of children, what happens next? In 1999 all persons who returned from the LRA were handed over by the UPDA to three non-governmental organisations (NGOs) – World Vision, Gulu Support for Children Organisation (GUSCO) and Kitgum Children's Welfare Association (KICWA) – for programmes of psychosocial counselling. Returnees are fed and clothed. The NGOs, working with the civilian authorities, trace family members and set in motion family reunification and community reintegration. They also take the returnees through a structured series of sessions where they encourage them to talk about what they have done and been through.

For the organisations their priority is the psychological health of the returnee. Within the limited resources available to them, counsellors spend quite a lot of time with the most disturbed children. Part of what they do is to provide a framework and safe context for the children to admit to things they have done. In part, returning to the theme of impunity, this can represent a form of confrontation with guilt. This is not, however, one of the aims of the counselling process from the perspective of the child protection agencies, and the process remains a somewhat individualised, if powerful, experience.

As time has passed child protection agencies have realised that working with returnees isolated from the community is not a sufficient or entirely effective way forward. The practical realities of the war mean, however, that working actually in the community is not always possible – World Vision and GUSCO operate out of buildings in Gulu town and KICWA is largely based in Kitgum town where there is a degree of safety. All make efforts to involve family members in the work of the centres. GUSCO in particular encourages other social and spiritual methods of confronting the consequences of having killed: for example, rituals of purification. In the words of the Programme Director of GUSCO: 'We are open to traditional beliefs. For example, children may experience the consequences of what they have done through spirit possession. We may be able to identify this is what is happening but it needs the family and community to deal with it. We may offer help, for example by giving money for a goat' (George Omona, Gulu, May 1998). However, it is unclear how often these rituals take place. It is not at all clear whether the community – especially in periods of serious disruption and dislocation when insecurity has forced large numbers of people into camps – is really able to deal effectively in this way with the consequences of killing, especially when the killings may have happened in distant places, ruling out rituals of reconciliation involving the relatives of the victim. Further, some children have killed many times.

In the end, the sheer number of returnees and the resources available to the non-governmental organisations means that none is able to give all children the kind of systematic attention and follow up that they would like to provide. In fact, perhaps one of the most important functions of the World Vision and GUSCO centres is not to be found in their actual programmes but in the movement through them in an officially and, to a degree, socially sanctioned rite of passage from the LRA to wider society. After passing through the centres, returnees are accepted by the authorities as genuine (they are, for example, given a passing out note for the local civil and military authorities). Once they have been through the centres they are not, usually, suspected of being LRA soldiers making a temporary visit to the community. Acceptance by the community also appears to be widespread.

The collective fiction of who is a child is not accepted by the child protection agencies. In part this is because the training and ideology of these organisations have been heavily influenced by the Save the Children Alliance, Western child psychologists and the important principles contained in the CRC. In part it is the product of empirical experience; having young former soldiers and older former soldiers together in the centres can cause problems. Often the structures found in the LRA are reasserted. For example, older former soldiers, some of whom may have been with the LRA for many years, have sometimes sought to reassert their rank. The regime in the centres is structured around the activities and needs of children, which can alienate adults, who may prefer to spend their time in nearby bars. GUSCO does not accept anyone that they suspect to be over the age of 18. Staff at World Vision would like to follow suit, but the authorities' failure to implement significant programmes for adults has meant that so far they have not found it easy to resist pressure from the UPDA and civil authorities to take any returnee that the army brings along. In 1999 World Vision used to transfer adults to a vocational training centre at Kiryandongo in Masindi District as soon as possible.

The lack of programming for adults points to the dangers of stretching a 'child' too far. Arguably, programmes of reintegration for adults could be set up in Gulu and Kitgum at least they could have been before March 2002 and the current huge degree of internal displacement. However, the authorities do not appear to want to confront the issue. Perhaps this is because they do not wish to divert resources from other budget lines. Perhaps they doubt they will get the same kind of NGO (and UN) support that they are able to mobilise around children. It might also undermine a rare area of agreement between many Acholi and the government – the social consensus that there should be some flexibility on the issue of responsibility for atrocities – by forcing confrontation with the fact that not all perpetrators actually are children. Doing this would involve making a particular criterion, chronological age, the defining characteristic of the status 'child'.

Confronting atrocities through a process of counselling, especially one that draws in people from the wider community, could be seen as a step towards addressing impunity. In northern Uganda, both by Acholi criteria and by chronological age, most perpetrators of violence are abducted children. Making a general truth out of this statistical fact may be contributing to the social acceptance of a low-key, individualised, nonpunishment-orientated approach to confronting atrocities. It may not, however, be an approach that in the long term enables the direct victims of violence to feel that justice has been particularly well served.

Further, the amnesty approach has the unintended side effect of posing dilemmas for how to deal politically with the LRA leadership. Setting up a category of 'innocents' (or the 'misled', as President Yoweri Museveni commonly refers to LRA returnees) presupposes a category of people who are knowingly guilty, the 'misleaders'. The LRA leadership, especially Kony and a small number of other key commanders, are frequently described by government and the media, especially the foreign media, in demonic terms that render almost unthinkable the notion that ending the war could involve negotiation with them.[3]

Looking more widely, the approach also sets up a number of anomalies that seem to cause other problems for the administration of justice in the legal sense. The first is that people who collaborate with the LRA, children or adults, for example by supplying them with food or information, may face far stiffer punishment in the government courts than LRA members who have killed and raped. The official rationale is that cooperation with the LRA (rather than membership) tends to be voluntary. From the perspective of the UPDA: 'It is different with a mature person who knows the effect of war. If such people are encouraging small boys, they should be dealt with like the LRA leaders... If I guide rebels or buy drugs for them, I'm doing it consciously' (Brigadier Edward Wamala Katumba, Commander 4th Division UPDA, Gulu, May 1998). However, this begs many questions, which are thrown into even sharper relief by the apparent decision to introduce a blanket amnesty. A key one is: how truly voluntary is 'voluntary'? Are villagers who provide support being coerced? Are the villagers who buy drugs for the LRA doing so to help the survival of close relatives? Perhaps more problematically, the discrepancy between not charging killers and charging supporters is perceived by many Acholi as unfair.

This paradox appeared to have been recognised in early 1997 when the courts in Gulu began systematically to throw out cases brought by the army against alleged rebel collaborators. The legal basis was the army's failure to collect evidence. Interestingly, the army and the police have not used criminal charges against persons involved in rebel activities to any great extent since 1997 (quite unlike the approach being followed in the war against the Allied Democratic Forces (ADF) in the west of Uganda, where hundreds of people have been charged with treason). When a rogue Kampala-based security operation arrested eleven men in Gulu in March and April 1998, illegally detained them, and eventually had them charged with treason, the Resident District Commissioner in Gulu – the President's representative in the district – led the protests. However, there is a real danger that the amnesty approach being followed closes down legitimate avenues for dealing with serious crime, thereby creating the circumstances in which security officers and the military may find the temptation to resort to extralegal means difficult to resist.

Indeed, the issue of justice also has to be examined from the point of view of government soldiers stationed in the north. If the enemy can commit atrocities and get away with it, why should comrades be brought to book? There is a big problem of impunity for soldiers who commit serious crimes. Between January 1996 and April 1998, eighty-two soldiers were charged with serious crimes against the person by the Gulu police. However, only four cases have been brought to court, three leading to convictions and one to an acquittal. In the course of working for Amnesty International, I collected information on approximately the same number of incidents over roughly the same period in which soldiers and police are alleged to have committed murder, rape or assault, but in which no arrests were made (Amnesty International 1999).

The Uganda Police report that they often have difficulty collecting evidence from soldiers. While it would be stretching things too far to suggest that the failure to bring the child perpetrators of LRA atrocities to justice in the legal sense is the cause of incidents of abuse by soldiers, anecdotal evidence suggests that army officers are mindful of the effect on their troops of what might sometimes look like double standards. There is a marked disinclination to pursue the prosecution of soldiers who commit human rights violations while on military operations. This brings us full circle – back to the cycle of violence and the collective Acholi sense of injustice.

Conclusion

In northern Uganda, government and Acholi society, if one can generalize about such heterogeneous terms, have apparently found a common interest in an expanded use of concepts of 'child'. Flexibility on the definition of 'child' means that people who have committed or been forced to commit atrocities while in the LRA are given sanctuary in a specially constructed moral space. To an extent this functions as a modern form of purification. In part, it is an amnesty and in part it is a form of quasi-religious confrontation with guilt, followed by absolution.

This process raises many questions – which is the point at which this chapter ends. Is it significant that the process is taking place through institutions of modernity, NGOs, rather than, apparently, through traditional Acholi institutions? Does this reflect the scale of the disruption and destruction in Acholi society? That is to say, has the problem of violence gone beyond the capacity of Acholi society to deal with it? Is this common ground around children and responsibility an interim measure in the current circumstances of war?

What time frame are people working on? Will the ancestors and spirits intervene to have their way later? What is the role of Christian churches and how might this develop? Will communal and individual demands for legally-based justice assert themselves more strongly in the future, once the threat of war has receded? Can a convenient fiction about what is a child carry the weight of so much violence?

Notes

1. An earlier version of this chapter was originally presented to a conference, 'Children in Extreme Circumstances', at the London School of Economics on 27 November 1998, and is available in L. Carlson, M. Mackeson-Sandbach and T. Allen, eds, *Children in Extreme Situations, Proceedings From the 1998 Alistair Berkley Memorial Lecture.* DESTIN working paper no. 00–05, London School of Economics and Political Science, March 2000, http://www.lse.ac.uk/depts.destin
2. In July 2003, after complaints from the Ugandan Government, the Sudanese authorities admitted that rogue army elements in Juba had again been supplying the LRA.
3. Since this paper was first written the Ugandan government introduced a bill to parliament to grant amnesty to all returning rebels for all crimes committed. After long delays the bill was eventually given parliamentary time and in 2000 became law. Meanwhile foreign governments exerted pressure on the Ugandan and Sudanese governments to end support for each other's rebel groups. In November 2000 the Sudanese made commitments to take action to demobilise the LRA. In 2001 the two governments restored diplomatic relations. However, the opportunity this presented to begin Sudanese facilitated dialogue between the Uganda Government and the LRA was still born. Instead, in March 2002 the Ugandan Government sent troops into Sudan (with Sudanese permission) to destroy the LRA. This military operation failed; the LRA withdrew into mountains on the border with Uganda and renewed intense military operations in northern Uganda leading to a humanitarian catastrophe.

References

Amnesty International. 1999. Uganda – Breaking the Circle: Protecting Human Rights in the Northern War Zone. Amnesty International, 17 March.
——. 1997. *Uganda – Breaking God's Commands: The Destruction of Childhood by the Lord's Resistance Army.* Amnesty International, 18 September.

Part IV

Children's Narratives

8

Children in the Grey Spaces Between War and Peace: The Uncertain Truth of Memory Acts

Krisjon Rae Olson

Already a fictitious past occupies a place in our memories, the place of another, a past of which we know nothing with certainty – not even that it is false.

(Jorge Luis Borges: The Circular Ruins)

Introduction

This chapter grows out of a need to make sense of truth and reconciliation in the aftermath of civil wars. These are armed struggles which make brother indistinguishable from stranger, family from a state of conflict. Such wars, marked by extermination and exodus which do not end with political treaties, both reveal and define the disquieting space in which we continue to live. I am particularly concerned with the ways in which acts of routine violence, practised on and by children between declared periods of war and peace, are treated within society. The following analysis examines the shifting narratives of children in the wake of armed conflict. By asking how children reconcile remembrance with forgetting, one also uncovers what is impossible to keep in conscious awareness.

The starting point for my inquiry is the memoir of a hidden child in France during the Nazi occupation. It is this occupation, of person and place, which frames my discussion of children in the grey spaces between war and peace. The child's experience of divided loyalties and shifting identity raises questions about how the past is understood and recalled. I turn from the individual narrative of the memoir to dialogues between children about the war, and prospects for peace, in Guatemala. At the close of the chapter, I grapple with the new and disturbing phenomenon of youth suicide in this same community. Throughout the chapter, suicide is explored as an act which demonstrates the sort of uncertainty that war and its aftermath bring about for young people.

While childhood has recently become the focus of significant academic scholarship (see for example Bluebond-Langner 1978; Mead 1930; Reynolds 1998; Scheper-Hughes 1992; Stephens 1995b), there is scant theoretical and empirical information on children's experiences of war. By exploring the narratives of children, in relation to their everyday practices, I take issue with an academic notion of childhood as a categorical space of recollection. Childhood is most often considered as the passed life of an adult person, something recalled but not present.[1] Maurice Halbwachs's seminal sociological work *Collective Memory* was among the first to establish childhood as a past, inseparable from memory. For Halbwachs (1941: 46–51) the significance of memories is intimately related to the communal and familial contexts in which children are inscribed. Instead, I suggest that children not only emerge from memories of the past, but also make the past memorable through their participation in social life. These are embodied memories, inhabiting gestures and emotions, which both discipline children and determine their view of their past. As violence past and continuing is examined in detail by truth commissions, textbooks and tribunals, children engage in the work of representing the past in the present. In this chapter, my critical anthropological approach to the intersecting problems of memory, truth and reconciliation raises questions about the social and political life of young people caught between war and peace. What does it mean to conceive of memory as something other than an archive, active in the youngest lives?

No One Can Defect: The Autobiographical Archive

The theory of the archive classifies secret and non-secret memories in a particular order. Jacques Derrida (1995: 2) explains, 'The concept of the archive shelters in itself, of course, this memory of the name *arkhe*. But it also shelters itself from this memory which it shelters: which comes down to saying also that it forgets it.' In war, order is no longer assured. Any truth of the archive is appropriated and manipulated. Silence and impunity often fall between the cracks of classification. The methodological importance of attending to the particular, the autobiographical, is often lost in the need to create order out of war. Reading the text of a memoir, anchoring ourselves in singular memories, is one way to understand the unstable truth of archives. Social analysts are often reluctant to understand such particular histories, instead making economic or political forces their point of departure, while anthropological analysis has most often pointed to public ritual or monument building as spaces of collective memory (see, for example, Connerton 1989; Halbwachs 1941). This section of the chapter is meant to raise different questions about which memories are privileged in the archives, and to caution against the creation of any single truth which naturalises the fractured experiences of war. I centre my preliminary discussion on an example from the Holocaust, the most investigated genocide of the twentieth century. My aim here is not to claim the Holocaust as the origin of all examinations of genocide. I maintain, however, that the narrative strategy of this autobiographical text provides a much needed escape from the dichotomy – implicit in nearly all studies of wartime memory – between individual (psychological) memory and anthropological (collective) memory.

Sarah Kofman's (1996) poignant memoir *Rue Ordener Rue Labat* is her recollection of childhood in France during German occupation. What happens when the narrative of the victim and perpetrator become one? Within Kofman's truth narrative, impunity contests culpability. It shows how truth arises out of the events, of which memory bears the trace, but is something new. It illustrates, it seems to me, how truth comes into being. In this slender book she confronts the absurdities of recalling and forgetting war. Beginning with the Gestapo sweep of Paris in 1942, Kofman questions her mother's wartime lies. Deceit cannot save her father from death in Auschwitz, prevent separating and renaming the family of six children or preserve their religious home. Like her father's prayer, in the moments before he was killed by the Kapo, Kofman's memory beseeches 'God for all of them, victims and murderers alike' (7). She recognises that those who survive war must be complicit in its violence. Kofman's story, suspended between her childhood home on Rue Ordener and her safe haven on Rue Labat, reveals that every contradiction is a struggle over the way in which the past is remembered.

Anthropological studies of memory tend to show how the different truths about the past coexist, often as a result of social conflict. Ultimately, even the available versions of truth are determined by struggles over power (see Bourdieu 1997 for an extended discussion). Kofman's suggestion is very different, in that she describes how an individual both remembers and forgets.[2] She invites us to think about memory as a way of world-making, a mode of relation.

Kofman is best known for her work as a French philosopher of Nietzsche and Freud. The clarity of *Rue Ordener Rue Labat* places Kofman firmly in the personal narrative realm. Her writing, however, departs from the testimonial tradition of Holocaust literature. Each chapter speaks for Kofman alone, her delicate memories, bathed in the profound isolation of violence. The sweet lucidity of Kofman's language provides the reader refuge without consolation. One is caught between a mother and child who are subject to the ambiguity of compliance, coercion and resistance in war. Kofman recalls the childhood incongruities of life on Rue

Labat with a Christian woman. The woman hides Sarah and her mother until the liberation of France in an act that saved the girl, but consumed the child. Tenants in the building never betray their place of refuge; instead it is Sarah who is filled with the guilt of treason. Her mother suffers in silence as the daughter defects from rituals of their past life together. Sarah violates territory established at birth by awarding her affection to Mémé – the woman who shelters them both.

Mémé christened the young girl with the name Suzanne, changing her hair and kosher diet, redeeming the child's small soul with anti-Semitic teachings. As Marshal Pétain went about the work of restoring family and fatherland to Vichy France, war separated Sarah from her mother. She remembers choosing the more beautiful of two cards for Mémé on Mother's Day. The woman who decided to keep her – within Jesus Christ, Bergson, Marx, great music and crossword puzzles – becomes the hero of Sarah's story. Slowly Mémé transforms the girl into an image of herself, a made-to-order daughter. How can we resist condemning the child for her betrayal? How do we escape misinterpreting her testimony?

The ultimate victory for the perpetrators of war is that the victims come to resemble them. Even after Paris is freed, Sarah never sheds her likeness to Mémé. Although the relationship is not congruous, victims able to exploit the system of the perpetrators do so through collaboration and corruption. Sarah collaborates with Mémé, acts as her daughter, in order to survive the war. When the war ends, she finds lying is easy, and returning to a life of refuge is expedient. The abuse of separation from Mémé is intolerable. When her daughter returns to live with that woman, Sarah's mother brings a lawsuit against Mémé. The mother loses custody because the Free French court discovers that she beats her daughter with a strap. Sarah is still plotting to survive, tinkering with the loyalties of mother and Mémé. This violence arises out of her ordinary thoughts, her fear of reconciliation. She is divided in the remainder of her narrative, desirous of absolution and needing to forget the trespasses of war upon her life. Such ambiguity cannot be shed with words. The expediencies of war remain. Is this position, at which people arrive after the war, confirmed by the truths of their past? Or is it the simple result of the extant structures of power which engulf them?

In an essay titled *The Drowned and the Saved*, Holocaust survivor Primo Levi (1958) developed his notion of the grey zone as a space which could not be seen as a simple dichotomy between the innocent and the persecuted. He suggests that within a person who has suffered such atrocity, 'his capacity for hatred, unfulfilled in the direction of the oppressors, will double back, beyond all reason, on the oppressed; and he will only be satisfied when he has unloaded on his underlings the injury received from above' (91). This dynamic notion of institutionalised violence is relevant in its explanation of the extreme behaviour of war. Giorgio Agamben

(2000: 40) further develops this space as a zone of indistinction between the inside and the outside of war wherein the possibility of deciding is flattened: 'human beings ... so deprived of their rights and prerogatives to the point that committing any act toward them would no longer appear as a crime'. Memories of the past, remembered or forgotten, are constituted by events in which a state of exception has become the norm. One cannot overestimate the importance of this paradoxical nexus between the state of exception and the way in which people make sense of the past.

The existence of this grey zone in *Rue Ordener Rue Labat*, the union of the perpetrator and the victim in Sarah, provides a nuanced depiction of one child's experience of war. Kofman is plagued by the nebulous character of choices she made in war. This pain takes the form of a childhood story, the threat of *Maredewitchale*, a flesh-eating character from Jewish folklore invoked by her mother when her siblings would not behave. Kofman 'pictured that ghostly and terrifying figure as a very old woman who would come to punish me by carrying me far away from home' (1996: 73). While the convergence of victim and perpetrator identities may not satisfy visceral yearnings for a plot resolution, this grey zone represents the absolute dehumanisation inherent in violent conflict. Ultimately *Maredewitchale*, the phantom of her mother's threat, consumes Kofman's flesh. As a student at the Sorbonne, she is unable to imagine a liveable past. She cannot be a daughter to her mother, or attend her Mémé's funeral. Mémé made a choice, to keep a small girl from the Holocaust. Did she kidnap Rabbi Bereck Kofman's daughter? Did she save a young Jewish child and mother? Is she a hero? *Rue Ordener Rue Labat* narrates a place and a time in which there are no heroes.

The narrative leaves us to grapple with the consequences. In the year that this memoir of war betrayals was published, Sarah Kofman took her own life (as Primo Levi is likewise believed to have done). Her suicide contests the notion that the pain of past truths can be talked out, confirmed and treated. It is an act which breaks the unbearable calm of torment within. We cannot escape the violence of mass murder by transforming it into the truth of human suffering and the universal possibility of reconciliation. The limits of suffering, some hidden sort of humanity, are ambiguous. The book remains as an articulate and candid reminder of the struggle that children face in the aftermath of war. Memoir, the archive of a single human life, is central to one understanding of some truth in war: no one can defect.[3]

People continue to live with what is unverifiable. It is this practice, of living with the past, into which children are drawn. In the remainder of this chapter I examine a different instance of internal war and peace, which has been the subject of my own work for several years. I describe the disposition of a particular community towards the past, and a history that children of the town live as ordinary. This is a preliminary attempt to explore truth as understood and enacted by children in the post-war period. And so I ask, how do children reshape the national reconciliation project in the aftermath of war to meet their interests and needs? My research addresses this question in the context of a post-war struggle occurring in the western highland mountains of Guatemala, within the Mayan Ixil community of Santa María Nebaj.

Remembrance of Things Past: The Truth Commission and a Guatemalan Town

In the course of a war which extended over thirty-six years in Guatemala (1960–1996), Nebaj suffered several periods of mass terror. In particular, during the regime of General Lucas García (1978–1982) and bombing of the Cuchumatanes mountain range (1985–1990). Of the 420 army massacres documented by the *Recuperation of Historic Memory* project (ODHAG 1998), more than one hundred occurred in the Ixil area, where Nebaj is a municipality.

Villagers describe the town itself as a common place. Tin metal covers adobe brick homes, the black smoke of cooking fires seeps into the cold morning light. The soundtrack from *The Godfather* meets marimba music during Sunday market. Rain marks seasons. Summer dust burns the whitewashed walls of the Catholic church in the central square. But how does one write into its history the hundred massacres? Narratives of truth and reconciliation are rooted in experiences of suffering which have not passed. A woman said of her dead son, 'He is not what we remember, but a spirit of the dead that remembers us.' Santa María Nebaj, situated in the verdant highland mountains of the northern department of Quiché, was the site of violence which cannot be copied into text. The people of Nebaj appear to be uncertain about the truth of having survived 'the violence' of this period of terror. They proceed in their daily routines, living within the absurdities of the truth. Thus, my purpose is to demonstrate the ways in which truth is both conformed by memory and claimed in the practices of everyday life.

To this end, I examine the dual objectives of the Guatemalan truth commission, both truth and reconciliation, in the aftermath of the war. Truth commissions have been established, in recent history, as an alternative archive in the wake of war.[4] While scholars have examined the broad implications of the Guatemalan peace process and truth commission, few have explored what this means in a particular local context. The archive fixed by the truth commission, while of critical importance, shows how desperate we are to impose order on the chaos of mass murder. The Guatemalan truth commission (1997–1999), in a twelve volume report, held the military state responsible for 93 percent of human rights violations committed during the war. The significance of writing these official atrocities into Guatemalan history cannot be underestimated.

But how do we begin to grasp the reality of this raw data? Recognising the initial importance of the documentation, we will see that such truth archives risk decontextualising violent social events not directly linked with military violations. In my estimation there are risks involved in understanding truth as a commission, an autonomous narrative of the past. Yet, it is equally important to acknowledge the dangers of divorcing material forces and power relations from the fragmented and individualised histories of truth. People in Nebaj are often most concerned with the collaborators and bystanders, their neighbours and friends, whose complicity in the violence is more difficult to evaluate. It is no longer adequate to examine the post-war era as a generalised transitional space of social reparation. Instead, critical inquiry of truth discourse suggests a tension between the archives of the past and the possibilities for reconciliation. In particular, attention to the narratives of children suggests that there are various authorised versions of memory and truth in the town. These truths continue to unfold in the lives of children.

Thirty-six years of war in Guatemala are in danger of vanishing like the 45,000 'disappeared' whose official histories remain deniable. Thirty-six years of atrocity are also within living memory, close enough to remember, and work into the future. The Guatemalan truth commission, named the 'Commission for the Historical Clarification of the Violations of Human Rights and Acts of Violence Which Have Caused Suffering to the Guatemalan Population' (CEH), is one archive of memory. The truth commission was born out of the protracted peace negotiations between the government and revolutionary forces. Signed in 1994, and administered by the United Nations between 1997–1999, the accord stipulates that the final report 'will not individualise responsibility, nor have any legal implications' (CEH 1999: 2). The weak language and coercive harmony of the agreement were widely criticised because it did not ensure reparations to those who had suffered, and also lacked judicial authority to bring offenders to justice.[5] Both the government and rebel forces negotiated to position their version of the truth at the forefront of history.

The commission report is an archive of truth, but it cannot be separated from its naming process. As a political compromise, it offers military and rebel forces amnesty for crimes against civilians and allows the perpetrators of crimes to remain in power. Such concession can dispossess the individual truths within people – victims, perpetrators, collaborators, bystanders – who practised resistance and collusion as survival strategies during a lifetime of war. While the commission laid out clear objectives, first to prevent future violations of human rights, and second to promote social healing, the implications of its truth are unclear. In the absence of juridical or social justice, it is a truth without a name. Is this archive simply another representation of the violence and capitulation which have determined Guatemalan history until the present? What is the purpose of knowing any truth, without the possibility of justice?

The truth commission urged Guatemalans that it was 'time to tell the truth'. During eighteen months, thousands of testimonies were taken by truth campaigns in rural communities. At the exhumation sites of mass graves, in local parishes and municipal offices people offered up the truth they remember. The truth on tape and written into notebooks was transported, in United Nations' jeeps, back to the security of the capital city. The truth was reviewed, verified and processed. The commission determined that ninety communities in the Ixil area, where Nebaj is located, 'were partially or totally destroyed by the army scorched earth policy' (CEH 1999: 345). The communities are listed6 in the final report, the names pile up on one another like bones in a graveyard. What does the list mean? I asked a friend in Nebaj and he replied, 'We know the truth about the list. They think it needs to be written down for it to be true. But we already know the truth. The truth is not in the list.' I ask again. Another reply: 'You already know about the list. You have been to Trapichitos and Xix, with your own feet on the land, to see the truth. You see people harvesting corn and carrying water. Other people you do not see. You do not need to look at the list, look at the land.'

The limitations of the empirical data, legal documentation of truth, are unearthed. In Guatemala the conflict over the truth continues as a war over land. Yet the truth commission does not document the testimony of children, whose land rights have been denied in the post-war period. It does not tell the story of young people who leave Nebaj in search of work in the capital city, when the land is exhausted. Representing the complexity of personal experience, in the face of historical denial, is a formidable task. As such, the commission raises important questions about who can lay claim to history. Does the archive of the truth commission respond to the everyday violence of life in rural communities that endured hegemonic state repression?

The mandate of the commission, to measure the fragile truth of war atrocity, created a particular political document. The effectiveness of the truth commission depended upon proving, with juridical certainty, that genocide had occurred in Guatemala. If such crimes against humanity were confirmed, experts argued that international legal action could be taken. The structure and content of the truth commission became part of a concerted effort to prove the realities of mass murder and violence, which the Guatemalan government had denied for decades. Just after the truth commission released its final report, General Efrain Ríos Montt was indicted on charges of genocide. The truth commission held his administration, in 1982 and 1983, responsible for 192 massacres and eighty percent of the documented human rights violations. Yet, a few months later, he revived his national political party, the Guatemalan Republican Front (FRG), and became the president of the Guatemalan congressional body.

As the leader of Congress, Efrain Ríos Montt has refused to recognise the conclusions of the truth commission. Upon taking office he effectively derailed the 'Code for Children', a government policy written in 1996 to provide youth with civil rights. When young people were denied their ancestral rights to land as they returned from refuge, youth became violent actors in rural communities. They claimed public parks through thievery, defaced municipal buildings and terrorised local markets in a language of refusal, creating a place for themselves even where one was not available. Children of poor displaced peasants emerged in the local news as a residual category of the war. In May 2000, President Alfonso Portillo of the FRG resorted to military intervention, calling thousands of troops into rural communities to combat the anarchy and disorder. Opinion polls in the national papers registered strong support from within the communities themselves. Given these circumstances, I concluded that the 'Code for Children' was generally perceived as a suspicious pretext which granted favours to common criminals. Children that I interviewed during this period often defended the violent attacks as an acceptable form of social control.

The complex realities in which children are engaged underscore the need for anthropological studies which develop an analysis of public policy in the post-war period. Several prominent events capture the ongoing controversy. On 7 April 2000, Mayra Guttierrez, a professor at the national university, disappeared. The brutalised body of Oswaldo Monzón, a union leader, was found several months later. Several leaders of popular rural organisations were killed in the weeks that followed. On 14 May 2000, armed men burned the cooperative store in Santa María Tzejá, Quiché. Members of the community had recently filed a legal action charging former dictator General Romeo Lucas García with genocide. All these crimes occurred in a supposed peacetime. While the Guatemalan truth commission produced a conclusive legal report, the recent resurgence of terror in the country calls the project of truthtelling and reconciliation into question. The archive of the truth commission is, by definition, hostage to the terms of its conception. Yet detailed accounts of the emergence of the truth commission in Guatemala, for instance, do provide us with one understanding of memory in the social and political context of Nebaj. Perhaps the singular explanation of genocide cannot represent the complexities of a war that changed people over time. The question becomes, what is forgotten within a truth commission?

Forgotten Justice

Guatemalan communities were disfigured by political violence in a series of violent truths that swallowed entire families, and transcended the cosmological possibilities of reality. The military archive remains to contest a mythic collective history: 'Our strategic goal has been to reverse Clausewitz's philosophy of war to state that in Guatemala, politics must be the continuation of war' (cited by Schirmer 1998: 1). A closer examination of the testimonies included in the volumes of the truth commission betrays a deep understanding, in local communities, that the truth of war is always worse than expected. The war is exposed as more than an ephemeral memory; it is also an agent of amnesia. A narrative from Nebaj, included in the truth commission, runs as follows:

> The Army listened ... they coordinated with the families, in this way they began to take control also. This is how they severed relations between families, they destroyed the customs, the very way of living... what there was between people. Because before the people always had a way to defend themselves, to make justice when there were problems between them. But then the war started, the violence, and there [during the war] this was forgotten. (collective testimony of people from Vicalamá, Nebaj, Quiché. CEH 1999: 334)

There is not a formulaic equivalence between memory and truth, social reparation and reconciliation. It was not simply mass killing, but the fabric of relations between people that was threatened and dismantled. Violence was not the tragic derivative of a just war, nor was it the utilitarian result of guns and beans.[7] Because the truth of the war is always worse than what is expected, the truth commission has a potentially powerful place within communities to describe what appears invisible and forbidden.

Between vengeance and forgiveness are friends and siblings, shopkeepers and lovers, neighbours and peddlers. One hot summer day I am sitting in town, eating watermelon with my coworker Julia. She has been on the staff at a local human rights organisation over the past twelve years, often working in communities controlled by the nearby military base. As we sit in the central square her brother approaches, dressed in army fatigues and extending a standard-issue rifle in our direction. Once he has walked past, she answers my confused inquiries in the most matter of fact tone. As with all of the dialogues which follow, names are pseudonyms and the translations are mine.

> Yes, he has always been stationed at the base. As far as I can remember, anyway. It is quite ordinary, something necessary. The killing, of course, was excessive. You know that. But he is still there. He is fine there. My sister is a nurse, remember. She was always seeing the bodies in the morgue. We are fortunate to have jobs in the same area though. If we were ever separated my parents would be sad.

Her explanation seems to be a contradiction. Yet, each Sunday afternoon she joins her brother and sister at church. Her brother often pauses in the doorway of our office as he patrols the town. As one of the field staff for the truth commission wryly remarked, 'It is impossible to identify the truth here. The person tells you something, but their words defy any understanding of what happened. What is recorded? Is it the truth, or is it a lie? Are we living a lie?' The indefinite character of truth in war, described by Primo Levi as a grey zone where the victim and the perpetrator mingle in a space of indistinction, seems relevant. The truth finds itself in constant conflict with the linear logic of everyday conduct. One begins to understand that a coherent master narrative of truth is an impossibility. This is particularly apparent in the conversations of children, as demonstrated in my ethnographic research. These dialogues between children provide a real possibility of examining the intersection between the personal and social. It is not only the significance of what children are saying, but also the relation with truth that their discussion forces upon the world here and now.

Perhaps what causes some to both love and fear, embrace and exclude children is their newness. While the vitality of their experience engages them so necessarily in social life, it also makes them dangerous and unpredictable. They are present – carrying water, herding cows, playing soccer and attending political rallies – in every routine moment. As representatives of a contested future and subjects of cultural policies, Ixil children often find themselves at the junction of divergent truths (Stephens 1995: 23). To understand what role young Ixil people play in formulating the politics of truth it is essential to document the structures of memory imprinted upon their lives. In this way one might understand the specific historical characteristics in which the way of being a person, considering oneself, was revised by complex institutional machinations.

In June 1982, the Guatemalan military adopted a plan called 'Operation Ixil' which called for:

> an intensive, profound and carefully studied psychological campaign to rescue the Ixil mentality … Respecting Ixil identity, customs and language, giving them an opportunity to contribute, together with the army, to the defence of their communities … Another [advantage] would be to neutralise the strategy of the enemy, utilising their own procedures [for defence] but with many more resources. (cited in Schirmer 1998: 104–5; and CEH 1999: 348)

This original army document foreshadows years during which military restructuring of cultural, economic and settlement patterns instrumentalised processes of social control over the most basic human needs in the Ixil area.[8] In an untitled pamphlet, the description of a local nongovernmental programme for youth, created to contest the military reproduction of Ixil identity, is remarkably similar: 'The young Mayan has suffered a total deterioration of his indigenous self-image ... and broken his true cultural ties. Our general objective is to help children living in the conflict zone to recuperate their own psychological identity ... revaluing, rescuing and promoting Ixil culture.'

As the military doctrine is translated into humanitarian propaganda, the original discourse is both reproduced and distorted. This process of appropriation alters the significance of both the signified and the signifier, suggesting that Ixil people might transcend the limitations of official history. Likewise the civil education programme used in Nebaj schools follows this first military precept: 'to cement and form a positive civic attitude'. In the community of Las Violetas, Nebaj children describe military marches that replaced traditional days of celebration during local festivals. Yet, in their drawings, the children sketch out the traditional red and yellow skirt of Ixil women, domesticating the patriotic enterprise. They show children talking, playing and sleeping. These activities subvert the official military order. Five-year-old Carolina explains her drawing of a march on independence day in 1993.

> For 15 September they [the military] do a parade. But it is very tiring because we arrive at the soccer field, feeling very tired, marching like soldiers in the national army. But we do not like it very much because it tires our feet. It is worse if we do not have shoes, then the rocks hurt our feet. Since most of the boys and girls of Las Violetas are hard up, most of us walk with bare feet.

The material existence of children is at stake in debates about civil rights, religious expression and ethnic identification. And while the form of military discourse may be reproduced over time, I suggest that children infuse these ideological truths with meaning that displaces the original discourse. When the domination of truth comes to its end, when the dichotomy of true and false can no longer be expressed, then knowledge of history and life moves to (re)inscribe itself. 'When knowledge is no longer a knowledge of truth, it is then that knowledge starts: a knowledge that burns thought ...' explains Maurice Blanchot (1995: 43). By focusing upon such transformations in knowledge, the politics of truth reveal themselves as both a risk and a resource for children.

Prior scholarship often cast children as unmitigated victims of war, offering only an analysis of brutal violence in Guatemala. Even while suffering the consequences of state-sponsored terror, children can reshape the discourse of truth for their own purposes. Interestingly, the conversations recorded by children below often directly contradict the history of the conflict in the Ixil area as written by academics.[9] This is suggestive of the idea that while one official, true history of Nebaj might be agreed upon in public, this narrative coexists with individual truths of parents and sisters. Few scholars, however, have sought children's interpretations of truth.[10] In August 1999, I became interested in the social means of participation available to children in the Ixil area.

I worked closely with ten young people between the ages of 10 and 13, in two communities, Las Violetas and Salquil Grande. These villages were selected first because of the existence of a community youth programme; second, their history as model villages for the military; third, current problems with youth suicide; and fourth, demonstrated interest on the part of children and parents in the community. With the help of a young Ixil woman I worked with the children in participatory workshops, covering topics such as research techniques, recording audio diaries and the practice of oral history, and together we developed a methodology for active listening.[11] We then gave the children tape recorders and the opportunity to express their lives as they understood them. The ten children created more than eighty hours of tape. Approximately half are thirty-minute interviews with friends and relatives. This group of young people decided to explore what it means to live in Nebaj at present, giving this working group the Ixil name *Xo'leb'al Chelem* (between young people). Over the course of our taped conversations we examined notions of politics, divinity and justice.

Each of the young people spent six months interviewing friends and companions on topics of interest to them. The result was a series of discussions that centre on ancestry; the question of origins; the effects of alcoholism; friendship; pollution; the obligations of parents; the rights of children; marriage; and the violent past. They also taped events such as church teachings, radio programmes, songs, soap operas, legends, school events and the omnipresent rain. After a year, more than one hundred children, in two communities, had participated in the project. The average age of a participant was 13. Their enthusiasm during this time remains a testament to their active social participation in Ixil society.

In my analysis of these conversations I do not make the distinction between children and adolescents. This is deliberate, and meant to underscore the fact that while youth now have unprecedented autonomy and constitute a distinct social category in Nebaj – as young workers, religious believers and social activists – they are not a homogeneous group in terms of age or life experience. For example, in the Ixil language, during casual conversation, one will refer to any unmarried person as 'child' regardless of age. In this case, to map age and the life cycle so directly onto young people would be deceptive at best. Precisely how and why and given what claims and conditions, the category of 'child' has emerged in Guatemala during the post-war period is an important aspect of my ongoing investigation. The scope of this part of the chapter, however, is limited to the way in which young people negotiate the truth of the past in these conversations. Their reflections on the processes of truth and reconciliation in Guatemala are what interest me here.

Descriptions of everyday life in Nebaj contest notions of truth set out by the archive of the Guatemalan truth commission. For these children, war has not occurred within the discrete parameters of the legal and illegal, true and untrue. More than half of the one million internally displaced in Guatemala were children. Young people comprised at least 60 percent of the returned refugees. Estimates suggest that 20,000 participated in army civil patrol units. Children represent one in three of the bodies exhumed from mass graves (ODHAG 1998: 80). But the peace accords do not recognise children as a vulnerable group with specific needs for support and protection. What consequences might children's experiences of war have for their sense of Ixil identity? How do their conversations change our understanding of childhood?

War has shaped the existence of parents, killed sisters and enveloped the beginning of young lives in Nebaj. So it was not unusual that the children who participated in this project often spoke about the 'deceptions of truth'. Although the violence of war had ceased in Nebaj three years earlier, participants explained that peace did not exist in Guatemala. Elena, who is 13 years old, describes the effects of the armed conflict on her community. 'The people are already sad. They don't leave their homes, they are still afraid. They can't make a fire anymore because they are thinking that people outside will see the smoke. Then they will be killed.' Children often speak about the origins of the violence in lynchings, alcoholism and assaults.

Catarina

What gives meaning to your life in the community?

Miguel

There is no feeling [*sentido*]. That is what I think. Because there are gangs that rob things. Just like happened here, a while back. They came from Chiuul to burn them [afterwards], to burn the ones from the gangs, because they had been stealing a lot of things that belonged to other people. They came to burn them with gasoline.

Manuel

Yeah, I felt badly. There are a lot of people who go around robbing. It isn't the same [as before], because you have to be afraid. Anyone can think that you are stealing things, and they might even burn you alive.

On various occasions the children related the everyday violence of life in Nebaj to the brutality of the war. Each form of violence generated social instability and limited freedom. As the everyday language of children is intertwined with official archives of truth, the ways in which historical remembrance interacts with everyday experience are apparent. How do children both internalise and resist available discursive practices?

Andres

> We are not safe anymore. We walk with fear. It is the same as when they killed so many people before.

Catarina

> What do you know about the past?

Andres

> That all of the people had to run. The soldiers wanted to capture them, and that is why people had to hide. The soldiers were very bad. They put bombs [mines] under the earth.

Jacinto

> And now people are coming to look for the bombs [mines]. Who knows if they have found any here [in the village]. But people are saying that in Nebaj they did find so many.

Diego

> The soldiers were very bad. They even stole the clothing from people's backs. People lost their clothing, they had to hide so often that they would leave it behind. Or sometimes people got into fights with their husbands or sons, everyone was so afraid. And when the violence ended sometimes they found their family, and sometimes they did not.

Ambrocio

> That is how it is. Because there are some that died of hunger and others that were killed. That is why they can't find them anymore. The people go, searching and searching, but they find no one because their family is dead.

Alvaro

> It was Lucas who started the war, he gave us all of these problems. And it was Ríos Montt who ended the violence. But the violence destroyed houses, corn and fields. And all of the things, all of the living beings, were hurt or killed.

Particular acts of violence become continuous and are transformed throughout the lives of individual children. They are deciding the guilt of one political leader, and the innocence of another. They easily associate their fear of crime to the experiences of displacement during the war. Children absorb the truth of state terror in 'all the things, all of the living beings, [which] were hurt or killed'. They are rethinking the terms of the past upon which Ixil people express membership in society. It is within their narratives that structures of coercion are superimposed on the daily habits of movement, dress and nourishment.

The violence of the war has translated into the crimes of impunity in peace. Daniel, who is 10 years old, phrases the absence of peace as a continuation of violence. 'Well, they already signed the peace into law, but the violence persists. They still walk about, killing people. There are still people who have nothing. This peace, no one will keep it.' He is not simply restating the official history; out of the violence Daniel constructs a recognisable image of himself. He is inventing a truth that people, caught in the archive, have not found. If they demand justice and security that the truth commission cannot secure, children also offer solutions. Noé, a child from Salquil Grande, has a clear idea of the measures necessary to stop the violence in his community. 'They need to put new laws in place, because the old laws are useless. Because, in the past, they put many mines in Tzalbal. That is why the war began. If they are going to make new laws, they should make them so that this history cannot repeat.' Noé and his companion Moisés agree that they do not want violence to return to their communities: 'If they return to such violence, if they put bombs in the homes of people, it is better that they kill those people for once and for all. Better that they kill the people who do such things,' explains Moisés. Despite the children's desire for peace in their communities, the discourse of truth offers them few nonviolent resolutions. A declaration that this is the inevitable result of violent factors which define Ixil children is oversimplified.

The knowledge of good and evil, to which the child is seduced, is best expressed in the grey zone of war violence. The truth commission documents explain that the army often invoked a biblical reference to judgement day in relation to extrajudicial killings (CEH 1999: 338). Nicolás, who is 13 years old, explains: 'To those who are guilty, to the ones that walk in the night, they should capture them and burn them. Nothing more. Do not question them. Just burn them for once.' The past is recalled: men strung up in the bell tower of the local church for 'sins against the Guatemalan people' (CEH 1999: 331). There were no questions. The answers demand only new questions. How does one determine the truth, or judge guilt and innocence in war? 'Maybe because we already know who is good and who is not. The people can come together and decide. And in this way, all that is bad will end,' explains 9-year-old Magdalena. The living memory of terror rises up in narratives of children as a part of quotidian life. The complex relationships between criminal violence, extreme poverty and social instability reveal the deep wounds of a war that rewarded victory at any human cost. During 1999 the department of Quiché, where Nebaj is located, had the greatest number of lynchings in the nation, with thirty cases registered with the United Nations for the year. Unfulfilled justice, the unrealised promise of truth and reconciliation, plague Nebaj. Children challenge us to consider that Guatemalan society has not been offered non-violent possibilities in the post-war period. How are children to understand a past that has devoured its own people?

Catarina

What problems do you see in the community?

Petrona

Well, there are gangs.

Jacinta

Thieves too.

Jorge

All of the people in the community should capture them, and burn them. Just like they did in Chiuul. That is what needs to be done here.

Petrona

When they burned the people in Chiuul we only saw the shoes of the person. They left the shoes thrown off in the middle of the road when they carried him away. They carried him with his hands tied behind his back, down the entire path. There was blood spilled along the way.

Jorge

Yeah. I used to shine shoes in Chiuul. There is an enormous hole, and poles dug in. In that hole, at the stakes, they burn people who are thieves or assault others. You can see it well when we pass by on the road.

José

That's right. And, do you know? When they burn them, the people are not dead. They are alive when they set fire to their bodies.

Catarina

And what do you think about it?

Francisco

It's a good thing. That way people won't act like vagrants. They won't rob and assault the rest of us.

Catarina

Is there any other way?

Ana

We can speak to the big people, to the oldest ones, because they know about so many things. They have seen many problems in the past. They know about escaping the problems.

Violence is transmitted and reinterpreted. Memories are recalled, in the bodies of dead sons and blood let into the earth. To what extent do children continue to live the cultural repercussions of genocide, even when they no longer experience the violence of war in daily life? Perhaps most difficult for children in the town of Nebaj is the lack of access to educational opportunities, hardships associated with extreme poverty and an absence of trust between community members. Children are denied the refuge of social history, their consciousness of the past does not allow them to avoid a disorientation of the present. It is their remembrance of the violence which is a most gentle foresight into the future. Their narratives are acute evidence of the interruptions children face in the aftermath of war; it is in their recollections that the past and present converge on what memory does not recall. Lawrence Langer (1998: 29) asks, 'What sense can we assign to the [Auschwitz] decree that *death begins with shoes*?' Death in Guatemala began where people walked, on the paths that took them to work in their fields; children continue to trace those same paths. En route something new also comes into being, not only a past remembered, but a present embodied in the youngest members of society. It is captured in their great ability to retrospect. What truth is derived from the notions of justice and reconciliation that Ixil children harbour? The discussions of children allow for some margin of hope, a promise that silence will not be kept. Children, like many of their families, neither accept nor refuse what has passed through their town.

How can we describe their absorption, being taken in, by the past? To what degree is openness to the past a property of childhood itself? To what extent are children open to any possible truth? Truth is something to which children are open, but that openness is not necessarily manifest. This openness, in some part, defines their capacity to make the world. It is both a structural moment and a space of possible creation. This means that through memory, and versions of the past which are either accepted or denied, children refuse totality and set limits on their world. In the refusal lies the possibility of something else. Perhaps it is the very possibility of something else, within the practices of children, which the reductive logic of the truth commission obfuscates. It does not account for these ongoing practices of both children and adults, in the here and now, that make memories possible.

Negotiating the Archives: The Grey Truth

In this chapter I have probed the darkness of truth and reconciliation posited by the archives of internal wars. The past appears in the fragments and contradictions of a memoir, a truth commission and in children's conversations in a small and ordinary town. Master narratives of truth are contested by partial memories, visible in the everyday exchanges between friends and neighbours. Truth cannot occur in isolation, with the text suspended in lists and legal proofs. Yet the historicity of truth is not entirely arbitrary. Truth can be seen to mediate material forces and human perception in the words of Ixil children. There is an interchange between the discourse of truth and the spirits of the past.

I am left with an official document from the National Civil Police Station 71-81 in Nebaj, printed on faint typing paper. It is signed and stamped, 1 February 2000, by Inspector Aurelio Gonzalez de León. The document reads:

> TEREZA PEREZ RAYMUNDO, 16 years old, single, educated, familiar with domestic duties. Native and resident of the Village Salquil Grande, daughter of TOMAS PEREZ RAYMUNDO AND JUANA RAYMUNDO. Of brown skin, round face, low forehead, black eyes, sparse eyebrows, thin nose, large mouth, thick lips, straight hair; measuring 1.45 metres in height, normal complexion. POSITION OF CADAVER: Head to the North, feet to the South. Left arm hanging, right arm hanging at the side. Legs stretched, face to the sky. LESIONS PRESENTED: Blood from the left orifice of the nose, stiff lips and tongue, discoloration around the neck due to suffocation by plastic tied around the same. Right arm stiff, left leg stiff. DRESS: White bordered blouse. A typical red, yellow and black skirt. Green plastic shoes. Woven belt, in black and white. A wristwatch and pink plastic bracelet. It is established that she died of asphyxiation by hanging at more or less 19:00 hours on 31 January 2000. After completing the formalities the body was returned to the family for burial.

Where does the death of this young girl come from? Was her death foretold in the extraordinary and violent history of the town? Could her suicide have been prevented? These were the questions asked by members of the community in Nebaj after more than twenty young people committed suicide over the course of only a few months. No person could remember a previous case of suicide by a young person in the town, and no one wanted to answer for such unjust deaths. What remains to be said about these deaths is not known. Will the truth of these suicides be included in the archive? Is it sufficient to understand these suicides in the context of wartime violence? Is death the only continuity between the past war and the present violence? The sum total of habits, good and evil misconceived, cross the town like shadows in the grey space of war. Perhaps the misunderstandings, the hesitations, that we see in the tension between truth and reconciliation expect, and create, violence.

The official testimony of the young girl's death is orderly. The truth of her life is written as injuries to her body which suggest, but do not confirm, that she could not bear to live with some version of her past. She has refused not only violence, but also the possibility of living within the contradictions between wartime and peacetime. She reminds us of the child hidden in France, during German occupation, a woman who later penned her memoir and also took her own life. It seems almost as if one woman could occupy, somehow, the place of the other. Yet, to consider suicide the predictable end of violent genocidal occupations is misguided. To understand a young person who withdraws from life in this way, we must also look to the episodes of criminality and vigilante justice which have young people among their perpetrators and victims. Of course the origin of this young Ixil woman's suicidal death is unknowable, not verifiable. Any reason we might ascribe to it, however rational, seems unjustifiable. To take one's own life is to occupy a forbidden space of undesignated death. What does it mean for children to be involved in this sort of protracted violence which extends from times of war into crimes of peace? By understanding how such violence is remembered and forgotten by the young we might begin to consider how memory acts, not only on the past, but also into the present.

What happens when children's narratives are forbidden, or made invisible? If we investigate only our convictions of childhood innocence, we risk never recognising the possibilities of children's perspectives on and active participation in social life. Taking the conversations of children seriously, it is no longer possible to describe the archive of the Guatemalan truth commission as original truth. If we uncover the truth of the youth suicides, perhaps we will only find the falsehood of the present. Children are faced with such impossible questions, and are left searching for knowledge of the forgotten, which precedes memory in the town of Nebaj.

Notes

1. Childhood is a contested category in our changing global order. Many shifts have occurred in the ideals and rights associated with childhood, as evidenced by Cunningham (1995) in his historical study of *Children and Childhood in Western Society Since 1550*, or Matthews (1984) in his philosophical approach to *Dialogues with Children*. The idea of the present has, very often, been collapsed within conceptions of children and childhood as a period of both potential and ideological innocence. The political and social struggles which define the contemporary situation of young people challenge such prevailing assumptions of childhood as a social category.
2. I consider this to be quite a different claim from the suppositions of Cathy Caruth, Dori Laub and Shoshana Felman that use a psychoanalytic frame to explain war memories as universally traumatic (cf. Caruth 1995: 1–61).
3. This phrase is taken from *Burger's Daughter* by Nadine Gordimer (1979), a novel which calls freedom into question as the protagonist struggles with the ideology of the South African Communist Party. She knows, 'No one can defect. I don't know the ideology. It's about suffering. How to end suffering. And it ends in suffering. Yes, it's strange to live in a country where there are still heroes' (332). Holding the ideology, acting on it, did end in suffering for many people. But it was not unreasonable, in the South African context, to believe that pain would give rise to freedom. It is made clear that no one can defect from humanity.
4. Internationally sanctioned truth-seeking has become an essential strategy in responding to the atrocities of wartime. There have been an estimated twenty-one official truth commissions established since 1974, with ensuing investigations of massive violence.

5. The Truth and Reconciliation Commission (TRC) in South Africa, another recent example of a negotiated truth archive, was charged with promoting a 'spirit of understanding' which would transcend past violence. The Guatemalan truth commission had a less public mandate, and focused its efforts upon covert research. The traditional norms of secrecy which have determined the disclosure of truth in Chile, Argentina and El Salvador also guided the compilation of testimony in Guatemala. As a result, the conclusions of the truth commission received little attention in the mass media, and only one public hearing during February 1998 was held over the course of its tenure.

6. Xix, Xolcuay, Batzal, Chacalté, Bitziquichum, Juá, Sotzil, Ilom, Xesaí, Chel, Xachimoxán, Estrella Polar, Covadonga, Xejuyeb, Santa Clara, Amachel, Cabá, Pal, Cimientos, Ti'aj'a, Tzotzil, Cajchixlá, Bitzich, Xeputul, Putul, Xaxboj, Xebitz, Cocob, Pexlá, Pulay, Río Azul, Xencuá, Jacaná, Bictoz, Cotzol, Vivitz, Acul, Xexuxcab, Xexocom, Chortiz, Xecocó, Janlay, Tzalbal, Xoloché, Tuchanbuc, Basuquil, Canaquil, Xeipum, Salquil, Parramos Grande, Parramos Chiquito, Tujolom, Xeo, Palop, Vijolom, Vicampanavitz, Vicamalá, Sumalito, Batzumal, Sumal Grande, Xeucalvitz, Trapichitos, Vilakam, Laguna, Batzchocolá, Viucalvitz, Ixtupil, Sacsihuán, Santa Marta, Talsumnalá, Xesumal, K'osonip, Vipecpalam,Viramux Bipaná, Kanakil Xepeum, Vitz, Piucual Pajilá, Asich, Namá, Cajixaj, Chisis, Quisis, Villa Hortensia, San Felipe Chenla, Chichel, Xeputul, San Marcos Cunlá (as documented in CEH).

7. The March 1982 coup, which placed General Efrain Ríos Montt in power, was known for its pacification strategy called 'Beans and Bullets'. The beans, a staple food in Guatemala, were meant to symbolise the military government's aid to national loyalists. Bullets were representative of the government struggle against communist insurgents (Schirmer 1998: 35).

8. This sort of coercive harmony, which eventually led to the mobilisation of indigenous former soldiers and former guerrilla irregulars during 1982 in the Ixil area, is neglected by Stoll's (1993) ethnographic study on the impact of violence in the area. What his description does not account for is that by initially linking food with locally obligated patrolling, the 'Beans and Bullets Programme', the military created a network of centrally controlled civil patrols which appeared as local support for the army.

9. Stoll (1993) reflects Guatemalan military rhetoric by blurring distinctions between guerrilla combatants, land activists and religious evangelists. He disregards the possibility that local perceptions of conflict change, particularly in a militarised context. In doing so he erases from history the ideological differences which Ixil people had with the military, from the start.

10. See Bluebond-Langner (1978) for an attempt to understand children as actors with knowledge of their own condition.

11. For a detailed description and materials see *Aprendamos por Medio de la Palabra* (NRM 2000) which has also been taperecorded in Ixil for use in community youth centres.

References

Agamben, G. 2000. *Means without End: Notes on Politics*. Minneapolis: University of Minnesota Press.

Blanchot, M. 1995. *The Writing of Disaster*. Ann Smock, trans. Lincoln: University of Nebraska Press.

Bluebond-Langner, M. 1978. *The Private Worlds of Dying Children*. Princeton:

Princeton University Press.

Borges, J.L. 1976. 'The Circular Ruins.' In D. Yates and J. Irby, eds, *Labyrinths*. New York: New Directions Press.

——. 1976. 'The Fearful Sphere of Pascal.' In D. Yates and J. Irby, eds, *Labyrinths*. New York: New Directions Press.

Bourdieu, P. 2000 [1997]. *Pascalian Meditations*. Cambridge, U.K.: Polity.

Caruth, C. ed. 1995. *Trauma: Explorations in Memory*. Baltimore: Johns Hopkins University Press.

CEH 1999. Guatemala: Memory of Silence. Tz'inil Na'tab'al. (12 vols)

Report of the Commission for Historical Clarification. United Nations Office for Project Services. http://shr.aaas.org/guatemala/ceh/

Connerton, P. 1989. *How Societies Remember*. Cambridge: Cambridge University Press.

Cunningham, H. 1995. *Children and Childhood in Western Society Since 1550*. London: Longman.

Derrida, J. 1998 [1995] *Archive Fever: A Freudian Impression*. Eric Prenowitz, trans. Chicago: University of Chicago Press.

Gordimer, N. 1979. *Burger's Daughter*. London: Penguin.

Halbwachs, M. 1992 [1941]. *On Collective Memory*. L. Coser, trans. Chicago: University of Chicago Press.

Kofman, S. 1996. *Rue Ordener, Rue Labat*. Ann Smock, trans. Lincoln: University of Nebraska Press.

Langer, L. 1998. *Pre-empting the Holocaust*. New Haven: Yale University Press.

Levi, P. 1958. *Survival in Auschwitz*. New York: Simon and Schuster.

Matthews, G. 1984. *Dialogues with Children*. Cambridge, MA: Harvard University Press.

Mead, M. 1930. *Growing up in New Guinea*. New York: Morrow.

Niños Refugiados del Mundo. 2000. *Aprendamos por Medio de la Palabra*. Paris.

ODHAG 1998. *Guatemala: Nunca Mas* (vols 1–4). Oficina de Derechos Humanos del Arzobispado de Guatemala. ODHAG.

Reynolds, P. 1998. 'Activism, Politics and the Punishment of Children.' In G. Van Bueren, ed., *Childhood Abused*. Aldershot, U.K.: Ashgate.

Scheper-Hughes, N. 1992. *Death Without Weeping: The Violence of Everyday Life in Brazil*. Berkeley: University of California Press.

Schirmer, J. 1998. *The Guatemalan Military Project*. Philadelphia: University of Pennsylvania.

Stephens, S. 1995a. 'Introduction.' in S. Stephens, ed., *Children and the Politics of Culture*. New Jersey: Princeton University Press.

Stephens, S. ed. 1995b. *Children and the Politics of Culture*.

Stoll, D. 1993. *Between Two Armies in the Ixil Towns of Guatemala*. New York: Columbia University Press.

9

Beyond Struggle and Aid: Children's Identities in a Palestinian Refugee Camp in Jordan

Jason Hart

Introduction

Conflict and displacement tend to encourage a discourse of monolithic and bounded identities. This may be especially true in the case of the young. As children's lives and bodies become objects for both political debate and humanitarian intervention, so the most immediate, most apparently pertinent or most expedient characteristic is taken up and stressed as singularly important. Young Hutu refugees in Tanzania, Bhutanese children in Nepal and Palestinians in Jordan are rendered as little more than that.

The rhetoric of political leaders and of international humanitarian agencies engaged with refugee children tends to give scant consideration to difference between individuals within the same group. Thus, the age, gender, social class, personal history, religious faith, political views, and so on, of individual children are rendered irrelevant within discourses which suggest that a single dimension – be it ethnicity, nationality or the simple fact of being a refugee – overwhelmingly determines their experiences, values and aspirations. Inevitably, prevalent views about the universality of childhood itself also militate against the contemplation of difference (Archard 1990; Boyden 1997; Jenks 1996; Woodhead 1997).

The authors and proponents of such discourse generally fail to distinguish between group identity and personal identity. In doing so they ignore the powerful arguments presented by social psychologists since the late 1970s. A core tenet of so-called 'social identity theory', which emerged with the work of Tajfel (1978, 1981), is that individual identities and collective identities are of a different order, informed in their construction by fundamentally different processes (Capozza and Brown 2000). That is to say, the attitudes and actions of the group are not merely an agglomeration of the attitudes and actions of individual members. Conversely, individual identity is not simply acquired through membership of the group. Indeed, as I shall argue, the identities of individual children – as manifest in their stated opinions, values and aspirations – may sprawl untidily across the neatly-drawn bounds of collectivities suggested by older generations.

I believe that this point is particularly important to consider in a situation of inter-group conflict (Cairns 1996: 6–8). The tendency to promote monolithic, rigid and static identities has serious implications for conflict resolution and reconciliation – potentially reinforcing a view of essential difference. Children are seen as and encouraged to become future advocates for group identities articulated around enmity, mistrust and opposition. Arguably, the UN Convention on the Rights of the Child (CRC) – in Articles 29 and 30 – offers a similarly static and bounded view of cultural identity that may, ironically, be used to justify such an approach. On the other hand, acknowledging the fluidity, contingency and open-endedness of children's processes of identity formation may nourish efforts at reconciliation, encouraging a focus on and strengthening of 'connectors': institutions, behaviour and values shared by the young across lines of conflict (Anderson 1999).

This is not to suggest, however, that conflicts, and the injustices and oppression which often give rise to them, can simply be brushed away by stressing commonalities amongst children. In line with current thinking within the sociology/anthropology of childhood, it is my conviction that children are active members of the societies in which they live (Prout and James 1997: 8). As such, their understanding and roles encompass the social, historical, political and economic aspects of those societies. Efforts at reconciliation should take this into account and avoid the trap of thinking that, simply by bringing young people together, enmity can be transcended since, 'ultimately, kids are all the same'.

Such a universalist and depoliticised view of the young is a common basis for the work of international humanitarian agencies. As I argue below, this view is, in its own way, as limiting and potentially inimical to children as that of political leaders who assume that the youngest generation is a replica of those preceding in terms of identity and aspirations.

It is my intention here to argue for an approach to the study of refugee children that anticipates – conceptually and methodologically – the contingency and historicity of the processes by which they develop their own individual and collective identities. Such processes are ongoing and informed by an array of influences from the very local to the most global.

I contend that the reluctance of politicians and international humanitarian agencies to acknowledge and respect these processes is potentially injurious to the best interests of children living in situations of conflict and displacement.

Ethnographic Context

The points outlined above are here explored in relation to a specific population of refugee children, namely Palestinians in Jordan. For a period of eighteen months in 1997 and 1998, I lived and conducted research in Hussein Camp, Amman, and the surrounding neighbourhoods in which Palestinian refugees currently reside. Given the timing of the fieldwork, it should be understood that I do not here consider the effects of the second Palestinian uprising or *Intifada* (started in September 2000) upon the ideas of children in Hussein Camp. Furthermore, it is important to bear in mind that whilst there are undoubtedly significant commonalities of background and outlook between the Palestinian refugee population in Jordan and that in the Occupied Palestinian Territories, after several decades of separation there are also important differences. Thus, for example, the children who assisted me with my research did not share with their peers in the West Bank and Gaza Strip the experience of wide-scale political violence.

Hussein Camp is one of ten established in Jordan in order to house Palestinians who fled their homes during the Arab–Israeli Wars in 1948 and 1967 (Finkelstein 1995; Masalha 1992, 1995; Morris 1987). At the time of research it was home to around 50,000 people, the majority of whom were refugees of 1948 and their descendants. Therefore, the young people with whom I worked were mostly 'third generation refugees' according to local definition: in other words the grandchildren of people originally dispossessed.

The Palestinians in the West Bank, Gaza, Lebanon, Syria and Jordan are unusual as a refugee population in that their principal support comes not from UNHCR but rather from the United Nations Relief and Works Agency (UNRWA). This agency was created in 1949 by mandate of the UN General Assembly for the specific purpose of assisting refugees and internally displaced persons from Palestine. Funded directly by governments, notably those of the U.S., Europe and Japan, UNRWA established the camps in Jordan. At present, its main services cover the areas of healthcare (through clinics and mother and child health units); women's activity centres; and the provision of emergency assistance to those of its clients deemed to be 'Special Hardship Cases'.

The largest share of UNRWA's budget (currently in excess of 50 percent of the annual total), however, is devoted to educational provision (Schiff

1995: 51) which includes ten grades of primary and secondary level schooling as well as kindergartens, colleges and vocational training centres. The avowedly 'humanitarian, non-political' stance adopted by UNRWA's top officials has important implications for the manner in which Palestinian refugee children are conceptualised by this organisation, an issue which I discuss below.

In fieldwork I particularly focused my research on children from 9 to 13 years of age, and boys and young men from 13 into their early twenties. Residence in Hussein Camp enabled me to become a neighbour, teacher, host and guest to at least one hundred children and young people. Most importantly, it made it possible for me to interact with them in a variety of physical and social settings and, in this way, witness a wide range of responses. Such long-term participant observation provided the framework for the employment of direct research methods, including drawing activities, role play, group discussions and photographic projects. I also spent a great deal of time with adolescent males over the age of 13, mostly chatting casually in the setting of our neighbourhood of the camp and in the local youth club. Regrettably, it was much harder for me to interact in this manner with their teenage sisters, due to local concerns about social contact between young women and unrelated men. It should, therefore, be clear that my observations about 'young people' refer particularly to males aged 9 upwards and females from 9 to 13 only.

In addition to this work with the young, I also conducted numerous interviews with parents, teachers, youth workers, UNRWA officials, religious figures and legal experts. These considerably enriched my understanding of the social and historical context in which the daily lives of young people were conducted.

By engaging with the young through these different methods and in a wide range of everyday settings, their complex relationship to processes of social change gradually became more apparent. In particular, I came to understand that any attempt on my part to create a simple coherence from the views which they expressed would be highly artificial. Whereas agencies, political leaders, journalists and even some parents and grandparents, may have wished to present a singular and uniform account of young Palestinian refugees' views, values and identities, the reality struck me as far more complex and contingent.

The Constraints of Humanitarianism

In situations of conflict and displacement, humanitarian agencies often play a vital role in supporting the efforts to provide basic services to civilian populations. In the case of UNRWA, its role in the lives of children is especially far-reaching since, as already mentioned, it has responsibility for the provision of schooling until grade ten. Despite enormous involvement with registered refugee children in this way, there is little actual engagement with them in the effort to learn about their own priorities, experiences and aspirations.

I would suggest that, in part, this lack of interest relates to their categorisation as refugees. As Liisa Malkki (1997: 224) has pointed out, both the practices and current ideology of humanitarian intervention function effectively to denude refugees of their history: 'to depoliticise the refugee category and to construct in that depoliticised space an ahistorical, universal humanitarian subject' (cf. Zetter 1991: 47). This is the consequence of a humanitarianism which, its executors maintain, can and should be kept distinct from issues of politics. Clearly refugees of all age groups are potentially liable to this process of dehistoricisation. However, I believe that this is particularly pronounced in the case of children, not least because of popular assumptions about the universality of childhood itself: a period of human life in which, it is commonly held, human beings have yet to acquire any meaningful history (Prout and James 1997: 7).

In the case of UNRWA, such dehistoricisation is manifest in their representation of Palestinian refugee children. *Palestine Refugees Today* is a thrice-annual glossy magazine in English and French produced by this organisation for public relations purposes, and is full of photographs from its own archives. My survey of back issues of the journal revealed a vastly disproportionate use of images of the young. In the period from 1968 to 1996, for example, around two-thirds of the issues had cover photos of children. In these shots we see pre-teenagers being fed, being given medical checks and treatment and, most commonly, at school. In the majority of pictures they are either represented as individual cases of need or else as an undifferentiated mass of humanity, often attired in uniform clothing.

In contrast to this abundance of images, accounts of young people's lives are, for the most part, narrowly restricted to their function as passive beneficiaries of UNRWA's assistance. We learn of their gratitude for the education, healthcare and food that they have received, while the difficulties of their lives are alluded to in vague terms. Frequent assurance is given that UNRWA's aid is making an important difference to their lives. For example, one issue informs us that 'for some 307,000 children, UNRWA means the chance of a brighter future' (1978: 2).

Towards the end of my fieldwork I invited a number of young residents of Hussein Camp to produce their own photographic images. Either as individuals or in small groups they were given a disposable camera and instructions to create a set of pictures which they felt conveyed important aspects of their daily lives and their values. I also asked the photographers to record in a notebook where, when and why they took each shot.

The images that the children produced in this project clearly demonstrated a dynamic relationship to their immediate social environment as well as to the wider economic, political and historical context. In the first place, they expressed the children's strong sense of belonging to social networks. Members of the neighbourhood community (*al-haara*) and of the camp (*al-mukhayyam*) were frequently represented along with photographs of kin. The bond between the children and others within these different, localised networks was explained by reference not only to emotional attachment but also to a common origin and history, and a shared experience of struggle as refugees. For example, one 11-year-old, Ahmed, included a photograph of his uncle who, in his words, 'taught me all about Palestine'. Nine-year-old Mounir chose to photograph a neighbour who had lost a hand due to an industrial accident. He told me that he had been eager to take this man's photograph in order to demonstrate 'the difficulties a man from the camp faces in earning money for his family'. Other images included a depiction of friends selling small items on the street, and one of a group of boys attempting to play football on a narrow and stony piece of ground by a busy road. The choice of such subjects was generally explained by reference to the particular struggles of being a Palestinian refugee in Jordan.

Thirteen-year-old Qusay produced several images – including the women's dress shop, the grocery store and the mosque – because they each, in different ways, suggested something to him about Islam. Above all else, he wanted people viewing his collection of photographs to understand that he was proud to be a Muslim.

The photographs produced by these children stand in stark contrast to the images contained in UNRWA's publication. They indicate the gulf that exists between the stereotypical perception of refugee children as passive cases of need and the self-perception of at least some of these children that they are social and economic actors as well as members of communities defined by history, politics and religious faith.

Despite the claims of UNRWA of political neutrality as a humanitarian agency, ignoring or overlooking the communal dimensions of children's lives is itself of profound political, and ultimately practical, significance. The idea that UNRWA can create 'a brighter future' for Palestinian refugee children without acknowledging both their engagement with the past and their interaction with circumstances in the present appears at best naive. A less charitable interpretation, suggested by many refugees themselves, is that UNRWA is merely a means for containing and ultimately redirecting the aspirations of young Palestinians away from the notion of return (in any form) and towards a future as skilled migrant workers, dispersed throughout the Middle East region and beyond.

The fact that Israel's greatest ally, the United States, is also the biggest single contributor to UNRWA's budget is often cited as evidence of this underlying intention. Certainly the role of the U.S. government suggests a glaring disparity in attitude towards Palestinian children in comparison with Jewish and Israeli children (cf. Stephens 1997). The former are treated, through UNRWA, as if history is of little relevance and the future is all that matters. In contrast, U.S. funding to the Israeli state ensures that Jewish children growing up in Israel and, potentially, anywhere else in the world are enabled to reside in the former territory of Palestine, with the explicit justification that it is their ancient homeland.

Political Necessities

The discourse of humanitarian intervention – as demonstrated by UNRWA – tends to overlook or implicitly negate the communal dimensions of Palestinian refugee children's lives, focusing instead on their uniform needs as individuals. In contrast, the dictates of Palestinian nationalism appear to demand an exclusive focus on these same children as members of a political community who share fully and completely in the nationalist struggle. This, in its way, is equally reductionist and, I would suggest, potentially inimical to children's own rights and interests.

In the history of the Palestinian national movement there has been a common tendency to vaunt the refugee camps as both symbols and centres of the struggle for return and nationhood. Political rhetoric contains numerous references to *sumud* (steadfastness) of which camp residents are depicted as the chief exponents. This view inevitably creates particular pressures on those living in camps – generally the poorest section of Palestinian society. For example, it renders those refugees who seek to improve their economic situation and leave the camps liable to stigmatisation as guilty of betrayal. I discern a similar pressure upon the young residents of refugee camps in the form of an assumption that they should consistently and solely express views which accord with the aims of the national movement. That is to say, there is no space allowed for the articulation of individual aspirations which diverge from those of the community as a whole. When children are invoked within the discourse of Palestinian nationalism it is generally to make a point about the nature of the struggle for return which is transmitted from generation to generation undimmed. The following quotation is illustrative of the kind of rhetoric employed:

> 'The future is for us,' says the camp, 'for the generations who have not forgotten the names of their villages and have remained tied to their soil, which is still waiting there in historical Palestine.' ... The camp knows the future, and it can read the message of the refugees' stones and the dreams of their children' (from Statement issued by Refugee Institutions and Popular Refugee Initiatives, Southern West Bank, Palestine Right-of-Return March. 16 September 2000).

In my discussion of the photographs taken by children I have already hinted at the sentiments expressed by the young which suggest their sense of membership in a (national) political community. Nevertheless, it is also important to acknowledge that their aspirations may not be confined solely to the aims of Palestinian nationalism. Children in Hussein Camp articulated aspirations that were both communal and individual, embracing a wide range of possibilities and demonstrating the influence of different sources of information and values.

Academic and Parental Assumptions

For the most part, researchers in the field of refugee studies have tended to share with humanitarian agencies and political leaders a lack of interest in the views expressed by refugee children. I would suggest that there are two main reasons for this. Firstly, there has been a tendency within this area of study to assume 'a universal refugee experience' which ignores the specificities and historicity of particular refugee communities (Stein 1981: 321; cf. Malkki 1995). Even where such a view does not prevail, it is possible that the lack of interest in young refugees is ascribable to abiding assumptions about socialisation. Although cogently disputed (James and Prout 1997; Mackay 1973; Toren 1996), the view that children come to take on the behaviour and ideas of adult society in a mechanical fashion appears entrenched (Toren 1996: 514). Accordingly, the ideas expressed by the young are rendered as inherently uninteresting, as, at best, incomplete statements of a society's values and ideals.

Of course, researchers are often not alone in assuming that children are incomplete repositories of extant (adult) views and consequently uninteresting. In my own fieldwork, this was certainly the belief expressed by most adult informants, including teachers and parents. I relate this, in part, to local assumptions about socialisation and the importance attached to mastery and precise replication of valued knowledge and behaviour in many areas of daily life. In the estimation of adults, there was little that the young could tell me that they themselves could not explain far better. The main purpose in talking to children, therefore, was to discover just how well they had absorbed certain prescribed facts, ideas and beliefs.

In these respects, the residents of Hussein Camp differed little from their non-refugee neighbours in Amman. However, I believe that, as refugees, my adult informants had a particular reason to stress reproduction of outlook amongst their offspring. This stems from the fact that hopes for return have become strongly and explicitly focused upon the youngest generation.

For many of the first and second generation refugees in Hussein Camp, the return to Palestine figured as a central aim of their lives. With the establishment of the Palestine Liberation Organisation in the 1960s this aim became the *raison d'être* of an organised struggle, requiring both military and political efforts. At the time of fieldwork, many refugees in their thirties and above spoke passionately to me about their wish to return to former homes and about their intention to maintain the struggle until this becomes a reality. People in this age category often described to me the youngest generation – their offspring and students – as the future redeemers of Palestine: they were *jeel al-awda* (generation of the return) and *jeel al-aqsa* (generation of al-Aqsa[1]). On innumerable occasions they assured me that the young shared their sentiments about Palestine and their *haniin* (longing) for return. To emphasise the point, parents and teachers sometimes requested children to tell me about 'their' village in Palestine: a request which generally elicited a familiar list of features ('the hills, the orange trees, the sea ...', and so on). This performance was apparently intended to impress upon me the unshakeable continuity of aspiration and feeling across the generations of refugees and, in this sense, accords with the aims and rhetoric of the nationalist movement described above.

Putting Identity in Context

My own research with children, away from parents and teachers, offered a more complex picture. On one hand, their acknowledgement of a significant relationship to Palestine was always in evidence. For example, even children as young as 7 or 8 would, without my prompt, ask one another *'min ayy balad inte?'* (from which town/village are you?).[2] However, it soon became clear that their ideas of belonging and their aspirations ranged far wider than adults generally suggested. In discussions about where they would like to live in the future, for example, only one third of the 100 or so 9 to 13-year-old boys and girls that I spoke with replied 'Palestine'. The remainder were roughly divided between those who imagined a life for themselves in Jordan and those who were attracted by the prospect of the United States or a Western European country. Amongst adolescent males ambitions to live in such places were expressed particularly often and with notable conviction.

The point I wish to emphasise here is that children and young people in Hussein Camp displayed a keen appreciation of the social context within which they were speaking. Statements about identity and aspirations differed depending on whether the speaker was alone or in a group; whether parents were present or not; and whether he or she was talking directly to me or in conversation with peers. The nature of ideas expressed also appeared to be influenced by wider events conveyed through the media. For example, violent incidents in the West Bank or Gaza were likely to elicit a certain mood amongst my young informants, clearly stimulating their identification with the communal struggle. At other, more peaceful times, such sentiments were less commonly expressed.

History and Social Change

In discussing the importance of context, my intention is to indicate that even children as young as seven or eight appeared able to articulate a range of responses in accordance with the particular circumstances in which they found themselves. This being the case, it is untenable to suggest that the identity of the young may be captured in a single 'truth'. On the other hand, this does not mean that all expressions of identity and aspiration are necessarily equally valid. Clearly some ideas are voiced more consistently than others and with greater emphasis and conviction. In distinguishing these we can begin to discern important differences between generations of refugees and, with that, the processes of social and historical change influencing and effected by children themselves.

Most significant to such processes of change, as evidenced in the ideas expressed by children, was the so-called 'Islamisation' of the society of the camp. This is a phenomenon noted in many countries in the Middle East, and of undeniable importance in Jordan and amongst refugee communities. At one level it was evident in the growing number of camp residents becoming observant of religious prescription. At another level, such Islamisation was apparent in the support for sociopolitical groupings espousing an ideology of pan-Islamism. Such groups generally championed Quranic education and the implementation of a highly conservative interpretation of religious injunction governing basic aspects of daily life.

The critical importance to children of their religion was expressed to me in various ways, not least through the pictures which many participants in the photographic project produced. Not only did photographs of the local mosque feature amongst most of the sets but the choice of other, apparently unrelated subjects, was explained by reference to some facet of Islamic teaching or history. For example, 13-year-old Qusay and his friends chose to photograph the local grocery store 'because the Prophet Mohammed, Praise be upon Him, was a merchant', while 12-year-old Samira included a picture of her school 'because this is where we learn about our religion'. Furthermore, when I asked some of the photographers to select the images by which they most wanted others to understand their lives, they generally chose those which alluded to the fact that they were Muslims.

Although the Islamisation of the society of Hussein Camp has involved residents of all ages, the engagement of the young was especially pronounced. At the time of fieldwork a growing number were attending the small centres of Quranic learning (*maraakiz haafez al-Qur'an*) dotted around the camp, most of which opened only in the last decade or so. The camp youth club, once a bastion for the activities of the various factions (*tanzimaat*) of the PLO, came under the effective control of refugees allied to the Islamist movement. In addition, a new, well-resourced Islamist youth centre opened just outside the camp, attracting large numbers of boys and girls from the camp and surrounding neighbourhoods.

Even children and adolescents who did not attend any of these institutions commonly professed strong interest in their religion and in Islamic history. In their neighbourhood groups, the ability to recite stories about the Prophet Mohammed and to guide the group's response to particular situations by quoting Islamic teachings were means to enhance personal status (Hart 1999). Conversely, children in the camp often deprecated others whom they considered lacking in respect for Islam: '*hum dayman bukfuru*' (they are always blaspheming) as one group of 7- to 9-year-old neighbours told me to explain their avoidance of children living a couple of streets away. In the estimation of some adolescents involved directly with the activities of Islamist groups, Palestine was lost because their grandparents were uneducated, particularly with respect to correct religious teaching.

Although many members of the second generation of refugees had become more observant in recent years (in some cases due to encouragement from their own children), they had generally not involved themselves with the Islamist movement as such, nor had they been greatly influenced by its ideology. In part this may be due to the fact that the Islamists tended to focus their efforts on grassroots educational and youth initiatives.

This difference between children and their parents and grandparents was also an undoubted consequence of divergent experiences of life in the camp as informed by wider historical events. For example, amongst the generation of parents were many who had been freedom fighters (*fedayeen*) and activists with the PLO. Although born in the camp, Palestine was made real to them by the stories of life there which were relayed to them in a consistent manner across a range of daily life settings. For this generation, Palestine was characterised as *ard jduudna* (land of our forefathers): an earthly paradise in which they had a birthright.

For the youngest generation, in contrast, Palestine was a more distant and abstract concept. Unlike their parents, they had generally not been regaled with stories of life in the pre-1948 towns and villages, nor of the exodus (Chatty and Hundt 2002). At the time of fieldwork the nationalist movement was a weak shadow of its former self, and the *fedayeen* no

longer heroes but sad reminders of a struggle which led to the unacceptable compromises of the Oslo Peace Process. Furthermore, the former
rural lifestyle of their grandparents did not commonly appeal to children
and adolescents growing up in a capital city and exposed to a wide array
of regional and global cultural products via satellite television, radio and
film.

At the same time, some of these young people directly encountered the
ideology of the Islamist movement within leisure, educational and religious activities. Here Palestine was characterised as *ard al-Muslimeen*
(land of the Muslims): a land that belongs to all Muslims equally and the
site of an ongoing battle of transhistorical proportions between the errant
and treacherous Jews and those who uphold God's teachings correctly. In
the context of a society that had become both more observant of Islam and
more disillusioned with 'secular' politics and diplomacy, such views
appeared not only to capture the imagination of those young people who
participated in the centres run by Islamists, but also to spread to the
majority of children who rarely, if ever, visited such centres.

To suggest that the young are particularly engaged with the activities
and ideology of the Islamist movement in Hussein Camp is, in itself, to
provide only a partial picture of the complexity of their lives and of the
distinctiveness of their generation from that of their parents and of their
grandparents. However, in their conceptualisation of Palestine itself, it
was possible to discern the influence of Islamist images intertwined with
those traditionally associated with nationalism (which were commonly
conveyed in the settings of home and neighbourhood). This is shown in
the following exchange which occurred in the context of a role-play exercise I conducted with a group of 12- to 13-year-old girls. The situation and
characters were chosen by the participants. In this discussion, 'Halima'
assumed the role of someone who had just arrived from Palestine. Using
a microphone and tape recorder, the others, as Jordanians, took it in turns
to interview her, thinking up questions as they went along. This is a section of their exchange:

Questioner: Before the Jews occupied Palestine did you live happily or in
           sadness?
Halima: We lived happily. The Jews came and brought misery to the
           country.

Q: Why did the Jews take our country?
H: Because it's beautiful and holy and it has Jerusalem. It's holy.

Q: Did you fight the Jews or not?
H: We fought them a lot but we had no chance.

Q: Who were greater in number? Them or you?
H: They were. That's why they conquered Palestine.

Q: What happened to the children in Palestine?
H: The young were killed. And the women and men too. The Jews had no mercy.

Q: The Jews took your houses?
H: They destroyed them and occupied Palestine. Destroyed all the houses.
Q: Why did they destroy the houses?
H: Vengeance.
Q: For what?
H: Because Palestine was beautiful, it was holy, it was all Muslim.

Q: Is there hope that you will return to Palestine or not?
H: I want to return to that country but the Jews occupy the land and I can't return. But there is hope.

Q: What did you like about Palestine?
H: It was all Muslim and our families were there. It had lots of orchards and ancient remains.

Q: Did people go to pray in Jerusalem?
H: A lot of people went to Jerusalem to pray.

Q: What other holy places are there besides Jerusalem?
H: The mosques.

Q: If you had to live somewhere other than Jordan or Palestine where would you like to live?
H: In Saudi Arabia.
Q: Why?
H: Because lots of people there go to pray. You can go on pilgrimage there.

This dialogue contains expressions that clearly fit with the notion of Palestine as both *ard jduudna* (land of our forefathers) as well as *ard al-muslimiin* (land of the Muslims). On one hand, there is interest in life in Palestine 'before the Jews', in family and in the physical attributes of the land. On the other, Halima shows immense appreciation of the holiness of Palestine: its Islamic character, the existence of Jerusalem, the fact that people prayed.

The exchange also indicates, I believe, the particular emphasis placed upon family by girls: as Halima states '[Palestine] was all Muslim and our families were there'. The importance of kin relations and the domestic sphere were expressed more often by girls than boys. In the photographic exercise, for example, the girls who participated tended to produce a far larger number of images of family members, close neighbours and the home setting than boys. This appears to be a consequence of the very different constraints on the movement of boys and girls within daily life. It may also be indicative of the different way in which boys and girls, in general, expressed their sense of identity. Amongst boys and young men

I detected a tendency to talk either in individualistic terms or in terms of an abstract community, whether it be the Palestinian nation or the community of believers. Amongst girls a less clear dichotomy was in evidence since the personal and the communal were strongly imbued with notions and sentiments of family.

My 12-year-old neighbour, Muna, offered an interesting example of this when she spoke with me about her ambitions for the future. An outgoing and very bright young woman she claimed that she wished to become an engineer when she grew up. As it transpired this wish partly arose from the fact that her maternal uncle, who had died fighting the Israelis before she was born, had followed that profession. Uncle Khaled had been her mother's favourite brother whom Muna referred to as a *shaheed* (martyr) for the cause of Palestine. As I understood it, the wish to follow in her uncle's professional footsteps represented a fusion of the personal, familial and communal that is indicative of the outlook commonly voiced by girls, in contrast to their brothers.

Media Consumption

In addition to discourses of national and religious community encountered in their immediate surroundings, young people were consumers of television programmes from around the world shown on both terrestrial and satellite channels. These programmes conveyed imagery of lifestyles and alternative realities and were a resource for the ideas and aspirations of the young residents of Hussein Camp. For example, during the time of my fieldwork the eponymous heroine of a Venezuelan soap opera, *Cassandra*, was a popular role model amongst many girls and young women. The dressmakers who supplied the clothes market in the camp endeavoured to keep abreast of the styles worn by Cassandra in order to meet the demand of their young female customers.

More poignantly, in several homes I sat with children and adolescents to watch programmes broadcast from Israel. These were presented by cheerful and attractive young hosts and showed a fashionable, carefree and affluent society. This was a far cry from the images of the 'treacherous' Jews depicted in the narratives of the Islamists, and the tales of Jewish soldiers' brutality described by the refugees from 1948. At times, several of the young men I knew in the camp expressed an ambition to visit Tel Aviv in order to take advantage of the opportunities for well-paid work and exciting leisure pursuits that they believed existed there. In the articulation of such wishes they appeared to make a conceptual separation between Israel as a modern place of opportunity in which they might reside, at least temporarily, and the land of Palestine which, at other times, they expressed a common determination to reclaim.

Amongst the few female contemporaries that I got to know well such aspirations were never articulated. It appeared that none held ambitions to leave their surroundings except in order to get married. Certainly, foreign travel was only discussed in relation to the possibility of marrying a cousin or other known person already living abroad – most commonly in a Western country or in the territories of the Palestinian Authority. I cannot assess, with confidence, whether the views expressed were tailored to the particular constraints of communication with an unrelated male or, as I suspect more likely, indicative of the constraints on the mobility of unmarried women in this society. Certainly, gender differences emerged even amongst preteenagers: boys were more likely to voice the desire to leave Jordan and the Arab world than girls.

Video games, pop music, action movies and American-style fast food also found great favour with the younger residents of Hussein Camp. In general, the attractiveness of such products fuelled interest about life beyond the Middle East, thereby complementing the stories of family members, friends and neighbours who have travelled or migrated to Europe, North America and Australasia.

In describing the engagement of young people in Hussein Camp with such consumer and media products, I am not suggesting that they focused their aspirations and sense of belonging solely around an amorphous notion of community based upon a globalised youth culture. Rather, I am indicating the need to acknowledge the wide array of sources of information and images that the young have access to, even within a refugee camp in a developing country like Jordan. The processes of conceptualising a relationship to the world around them were inevitably informed by such sources, together with the ideas and values presented directly to the young by family members, teachers, youth and religious leaders. In order to account for difference between generations in terms of values, aspirations and self-identity it is vital, I believe, to embrace this broader context of young people's lives, even amidst the precarious conditions created by conflict and dislocation.

One 13-year-old

Conducting research with 13-year-old Qusay made this point abundantly clear. My understanding of Qusay's views grew out of engagement with him in various settings and through his participation in several research activities. He was one of the photographers in the project described above and he also produced several drawings for me. Qusay joined in group discussions which I organised with a small number of his friends and we held numerous informal one-to-one dialogues over the fifteen-month period of our acquaintance.

At times Qusay expressed his identification with Palestine in passionate terms. In front of his father and for my benefit, he demonstrated his broad knowledge of that country's history and geography. He also displayed the greatest awareness of Palestinian folklore of all the boys and adolescents I met. Like the overwhelming majority of his peers, he was a stout supporter of the *Wihdat* football team in the national league for the two reasons commonly given, namely that it was 'the best' and it was 'Palestinian' (Hart 1999).

In seeming contradiction to such identification, however, he once made the following remark: 'Look, Palestine is the country of my forefathers and my father but I was born here, I eat and drink from Jordan and I am clothed from here. So it is my country and I must support it.' This occurred in the setting of a group discussion with around eight or so of his peers and, despite their objections, Qusay remained adamant in his endorsement of Jordan.

The photographs which he produced for my project suggested a further important dimension of Qusay's sense of belonging. As I have already described, many of his subjects were chosen due to a connection which he had made with Islam.

On several occasions Qusay also demonstrated an interest in Western pop culture.[3] He told me that he was a great fan of Michael Jackson and that he secretly watched his videos and listened to his tapes when his father was not around. On a daytrip out of town, Qusay sported a stars-and-stripes bandanna, cutoff shorts and sunglasses: an unusual look in the setting of the camp and one that he modelled on performers, such as Bryan Adams, whom he sometimes saw on television. He was keen for me to take his photograph dressed in this fashion, and when I later handed him the developed picture he took care to hide it from his father.

That Qusay should, in different settings, express identification as a Palestinian, as a Jordanian and as a Muslim, and that he voiced his appreciation for Western pop culture did not surprise me greatly. However, I was taken aback when he first spoke of his concerns about the environment. In response to my question about his aspirations for the future, Qusay told me: 'I don't know. In any case, it's pointless to think about the future since there isn't going to be any future. There will be no more water in Jordan because the Jews are going to take all the water from the River Jordan and the air will become unbreathable.'

When I asked him how he knew all of this he answered simply '*mbayyin*' (it's obvious). On a later occasion, however, he told me that even Bill Clinton, on a visit to Jordan, refused to drink the water because he knew, quite rightly, that it was dirty. For Qusay, this was clear validation of his beliefs.

I am not suggesting that Qusay's views are necessarily representative of young people of his age in Hussein Camp, although I did encounter the range of ideas which he expressed from different children and adolescents at various times during the course of fieldwork. My point in discussing Qusay's responses is to demonstrate the range of concerns, interests and values that one young refugee may express. As should be clear, these include, but are not confined to, the issue of Palestine and the situation of life in a refugee camp. Qusay clearly demonstrated a strong identification with the land from which his grandparents had been exiled and with the Palestinian national community. This identification diverged from that of his father, not least because his environment and experiences growing up in Amman at the end of the twentieth century inevitably differed from those of his father at the same age.

Conclusion

Whatever the particularities of the Palestinian case, the fact that they have been a refugee population for several decades makes them far from unique. In many other parts of the world, including East Africa, South and South-east Asia, there are new generations being born into settings created as a direct consequence of displacement and exile. I argue that the consideration of generational difference, changing values and identities amongst children in such situations merits widespread attention. Despite a few notable examples, which relate to refugee children whose families have settled in industrialised countries, this topic has attracted little attention.[4] However, it is my certain contention that sustained research with the young will bring to light issues of generational difference which have important practical, theoretical and moral implications.

In her discussion of the 'cultural-identity formation' of British-Sikh teenagers in Leeds, Kathleen Hall (1995) has alerted us to the problem inherent in the UN Convention on the Rights of the Child in its assertion of a child's right 'to his or her own cultural identity' (CRC Article 29, section 1, paragraph c). Such a statement clearly begs questions about who determines a child's cultural identity and according to what principles. There is a suggestion here of fixity and determinacy which appears to take little account of young people's role in the ongoing reworking of their own identities and values. Quoting Veena Das (1992: 20; quoted in Hall 1995: 244), the author argues that it should be the right of children to 'cultural innovation, play with other identities' which is protected. The approach suggested by the CRC, in contrast, all too easily lends itself to 'cultural authoritarianism' (Das 1992), by which attempts are made to constrain the young within reified value systems.

For children growing up in a refugee camp anywhere in the world, the possibility to challenge and step outside the values of the society, to develop values and aspirations that do not accord with those of older generations, is likely to be limited. Nevertheless, I argue that it is the inherent right of each child and every generation to engage creatively with the world in this way. The view that children are not simply the passive recipients of culture but actors and participants in society implies the necessity that we allow the space, conceptually and practically, for the young to make choices that may not fit with our own aspirations or beliefs.

In a situation of conflict and displacement, which inevitably is fraught with enormous political complexity, it may be especially hard to allow such space. In this situation the young, more than ever, are required to serve as vehicles for the hopes and ambitions of their elders. Thus, for example, while it may be perfectly acceptable for an English or French child – inspired by images from television or the cinema – to express the desire to live in America one day, in my experience political activists and those who wish to stand in solidarity with the Palestinian people tend to balk at the idea of a child in a refugee camp (who views the same images) sharing this wish.

At the same time, I have also suggested that children in Hussein Camp are not isolated from the aspirations of their community. As social actors they are inescapably and dynamically connected to the history of that community, including the history of struggle. The challenge for humanitarian agencies, in particular, is to embrace this point meaningfully in their programming and advocacy work while attending to the immediate needs of the young for education, healthcare and leisure activities.

To argue that all children are, and should be seen as, both individuals with a right to their own personal views and aspirations, and active participants in the families and communities in which they live, challenges the traditional division between political solidarity and humanitarian assistance. I would assert that to promote fully the best interests of the young living in a situation of conflict and displacement, we have to move beyond this dichotomy and engage with the complex processes of identity construction in which actual children engage.

Notes

1. This expression refers to the mosque of al-Aqsa in Jerusalem, the third holiest site in Islam. The youngest generation are vaunted as the redeemers of this mosque (and, by extension, the whole of Palestine) from Israeli control.
2. When introducing themselves to one another, children generally alluded to the village or town in pre-1948 Palestine from which their father's family came. As Joseph Massad (1995: 472) has explained, a child's relationship to Palestine, both as a place and as a national community, is figured through the patriline.

3. To be precise, young people in Hussein Camp do not generally refer to pop music as Western but rather as ajnabiyy (foreign), in contrast to arabiyy (Arabic). Most of those I knew, especially the boys and young men, expressed appreciation of both.

4. My own literature search has led me to two fairly recent articles about young refugees which explore the issues that I allude to here. John Knudsen (1995: 28), in his discussion of Vietnamese refugees in Norway, considered the young people with whom he conducted research to be 'like bricoleurs, trying to integrate the new with the old ... They simply resist being victims of culture – whether Vietnamese or Norwegian'. In a similar vein, Linda Camino (1994: 30) wrote of the adolescent Latin American refugees whom she met at a drop-in centre in a large U.S. city as follows: '... this population of youth developed new collective ethnic identities that presented themselves rather systematically depending not only on the young person's sense of homeland, but also in response to present contexts and situations'.

References

Archard, D. 1990. *Children: Rights and Childhood*. London: Routledge.

Anderson, M. 1999. *Do No Harm: How Aid Can Support Peace – or War*. London: Lynne Rienner.

Boyden, J. 1997. 'Childhood and the Policy Makers: A Comparative Perspective on the Globalisation of Childhood.' In A. James and A. Prout, eds, *Constructing and Reconstructing Childhood: Contemporary Issues in the Sociological Study of Childhood*. 2nd edn. Basingstoke: The Falmer Press.

Cairns, E. 1996. *Children and Political Violence*. Oxford: Blackwell.

Camino, L. 1994. 'Refugee Adolescents and Their Changing Identities.' In . L. Camino, ed., *Reconstructing Lives, Recapturing Meaning: Refugee Identity, Gender and Culture Change*. Washington DC: Gordon and Breach.

Capozza, D. and Brown, R. 2000. 'Introduction.' In D. Capozza and R. Brown, eds, *Social Identity Processes*. London: Sage.

Chatty, D. and Hundt, G. eds. 2002. *Children and Adolescents in Palestinian Households: Living with the Effects of Prolonged Conflict and Forced Migration – A Regional Study*. Oxford: Refugee Studies Centre.

Das, V. 1992. 'Ironic Negation and Satire: Children's Talk on Politics.' Paper presented at the conference 'Children at Risk'. Bergen, Norway.

Finkelstein, N. 1995. *Image and Reality of the Israel–Palestine Conflict*. London: Verso.

Hall, K. 1995. 'There's a Time to Act English and a Time to Act Indian: The Politics of Identity among British-Sikh Teenagers.' In S. Stephens, ed., *Children and the Politics of Culture*. Princeton: Princeton University Press.

Hart, J. 1999. '*Growing Up Mukhayyamji*: Boyhood in Hussein Camp, Amman.' Paper given at conference The Uncertain State of Palestine: Futures of Research, University of Chicago.

Jenks, C. 1996. *Childhood*. London: Routledge.

Knudsen, J. 1995. 'When Trust is on Trial.' In V. Daniels and J. Knudsen, eds, *Mistrusting Refugees*. London: University of California Press.

Mackay, R. 1973. 'Conceptions of Children and Models of Socialisation.' In H.P. Dreitzel, ed., *Childhood and Socialisation*. London: Collier-Macmillan.

Malkki, L. 1995. 'Refugees and Exile: from "Refugee Studies" to the National Order of Things.' *Annual Review of Anthropology* 24: 495–523.

——. 1997. 'Speechless Emissaries: Refugees, Humanitarianism and

Dehistoricisation.' In K. Fog Olwig and K. Hastrup, eds, *Siting Culture*. London: Routledge.

Masalha, N. 1992. *Expulsion of the Palestinians: The Concept of 'Transfer' in Zionist Political Thought 1882–1948*. Washington: Institute of Palestine Studies.

——. 1995. *A Land Without a People: Israel, Transfer and the Palestinians 1949–96*. London: Faber and Faber.

Massad, J. 1995. 'Conceiving the Masculine: Gender and Palestinian Nationalism.' *Middle East Journal* 49 (3): 467–83.

Morris, B. 1987. *The Birth of the Palestinian Refugee Problem*. Cambridge: Cambridge University Press.

Prout, A. and James, A. 1997. 'A New Paradigm for the Sociology of Childhood? Provenance, Promise and Problems.' In A. James and A. Prout, eds, *Constructing and Reconstructing Childhood: Contemporary Issues in the Sociological Study of Childhood*.

Schiff, B. 1995. *Refugees Unto the Third Generation: UN Aid to Palestinians*. Syracuse: Syracuse University Press.

Stein, B.N. 1981. 'The Refugee Experience: Defining the Parameters of a Field of Study.' *International Migration Review*: 320–30.

Stephens, S. 1997. 'Nationalism, Nuclear Policy and Children in Cold War America.' *Childhood* 4 (1): 5–17.

Tajfel, H. 1978. *Differentiation Between Groups: Studies in the Social Psychology of Intergroup Relations*. London: Academic Press.

——. 1981. *Human Groups and Social Categories*. Cambridge: Cambridge University Press.

Toren, C. 1996. 'Socialisation.' In A. Barnard and J. Spencer, eds, *Encyclopaedia of Social and Cultural Anthropology*. London: Routledge.

Woodhead, M. 1997. 'Psychology and the Cultural Construction of Children's Needs,' In A. James and A. Prout, eds, *Constructing and Reconstructing Childhood: Contemporary Issues in the Sociological Study of Childhood*.

Zetter, R. 1991. 'Labelling Refugees: Forming and Transforming a Bureaucratic Identity.' *Journal of Refugee Studies* 4 (1): 39–62.

Part V

Research Methodology
and Methods

10

Researching Young People's Experiences of War: Participatory Methods and the Trauma Discourse in Angola

Carola Eyber and Alastair Ager

Introduction

Young people's experiences of armed conflict and displacement have formed a focus of research within the discipline of psychology for many decades. Psychologists and psychiatrists have conventionally studied the effects that these experiences have on children's emotional wellbeing, as well as the factors that mediate these effects: for example, the presence of a caregiver, or the age and personality of the child. A dominant trend in such research has been to take vulnerability rather than resilience as a starting point, based on assumptions about the difficulties which children and young people have in coping with the distressing experiences of armed conflict (Cairns 1996). Such assumptions are derived from popular conceptualisations of childhood in the West, where children are frequently regarded as vulnerable, passive beings who need to be protected and cared for, rather than as active members of their communities (Hwang et al. 1996).

A second factor which has contributed to the portrayal of children and young people as victims is the rise of trauma discourse in the West over recent decades. This discourse is based on the notion that adverse experiences which actually or potentially involve death or injury, may lead to negative, long-term psychological consequences for those exposed to such incidents. The concept of post-traumatic stress disorder (PTSD), which was developed during and after the Vietnam War when relatively large numbers of returning soldiers reported a range of psychological problems and symptoms, is now frequently used in connection with understanding the impact of war on individuals and communities (Young 1995). PTSD was officially recognised as a psychiatric diagnosis in 1980 when it was included in the Diagnostic and Statistical Manual of Mental Disorders (DSM) III, the formal classification system of the American Psychiatric Association. Since then the word 'trauma' has become part of everyday vocabulary in many Western countries, 'invading the social and cultural arena through television, commercial movies and even talk shows' (Nashat 2001). The media have reported the events of 11 September 2001 in New York and Washington, for instance, by making frequent use of the psychological vocabulary of trauma discourse.

Many psychological professionals have used a trauma framework to understand the experiences of war in different countries around the world. This approach has come under increasing criticism over the past few years, with scholars pointing out that the concept of trauma originated within a specific (American) cultural setting, and does not translate into other social, cultural and political contexts (Bracken and Petty 1998; Summerfield 2001). Proponents of PTSD have largely ignored the role that culture plays in issues of distress and mental health, interpreting people's suffering by means of predetermined psychiatric categories and symptom checklists, instead of starting from people's own perceptions and the meaning they attach to events. At times Western models of trauma may be in direct opposition to local understandings of distress or local cosmologies, norms and values (Wessells 1999). The trauma discourse continues, however, to dominate many of the discussions and practices of mental health professionals and researchers who investigate and seek to provide assistance to war-affected children.

The Study: Three Methods Used

The study on which this chapter is based was undertaken by the first author amongst war-displaced communities in the south-eastern province of Huila in Angola during an eight-month period in the year 2000. The youths who participated in the study were between the ages of 13 and 19. The main aim was to give voice to young people themselves by involving them as primary informants on their lives, exploring their perspectives on the experiences of armed conflict and displacement, and focusing on the ways in which they cope with these experiences. Rather than viewing young people as passive victims, the assumption guiding this research was that they are active agents who contribute to, transform and influence the situation and environments in which they find themselves. The main research approach used to achieve this was ethnographic and included observation, focus group discussions, semistructured interviews and informal conversation.

The study was conducted in two settings: in the town of Lubango and in the centres for the internally displaced in the east of Huila province. Initial entry into the communities in Lubango was facilitated through a non-governmental organisation (NGO) engaged in youth activities, whose local staff members had good knowledge of the area and extensive contact with community members. The first group of young people with whom a relationship was established consisted of girls and boys who participated in the youth activities of the NGO and who were involved in sports, drama and discussion meetings. Gradually a core group evolved with fourteen to sixteen members with whom the first author had more in-depth conversations, spending time with them in the public spaces where young people in the community met, for instance at the river, at the markets and near sports fields. Through this group it was possible to meet other youths who did not participate in the NGO activities, thereby broadening the study to include young people who, for example, were engaged in full-time income generation at the markets, and those living on the streets of Lubango.

In the centres for the internally displaced, initial contact with young people was made through general ethnographic work in the community which focused, amongst other issues, on their approaches to coping with distress and illness. From this, more in-depth relationships developed with a number of young people, predominantly boys, who also served as facilitators of further contacts with other youths.

In both situations establishing an initial relationship with the young people was relatively easy, as they were interested in outsiders and saw the researcher as a source of information about a variety of topics, including politics and popular youth culture. Angolan society is frequently characterised as being open and informal, with Angolans readily engaging with foreigners and including them in their social networks (Matloff 1996).[1] Building confidence and trust with the youths was, however, a far more challenging process. The researcher is a white woman from a country (South Africa) which had waged war with Angola in the not so distant past, and many respondents, both young and old, asked questions regarding her political convictions and personal view of these events. These questions not only provided opportunity for reflexivity[2] on the part of the researcher, but also often led to further discussion of what had brought her to Angola. The youths were also initially hesitant to discuss specific aspects of their lives, for instance certain cultural beliefs about witchcraft, and certain activities that adults in their communities viewed as negative, such as smoking cannabis or stealing. By giving examples of cultural traditions and what young people in the researcher's home country do, such barriers were broken down slowly, leading to a level of trust being established. While it is, of course, clear that the youths did not share all their concerns and thoughts with the researcher, it was possible to gain insight into many aspects of their lives and to discuss with them some of the observations made during this process.

The second methodology used was participatory rapid appraisal (PRA). There were two main reasons for this. Firstly, it yielded relevant information about aspects of the lives of the youths that would have been more difficult to obtain through other methods, or that would have taken a far greater amount of time and resources to ascertain. An example of this is the range of illnesses the young people suffer from and the health care options that they use. Secondly, PRA allowed the respondents to conduct their own research into issues that affect them, thus providing opportunities for their participation and for the development of certain skills. PRA facilitates discussion of issues and the development of ideas amongst both participants and researchers.

A small number of youths were trained to facilitate the investigation of a range of topics such as health, education, work and leisure activities, their communities, and their views on the future and on life as a displaced person. Each facilitator then conducted some of these participatory activities with groups of other displaced youth and general meetings were held afterwards where they could report back on the process, discussions and results. Examples of the activities are:

1. *Issues Matrix*: This is a table which captures in summary form the issues of concern to participants, allowing for a differentiation between different subgroups within a community (Mukasa and Mugisha 1999). The youths, for instance, identified groups such as boys and girls, local people and *deslocados* (displaced), workers and students, and indicated how severely affected each of the groups were by a specific problem.
2. *Health Curative Matrix*: The matrix provides information about the most common physical and mental illnesses that the youths suffer from as well as the treatment options available in their communities, such as the clinic, the hospital, the *curandeiro* (traditional healer), the *adivinhador* (diviner) and home remedies. This provided insight into common perceptions about the effectiveness of health care options and raised issues about access, effectiveness and the differences between explanatory models (de Koning and Martin 1996).
3. *Body Maps*: Each participant drew a person on a piece of paper and then marked on the drawing all the illnesses they had personally had over the last two years, as well as where they went for treatment for each illness. During the report-back sessions the body maps were also used to discuss general effects of the war on people's health, where the youths marked all the illnesses that could result from violent conflict and displacement (Institute for Development Studies 1996).

4. *Spider diagrams* on war and displacement: In groups the youths discussed the various consequences of war and displacement for themselves and for their communities, filling in spider diagrams about issues related to health, survival, emotions and education, amongst others.
5. *Radio programmes* about their experiences of displacement: The youths designed short radio programmes about how young people are affected by war and displacement. They used tape-recorded interviews, drama, songs and speeches to convey their experiences and thoughts.

A further aim of the research was to investigate how young people's experiences are conceptualised and understood from within a trauma perspective in order to see what contributions this makes to understanding and gaining insight into pertinent issues. This was done by using a PTSD scale with a group of youths, measuring the numbers of symptoms of trauma they reported, and assessing whether they would qualify for a diagnosis on the basis of symptoms reported. The scale, called the EARAT (*Escala de avaliação da reposta ao acontecimento traumatico, versão adolescentes*), was employed with 102 youths. The EARAT was developed by McIntyre and Ventura (1996) in Portuguese and is based on Saigh's (1987) Children's PTSD Inventory (for details see Ventura 1997). The main section of this scale consists of seventeen questions that cover the three categories of symptoms of PTSD that are provided in the American Psychiatric Association's manual DSM-IV.

1. Reliving of the experience (for example, having nightmares about the traumatic event).
2. Avoiding reminders of the traumatic experience (for example, trying to avoid thinking about it), and a numbing of responsiveness (for example, being unable to think about the future).
3. Increased arousal (for example, having problems concentrating).

The EARAT is a structured diagnostic questionnaire and the questions are framed in terms of a yes–no dichotomy, establishing either the presence or the absence of a symptom.

This chapter reports on some of the findings of the three different methodologies used – the PTSD scale, observation and PRA – and reflects on the insights gained from these varying perspectives. First, the historical and political context within which this study took place is given by briefly outlining the history of the conflict in Angola. This is followed by a discussion of the concept of youth and the changing relationships between adults and young people in Angola, as this forms part of the context within which the research needs to be understood. Some of the findings of the different research approaches are then presented: namely the perspectives of young Angolans on the war and displacement as obtained through observation and the PRA exercises; and the results of the PTSD scale employed with the youths. The chapter concludes with some reflections on the contributions made by the various research methodologies.

Definitions and Contexts: War, the *Deslocados* and Youth

The Angolan War(s)

Angolans refer to specific periods of the almost forty years of continuous war in their country in terms of numbers.[3] The First War was the War of Independence which began in 1961 and was fought against the Portuguese colonialists. In the 1950s and 1960s, African national feeling led to the formation of three political groups which fought for independence: the Popular Movement for the Liberation of Angola (MPLA), formed by Agostinho Neto in 1956; the Frente Nacional de Libertação de Angola (National Front for the Liberation of Angola, FNLA), established by Holden Roberto in 1962; and UNITA, founded by Jonas Savimbi in 1966. Independence was achieved in 1975 and an agreement was signed by the three independence movements to form a transitional government.

However, ideological differences and mutual suspicion among the MPLA, UNITA (National Union for the Total Independence of Angola) and FLNA resulted in outbreaks of fighting between the movements in July 1975, and led to a breakdown of the transitional government. This initiated the Second War, also known as the Cold War, which was to last from 1975 until 1990. Various other countries which had ideological, political and material interests in Angola gave their support to the parties, with the Soviet Union and Cuba aiding the socialist-orientated MPLA, and South Africa and the U.S. assisting UNITA. Angola became a battleground in the world powers' fight for influence in southern Africa, bound up with the liberation struggles of its neighbours, such as Namibia, Zimbabwe and South Africa. The war was initially confined to the southeast, but UNITA tactics created insecurity in around 80 percent of the country, severely affecting the productive life and the socio-economic situation of the population. Negotiations involving South Africa, Cuba, the U.S., Portugal and the warring factions finally culminated in the signing of the Bicesse Peace Accord in 1991.

Elections were held in September 1992 with a turnout of 91 percent (CCR 2000). When UNITA lost these elections, Savimbi rejected the results as biased and manipulated, and returned to war with largely-intact troops. This marked the beginning of the Third War or the Election War, which lasted from October 1992 until November 1994. This war proved to be more destructive and all-encompassing than the first two wars, and became known for its systematic violations of the laws of war by both the government and UNITA (Human Rights Watch 1994). UNITA went on the offensive in provinces throughout the country. Indiscriminate bombings by the government, the laying of land mines and the entrapment of civilians in cities under prolonged siege resulted in extremely high losses of civilian lives (Tvedten 1997). The UN estimated that 1,000 people were dying every day in Angola during 1993, more than in any other conflict in the world (Human Rights Watch 1994). Tens of thousands of people were displaced from the countryside, fleeing to towns and cities where they lived in conditions of abject poverty, cut off from food supplies and from basic sanitary and hygiene provisions.

New peace talks began towards the end of 1993 and the signing of the Lusaka Protocol in November 1994 formally marked the end of the Third War. Almost from the start, UNITA failed to comply with the obligations of the Protocol such as demilitarisation and demobilisation of soldiers, and small scale conflict continued to flare up in various parts of the country, increasing to incidents of serious violations of the ceasefire in 1997 (CCR 2000). Throughout 1998 both the government and UNITA prepared for a new war, which broke out in December of that year. UNITA, which financed its military exploits through diamond revenues from its territories in the north and the east of the country, found itself increasingly isolated internationally, experiencing the effect of the UN sanction packages imposed on it. The MPLA government used the country's oil resources to fund its war efforts. The killing of Jonas Savimbi by government troops during a combat operation in February 2002, and the signing of a peace accord in April, have given renewed hope to achieving an end to the four decades of almost continuous conflict in the country.

The Situation of the Deslocados *(war displaced)*

The effects of this ongoing conflict on the civilian population have been severe. Death and injury result not only from direct combat but also from the estimated 10 million land mines planted throughout the country; and from non-existent or inadequate health services available to those affected by illness and disease. Angolan conditions fulfil most classical indicators of poverty and vulnerability, with a life expectancy at birth of only 45 years, and 320 out of 1,000 children dying before they reach the age of 5 (Norwegian Refugee Council (NRC) 2001). In 1999 UNICEF described Angola as 'the country whose children are at greatest risk of death, malnutrition, abuse and development failure' (Office for the Coordination of Humanitarian Affairs (OCHA) 2001), leading many organisations to conclude that Angola is 'the worst place in the world in which to be a child' (NRC 2001). Malnutrition rates amongst children are high: according to

government statistics 35 percent of the country's children are malnourished, with rates as high as 46 percent recorded for infants amongst the
war-displaced in provinces such as Bié (OCHA 2001). No aspect of life has
been left unaffected by the war: the infrastructure has been seriously damaged and public services in the area of education are minimal.

UNHCR considers approximately two million people to be internally
displaced in Angola as a consequence of the war (NCR 2001). *Deslocados*,
the Portuguese term used to refer to war-displaced people, usually follow
one of two settlement patterns: they may be settled in government-run
centres on a temporary or permanent basis, or they may become self-settled in nearby towns or cities. The research on which this chapter is based
was conducted in both situations in the province of Huila: amongst self-
settled *deslocados* in the town of Lubango and its surrounding areas, and
amongst government-settled *deslocados* in two IDP centres near Matala.
The latter group of *deslocados* originated from the municipality of Ndongo
in the north-east of Huila province, where they had been attacked in the
middle of August 1999 by UNITA forces. This resulted in a mass displacement of approximately 12,000 to 13,000 people who fled towards
Matala. Their condition upon arrival was extremely poor, as the flight had
been long and exhausting, and many people succumbed to illness and
malnutrition. People arrived with no or few possessions, being reliant on
external assistance for essential items such as blankets, kitchen utensils
and clothing.

Economic survival is a constant concern and high priority for both the
self-settled *deslocados* and those living in the centres. The *deslocados* do not
have access to farming land around the centres, and are thus deprived of
their previous methods of subsistence through agriculture and animal
husbandry. The monthly food provisions of the World Food Programme
(WFP) sustain families for approximately two weeks. Additional sources
of income are sought through a combination of kinship exchange, petty-
commodity production, collecting and selling firewood and preparing
food and drink. Women also work in the fields of local residents in
exchange for food, usually paid in the form of maize. Assets such as emergency items and food provided by aid agencies are routinely exchanged
or sold as part of the coping strategies of the population, and it is common
to see WFP sacks of maize meal in the marketplaces of surrounding villages after food distribution has taken place in an area (NRC 2001).
Despite these initiatives, people live in a state of acute poverty, unable to
cope with disruptions to their survival strategies through illness or other
events. Households headed by elderly widows seem especially vulnerable and fragile, with high rates of malnutrition and visible destitution
common among them (OCHA 2001).

Youth and Young People

Angola's age distribution is typical of many developing countries, with an estimated 45 percent under the age of 15 in 1993, and more than 50 percent under the age of 25 (OCHA 2001). Young people thus make up a considerable proportion of the general population, as well as of the displaced. In this section we briefly discuss the way in which young people are perceived in Angola and what role they are accorded in society.

Within the discipline of psychology, emphasis has often been placed on the notion of the universality of the processes of development and change that adolescents undergo, following theorists such as Anna Freud (Blos 1967) and Eric Erikson (1968). The central notion is that all youths undergo similar developmental stages, irrespective of the cultural, economic or social contexts within which they live (see for instance Noller and Callan 1991; Offer et al. 1988). This perspective has been criticised by social constructionists who argue that the categories of adolescence, youth and adulthood are social and cultural constructions of particular phases in the life course, rather than universal categories. All societies have ways of defining what constitutes adulthood and how one attains it, and these may be age-related or may be determined by physical, social and/or religious rites (La Fontaine 1986). The concept of adolescence is not present in all societies, for example, and often childhood and adulthood are the only two defining phases in the life cycle. A central argument of the social constructionist perspective is that young people cannot be considered in isolation from other social groups within communities and societies, and that social, cultural and political issues should be foregrounded, rather than biological or intrapsychic processes (Scheper-Hughes and Sargent 1998).

Amongst many ethnolinguistic groups in Angola the transition from childhood to adulthood is generally marked by initiation rites performed around the time of puberty (Mbiti 1989). These rites are of utmost importance in the communities as initiation is accompanied by a change of status for the youths and is essential in order to be considered a man (amongst some ethnic groups, for a girl to be considered a woman also) (Milheiros 1967). However, after the rites the initiate is still considered a *jovem* (youth) as opposed to an *adulto* (adult) for some time. The concepts of *juventude* (youth) and *jovens* (youths) are commonly held notions in Angola that are in some ways unrelated to definitions of adulthood. They include anyone who is no longer a child up to approximately 35 years of age, thus including young adults. Adogame (2001: 2) notes that in African societies the 'youth age range is usually wide and somewhat elastic', where the term 'youth' can indicate a particular position in society, for instance unmarried status, certain political views or specific lifestyles. Clear distinctions between a child and a youth, and between a youth and an adult are thus not necessarily easy to make in many social situations. In the research reported on here, participants ranged between the ages of thirteen and nineteen, and they are referred to as 'youths' rather than as adolescents in order to reflect Angolan use of terms more closely and to emphasise the social and cultural meanings attached to the concept.

In Angola a recurrent theme in adults' conversations about youth is the issue of the increasing 'unruliness' of young people who disregard the authority of the elders. This resonates with the age-old perception of youth as a problem (Griffin 1993). In many countries, both in the north and in the south, youths are represented and perceived as a threat. Adogame (2001) argues that in many modern African societies youth have been a source of constant criticism and protest against institutions and the social, economic and political boundaries of states and have been stigmatised as a consequence: 'Societies have a tendency to stigmatise those who represent such a threat to their symbolic orders. Thus, youth represent various forms of threat: new ideas, new ways of life, and independence of judgement. To identify and isolate the threat, societies place a kind of stigma on the person(s)' (Adogame 2001: 3).

In societies where there are large numbers of poor, jobless youths the ruling elite may have concerns and fear for economic and political control (see Richards 1996). Especially, young displaced people who migrate to cities instead of remaining in designated camp areas, are perceived as being a destabilising factor, contributing to crime and insecurity, despite evidence to the contrary (Sommers 2000). Angola is no exception to the phenomenon of young displaced migrants who crowd into urban areas where they are regarded by adults as a danger and a major factor in crime.

Young Angolans are critical of the way in which adults have handled the political and social problems of their country. Traditional ways of resolving problems are perceived by some youths as irrelevant, as they have not managed to halt the destruction and violence. This discord between old and young is reflected in a statement by a displaced elder from the province of Huambo: 'Our problem now is that we, *os mais velhos* [the elders] here, are also struggling with life ... The young people say that our traditions are outdated. But the reason why we don't manage to resolve our problems is because of the war' (CCF Report 2000).

The traditional relationships between adults and youths, which have been partially founded upon respect for the authority of the elders, are being seriously challenged by the radical shift resulting from the large-scale displacement and economic desperation of both youths and adults. In urban areas youths often become the main income generators in households through their involvement in the informal trading sector, and therefore become more powerful and influential in relation to the adult members of the households. In addition, some youths who return from war, where they have been expected to be strong and fearless, may experience difficulties in submitting to the traditional gerontocratic power structure.[4] Relationships with parents and other adults were at times characterised by conflict. The generally authoritarian parenting style of Angolans includes corporal punishment, especially of boys, and is deeply resented by many youths. They reported that they were often being judged unfairly by adults who tended to stereotype as *bandidos* (criminals, thieves, thugs) anyone who questions their authority.

Living as *Deslocados*: Perspectives of Young Angolans

Nordstrom (1997) notes that whereas adults tend to treat children as if they have no philosophies or feelings on the war themselves, often children do develop remarkable social commentaries on the situations in which they find themselves. In this section we present some of the youths' perspectives on life as *deslocados* and the concerns and worries they have, findings which were obtained through observation and the PRA activities.

The participants were two groups of young people: one group of *deslocados* in Lubango who were either living on their own or with relatives in the town, and another group living in the internally displaced persons (IDPs) centres in the rural areas in the east of the province, described above. The groups consisted of boys and girls with various experiences of war and displacement: some had been displaced five to eight years previously during the Second and Third Wars, and some had only fled recently. Amongst them were youths who had been forcibly recruited by UNITA soldiers and had managed to escape, while others had fled with family members and avoided capture. All had experienced the violence of war for extended periods, as described in the following statements about preflight life in a rural area of the province:

> People don't sleep inside the houses. Sometimes, at night, when you are sleeping in the huts you just hear other people screaming and you can't say or do anything. If they [UNITA soldiers attacking the village] hear your voice, they will take you and put you in the fire and kill you ... At times the troops from MPLA and UNITA meet and they fight. The troops don't always die – it is the people who die. At times when UNITA leave, they leave mines in the countryside. At times they hide nearby in the countryside. They wait until you go to fetch your maize from your fields. And when you go there they catch you and cut your throat. (Zacarias, aged 15, Lubango)
>
> In the villages we couldn't sleep well, because we had to think about the enemy, if they were coming or not. We always felt oppressed. They could have come during the day, in the morning or in the night. No one knows their hour. We only waited for them, the hour when they come. These are things that we thought about a lot: 'are they coming, today?' or 'could I die today?' (Beatriz, 16, IDP centre).

The lifestyles of the youths varied, depending on their economic, educational and personal circumstances. The majority were involved in some form of income-generating activity, with girls in the IDP camps often working on the farms of the local residents in exchange for food, and both sexes working as *negociantes* (traders) in the market places in Lubango, selling items such as cooking oil, cigarettes, soap, soft drinks or home-brewed alcoholic beverages. Girls in both settings were much more involved in performing household work, such as washing clothes, pounding maize, taking care of younger children, cooking and cleaning. Some youths attended school during the day or at night in addition to pursuing their other activities. Leisure time was predominantly spent in the company of friends, and involved 'hanging out' in certain spots in the neighbourhood, playing sports and games.

Unlike the stereotype of disenfranchised and angry young men hanging around the streets looking for trouble, the vast majority of male youths who participated in the study had relatively structured lives that involved juggling many different daily commitments. Most boys and girls engaged in a range of education, work and sports activities on a regular basis and with a sense of seriousness and responsibility for what they did. The research shows that the youths make decisions about their lifestyles and their futures, explore options, contribute to their families' livelihoods, develop their own opinions and perspectives and live multifaceted lives.

When the youths talked about their worries and difficulties and constructed spider diagrams they seldom mentioned the war directly as a problem or a concern, or distressing experiences such as the killings and attacks they have witnessed. The war was, however, an ever-present feature of their lives, much as it was for adults, and one which they saw as being not only the direct cause of their own displacement and misery, but also of general problems in the health and education sectors of society. The loss of home and possessions and the accompanying hardship was a frequent theme and one that was inevitably discussed. It signified, amongst other things, the loss of the protection of their families and parents and implied having to fend for themselves. Many of the youths lived lives of extreme hardship, and sometimes of neglect and abuse, on the streets of the town where they found themselves after displacement:

> I was only 12 years [when they killed my mother]. I was very sad and I was thinking how will I live. I am the oldest of the siblings and I need to take care of all of them ... Here I live with the sister of my father. ... If my mother had not died I would be living differently, I would be living well. (Ngongo, 15, Lubango)

The loss of home and possession also meant a change in status for the youths in terms of standard of living and lifestyle: 'When I lived with my father, he didn't let me do the kind of work I am doing here now. When I arrived here, I didn't manage to live like I did before. I have to do other things in order to get what I need' (Sousa, 17, Lubango).

Another major source of distress for the youths is unfulfilled burial obligations to members of the family killed during the conflict and left behind unburied. This finding echoes similar reports from Zimbabwe (Reynolds 1996) and Mozambique (Honwana 1997), where great importance is attached to showing respect to the deceased as well as to preventing trouble with the spirits in the future, caused by unfulfilled obligations to the dead. When the youths spoke about the killing and deaths of family members, they worried a great deal about whether or not the family had managed to perform the funeral for that person. A few youths spoke about the need for their family to perform these rites at some point in the future in order to pay respect to the dead person: 'When my brother died from a mine we didn't manage to do the funeral. We are not going to manage to do this because you need some money to do this. This is a problem' (Baptista, 14, IDP centre).

The youths also spoke about poor health and illness that result from worrying about their present situation and remembering their past lives. Body maps revealed that they made a strong connection between emotional wellbeing and physical health, as demonstrated in the following remarks by Ornelio:

> My health is not good because I think a lot. I am a *deslocado* without any family in Lubango. When I stay at home not doing anything, I think too much. Sometimes the others get up early to go to school or to work, some go to market, and I stay behind thinking a lot with nothing to do. Because of that my health is not good, because if I had some money or some work I wouldn't have these bad *pensamentos* [thoughts, memories]. It's these *pensamentos* that provoke one to steal or to look in the rubbish on the streets. (Ornelio, 16, Lubango)

A further pressing concern identified through the issue matrices was the lack of clothing and shoes. In Lubango local youths make fun of the *deslocados*, who are poor and wear old, torn clothing. Having appropriate clothing prevents one from being immediately identified as a *deslocado*, from being branded even more of an outsider, and helps facilitate integration into friendship groups. The youths also often outgrew their clothes quickly and were embarrassed about having to wear clothes that were too small for them. They no longer identified themselves as children, and part of representing this was by dressing in a way that they perceived reflected their new status; for instance, boys wanted to wear long trousers and everyone wanted to own a pair of shoes. The youths were also concerned about looking attractive in order to find a girlfriend or boyfriend. In Lubango this had much to do with fashion and what the trends from

Luanda, the capital, dictated. In the centres there was not much concern with issues of fashion, but looking good and wearing clean clothes was seen as an important factor in attracting the attention of a member of the opposite sex. The difficulty in obtaining soap to wash their clothes was a problem for the youths in the centres.

These issues were frequently occurring themes in their conversations, in interviews, focus groups and in the PRA exercises. There were many other issues which the youths talked about in relation to their lives and the difficulties they face, for example, the lack of educational opportunities, not having enough food and no variety in their nutrition, amongst others.

The Trauma Discourse and its Implications

Turning to the results of the EARAT PTSD scale, 71 percent of the young people who participated in the research had scores that suggested the presence of PTSD (see Eyber 2001 for more details). Questions that were answered with 'yes' by over 80 percent of the youths included items such as the following:

1. 'My body reacts with sweating, shaking or my heart beats faster when I have an experience similar to the traumatic event';
2. 'I feel nervous or strange when I see or hear something similar to the traumatic event or that makes me remember it';
3. 'at times I feel so sad and alone that I can't speak nor cry';
4. 'I have problems falling asleep or staying asleep'.

Within the trauma discourse the overall results of the EARAT scale would indicate that the youths were traumatised by their experiences to such a degree that it is likely that they may be suffering from a psychiatric disorder. How does this finding relate to the experiences of the youths reported above?

As noted earlier, the youths did not directly mention their experiences of violence, death and destruction as problems or concerns that currently worried them, nor did they mention their own emotional or physical reactions to these experiences as disturbing. Instead, they considered the actual situation in which they and their families found themselves to be the central issue that provoked worry and anxiety. The vast majority of youths reported that they still felt sad when they remembered their experiences of war and displacement but that they now felt fine or 'normal' because some time had passed since the attacks. They stated that although they did experience *pensamentos* (thoughts or memories of the war) and nightmares sometimes, these did not prevent them from doing things nor were they worried about experiencing them. The question of the usefulness of the PTSD diagnosis and the concept of traumatisation arises, as the majority of youths seemed able to adapt themselves effectively to living with their symptoms of 'trauma', without it impacting significantly on their lives.

The war thus affected the young people in ways which are different from those that trauma experts have identified as pertinent. For example, rather than being worried about having nightmares or memories of violent incidents, the youths (and their families) were primarily distressed about unfulfilled burial obligations to the dead. This issue does not feature on PTSD scales, and thereby a crucial cause of distress for the population is excluded from consideration. A further example is that according to the criteria for PTSD, the loss of home and possessions is not categorised as a 'traumatic event' as it does not involve 'actual or threatened death or serious injury, or a threat to the physical integrity to self or others' (DSM-IV 1994). Yet the youths consistently identified this as one of the most distressing aspects of their experiences. The importance of culture and context in understanding the experiences of war cannot be underestimated, issues which are frequently absent from the trauma discourse.

In order to diagnose someone with PTSD, 'impairment' of function or 'clinically significant distress' needs to be present: 'The disturbance causes clinically significant distress or impairment in social, occupational, or other important areas of functioning' (Criterion F for PTSD, DSM-IV 1994). This criterion of functionality is often ignored by researchers who employ a trauma discourse as more attention is paid to the number of symptoms present rather than on how these symptoms affect the daily lives of people. Frequently, assumptions are made about the impact of 'trauma' on people who are represented as passive and helpless victims unable to engage with the tasks of life without assistance. The youths in this study did not fit the stereotype of passive victims, as they were functioning well on social and occupational levels by maintaining active social lives with peers, engaging in community activities and involving themselves in income-generating tasks. They went about their lives, drew on a number of available resources in their communities and interpreted, adjusted to and changed the situations in which they found themselves. The exercises in which the young Angolans talked, drew and wrote at length about their perceptions, feelings, activities and hopes for the future, showed a reality that was far from being 'disordered'. The vast majority of the youths engaged actively on emotional, spiritual and intellectual levels with the situation in which they, their families and communities found themselves. They lived full, multidimensional lives that involved work and educational leisure activities as well as maintaining relationships within and outside of their household circles.

An example of functionality is the range of different coping strategies which the youths employed to deal with the difficulties they faced, including social and personal strategies, religious, traditional, political and economic ones (Eyber 2001). The trauma discourse does not give voice to the diverse ways in which war-affected people cope with the difficulties they face, as it is predominantly a discourse of victimhood. Summerfield (1999: 41) suggests that: 'A diagnosis of PTSD alone is poorly predictive of the capacity to pay the psychological costs of a war, to keep going despite hardship, nor a reliable indicator of a need for psychological treatment'. These assertions are not to deny that children and young people experience fear and suffering as a consequence of their experiences of armed conflict, or that there were some youths who were severely depressed and anxious as a result of their experiences. Some of these youths were described by members of the communities as extremely aggressive, others as withdrawn and suffering from too many *pensamentos*. These youths needed help, and various forms of treatment and assistance were available locally, for example, through traditional healing and religious ceremonies (Eyber 2001; Honwana 1998).

It is also important not to romanticise people's ability to cope with the consequences of war; important social and communal functions are disrupted, destroyed and transformed during violent conflict. While war-affected communities have resources on which they can draw, the reestablishment of communal structures such as meeting places and churches, and providing access to health care are, amongst others, vital forms of assistance. However, to pathologise the war-displaced as traumatised victims is incorrect as it ignores their abilities and efforts to rebuild their lives and their social worlds, as demonstrated in this chapter by the way in which the youths participated fully in social, communal and occupational activities. Labelling war-affected people as passive victims may also have a negative impact as international organisations may assume that they already know what is needed and attempt to provide assistance without taking the actual needs, priorities and coping strategies of the people themselves into account.

A further issue in relation to the trauma discourse is that it is focused predominantly on the past, that is, on distressing past events. As is clear from the concerns voiced by the youths, they were not predominantly concerned with the past but with their present lives and their prospects for the future. The trauma discourse often sees the traumatic incidents that occurred as central to children's lives, as if nothing else is happening in the child's life (Dawes and Cairns 1998). However, other factors and issues are causing the youths more distress, anxiety, worry and depression than the incidents of violence, including their means of survival, unfulfilled burial obligations and the lack of educational opportunity associated with successful future development. Attention should be focused on providing them and their families with assistance in these areas rather than on issues identified by professionals with pre-determined PTSD checklists.

Concluding Reflections on Research Methodologies

What implications do the findings of this study have for approaches to studying the impact of war on children and young people? Three research methods were used, each contributing certain information about the situation of young people in the province of Huila. The data obtained from observations and the PRA-type exercises provided information about a variety of aspects of the youths' lives, including their daily concerns and routines, health problems, resources in the health care system, coping strategies and their thoughts and feelings about the war. The exercises served as starting points for discussions and opened up a number of different channels of information which would have been harder to achieve through more conventional interviewing methods. The youths enjoyed engaging with the tasks and exercises, especially when they themselves acted as facilitators. This is important as participatory research with young people is likely to yield better results when it is based on participants' active engagement with the process and simultaneous enjoyment of the activities.

Most importantly, however, the participatory approach allowed the voices of the youths to be heard, as they themselves identified the issues that concerned them without the predetermined agendas of adult researchers interfering in the process. This yielded some unexpected results in terms of the issues the youths found distressing, for instance the centrality of experiencing the loss of homes and land, which they saw as the most distressing event, and the importance attached to having appropriate clothing and shoes. The findings also showed that the youths in this study were astute analysts of their situation and had insight into the interrelatedness of factors, as was demonstrated in the quotation by Ornelio (above) on the relationship between ill-health, *pensamentos* and poverty. Approaches that view children predominantly as passive recipients of aid and care frequently do not recognise this ability of the young to contribute valuable perspectives on the dimensions of war.

As discussed above, according to the results obtained from the PTSD scale employed in the study, most of the youths are not only traumatised but may be deemed to be suffering from a psychiatric disorder. If this method had been used as the only means of investigating the experiences of young *deslocados* in the area, significant information would have been missed relating to the causes of distress in their lives. In addition, conclusions regarding their inability to function in daily life may have been reached, contributing to a discourse of victimhood which has been contradicted by other findings. A PTSD scale in itself is thus insufficient for understanding the meanings attached to certain causes of distress as well as for gaining insight into the explanatory models held about certain symptoms, for instance the spiritual aspects of illnesses. These findings indicate that the use of a psychometric measurement based on PTSD criteria is inadequate, on its own, for understanding issues of war-related distress, as the *a-priori* determined symptoms of trauma do not yield insight into what the displaced themselves consider to be important aspects of their distress.

The trauma discourse does not, of course, base itself only on the concept of PTSD but also draws on a variety of other ideas and aspects. The notion of trauma remains a dominant 'lens' through which the impact of armed conflict on people is interpreted. The danger of employing such a lens is that it filters out important information about people's experiences of war, experiences which always take place within a specific cultural, social and political context. This chapter has argued that it is vital to employ such a contextual analysis when seeking to understand young people's experiences of armed conflict, in order to gain insight not only into the issues they define as difficulties but also into their coping strategies and strengths.

Notes

1. Given the history of armed conflict in Angola, suspicion of political motives was high during the time period when the research was conducted. In addition, urban and semi-urban communities typically display more openness and inclusion towards outsiders than rural communities.
2. Reflexivity: critical and constant reflection of the researcher on how his or her characteristics, theoretical orientation and those of the participants impact on the interaction in the field.
3. The history of Angola does not, of course, start with these wars. Angola's pre-colonial history and the impact of more than 300 years of slave trade which 'drained the country of human and material resources and left scars in the basic fabric of society that are still not healed' (Tvedten 1997: 8) are central to national identity.
4. Many demobilised underage soldiers do not seem to experience such problems. However, cases exist where this does occur (Monteiro 1996).

References

Adogame, A. 2001. 'Tomorrow's Leaders of Today: Youth Empowerment and African New Religious Movements.' Paper presented at the conference 'Africa's Young Majority: Meanings, Victims, Actors.' 23–24 May 2001. Edinburgh: Centre for African Studies, University of Edinburgh.
Blos, P. 1967. 'The Second Individuation Process of Adolescence.' *The*

Psychoanalytic Study of the Child. Vol. 22. New York: International Universities Press.

Bracken, P. and Petty, C. eds, 1998. *Rethinking the Trauma of War*. London: Free Association Books.

Cairns, E. 1996. *Children and Political Violence*. Oxford: Blackwell.

CCF Report 2000. *Diagnostico da Communidade de Lalula*. Lubango: CCF (Christian Children's Fund).

CCR (Centre for Conflict Resolution, Cape Town) 2000. 'Angola: Forty Years of War.' Occasional Paper, Track Two 9 (2).

Dawes, A. and Cairns, E. 1998. 'The Machel Report: Dilemmas of Cultural Sensitivity and Universal Rights of Children.' *Peace and Conflict: Journal of Peace Psychology* 4 (4): 335–48.

de Koning, K. and Martin, M. eds, 1996. *Participatory Research in Health. Issues and Experiences*. London: Zed Books.

Diagnostic and Statistical Manual of Mental Disorders (3rd edn) 1980. Washington: American Psychiatric Association.

Erikson, E. 1968. *Identity: Youth and Crisis*. New York: Norton.

Eyber, C. 2001. 'Alleviating Psychosocial Suffering: an Analysis of Approaches to Coping with War-related Distress in Angola.' Ph.D. thesis, Queen Margaret University College, Edinburgh.

Griffin, C. 1993. *Representations of Youth*. Cambridge: Polity Press.

Honwana, A. 1997. 'Healing for Peace: Traditional Healers and Post-war Reconstruction in Southern Mozambique.' *Peace and Conflict: Journal of Peace Psychology* 3 (3): 293–305.

——. 1998. 'Okusiakala Ondalo Yokalye, Let us Light a New Fire: Local Knowledge in the Post-war Healing and Reintegration of War-affected Children in Angola'. Luanda: Unpublished consultancy report for Christian Children's Fund (CCF).

Human Rights Watch 1994. *Angola: Arms Trade and Violations of Laws of War since the 1992 Elections*. New York: Human Rights Watch.

Hwang, C.P., Lamb, M. and Sigel, I. eds, 1996. *Images of Childhood*. New Jersey: Lawrence Erlbaum.

Institute of Development Studies 1996. *PRA Health Pack*. Brighton, U.K.: IDS.

La Fontaine, J. 1986. 'An Anthropological Perspective on Children in Social Worlds.' In M. Richards and P. Light, eds, *Children of Social Worlds*. Cambridge: Polity Press.

Matloff, J. 1996. *Fragments of a Forgotten War: Angola*. Johannesburg: Penguin.

Mbiti, J. 1989. *African Religions and Philosophy* (2nd edn). Oxford: Heinemann.

McIntyre, T. and Ventura, M. 1996. 'Escala de Avaliação da Resposta ao Acontecimento Traumatico: Versão Adolescentes.' Unpublished paper: University of Minho.

Milheiros, M. 1967. *Notas de Etnografia Angolana* (2nd edn). Luanda: Instituto de Investigação Cientifica de Angola.

Monteiro, C. 1996. 'Cultural Issues in the Treatment of Trauma and Loss: Honoring Differences.' Unpublished paper: Christian Children's Fund (CCF).

Mukasa, G. and Mugisha, G. 1999. 'Beyond the Good Discussion: the Issues Matrix for Analysing Intra-communal Difference in PRA.' *PLA Notes* 34, February.

Nashat, S. 2001. 'Anthropological and Psychoanalytic Perspectives on PTSD: A Complementary Approach.' Paper presented at the 7th European Conference on Traumatic Stress, 26–9 May, ESTSS, Edinburgh.

Noller, P. and Callan, V. 1991. *The Adolescent in the Family*. New York: Routledge.

Nordstrom, C. 1997. *A Different Kind of War Story*. Philadelphia, PA: University of Pennsylvania Press.

NRC (Norwegian Refugee Council) 2001. Global IDP Database. Angola. Electronic document: http://www.idpproject.org.

OCHA (Office for the Coordination of Humanitarian Affairs) 2000. *Angola: Report on Rapid Assessment of Critical Needs*. Luanda: United Nations.

Offer, D., Ostrov, E., Howard, K. and Atkinson, R. 1988. *The Teenage World: Adolescents' Self-image in Ten Countries*. New York: Plenum Medical Books.

Ramphele, M.A. 1997. 'Adolescents and Violence: "Adults are cruel, they just beat, beat, beat."' *Social Science and Medicine* 45 (8): 1189–97.

Reynolds, P. 1996. *Traditional Healers and Childhood in Zimbabwe*. Athens, Ohio: University of Ohio Press.

Richards, P. 1996. *Fighting for the Rain Forest: War, Youth and Resources in Sierra Leone*. Oxford: James Currey.

Scheper-Hughes, N. and Sargent, C. eds, 1998. *Small Wars: The Cultural Politics of Childhood*. London: The University of California Press.

Sommers, M. 2000. 'On the Margins, in the Mainstream: Urban Refugees in Africa.' In S.C. Lubkemann, L. Minear and T.G. Weiss, eds, Humanitarian Action: Social Science Connections. Occasional Paper 37. Providence, U.S.A.: The Thomas Watson Institute for International Studies.

Summerfield, D. 1999. 'Sociocultural Dimensions of War, Conflict and Displacement.' In A. Ager, ed., *Refugees: Perspectives on the Experience of Forced Migration*. London: Pinter.

——. 2001. 'The Nature of Conflict and the Implications for Appropriate Psychosocial Responses.' In M. Loughry and A. Ager, eds, *The Refugee Experience: Psychosocial Training Module* 1 (2nd edn). Oxford: Refugee Studies Centre, University of Oxford.

Tvedten, I. 1997. *Angola: Struggle for Peace and Reconstruction*. Boulder, Colorado: Westview.

United Nations Security Council (UNSC) 2000. *Report of the Secretary-General of the United Nations Office in Angola*. Luanda: UN.

Ventura, M. 1997. 'O Stress Post-traumatico e suas Sequelas nos Adolescentes do Sul de Angola.' Ph.D. diss. Minho, Portugal: Instituto de Educação e psicologia, Universidade do Minho.

Wessells, M. 1999. 'Culture, Power, and Community: Intercultural Approaches to Psychosocial Assistance and Healing.' In K. Nader, N. Dubrow and B. Stamm, eds, *Honoring Differences: Cultural Issues in the Treatment of Trauma and Loss*. Philadelphia: Bruner/Mazel.

Young, A. 1995. *The Harmony of Illusions: Inventing Posttraumatic Stress Disorder*. Princeton, New Jersey: Princeton University Press.

11

Fluid Research Fields: Studying Excombatant Youth in the Aftermath of the Liberian Civil War[1]

Mats Utas

> The architecture of this work is rooted in the temporal. Every human must be considered from the standpoint of time.
> (Frantz Fanon: *Black Skin, White Masks*)

Introduction

Methodology is a rather neglected topic in studies of under-age combatants. Research in this field generally employs a quantitative approach and is based on short-term fieldwork in which encounters with respondents are often limited to one, or at most a few, and interviews are generally carried out with a tape recorder. Moreover, research is often done from within aid organisations. These approaches normally yield responses in victim modes and tend to conceal many important aspects of lived experience (see, for example, Brett and McCallin 1996; Fleischman and Whitman 1994; Goodwin-Gill and Cohn 1994). That is to say, respondents display what I term 'victimcy', expressing their individual agency by representing themselves as powerless victims (Utas forthcoming). This is a strategy that may also be employed by refugees and internally displaced people. 'Victim' responses often form the raw material for standardised and collectivised discourses of, for instance, survivors of war or repressive regimes (see, for example, Jackson 2002; Tiljander Dahlström 2001; Handelman 1997). Victimcy is a tactical manipulation, in part, aimed at presenting an image in line with cultural ideals. However, victimcy is also a political response to real security threats, as well as an economic strategy in relation to humanitarian aid projects, and as such is an obstacle to research. Hence, it is essential to find alternative modes of data collection.

There is an established tradition of social research in Liberia that has generally involved long-term periods of fieldwork and frequent revisits. High profile scholars such as Bellman (1975, 1984), Bledsoe (1980), Clapham (1976), d'Azevedo (1962, 1969–70, 1972, 1989, 1994), Liebenow (1969, 1980, 1984), Moran (1990) and Tonkin (1992) have considered many different aspects of Liberia. Regrettably, however, they have been quite silent in research about the Liberian Civil War; instead, it appears that along with emergency aid comes a set of emergency researchers. The war researchers copy the rapid response methods of medical teams like Médecins sans Frontières or Merlin, much to the detriment of the final product. To a large extent it is the staff or consultants of international non-government organisations (INGOs) or government agencies that carry out social research in conflict zones.[2] In 1992 Hiram Ruiz, employed by the U.S. Committee for Refugees, wrote a report on the refugee situation in Liberia (Ruiz 1992). In eleven years (1988–1998) Ruiz covered at least eight other conflict zones, on three continents, and released reports very similar to the one on Liberia. What insights can we expect to find in such work? Research methods need to be modified when we study war-torn societies, but cannot be neglected altogether. Long-term approaches are difficult to carry out in times of conflict, but they are of no less importance. In order to understand individual and collective motives and perspectives underlying child and youth participation in civil wars, scholars need long-term personal contacts with the research subjects, as these particular issues are especially delicate. They are delicate for many reasons, some of which I point out in this text. Long-term fieldwork and participant observation 'are better suited than exclusively quantitative methodologies for documenting the lives of people who live on the margins of a society that is hostile to them. Only by establishing long-term relationships based on trust can one begin to ask provocative personal questions, and expect thoughtful answers' (Bourgois 1995: 12f.). Victimcy becomes transparent during long-term ethnographic fieldwork. However, even long-term fieldwork conceals problems and shortcomings, some of which I will discuss using my own experiences from fieldwork among excombatant youth residing in urban Liberia.

Entering the field for the first time, getting access and becoming accepted is generally a painstaking business. Anthropologists tend to create an air of mystique around this topic. In ethnographic work the entry is often treated as a rite of passage (see, for example, Hannerz 1969; Jensen 2001; Whyte 1993) although it is often what is unplanned that suddenly opens the way. Clifford Geertz's (1973) account, in *Deep Play: Notes on the Balinese Cockfight*, captures the drama and the abrupt change: Geertz describes how he went to an illegal cockfight which was raided by the police, whereupon he ran into hiding together with the villagers. In the next sequence he realises that the moment of inclusion was in the communal activity of running and hiding from the officers. My own inclusion into the field was not as dramatic, but nonetheless of great importance. It is discussed in some detail below. However, I want to push the discussion on inclusion a step further. Researchers tend to see inclusion as a permanent state – once you are inside, it is forever – whilst in a turbulent field such as that of conflict or post-conflict the promise of inclusion is permanently threatened. People are constantly on the move, power is utilised in so many brutal ways, criminal livelihoods and dangerous military pasts challenge the researcher's position on a daily basis. In retrospect my eventual exclusion was inevitable.

Humanitarian aid agencies tend to make a fetish of childhood as a closed, age-bound category of agency-free individuals. In contrast, I approach childhood and the liminal phase of adolescence as an open-ended process of adult formation (cf. for example, Kaplan 1984). Age is social in the sense that members of an age group can 'outgrow their chronological age but not its chronological behaviour' (Momoh 1999: 17). One can stay within the youth category for a prolonged time period. As the youth category is a social effect of power (Durham 2000), it follows that individuals who have not managed to establish themselves as adults, with the socio-cultural implications which this entails, remain in the category to ages far beyond our general understanding of youth. Below I include the story of Washington. He is 36, but I argue that he is still part of the youth category. Likewise, at the other extreme, 11- or 12-year-old rebel fighters live lives that disqualify them from forming part of childhood, as we want to understand it, but designate them rather as youth. To my mind we need to discuss young soldiers in Liberia as an integrated part of a 'crisis of youth' (Richards 1995). By talking about youth in this loose sense we do away with the label 'child soldiers' which invokes the image of passive victim.

In what appeared to be the aftermath of the Liberian Civil War many young excombatants ended up homeless on the streets of cities and larger towns. In the capital, Monrovia, they were found squatting in vacant and damaged housing complexes, office buildings, shops, hospitals and hotels. This chapter focuses on a small group of youth who lived in a deserted petro-chemical factory (nicknamed 'the Palace'), right on the beach in central Monrovia. All of them had actively participated in the civil war as combatants, and at the time I got to know them were living rough (this social category has been described elsewhere as 'lumpens': Abdullah 1997, 1998; Abdullah and Bangura 1997; Rashid 1997). In early 1998 normality was slowly returning to Liberia. Excombatants from most factions, with the exception of some from President Charles Taylor's own rebel army, had been made redundant and were desperately looking for work. The peace proceedings from late 1996 up to the election in July 1997 had reduced them from masters to subjects, returning them to the lowly social position they had occupied at the onset of the war.

Participating in the civil war was to many of these young men and women an active move towards power and influence. Peace was thus often seen as an immediate loss. In fact one could argue that for many excombatants the peace that followed the civil war was experienced as a more challenging and dangerous situation than the war itself, due to a tremendous increase in hardship; in other words, 'war is peace', to paraphrase the slogan of George Orwell's 1984. From time to time Palace youth would say to me that they wished that war would break out again. As one of them put it, with war 'the shelves of Stop and Shop [a supermarket situated nearby] are again filled to the brink' and by taking up their guns once more they would regain respect, food and commodities and become masters of at least a part of Liberian society.

The Liberian Civil War

The Liberian Civil War started on Christmas Eve 1989, when a group of about 150 ill-equipped rebel soldiers, supported by Libya and Burkina Faso (Ellis 1999), crossed into Nimba County in Liberia from adjacent Ivory Coast. The group, who became known as the National Patriotic Front of Liberia (NPFL), initially enjoyed massive popular support. Young men and women joined the NPFL, armed with single-barrel guns and at times sticks, and the government forces — Armed Forces of Liberia (AFL) — were soon driven out of Nimba County. Following an internal struggle, the NPFL split into two: NPFL led by Charles Taylor, and Independent National Patriotic Front of Liberia (INPFL) under Prince Y. Johnson. Taking different routes, but at times fighting each other, both defeated the AFL and reached the Atlantic coast and Monrovia in July 1990. By that time a West African peacekeeping force, ECOMOG, had been created under the leadership of Nigeria and sent to take control of the situation in Monrovia. Prince Y. Johnson struck a deal with the peacekeepers and lured President Doe into a trap, caught him, tortured him in front of a video camera and eventually killed him. The struggle that at the outset was viewed as a popular rebellion by the Gio and Mano ethnic groups in Nimba County turned the whole of Liberia into a war zone. Young rebel fighters not only fought each other but terrorised, looted and committed gruesome atrocities against the entire civilian population.

The INPFL was dissolved after killing President Doe, but soon several other rebel factions appeared. The United Liberation Movement of Liberia (ULIMO) was formed in Freetown, Sierra Leone, with assistance from the Sierra Leonean government. Soon ULIMO split into two; ULIMO-J (Johnson Branch) and ULIMO-K. AFL (Kromah Branch) continued fighting but was aided by another faction, the Liberian Peace Council (LPC) originating in the south-east. Often enjoying regional support, other factions, such as the Lofa Defence Force (LDF) and the Congo Defence Force

(CDF), came and went. The main incentive to continue the war was financial. Soldiers fought to obtain loot while the warlords aimed to gain control over areas rich in resources, especially those with gold and diamonds, but also timber and rubber, coffee and cocoa. Rebel movements kept some amount of popular support by feigning to protect the interests of particular regions and ethnic groupings, which were further politicised by the war itself (Atkinson 1999). In reality, their brutality towards the very people they claimed to serve kept civilians submissive. Dubious international businessmen,[3] conglomerates of West African states and at times foreign departments of powerful Western states supported the warlords (Keen and International Institute for Strategic Studies 1998; Reno 1996).

After seven years, the war came to a halt, culminating in democratic elections in 1997. Ironically, in what Jimmy Carter, former president of the U.S.A., called the most just election in African history, Charles Taylor and his National Patriotic Party (NPP) – formed out of the NPFL – won a landslide victory and thus succeeded in what they were not able to accomplish through warfare (on Taylor's political career see Harris 1999). The war had by then caused between 60,000 and 200,000 deaths.[4] Without relying on uncertain statistics, it is true to say that during the course of the conflict most Liberians were displaced at one point or another. Areas across the borders, in Sierra Leone, Guinea and the Ivory Coast, were at times flooded with refugees (see Utas 1997). Internally displaced persons (IDPs) moved up and down between temporary safe havens in search of the protection of some form of authority. The coastal cities of Monrovia and Buchanan, zones guarded by the peacekeepers, received most IDPs and today Monrovia has twice the number of inhabitants it had before the war.

During 1998 and 1999 the security situation in Liberia remained uncertain. Parts of the country experienced moments of unrest verging on outright war, with heavy shooting and civilians fleeing at will. Even so most observers regarded the war as over. Yet in late 1999, upper Lofa County experienced the first of a series of armed incursions. By mid 2000 groups of subversive soldiers were entering from neighbouring Guinea on a regular basis. Liberians saw the birth and growth of a new rebel movement, ironically named Liberians United for Reconciliation and Democracy (LURD). LURD rebels have, since then, gradually worked their way down through Lofa County towards the coast. During the first half of 2002 LURD made a series of successful raids in Bong, Bomi and Montserrado Counties, temporarily taking control of major towns, Gbarnga, Tubmanburg and Klay Junction, before troops loyal to the government were able to recapture them. In mid-May an attack on President Taylor's native town of Arthington, less than 20 kilometres from Monrovia, caused widespread panic in the capital. With a core of soldiers recruited from among exiles in Guinea, LURD have also been able to enlist young people within Liberia. Similarly the AFL, the various governmental security forces and pro-governmental paramilitaries, have also succeeded in drawing fresh support by recruiting among young Liberians, mainly from Monrovia and surrounding counties. It is conceivable that many of the young men and women present in this text have taken part in these new proceedings of the civil war.

Children and Youth in the Civil War

The number of combatants from 1990 to 1997 is estimated at 40,000 to 70,000, peaking in 1991 (Brett and McCallin 1996; Fleischman and Whitman 1994; internal statistics from SCF-UK and UNOMIL). The estimated ratio of child soldiers varies considerably, from 10 to 40 percent, depending partly on whether a child soldier is defined as under fifteen or eighteen (Fleischman and Whitman 1994). During the demobilisation exercise, from November 1996 to February 1997, UNDHA (United Nations Humanitarian Assistance Coordination Office) found that child soldiers made up 24 percent of the total. The LPC had the highest number at 37 percent. The modal age of demobilisation was 20. If, for instance, a soldier had fought the entire war and was 20 years old at demobilisation, he or she had joined at 14, thus clearly falling within the category of child soldier. The value of these statistics is not entirely clear.[5] According to my own observations during the April 6 fighting[6] a majority of those who fought in Monrovia were boys and girls[7] under 18. I estimate the average age of conscription to be around 14 to 16, but some rebel soldiers were as young as 9 (Brett and McCallin, 1996, have recorded fighters as young as 6).[8] Commanders often state that soldiers of this age are more reliable, loyal and less fearful than older ones (Goodwin-Gill and Cohn 1994). In the type of war fought in Liberia and many other African countries, very young soldiers can be used because the weaponry is mainly light and simple enough for a young person to handle.

   Even if forced conscription took place in Liberia most young combatants joined out of 'free' will.[9] At the onset of war, as noted above, the people in Nimba County viewed it as a rebellion designed to free them from a repressive government seen as anti-Nimbadian. Parents sent their children off to fight in a righteous war. But young people also saw it as a youth revolution, a chance to get rid of an elitist urban leadership of autocrats that showed little concern for the young of Liberia (cf., for example, Clapham 1976, 1988; Liebenow 1987), as well as the local gerontocratic leadership (cf., for example, Bellman 1984; Murphy 1980). In this way war was fought by marginalised youth, who saw combat as the only opportunity to move from the margin into the centre of politics and economy. Large parts of the contemporary young generation in West Africa are only offered subsistence on the margin. Thus, Cruise O'Brien (1996) has dubbed West African youth 'a lost generation' and Richards (1995) has seen the origin of the wars in Sierra Leone and Liberia in a general 'crisis of youth'. Young Liberians' performance bears witness to and validates such a perspective.

The war changed its form and, as rebel groups increased terror against civilians and looting missions increasingly became the *raison d'être* for war, the reasons for enlisting also changed. Many young excombatants state that it was the benefits that drew them to join up, both the direct gains and also escaping the disadvantages of being a civilian. Direct advantages include loot from raids; bribes during security assignments; and payoffs from protecting locals and the acquisition of power in local communities. The leap from being a powerless young boy, under the authority of parents and elders, to being a commander with a gun is momentous. Being a soldier would also imply having girlfriends, often many at a time, and taking a girlfriend for the night as often as one would like (Utas forthcoming). On the other hand, escaping the disadvantages of being a civilian would primarily involve preventing other rebel soldiers from harassing oneself and one's family. During the war it was crucial for every family to have someone – a son, an uncle or another close relative – in the rebel army in control of the area; otherwise, family members would constantly be harassed and farms and property looted.[10] Finally, young Liberians would at times join the rebel forces in order to avenge family members killed by other rebel factions. At an early stage my informants stated that vengeance was a main motive for joining the war, but as our relationship gained in depth, vengeance motives often disappeared behind other objectives. Most Liberians lost close relatives in the war but very few of them took up arms for that reason.

In early 1998 excombatants moved around uneasily. Peace was still fragile and many excombatants had no clear vision of their lives in post-war Liberia. Some of them returned to their home towns and villages. However, large numbers of demobilised fighters remained behind in cities and towns. The relative anonymity and distance from kin gave them breathing space and time to think about their future. In towns all over Liberia, groups of excombatant youth would be found squatting in deserted buildings, or occasionally, living in rented accommodation. For greater security, living in collective houses along with other excombatants, girlfriends and children seemed to be the norm for the immediate post-war period. The Palace is but one such setting.

Entering the Palace

For a researcher, the general procedure for establishing contact with excombatants is via the demobilisation and reintegration programmes offered by a plethora of national and international aid organisations found on the ground in Liberia. Initially, when I arrived in Liberia, I explored this path. Visiting a few of the NGO/INGO projects brought me close to possible informants, yet placed me in a problematic category. Inevitably, my association with aid agencies predetermined my relations with those I wanted to understand. Every single person I talked to saw me as a donor, and responses to my questions were tailored to that imagined identity. It became a straightjacket I could not escape. They made the most of presenting themselves as victims: victims of war, devoid of any other agency than asking the donor community for aid. Far from satisfied with these victimcy-modelled responses, I went looking for something else.

During my search for another entry I came across a local social-field-worker employed by one of the INGOs, who was also active in the field outside the specific projects. He took me to some of the spots in town where excombatants were squatting. Our second visit was to 'the Palace'. In contrast to the first place we visited, I was well received, undoubtedly because they took me for a donor, even if I did what I could to deny it. The paradox occurred to me that my donor status was an advantage to be let in, in the first place, but a clear disadvantage if I wanted to do nonvic-timcy biased research. I needed to do away with the donor status, but only at a pace slow enough to be able to establish personal trust. As I was living nearby, I scheduled another visit the next day without the social worker. I was now on my own and I had found a place I could visit on a daily basis, spending all the time I wanted with my research subjects. Better still: at least half the group remained idle and readily available for chats during daytime. Entering the Palace I discovered a clandestine world of excombatants; a realm of combatants unified, but also one with broad chasms due to separate experiences and liaisons in the Liberian Civil War. Intertwined clandestine networks shared the same marginal space, yet beneath the surface they competed fiercely over limited resources in the extreme margin of post-war economics.

The Palace was a placed feared in the neighbourhood. People dared not enter the premises and rumours were rife that the inhabitants were can-nibals. Even a European aid worker living in a neighbouring building told me that she had seen people in the Palace bringing in a big basket with human flesh – presumably for consumption.[11] People entering the Palace included army soldiers escaping from the nearby barracks to buy mari-juana, or just to smoke a joint, or arrange some deal with the Palace dwellers. Civilians also bought marijuana from dealers in the Palace, but not just any person would enter the premises. In fact, at the beginning of my research, traders who wanted to sell their goods halted at an invisible line and waited for the people inside to come out. The gate to the build-ing had disappeared a long time ago and the entire building was physi-cally open, but socially it remained closed.

Under these circumstances it was quite a delicate matter to get under the skin of the Palace youth – a skin considerably encrusted by all perceived betrayals from early on in life, through the war years, to the current outcast mode. At a time when everybody else seemed to ignore their very existence, I believe that initially it was their curiosity about why I was interested in their lives that made them accept me. During the war years they had all experienced international journalists and had been let down by their promises.[12] I came with no promises. But visiting them day after day slowly convinced them of my earnest interest in their lives. That they were shunned by the larger society made my endeavour the more important. In that vein my presence was also a status symbol for Palace youth. I had imagined that my ethnographic knowledge of Liberian society and good orientation in contemporary Liberian war history, with specific reference to issues of youth, would give us a common ground for discussions. Yet what turned out to be my premium asset was that I had been in Monrovia during the April 6 battle in 1996. Back then I was caught for a few days in a downtown flat before I managed to get across to the U.S. embassy where I was eventually airlifted out of the country. I had not fought, but I had experienced wild bullets whistling around and grenades detonating. I had experienced the grip of panic, abysmal fear and indeed witnessed young people, like those I later met at the Palace, acting out the very war. I had experienced a little piece of 'their war' and it was enough, my rite of passage, which made my transition from stranger to peer possible. I was constantly reminded of this fact when they introduced me to friends in their social networks with an opening line such as: this is our friend; he was here during 'April 6'. I shared the experience of their war and thereby they let me into their lives.

Moreover, I gained trust by keeping my house open to them. My closest friends from the Palace would drop in for a chat, some food or a game of cards. Together we started to plan other activities. First we proposed a small project to an INGO. We got some money for a basketball court and cleared the yard inside the Palace. This had a tremendous effect on the neighbourhood. Within days youth started to come from all around to play basketball on 'our' ball ground. Flowers grew out of the concrete. Sammy, one of the leaders in the Palace, even got himself a girlfriend from the neighbourhood. We later went on with another small-scale project to put up a small carpentry workshop; this time, however, it grew out of our hands and eventually collapsed.

Even with the tremendous effort I put into gaining their trust and cooperation it was a delicate matter to succeed in, and certainly I failed in some areas. My main focus on their activities during the war years turned out to be the most sensitive area. On these issues I could get one answer before lunch and another after. Sometimes they told me that they had been fighters, only to withdraw their statements during our next discussion. However, after some time I had a pretty clear picture of who had done what. But who had they fought for? This appeared to be a pretty straightforward question and I was initially satisfied with the answer that most had fought for the NPFL. However, near neighbours told me otherwise. They said that most Palace youth had been part of the ULIMO-J in the 1996 fighting. Many had indeed fought for NPFL or INPFL at some point - change of faction was very common in the civil war and many excombatants had experiences from more than one faction – but they omitted that they had any relationship with ULIMO-J.[13]

During 1998 ex-ULIMO-J fighters were still a source of unrest in Monrovia. High tensions remained around their leader's house and several skirmishes took place between ULIMO fighters and government security forces. On 18 September these tensions brought Liberia back to the brink of civil war. Large parts of downtown Monrovia were again turned into a battlefield when fighting broke out between security forces and irregulars loyal to the ULIMO-J leader. When government forces got back in control, changes also occurred in the Palace. One of the younger boys in the Palace turned out to be in the ULIMO-J leader's bodyguard. He fled with the leader to the U.S. embassy and was later airlifted, together with the ULIMO-J elite, to Nigeria. Thus it became obvious why he had refused to participate in our 'lecturing' and why he always kept a low profile in my presence. Further, Scarface, one of the seniors in the Palace, a corporal in the army and a ULIMO-J soldier during the war, was picked up by security forces and taken to the military barracks where he was first interrogated and eventually executed.[14] By then it was pretty clear to me that most of the Palace youth had fought for ULIMO-J during the April 6 war, and the tragic death of Scarface made it extremely clear why war issues were not discussed with an outsider and possible infiltrator like me.

Palace Geography

Like a fortress overlooking the ocean, the Palace is the concrete remnants of a factory situated right on the beach, at the far end of one of the main streets in downtown Monrovia. Immediate neighbours are two rather superior apartment buildings, inhabited by expatriate NGO staff and naturalised Lebanese businessmen. A deserted car park with an old garage is situated in between these complexes, occupied by another band of homeless youth. Behind the Palace is a dusty football field, full of activity in the late afternoons when the sun is going down. And then there is the beach nicknamed the 'Puh-puh-cana', because people living nearby use it as their toilet – ocean waves flushing away the human excrement. On the beach at the far end of Randall Street is a rubbish dump where Palace youth frequently go scavenging.

Inside the Palace fence one enters the building via the old loading bridge. The main door is closed by a pile of concrete blocks, probably a remnant from the war, when it was used as headquarters for militias and only one entrance was preferred for security reasons. Old concrete blocks and other debris litter the rooms on the ground floor except one inhabited by three of the most junior residents. A big open space between the L-shaped building and the outer walls was initially also covered with debris but in a joint effort we cleared the area to turn it into a basketball court. Upstairs there are six rooms, inhabited by the rest of the Palace youth. The most senior boys occupy the small rooms with no or very small window apertures. They prefer these for security reasons. Old cloth or plastic covers the doorways. The 'beds' are mainly made up of a few pieces of cloth spread out on the concrete floor. The rooms are furnished with items from the rubbish dump – primitively repaired chairs and tables, a refrigerator door functioning as a shelf. Surprisingly, much is done to make the place tidy: some tables have a tablecloth and in one of the rooms a plastic flower is stuck in an old beer bottle. Palace youth dream of a decent life and feed their dreams with magazine pictures of consumer goods plastered on their walls. Palace youth do not have many possessions; they need to keep things in close proximity or they will be stolen and sold by other residents. Theft is punished, but it is hard to determine the culprit, and residents are often so hungry that an extra meal is worth the punishment.

Palace Youth

Palace youth are a constantly changing population. Some stay only for a few weeks, others for longer. At the onset of my fieldwork in the Palace there were twenty-one residents, only five of them female, with an age range from 15 to 36. On average they left school in the fifth or sixth grade, but some have no education and one says he has finished tenth grade. Although the onset of war may have cut studies short, leaving school in the fifth or sixth grade was also rather average in urban Liberia before the war.[15] About half the Palace youth were born or grew up in Monrovia. The rest grew up in mining and plantation communities up-country (a typical recruiting area for rebel armies, see Muana 1997; Richards 1996). In the pre-war setting their parents worked mostly in the wage labour sector. Most Palace youth have stable family backgrounds and most probably would not be living rough if the war had not disrupted their life realms. In the post-war era they have little contact with parents and siblings even if they are alive. Those who have relatives in Monrovia rarely, if ever, make visits and little effort is spent reinstating contact. None of the Palace residents receive any economic assistance from relatives, even though thirteen of them have relatives abroad (mainly in the U.S. but also elsewhere in Africa).[16]

Half of the males have experience or training as skilled workers (mainly carpentry), but nurture little hope of finding employment as skilled labour (see below). Most of them, and two or three of the females, fought during the war. One girl proudly told me how she used to slit the throats of the enemies with her hunting knife. As mentioned above, I have not been able to verify in which factions every individual fought during which part of the war, although I have good evidence of their participation in ULIMO-J during the 1996 battles. Their ranks and the units they fought in were also classified information, even if it was a topic often debated in informal discussions.[17] Palace youth fought over large areas of Liberia. Those who fought with the NPFL, AFL and ULIMO-J have often been everywhere in Liberia as well as in Sierra Leone. They were generally armed with AK47s (Kalashnikovs) but a wide range of guns were used – light machine guns, belt guns and RPGs. Twelve out of twenty-one in my survey had bullet or grenade wounds from combat.

On Returning Home

All the individuals in the Palace have personal reasons for not returning to their families and place of origin. Circumstances in the original opportunity structure, for instance inheritance, access to land and resources, marital status, play a crucial role in choosing whether or not to return home. Relationship with parents, as well as associations with other people in the local setting, determine whether the ex-fighters go home or stay in the cities. In some cases Palace youth do not know where to start looking for their parents or they have found out that they lost them during the war years. Others are aware of the fact that they have grown too old to depend on the parental generation and / or that their parents or other close relatives themselves have no or limited means of subsistence. 'In post-war Liberia you have to fight for yourself', Palace youth often say. Many have committed crimes and atrocities in their communities and thus fear the way they would be received. Another important reason for staying away is a prevalent sense that to go back you need some proof that the years away have not been wasted. To prove success on return is of immediate importance and can be done by returning in nice clothes, with money in the pocket, a car or a complete education.

Earning One's Livelihood in the Street: the Nuku Hunt

Nuku is street slang for money and the daily hunt for *nuku* preoccupies Palace youth. Life in the Palace is a fight for survival. Luxuries are only available in imaginary returns to the 'glorious' days of the civil war. In de

Certeau's (1984) terms, Palace youth rely on short-term 'tactics' rather than long-term 'strategies'. If someone is successful in obtaining some *nuku*, then they will often buy food and cook for everybody. A big pleasure for all, it simultaneously functions as the glue keeping Palace youth together. Except for food, Palace youths' needs are limited. Soap for laundry and personal hygiene is one of the few necessities and generally laundry soap is used for both purposes. A one-portion bag of laundry soap costs 10 Liberian dollars (L$10). In addition, cigarettes (at L$5 for four), marijuana (an affordable L$5 – harder drugs are more costly), and occasionally some home-brewed spirits (cane juice) for the night cover the rest of their basic needs. Youth in the street can live on L$15–20 (U.S. $0.35–0.50) a day.[18] Even so, many of the young dwellers in the Palace find it troublesome enough to get that amount of money. People often call attention to the lack of even the smallest funds as characteristic of the post-war era, and talk with nostalgia of the 'sweet' life of 'normal day' (pre-war). To excombatants, however, 'sweet' life was rather located *in* the war years.

Generally the *nuku* hunt is a combination of both day and night shifts. Among the legal (daytime) activities, one of the most lucrative is hauling sand from the beach, which is used for construction everywhere in town. The rubbish dump, on the beach, is another main source of income, yielding among other things copper, found inside old engines and cables, and rubber from tyres or slippers (made from tyres). The proximity to the INGO living quarters also means that furniture and other items only slightly damaged appear on the rubbish dump. These are repaired and resold, for instance at the Go-by-shop market (for a definition of Go-by-shop see below) in Johnson Street. Less valuable than copper but still useful is scrap metal, mainly from freezers and refrigerators, which is used to make coal pots (cooking stoves fuelled with charcoal used by a majority of the urban population). Making coal pots is one of the main income-generating activities for Palace youth. Scrap metal is at times also bought in bulk. Palace youth are occasionally employed as day labourers, on construction sites, offloading trucks or as night watchmen. Since they have a reputation for being unreliable, they will only be employed for short periods and under keen supervision.

Being a young excombatant has few advantages in post-war Liberia. However, one is that there are a lot of NGOs and INGOs catering for excombatants. During the civil war, projects for reintegration and reconciliation mushroomed in cities all over Liberia. Most of these projects are found in Monrovia. Palace youth are well acquainted with these and most have been through at least one such programme during or after the civil war. The projects catering for excombatants offer skilled training programmes in carpentry, construction, mechanical craft, etc. Some offer courses in drama and music or a continuation of ordinary school. Palace youth know all too well that no matter what skills they obtain, they have few or no chances of getting employed after their training. INGO programmes are still very popular, giving homeless youth an opportunity to get off the streets, have a stable supply of food and, maybe, some pocket money, for up to two years.

Illegal Livelihoods

Selling cigarettes is on the surface a legal activity that the Palace youth are involved in. However, they generally sell drugs, principally marijuana, as well. The Palace is called a Bob Marley house, 'Bob Marley' being a nickname for marijuana, where outsiders go both to buy their supplies and to 'chill out' with a joint. Other drugs distributed are 'Mr. White' or Brown-Brown, low quality crack cocaine; and sleeping pills, Valium 5 and 10, nicknamed 'bubbles', or 'blue boat'. Pharmaceutical drugs, in high doses, are taken in combination with alcohol to make the user utterly fearless in criminal activities such as night-time robberies. Drug abuse was often built up during the war years, when drugs were readily available to most combatants.

The Palace functions as an illegal petrol market where night watchmen and others sell petrol stolen from the generators in nearby expatriate housing and offices. Homeless youth also form the lower echelon of patron–client networks, carrying out illegal activities on behalf of patrons (see Momoh 1999 on Nigeria). Many of these activities are carried out in collaboration with army personnel, where Palace dwellers have retained links from their background in ULIMO-J and AFL.

Other homeless groups in Monrovia have similar arrangements with, among others, the National Police Special Operations Division (SOD), the Special Security Service (SSS), the President's own Special Security Unit (SSU) and Anti Terrorist Unit (ATU). These groups generally consist of ex-NPFL fighters, who have kept close ties with their excommanders who in the post-war setting have been employed in the reconstructed police and security forces. Go-by-shop robberies are the most notorious type of criminal activity. Even if not directly sanctioned by the government, fully uniformed and armed police or security units will enter any store and empty it for commodities – keeping their war mentality intact they will literally 'go by and shop', picking up anything they want but neglecting to pay. At times go-by-shopping will occur in broad daylight. Homeless youth play important roles in these robberies, often doing the most dangerous parts of the work, but due to their inferior position they will only get a small portion of the earnings. Being in opposition to the government, Palace youth will seldom participate in go-by-shops, but in all other forms of burglaries.

Girls in the Palace

Girls in the Palace make their own contributions. Regularly or intermittently they will work as prostitutes (Utas 1999). If successful, they are often able to make much more money than their male partners do. How much they earn depends on the clientele; generally Palace girls are active in West Point, the poorest area downtown, and are paid accordingly. Rates are from approximately U.S.$1 upwards.[19] When Rose returns to the Palace after a night having earned U.S.$10, everybody is overjoyed as she arranges a great meal for all Palace dwellers. It is, however, rare that anyone brings home that amount of money. The Palace girls generally take the same kind of drugs as the boys so as to be brave and daring in their work.

Episodes of Peace and War

In this section I relate specific episodes which occurred during my time in the Palace, and which show why Palace youth are so careful about how they present themselves, to whom they expose their life realities, and how they deal with issues relating to their time as combatants. The constant threat of violent reprisals is one reason why Palace youth do not talk openly. Violence is a risk both inside and outside the Palace walls. As the story of Washington will show, evidence of past injury can also jeopardise the future. Evident in Sammy's story, is the fact that truth comes in many layers. In the precarious position of many of the Palace youth, being able to present themselves and their lives in different ways to different people is a necessary tactic.

Stealing

There is a clear moral code maintaining order within the Palace. Stealing outside the Palace is acceptable as long as no tracks are left leading to the Palace or to Palace residents. However, it is taboo to steal within the walls of the Palace. (There is also an informal code of sharing, mainly of food.) The police and other security forces often raid the Palace. They will generally loot everything they stumble over and pocket the little money they find. Thus it is easy to understand that Palace youth react forcefully to anyone leaving tracks leading to the Palace. If a suspect is caught, the seniors in the Palace decide on a punishment, which may then be carried out by anyone. Commonplace offenders are beaten. During my time in the Palace they avoided punishing people in my presence. On one occasion, however, I found an outsider tied up and stripped to his underwear. Being part of their large social network, the outsider had arrived the night before asking to be lodged for the night. The police came looking for him early the next morning and raided the Palace, but he managed to escape. Now furious, the Palace dwellers tracked him down, brought him back to the Palace and tied him up. When I arrived he was lying on the concrete floor begging for forgiveness, while they continued beating him mercilessly with a cane. After being punished according to 'the Palace law' he was handed over to the Military Police (MPs), as the Palace has connections with the military and not the ordinary police.

Things go missing in the Palace. The two leaders of the Palace, Sammy and Noah, investigate every incident. Rumours are rampant and if the stolen items cannot be found and nobody has seen anything suspicious, the youngest boys and Hawa, an outcast girl, will generally be blamed. But at times the suspect will react violently. When Noah accused Small Kamara of theft, Small Kamara really got upset and started a fight, despite being half Noah's size. Noah shoved Small Kamara into a corner, temporarily ending the fight. Within minutes, however, Small Kamara returned with a knife and with an earlier unperceived rage. His friends explained his hyperaggressive behaviour. He had gone up to his room to inhale crack cocaine and gain the illusion of being an immortal fighter, just as he had repeatedly done during the war prior to a battle. Everybody jumped on Small Kamara, preventing him from doing any harm, and he eventually got his punishment.

Risking Jail

Disclosing matters of everyday life in the clandestine world is hazardous for many reasons. For instance, information in the wrong hands might entail prison. Palace youth talk about prison as a 'cool' thing, but this covers a sense of fear. Ending up in prison lacking the right connections is potentially fatal. Still they all spend time in jail now and then. Getting caught for some minor crime might lead to prison without any hope of a trial whatsoever. To get out of jail cash is needed to bribe officers, and Palace youth seldom have the amount of money they demand. Noah is jailed at Central Police Headquarters. Succeeding in getting out after just forty-eight hours he states that 'inside there is a completely different kind of government'. Some inmates have been in jail for more than three months and, inevitably, crude hierarchies are in place. Prisoners beat each other up and new arrivals are robbed of all valuables and at times stripped to the skin. As Noah is caught just outside the Palace he enters jail bare-chested, wearing only a pair of old trousers, and the small bag in which he always carries his cigarettes and drugs for sale is soon confiscated by his cellmates. Those in jail do not get any food unless relatives or friends bring it, and the chances are that it will end up eaten by the senior inmates. The drinking water is brown. According to Noah a few of those interned are so weak that they must be propped up when they walk. He does not believe that they will stay alive for long. Sammy visits Noah and describes how he has to pay a bribe at every desk he passes until he reaches Noah's cell. After negotiations Sammy manages to get Noah out of the jail after two days by promising a police officer 'beer money' and borrowing the L$75 required (approximately U.S.$2).[20]

Washington's Story

Although Washington was born in Margibi County (in central Liberia) and grew up in Monrovia, the war still put him in a precarious situation as his parents were from the Krahn ethnic group – Krahn being portrayed as the main enemies of the NPFL and INPFL. When these two factions advanced into Monrovia he saw no other hope than to join forces with them. Keeping a low profile he succeeded in getting employed in the kitchen for some senior NPFL commanders and ended up in the port of Buchanan. However, after some time the commanders were informed that Washington was a Krahn and he was taken to the beach one night to be shot. He was shot in the left hip and left to bleed to death. After three days he got to a doctor, with a badly infected wound. He recovered fully and today he walks with only a slight sway, but enough to be suspected of participation in the war and to remain without stable employment.

At 36, Washington is the oldest inhabitant of the Palace. From a chronological perspective he would hardly be labelled youth, but from a perspective of social age he is well within the youth category. Having no official house, no official wife and no substantial income restrains him from entering adulthood. Washington's life is an ongoing struggle to become an adult, to get out of the youth category. Trying to leave the criminal sector behind, he has to start from the very bottom of society. He is employed by the MCC (Monrovia City Council) as caretaker of two rubbish containers on a side street a few blocks away from the Palace. Civil servants in Liberia are paid ridiculously little and on an irregular basis, if at all. But to Washington it is a window of opportunity to enter the accepted world. Washington has a fiancée, whom he plans to marry. Because of the security situation in the Palace, Washington keeps her away from there as much as possible. In line with his aim of leaving the youth category, Washington and his fiancée are expecting a baby. He takes every opportunity to get a better job, which will enable him to rent a small place for them both. But although he is a trained carpenter, every potential employer he contacts asks him to strip to check if he has war related scars – a common practice. Being wounded in the war he will generally be dismissed instantly. Washington, as the story of the powerless often goes, fails to get a better job, and loses the one at MCC (after stealing two wheelbarrow tyres); finally his fiancée walks out, leaving him with his shattered dream.

Sammy's Story

Sammy could speak rather openly about his life, because of his position as a senior in the Palace. Moreover, he was the person I built up the closest relationship with. Matters concerning the war, however, were more delicate and he remained reluctant to go into detail throughout our time together. Sammy was born in Monrovia to a Sierra Leonean father and a Liberian mother. He was one of nine siblings living with his divorced mother. I pick up the story from a day in 1985, when Sammy was fifteen years old. He says he was going to school in central Monrovia. One day after school he was walking through Waterside market with a friend of his, when they stumbled on a U.S.$50 bill on the ground. This was a large sum and they instantly decided to keep it. However, they felt anxious going home to their parents, because they knew that sooner or later they would find the money and suspect them of having stolen it. That afternoon, says Sammy, they tried to spend as much money as possible, but this only increased the difficulty of hiding their catch. Then in bravado his friend proposed that they should leave the country. Since Sammy had previously attended school in Freetown, Sierra Leone, this was where they went. Needless to say they soon ran out of money. For several years Sammy worked as a *poda-poda* (minibus) apprentice in Freetown. Through his father's efforts he was reunited with his family after three years. The war had not yet begun and during his absence his mother had progressed from being a small-scale baker to a big business woman running the most popular nightclub in Gardnersville (a suburb of Monrovia). From living a marginal and difficult life in Freetown he returned to wealth in Monrovia. When the war started his mother's property and club were looted, and for revenge and to regain what the family had lost he joined the INPFL.

I am doubtful about parts of Sammy's account. Sammy's mother was poor before the war and according to Sammy his father did not aid his former wife in any substantial way (Sammy's father is upper-middleclass – as I could observe during a visit to his house). Probably Sammy did not go to school, and most likely he stayed with other boys in the market area looking for opportunities. The U.S.$50 – a huge sum for a poor 15-year-old – was that opportunity. In his story he emphasises that the money was found but it is likely that they saw an opportunity to snatch the money. Someone probably observed them or could link them to the stolen money, hence they felt constrained to leave town for some time. Freetown became a natural choice for someone with Sammy's background. According to Sammy he returned to his mother in Monrovia after three years. In that time she had gone from baking bread at home in the morning (and sending her children out to sell it during the day) into being a big-business woman. Such a transformation would be rather unlikely during ordinary circumstances. But if, instead, it occurred during the first phase of the war, if she became close to a high-ranking commander of the Liberian army or any of the rebel forces, it turns into a rather commonplace story of upward social mobility in war times, which happened to many women. I believe that Sammy returned to his nouveau riche mother during the war.

Sammy was 19 when the war started and most probably he joined the rebel force ULIMO in Freetown, Sierra Leone, at the time it was formed in 1991. At this time many Liberian boys and girls in Sierra Leone were recruited by ULIMO and trained in camps there.[21] According to him he fought for INPFL during 1990 and 1991, but this seems doubtful. At the time of my fieldwork, 1998, Sammy is 27. Well behaved and articulate, he makes his living as a con-artist (*picaro*) (Austen 1986) in the post-war setting. Sammy developed these skills during the course of the war. For instance, he described how during 1992, he used a bogus identification card distinguishing him as a captain in the police force to arrest people who had just arrived in Monrovia and squeeze money out of them. In the Palace, Sammy maintains a leading position next to Noah. He is active in keeping law and order inside the Palace, something of a contradiction to his other activities. My friendship with Sammy ends abruptly as he shows his *picaro* character. As the right opportunity occurs, the first time he gets his hand on some of the money in our development project for the Palace (see above), he runs away with it. He keeps hidden from the other Palace inhabitants for quite some time, being aware of the vengeance they will take if they catch him. It takes several months until the others in the Palace give me reports of his whereabouts, at which time he has apparently already abused the trust of another group in one of the Monrovian suburbs, and is again a fugitive.

Doing Research among Petty Criminal Excombatant Youth

Entering the field and the Palace I stumbled into many methodological problems ranging from ethical issues, issues of acceptance and personal security, to how to classify stories in relation to their truth. Expecting that my fieldwork would be quite different from most fieldwork carried out in West Africa, during a stopover in Abidjan I read Philippe Bourgois' Harlem study on young Puerto Rican drug dealers (1995). Methodologically, the field of my study showed greater similarities with Bourgois' work, or Rodgers' (2000) and Jensen's (2001) dissertations on gangs in urban Nicaragua and South Africa respectively, than, say, Zetterström's ethnographic account of the Yamein Mano in Nimba County, to take a Liberian example (1976). The fieldwork presented me with a whole host of methodological dilemmas.

Personal Security

Initially I experienced my own personal security as a problem. People told me time and again that Palace youth were dangerous. I took some precautions: for instance I did not stay in the Palace overnight. However, after some time in the Palace I felt that I could trust most of the Palace youth and in some cases they even protected me: instead of viewing Palace youth as potential risks I came to view them as assets. Accompanied by my friends in the Palace I could venture to places where ordinary Monrovians dared not go. For instance, we went to bars in West Point, the poorest downtown area, at night. I genuinely enjoyed myself and due to the presence of my companions did not think of myself as being in danger. At one time the entire expatriate community was advised to move near the U.S. embassy for security. There were problems around the ULIMO-J leader's house with nightly armed skirmishes in the vicinity (one night they were shooting just behind my house). I asked the Palace youth for advice and was assured that there was no real danger and they would inform me if there was. I took their advice and as time went by I started trusting them more than the U.S. intelligence that the INGO community relied on.

Informants' Security

Even if Palace youth avoided bold accounts from the war years or their contemporary lives, I had to be careful with my own material. At the outset of my research, government security staff took a keen interest in me. I was arrested and intimidated. It was mainly a way to extort money from me, but I had to take precautions. In my notebooks I used aliases for all informants and every week I went to an NGO office to enter my notes on a computer. I burnt the notes and kept the disk in their safe. To avoid the risk of security personnel confiscating my material when I left, I sent it home in portions by e-mail. This text also uses aliases for my informants.

An ethical matter that I have not resolved is a few eyewitness accounts that I have taped. In one, a young boy gives details about the murder of five American nuns in which he participated.[22] It is not clear to me whether he told me this because he wanted to share the information or in order to make a personal confession as a means of coming to terms with what he had done. I also have accounts of women who have been raped by people currently in high positions within the government and civil service. To protect my informants I have not been able to use these accounts.

Getting in

As explained above, gaining acceptance was a delicate task. In this case my rite of passage was that I had experienced the Liberian Civil War myself. Even so, some topics were exceptionally difficult to discuss. My informants intentionally blurred everything related to participation in the civil war. Illegal activities carried out in daily life remained difficult to pinpoint. Initially, I learned about these issues from Palace youth who liked to gossip about others while maintaining a moral façade. In time, however, some began to relax this attitude and started telling me more. How openly they related issues to me depended on several factors.

Age and Social Network

One factor was age. During my stay in the Palace I found it much harder to get detailed information out of the younger ones. Their tactic would generally be to change their accounts time after time, leaving me with little substance in the end. Part of the passage to maturity is being able to judge what is personally dangerous to talk about and what is not. The younger informants were the more likely to present themselves as victims and passive nonagents in their accounts. This became especially evident when I took on the task of making semi-structured taped interviews with a group of excombatants aged ten to fifteen within a reintegration project in Ganta.

The older Palace youth often abandoned the extreme victim mode as we deepened our relationship. Indeed their position in the social network in and around the Palace also played its part. The leaders established a much more confident tone in our discussions, while the subordinate youths watched their tongues so as not to give details on issues that would displease their seniors. A young Palace dweller could be beaten up severely for any small matter, as in the case of Small Kamara described above. Just how open one could afford to be was also dependent on contacts outside the Palace; having good contacts with patrons, big men, in larger society had its implications for what one dared to say, and to whom. For instance, on the issue of illegal activities, youth with good contacts within the police dared to be fairly open about their activities because they could count on aid if they were caught. Getting caught by police and ending up in jail could be very dangerous without such contacts. In the incident related above, Noah was lucky to get out of jail so quickly.

Which rebel army they had fought for was also of great importance. Being an NPFL fighter during the April 6 war makes life easier in the post-war setting. In post-war Liberia it is only NPFL soldiers that dare to talk openly about all issues of war. Only a change in government would have allowed Palace youth to be frank with me, thus after four months in the Palace I knew that I had to change to another setting to get to the heart of war issues. By moving up to Nimba County, NPFL heartland, I later managed to locate a set of young people that dared to talk about their everyday life in wartime Liberia.

Multi-layered Stories

Doing research among groups of people living in a disturbed environment, such as Palace youth, is inevitably a navigation through multilayered stories. The production of different stories for different audiences is a method of survival in dangerous life realms. During the time I spent in the Palace, the youth categorised me in different ways at different times; thus the stories they related to me varied from occasion to occasion. After some months, when their trust of me had deepened, some of the youth came closer to relating their own honest versions of their experiences. Time was the most important ingredient in this arrangement. The story told by Sammy highlights this. The full version was given to me quite early in our friendship. In due time he gave me other pieces of information. With these bits and pieces I patched together an alternative story – it is not the 'true story' but it is a story that lies closer to reality than the one that he presented to me earlier on.[23]

During my time in Liberia I did some work for an INGO. We spent five days in Southern Liberia conducting close to 100 taped semi-structured interviews with young people, many excombatants. It amounted to an impressive set of data. As a comparison, after four months in the Palace I had not done a single taped interview. In retrospect I can see that the taped interview material I collected in Southern Liberia was almost entirely wasted effort; every interviewee complied with one of the preset frames of victimhood. To tape any interviews in the Palace was out of the question as their life realms were just too insecure. Such is the case in most Liberian post-war settings and indeed excombatants worldwide would not directly discuss issues involving their war crimes with just any outsider. My work in the Palace came, to a large extent, to revolve around topics of everyday life played out in front of me by the Palace youth. In due time trust increased and I believe that we jointly managed to produce a unique picture of everyday life for excombatant urban youth in post-war Liberia.

The Temporal: 'It all Chakla'

The Palace as research space highlights the temporality of research itself. The social framework of the Palace showed both extreme elasticity and rapid transformations. Persons who, at the onset of the fieldwork, only had an outsider status as occasional visitors, turned into core Palace dwellers. Likewise, within a few months, some of my central informants left the building and were replaced with new ones. The fluidity made it difficult to establish stable relationships. My prime informant, Sammy, for example, took some material and money from our micro project and left never to return. Less than a month later, two of the other leaders of the group moved to another building. Even if I had kept in contact with them, it could never have been with the same frequency as before.

As smoothly as the gate once opened when I first arrived at the Palace, it closed in front of me. After four months in the Palace I was absent for a month. When I returned I found a new leader in control. Still having some of my closer contacts among the Palace youth, I thought I had a fair chance to reestablish my presence in the building. However, the new leader did not like my presence and managed to turn some of the Palace youth against me. At this difficult moment I had brought my sister (a free-lance filmmaker) with the intention of recording the Palace and maybe making a television documentary about it. The new leader, however, seized the initiative and convinced most of the Palace youth that I would make a lot of money by producing a movie of their lives and that I would not let them take any of the profit. Within a single day they turned from friends into strangers. In the morning we were shooting footage and then, when we returned after lunch, they confiscated the camcorder and took me as a kind of hostage until my sister could pay for our release. As I was moving upcountry to continue my research it was not a disaster from a research point of view. I had managed to get an INGO interested in developing the micro-economic project that we had established in the Palace, so I knew there was some actual hope for the Palace youth for whom I had found great sympathy. Yet I was sitting there on the ground of the basketball court we had once cleared together. It was rather pathetic. My sister (in shock) eventually came with the money. All in all they had only demanded L$800 (about U.S.$20). I made a last effort to distribute the money equally to all, but the new leader had a different idea. He selected a 'trusted' member of the group to keep the *nuku* for the time being. Conniving with the leader the boy snatched the *nuku* and dashed out of the Palace followed by a wild bunch of his deceived friends. Later on I came back for visits as a friend, but by this time the Palace as research space was unconditionally closed. I had been excluded, again turned into an outsider. Palace youth would say 'it *chakla*' – it fell apart.

Notes

1. This paper is dedicated to Scarface who was, due to his war history, tragically executed during the course of my fieldwork.

2. Political scientists who use personal contacts within political networks as a base for their analysis are less troubled by wars (see e.g. Reno 1995, 1996, 1997, 1998, 2000; Ellis 1995, 1998, 1999).

3. One of the best known is the Dutchman Gus Kouwenhoven, a large-scale drug trafficker who has made Liberia a base for his illegal operations in drugs, arms, diamonds and timber (see Global Witness 2001).

4. Popular estimations point towards 200,000 deaths, but in a recount Ellis (1999) argues convincingly for a much lower figure (60,000).

5. A former UNDHA employee states that the demobilisation exercise was merely a numbers game (e-mail communication).

6. 'April 6' is the name used for the last part of the civil war. Renewed fighting on 6 April, 1996, in Monrovia signalled the onset.

7. The fighting forces consisted only of about 2–4 percent women (David 1997; UNDHA–HACO 1997).

8. Children at such a young age did generally not form part of the regular troops and would more often function as assistants to older soldiers, forming a first step in a military career.

9. I place 'free' in quotation marks because structural constraints tend to be more limiting in times of war than in peace.

10. I have elsewhere shown that it might be equally effective for a family if a daughter is going out with an important commander (Utas forthcoming).

11. Stories of cannibalistic rituals among combatants during the civil war were widely told and most Liberians never doubted their validity. Clearly such rituals took place, but it appears to me that the regularity is exaggerated by Liberians, by international media and in some academic writing (as for instance in Ellis 1999).

12. One American journalist had recently visited the Palace and promised them all that he would send them beds to sleep in. He also talked about establishing long-term contacts, which might one day lead to a visit to the U.S.

13. One thing that signalled their ULIMO-J status was that they had red nail polish on one fingernail. When I asked about it, they agreed that it had been a marker for ULIMO-J affiliation during the war but that in the post-war setting it was mere street fashion.

14. After his death I made some investigation in the matter among my acquaintances within the security forces. According to those familiar with the case it was quite clear that he had not played any active part in the 18 September unrest.

15. In Liberia as a whole, primary school enrolment is 51 percent for boys and 28 percent for girls. Secondary school enrolment is 31 percent for boys and 13 percent for girls (UNFPA 1999, based on prewar surveys).

16. Economic assistance from abroad is one of the main sources of income in post-war Liberia.

17. Ranks were often given to soldiers as proof of bravery rather than commanding position, hence many of the fighters obtained unusually high ranks. For instance, one of the youngest of the Palace inhabitants (15 years old in 1998 but only seven at the onset of the war) had a captain's rank.

18. Since the Firestone deal in the 1920s, U.S. dollars have been the main currency in the country. During the early 1980s a national currency was introduced but only in coins, while U.S. bills were widely used. Today Liberia has its own currency system but U.S. currency is still used in parallel.

19. Expatriate workers at Save the Children Foundation in Monrovia say that as little as L$5 (less than 10 U.S. cents) is paid.

20. 'Beer money' signals the size of the bribe not its employment. If someone wants a smaller bribe they will ask for 'cold water'.
21. As a consequence of NPFL flushing out people associated with the Samuel Doe government during the early phase of the war, many people with origins in southern Liberia were forced into exile. Earlier, similar cleansing exercises were carried out by the Doe administration.
22. This incident has been widely reported. Some witness accounts have been made publicly available, see for instance *Liberian Studies Journal* (2001).
23. A cultural ideal of secrecy (Bellman 1984) also makes it hard to get a straightforward account. As Mariane Ferme has noted among people inhabiting the forest regions of Sierra Leone, Guinea and Liberia 'truth is what lies under multiple layers of often conflicting meanings' (2001: 7).

References

Abdullah, I. 1997. 'Introduction: Special Issue on Lumpen Culture and Political Violence: the Sierra Leone Civil War.' *Africa Development* 22 (3/4): 5–18.

——. 1998. 'Bush Path to Destruction: the Origin and Character of the Revolutionary United Front/Sierra Leone.' *Journal of Modern African Studies* 36 (2): 203–35.

Abdullah, I., and Bangura, Y. 1997. 'Lumpen Youth Culture and Political Violence: Sierra Leoneans Debate the RUF and the Civil War.' *Africa Development* 22 (3/4): 171–216.

Atkinson, P. 1999. 'Deconstructing Media Mythologies of Ethnic War in Liberia.' In T. Allen and J. Seaton, eds, *The Media of Conflict: War Reporting and Representations of Ethnic Violence*. London: Zed Books.

Austen, R.A. 1986. 'Social Bandits and Other Heroic Criminals: Western Models of Resistance and their Relevance for Africa.' In D. Crummey, ed., *Banditry, Rebellion and Social Protest in Africa*. London: James Currey.

Bellman, B.L. 1975. *Village of Curers and Assassins: on the Production of Fala Kpelle Cosmological Categories*. The Hague: Mouton.

——. 1984. *The Language of Secrecy: Symbols and Metaphors in Poro Ritual*. New Brunswick, NJ: Rutgers University Press.

Bledsoe, C.H. 1980. *Women and Marriage in Kpelle Society*. Stanford, California: Stanford University Press.

Bourgois, P.I. 1995. *In Search of Respect: Selling Crack in El Barrio*. Cambridge: Cambridge University Press.

Brett, R. and McCallin, M. 1996. *Children the Invisible Soldiers*. Stockholm: Rädda Barnen.

Certeau, M. de 1984. *The Practice of Everyday Life*. Berkeley: University of California Press.

Clapham, C. 1988. 'The Politics of Failure: Clientelism, Political Instability and National Integration in Liberia and Sierra Leone.' In C. Clapham, ed., *Private Patronage and Public Power: Political Clientelism in the Modern State*. New York: St. Martins Press.

Clapham, C.S. 1976. *Liberia and Sierra Leone: an Essay in Comparative Politics*. Cambridge and New York: Cambridge University Press.

Cruise O'Brien, D. B. 1996. 'A Lost Generation? Youth Identity and State Decay in West Africa.' In R. Werbner and T. Ranger, eds., *Postcolonial Identities in Africa*. London: Zed Books.

David, K. 1997. *The Disarmament, Demobilization, and Reintegration of Child Soldiers in Liberia 1994–97*. Monrovia: UNICEF–Liberia.

d'Azevedo, W.L. 1962. 'Common Principles of Variant Kinship Structures Among the Gola of Western Liberia.' *American Anthropologist* 64 (3): 504–20.

——. 1969–1970. 'A Tribal Reaction to Nationalism.' *Liberian Studies Journal* 1, 2, 3 (2,1,2,1): 1–21, 43–63, 99–115, 1–31.

——. 1972. *Gola of Liberia*. New Haven, CT: Human Relations Area Files.

——. 1989. 'Tribe and Chiefdom on the Windward Coast.' *Liberian Studies Journal* 14 (2): 90–116.

——. 1994. 'Gola Womanhood and the Limits of Masculine Omnipotence.' In T.D. Blakely, W.E.A. van Beek and D.L. Thomson, eds, *Religion in Africa: Experience and Expression*. London: James Currey.

Durham, D. 2000. 'Youth and the Social Imagination in Africa: Introduction to Parts 1 and 2.' *Anthropological Quarterly*. 73 (3): 113-20.

Ellis, S. 1995. 'Liberia 1989–1994: A Study of Ethnic and Spiritual Violence.' *African Affairs* 94: 165–97.

——. 1998. 'Liberia's Warlord Insurgency.' In C. Clapham, ed., *African Guerrillas*. Oxford: James Currey.

——. 1999. *The Mask of Anarchy: the Destruction of Liberia and the Religious Dimension of an African Civil War*. New York: New York University Press.

Ferme, M.C. 2001. *The Underneath of Things: Violence, History, and the Everyday in Sierra Leone*. Berkeley: University of California Press.

Fleischman, J. and Whitman, L. 1994. *Easy Prey: Child Soldiers in Liberia*. New York: Human Rights Watch.

Geertz, C. 1973. *The Interpretation of Cultures: Selected Essays*. New York: Basic Books.

Global Witness 2001. *Taylor-made: the Pivotal Role of Liberia's Forest and Flag of Convenience in Regional Conflict*. London: Global Witness/International Transport Workers Federation.

Goodwin-Gill, G.S. and Cohn, I. 1994. *Child Soldiers: the Role of Children in Armed Conflict*. Oxford and New York: Oxford University Press.

Handelman, D. 1997. 'Absence Rising: Telling Little Holocaust Stories in Israel.' Unpublished paper.

Hannerz, U. 1969. *Soulside: Inquiries into Ghetto Culture and Community*. New York: Columbia University Press.

Harris, D. 1999. 'From "Warlord" to "Democratic" President: How Charles Taylor Won the 1997 Liberian Elections.' *Journal of Modern African Studies* 37 (3): 431–55.

Jackson, M. 2002. *The Politics of Storytelling: Violence, Transgression, and Intersubjectivity*. Copenhagen: Museum Tusculanum Press, University of Copenhagen.

Jensen, S. 2001. 'Claiming Community – Negotiating Crime: State Formation, Neighbourhood and Gangs in a Capetonian Township.' Ph.D. thesis, Roskilde University.

Kaplan, L.J. 1984. *Adolescence, the Farewell to Childhood*. New York: Simon and Schuster.

Keen, D. and International Institute for Strategic Studies 1998. *The Economic Functions of Violence in Civil Wars*. Oxford and New York: Oxford University Press.

Liberian Studies Journal 2001. 'How Five Nuns were Killed in "Octopus".' *Liberian Studies Journal* 27 (1): 120–24.

Liebenow, J.G. 1969. *Liberia: the Evolution of Privilege*. Ithaca: Cornell University Press.

——. 1980. *Liberia: the Dissolution of Privilege*. Hanover, NH: American Universities Field Staff.

——. 1987. *Liberia: the Quest for Democracy*. Bloomington: Indiana University Press.

Liebenow, J.G. and Universities Field Staff International 1984. *Liberia – 'Dr. Doe' and the Demise of Democracy: Part II, Re-establishing the One-party State*. Hanover, NH: Universities Field Staff International.

Momoh, A. 1999. 'The Youth Crisis in Nigeria: Understanding the Phenomenon of the Area Boys and Girls.' Paper presented to the conference on Children and Youth as Emerging Categories in Africa. Leuven, 1999.

Moran, M.H. 1990. *Civilized Women: Gender and Prestige in South-eastern Liberia*. Ithaca, NY: Cornell University Press.

Muana, P. 1997. 'The Kamajoi Militia: Violence, Internal Displacement and the Politics of Counter-insurgency.' *Africa Development* 22 (3/4): 77–100.

Murphy, W. 1980. 'Secret Knowledge as Property and Power in Kpelle Society: Elders Versus Youth.' *Africa* 50: 193–207.

Rashid, I. 1997. 'Subaltern Reactions: Lumpens, Students, and the Left.' *Africa Development* 22 (3/4): 19–44.

Reno, W. 1995. 'Reinvention of an African Patrimonial State: Charles Taylor's Liberia.' *Third World Quarterly* 16 (1): 109–20.

——. 1996. 'The Business of War in Liberia.' *Current History*. May: 211–15.

——. 1997. *Humanitarian Emergencies and Warlord Economies in Liberia and Sierra Leone*: Helsinki: UNU/WIDER.

——. 1998. *Warlord Politics and African States*: Boulder, CD: Lynne Rienner.

——. 2000. 'Liberia and Sierra Leone: the Competition for Patronage in Resource-rich Economies.' In E. W. Nafziger, F. Stewart and R. Väyrynen, eds, *War, Hunger, and Displacement: the Origins of Humanitarian Emergencies*. Oxford: Oxford University Press.

Richards, P. 1995. 'Rebellion in Liberia and Sierra Leone: A Crisis of Youth?' In O. Furley, ed., *Conflict in Africa*. London: Tauris Academic Studies.

——. 1996. *Fighting for the Rain Forest: War, Youth and Resources in Sierra Leone*. Oxford: James Currey.

Rodgers, D. 2000. 'Living in the Shadow of Death: Violence, Pandillas, and Social Disintegration in Contemporary Urban Nicaragua.' Ph.D. thesis, University of Cambridge.

Ruiz, H.A. 1992. *Uprooted Liberians: Casualties of a Brutal War*. Washington, DC: American Council for Nationalities Service.

Tiljander Dahlström, Å. 2001. 'No Peace of Mind: the Tibetan Diaspora in India.' Ph.D. thesis, Uppsala University.

Tonkin, E. 1992. *Narrating our Pasts: the Social Construction of Oral History*. Cambridge: Cambridge University Press.

UNDHA–HACO 1997. 'Demobilisation in Liberia: 22 Nov 96 – 09 Feb 97' (unpublished). Monrovia: UNDHA-HACO.

UNFPA 1999. 'The State of the World Population'. New York, United Nations Population Fund.

Utas, M. 1997. *Assiduous Exile: Strategies of Work and Integration among Liberian Refugees in Danane, Ivory Coast*. Working Papers in Cultural Anthropology, no. 6: Uppsala University.

——. 1999. 'Girls' "loving business": Sex and the Struggle for Status and Independence in Liberia.' *Antropologiska Studier* 64/65: 65–76.

——. forthcoming. 'Agency of Victims: Young Women's Survival Strategies in the Liberian Civil War.' In F. de Boeck and A. Honwana, eds, *Makers and Breakers;*

Made and Broken: Children and Youth as Emerging Categories in Postcolonial Africa. London: James Currey.

Whyte, W.F. 1993. *Street Corner Society: the Social Structure of an Italian Slum.* Chicago: University of Chicago Press.

Zetterström, K. 1976. 'The Yamein Mano of Northern Liberia.' Ph.D. thesis, Institutionen for allmän och jämforande etnografi vid Uppsala Universitet.

12

Anthropology Under Fire: Ethics, Researchers and Children in War

Jo Boyden

Introduction

As one of the most horrifying and momentous experiences known to humankind, war is of major theoretical and empirical interest to many scholars in the social sciences. International relations, economics, sociology and political science have been at the forefront of research in this field. Anthropologists, however, have tended to neglect the topic of war. In so far as the normal condition of human society is taken to be one of order, stability and equilibrium, anthropology tends to regard armed conflict as an atypical and calamitous state that, as such, merits little theoretical or empirical scrutiny. This outlook can be attributed in part to the influence of Marcel Mauss, whose theory of gift exchange promoted the idea that human interaction is founded on mutual interest and peaceful transaction. It has, however, been criticised in recent decades by those who suggest that it exaggerates both the accord and consistency of societies at peace and the anarchy of war (Allen 1989; Colson 1989; Davis 1992; Nordstrom 1997; Reynolds-White 1998). The critics stress instead the order that prevails within the disorder of war. They highlight the morality that persists in an immoral context and the culturally encoded meanings that structure and regulate individual and collective experience even in communities exposed to extreme violence and discord. They understand armed conflict not as a societal aberration, but as growing out of either a specific form of social organisation or a specific cultural phase. Some call for greater attention to conflict, or for the development of what John Davis has termed 'the anthropology of suffering'.

That said, for the anthropologist who is interested in war there are many challenges and dilemmas not merely with regard to theory, conceptualisation and analysis but also in terms of practical constraints, methodology, methods and ethics. Personal security, access to research subjects over time and integrity of data are all threatened by armed violence. In certain cases, research is itself a major source of risk to war-affected populations. In this chapter I explore some of the practical, methodological and ethical difficulties I have confronted during research with war-affected and displaced children and communities in several parts of the world. I highlight some of the compromises I have been forced to make and their implications both for the research and for those involved in it. This in turn leads to a deeper questioning of the role of research in the reporting and mediation of human misfortune and distress.

Risk and Restraint

During war, the researcher struggles against the odds to create the ethical and practical conditions that are normally thought of as essential to good ethnography. The circumstances of conflict are hardly conducive to sound fieldwork and commonly make participant observation, the basic tool of the anthropologist's trade, impossible. Areas affected by conflict are generally subject to complex governance arrangements in which military and security concerns are predominant. In many cases the power of military and law enforcement bodies to contain conflict is enhanced through draconian legislation that bears down heavily on civilian populations. Frequently, the breadth of these legal instruments and the degree of authority accorded within them means that the range of situations that can be construed as a threat to security and acted upon with the impunity of defence forces is considerable. Not only does this impinge directly on the lives of children and communities, but it also undermines research, which in the more extreme cases may be outlawed altogether. At the very least, researchers must normally obtain clearance to carry out their work, whether from government, the armed forces, insurgents or in, 'grey zones' that fall under the influence of more than one party to the conflict, both state and nonstate actors.

Aside from security constraints there are the volatile working conditions to contend with. Population mobility, an essential survival strategy and a key feature of civilian life in many war zones, is a major obstacle to research. Often it is easier to research conflict in its aftermath when the fighting has ceased. Often it is easier to study displaced populations contained in camps for refugees or internally displaced persons (IDPs), rather than those populations that remain in areas of conflict. Shelling and attacks by ground troops may be daily or nightly, and civilian evacuations may occur with the same frequency. Sometimes respondents disappear without warning and for reasons not obvious to the researcher.

Other difficulties include the frequent interruption of national and subnational information retrieval systems and destruction of crucial demographic, health and social records. Another problem is the overt manipulation of data: many of the statistics that researchers rely on for contextual detail are in effect spurious. Hence, official statistics on refugee populations are commonly compiled not through demographic surveys but through negotiation with warring parties, host governments and the like. The figures arrived at are more likely to reflect political expediency than actual population numbers. At another level, refugee deaths may be significantly underreported as families who depend on rations of deceased members bury their dead in secret. Thus in Rohingya camps in Bangladesh, the offer of a free burial shroud proved an insufficient incentive for inhabitants to disclose deaths, for it did not provide adequate compensation for rations forgone. Camp officials only learned about the true extent of mortality when they took to standing vigil around the clock and counting the dead as they were brought to burial grounds by relatives (Pat Diskett, personal communication).

I first confronted some of the complexities of research in conflict in 1990 when I conducted a study in the Kentung area of East Shan State, Burma, with girls who had been trafficked into the sex trade in Thailand. Located in the notorious Golden Triangle, the region had long been exposed to the destabilising effects of the opium trade, and for forty years had been subject to armed conflict between the army and insurgent forces led by powerful warlords. The ceasefires of 1989 had brought a semblance of peace to the area but also heralded a period of highly repressive rule by central government, the State Law and Order Restoration Council (SLORC). Access to the region had to be negotiated with both the Burmese military and the warlords. My presence there was made conditional on staying at a military camp – to which the research team returned each night – and being accompanied continually by armed guards.

Due to these security arrangements, an inordinate amount of time was wasted travelling to and from research sites. More seriously, given the presence of armed soldiers, the impossibility of staying in any one village for an adequate period of time and language barriers, it was not feasible to build the kind of relationships with respondents that are normally regarded as an essential ingredient of good fieldwork. Graver still were the ethical considerations that dogged me throughout, such as the possibility that our visits could expose civilians to interrogation or reprisal. There was a very real risk that their safety could be jeopardised by information unwittingly divulged to us. I was also troubled by how people would interpret our association with the military. The SLORC was profoundly unpopular in this region and I feared that whatever explanations were given, our apparent cooperation with the army would be taken as voluntary. Of greater concern was the possibility that we would be perceived as spies. The most worrying experience I had during my time in Burma was being followed into a preschool classroom by a soldier with a Kalashnikov strung over his shoulder and a belt of hand grenades around his waist. Incidents such as these brought home to me the importance of researchers in war having a heightened awareness of the potential impact of their actions on public perception and feelings. A chance encounter on the street, an unguarded statement, or an interview or an imprudent friendship with someone who has secret links with the enemy, can mark the researcher as foe, thereby destroying research relationships.

In the event, most of the fieldwork in Burma was conducted through a kind of subterfuge in which researchers and respondents operated in collusion to deceive the authorities. I acted as a decoy, wandering one way with the soldiers following me, while my local colleagues carried out the investigation by moving in the opposite direction. They took to jogging outside the camp in the early mornings and shopping in the local town in the evenings as a means of normalising their presence in the area and legitimating their interactions with the local population. One of the team members, a medical practitioner, conducted interviews whilst attending patients at impromptu clinics set up in villages and homes. Medical settings provided one of the few contexts in Burma in which civilians were granted respite from military surveillance. Despite these efforts, however, and even with the guarantee of respondent anonymity and explicit and clear discussion of the potential hazards of taking part in the research, involvement in this project inevitably presented some risk to all concerned. As the outsider in this context, I was particularly worried about being so dependent on others for security assessments and found this dependence especially difficult to reconcile with my responsibility as lead investigator for the overall safety of both researchers and researched.

A study undertaken with colleagues (Boyden et al. 2002) recently in the north and east of Sri Lanka posed similar problems, particularly in relation to achieving continuous access to and unimpeded communication with respondents. Strict security procedures have for many years acted as a major constraint to research in these areas. Prior to the 2001 ceasefire, people living in the north and east were made liable to a plethora of restrictions on mobility, access to income and services and interaction with outsiders. When permission to travel was granted, civilians in many areas faced severe delays, harassment, extortion and violence at army checkpoints. For their part, outsiders seeking access to the north and east had to negotiate with the government, the Sri Lankan Army and in some places the insurgent forces of the Liberation Tigers of Tamil Eelam (LTTE). Even though our fieldwork took place following the ceasefire when many of the restrictions had been relaxed, there were major obstacles still to be overcome. There was a palpable tension in quite a few of the camps and villages we visited. This was partly due to the animosity between civilians (especially the displaced) and government officials, the oppressive presence of military personnel, political encroachment by the LTTE into government-controlled areas and the continued violations, especially the abductions of children by the LTTE and infringements committed at checkpoints. Government and law enforcement officials were still very much in control of the IDP camps in some areas and we learned from inhabitants that people who had in the recent past tried to speak out about the poor conditions or other problems were either expelled or arrested and detained. In general, civilians were not at all confident about the efficacy of the ceasefire agreement.

Arising from all of this, civilians in the north and east had become accustomed to severely curtailed interaction with outsiders. Government officials and staff members of humanitarian agencies were among the few groups to enter these areas on a regular basis. The agencies had grown used to organising programmes around the constraints of curfew, security clearances, checkpoints, minefields and intelligence operations and had fallen into a habit of confining contact with aid recipients to rather formal and brief workshops and meetings. Informal and more regular and long-term exchanges with civilians were discouraged for fear of attracting the attention of the authorities or raising unrealistic expectations of aid. Despite attempts to counteract these tendencies, our fieldwork soon fell into a similar pattern, with adverse consequences for both the research process and the findings.

Ethical Minefields

Trust

One of the chief prerequisites of effective ethnographic research is building a degree of mutual understanding and trust with respondents. But herein lies the first major challenge, for in intrastate conflicts, such as those in Burma and Sri Lanka, relations between researcher and researched are generally mediated by political and security forces whose intercession is highly oppressive and restrictive. More fundamentally though, internal conflict commonly undermines the very fabric of society, creating social worlds that become permeated by misunderstanding and mistrust.

During fieldwork in Cambodia in 1995, war survivors reflected on the long-term effects of the despotic Pol Pot regime which had, in just four years, visited widespread devastation, brutality and far more on the country. On assuming power, Pol Pot and his Khmer Rouge forces mounted a national project that entailed overthrowing Cambodian society and polity and installing a new political order led by the revolutionary organisation Angka. A Khmer metaphor, 'Angka has the eyes of a pineapple', captures the sense of fear instilled by this organisation: 'Briefly stated, it means that ... Angka, knows everything that is going on – it can see in all directions, just as the eyes of the pineapple point in all directions' (Marston 1994: 114–5). Named Democratic Kampuchea, the new state was fashioned after the ancient Angkor kingdom that had reached its zenith in Cambodia between the ninth and thirteenth centuries. The economy was restructured – with devastating effect in terms of starvation, morbidity and mortality – and the population subjected to widespread terror, genocide, forced relocation, displacement and family separation. Through these mechanisms, a conscious attempt was made 'to sever the usual bonds of allegiance and trust which bind a society together ... The society was systematically dismembered ... All the usual means of socialization were removed or undermined' (Taylor 1994: 28; see also Uimonen 1994: 6).

The social engineering and violence of this time effectively dismantled relationships within local communities and led to a profound loss of confidence in self and others. During our research respondents expressed deep ambivalence about friends, neighbours and kin, among whom figured wrongdoer and wronged, betrayer and betrayed, victim and perpetrator (Boyden and Gibbs 1997). Most poignant of all was the mistrust – and indeed fear – of children, for the Khmer Rouge forces had used the young as spies, fighters and leaders to humiliate, manipulate and ultimately incapacitate adult civilians. Paradoxically, while our attention was focused on the suffering of children in conflict, respondents were often more concerned about the atrocities they had committed. They expressed a sense of foreboding about the young, a fear of what they had done in the past and of what they might do again in the future. From this study we understood that whatever effort the researcher makes to build a sense of mutuality and confidence with respondents, these cannot override relationships fractured by war. Research is ultimately an act of disclosure that in war creates a gulf with everyday realities which are marked by secrecy, suspicion and the isolation of individuals one from the other.

Nevertheless, surprisingly, even taking the many risks and difficulties into account, populations that have been exposed to armed conflict are often more than willing to take part in research. In fact, given the dreadful circumstances under which they live, it is striking just how enthusiastic people sometimes are to talk to researchers. There was very little reservation about engaging in our study in Cambodia, for example. This observation should not, however, be taken at face value. Respondent attitudes towards research are influenced by a variety of factors, the most important commonly being perceptions about the purpose of the exercise and of the researchers themselves. Examination of how these perceptions come about raises important questions concerning the efficacy of the notion of informed consent. Most accepted ethical codes and guidelines emphasise consent as a fundamental condition of social research, and yet it turns out that this is not a free value but one that is bound up in a highly complex web of expectations, norms and meanings and as such can be hard to achieve in practice.

The Researcher in War

Take the issue of respondent perceptions of researchers for example. At one time, the scientific credibility of anthropology was thought to depend on researchers adopting a socially designated role within the research community, and thereby rendering themselves 'invisible'. The intention was for the scholar to become a neutral component in the research process and hence to minimise his or her influence on the findings. This line of thinking has now given way to a far more reflexive mode in which the personal manner and characteristics of researchers, and particularly social attributes like gender, generation and ethnicity, are regarded as critically influencing research outcomes. Hence, it is now accepted that the researcher's social status can have a major impact even on participation in research. For example, in the caste-bound Tamil communities of northern and eastern Sri Lanka, relations between people in different social categories tend to be both hierarchical and prescriptive. Strict codes of conduct dictate that when people of low caste are invited to attend a meeting or other event by those of higher status or caste they cannot reasonably refuse. Consequently, as a mixed group of foreigners and comparatively high caste, educated, urban Tamils, our research team was seriously disadvantaged with regard to the issue of consent. Certainly villagers would turn out for our sessions in large numbers and certainly they appeared content to work with us, but, given the social constraints, could this really be considered 'consent'? We remained concerned throughout our time there that prescription was prevailing over volition.

There is nothing particularly novel about this observation and many others have acknowledged the power imbalances inherent in research. Robert Chambers' work on participatory methodology and methods has proved particularly influential in attempts to overthrow orthodox research paradigms. His intention has been to empower the researched by encouraging researchers to act as facilitators rather than extractors of information, and to respect the authenticity of respondents' voices by having them, as far as is possible, devise research agendas and control the production of findings. Based on notions of inclusiveness and transparency, he has encouraged use of tools and methods that are apparently accessible to illiterate, low status, populations. Group discussion, mapping and ranking exercises are employed as an alternative to interviews, with the aim of capturing information built on collective knowledge and experience. The findings are represented in highly accessible visual forms – through diagrams, charts, maps and drawings – that are often made up with natural materials that are both familiar and status free.

Participatory methods have been employed with considerable effect in many parts of the world, especially in rural areas and in research on the distribution and utilisation of physical resources and assets. But, for a number of reasons, their applicability in areas of conflict is far more limited. First, when kin are set against kin and neighbour against neighbour, this makes a mockery of notions of a collective. Consensus that is often hard earned during peacetime may be entirely elusive during conflict. In fact, collective research methods have the potential to incite further disharmony in areas affected by war since they lay bare divisions, tensions and contradictions that might otherwise remain dormant.

Second, in wartime there may be great risk in offering up information in public. For example, research findings recorded and shared in visual form can be treated as evidence and used against respondents. A social map prepared by a community in eastern Sri Lanka initially generated a great deal of excitement, for it was the first time that the villagers had seen a graphic depiction of their social world. However, once the map was completed and laid out on the ground before them, they realised that it could easily be used by the LTTE to facilitate abductions of local children, since it identified all the inhabitants of the community and the dwellings in which they lived. An urgent discussion among the men led to a decision to destroy the map (Mandy Stephens, personal communication).

Third, the privileging of collective over individual knowledge is in itself problematic because it somehow presumes that the whole is constituted merely by the aggregation of its constituent parts. In this presumption lies the negation of the many individual testimonies of war that are highly personal and distinct and that cannot be told in public fora. Time and again I have been struck by the richness and complexity of children's narratives that remain hidden from families and communities and often contradict the stories told by them.

One of the defining features of war research is the reporting of events – social, political, criminal and personal – generally conceived of as major transgressions against individuals and/or society. Given this circumstance, it is unsurprising that the political values and affiliation of scholars can have a greater impact on research than their social status. Yet the issue of political affiliation or the role of research in the political process more generally has been rather neglected in anthropology. This may be because scientific validity is thought to rely on the impartiality of the researcher. But war research has profoundly political overtones and impartiality is a luxury few can aspire to in such an environment. In many situations of war local researchers have certain advantages over outsiders, due to their ability to merge with the research population and the likelihood that they will be more aware of the political allegiances or partialities of respondents. This was brought home to me very clearly in both Burma and Sri Lanka. On the other hand, as stakeholders in the country's political direction, with inevitable interests in the outcome of the conflict, nationals are often compromised in the role of investigator. Foreign researchers tend not to have associations with particular groups or interests. This frequently enables them to move around more freely and to address parties to the conflict more directly than their nationally recruited colleagues. Hence, in Cambodia, the trust implicit in the bestowal on us of powerful personal testimonies was most likely connected with the fact that we were outsiders to the society and separated from its ordeals (see also Swaine with Feeny, chapter 4, this volume).

Uses of Data

Beyond the issue of attributes and allegiances of researchers, how research is framed and used has profound ethical implications. Indeed, because of threats to the security of all involved, use of data is one of the most pressing ethical concerns in war research. During armed conflict, research information becomes a source of inordinate power and vulnerability. Information that to the researcher may appear benign can assume the status of military intelligence, or be used to imprison, extort money from or otherwise coerce the person who has divulged it. Since they often have insights into the dangers they confront and ways of dealing with them, respondents can frequently be relied on to steer conversations away from hazardous topics. This is one reason why researchers should make a conscious effort to explore events through the respondents' lens rather than through researcher-directed instruments such as stress exposure ratings and impact scales that are the typical fare of mental health research. Unless they pay great attention to the insights of affected populations, researchers are unlikely to be cognisant of the dangers involved or able to anticipate the full consequences of dissemination of their findings. Nevertheless, it would be naive to think that this is a sufficient guarantee of safety, and it could be argued that in the case of children researchers have a particular obligation to verify the risks entailed.

There are ethical concerns that research and consultation with war-affected populations may raise expectations that cannot be fulfilled. This is an important consideration for scholars. But it is also true to say that the ethical codes that typically guide research tend to ignore the agency of respondents who may take advantage of, manipulate, or possibly even actively abuse research, sometimes with adverse consequences – intended or unintended – in terms of security. The focus of such codes is on preventing infringements of one sort or another by researchers: it is seldom acknowledged that respondents may use the research process for their own ends. Yet all research involves a contract between researcher and respondent, whether implicit or explicit, and inevitably both parties attach expectations to this contract. In war research the stakes are high. At the very least, respondents may hope that research will lead to some form of practical assistance. Because of constraints on mobility and access to civilians, researchers are seldom able to act autonomously in war. Many rely on the aid community for initial contact with research populations, and occasionally for transportation and accommodation. Often the unanticipated effect of negotiating entry into an area through an aid agency is the perception that the research exercise is merely a forerunner to programmatic intervention. Under these circumstances, responses to research questions are likely to be influenced by the desire to elicit agency assistance and hence, to be framed in terms of deficits and needs (see Utas, chapter 11, this volume).

Another of the more compelling reasons why war-affected populations consent to research is the desire to testify to and archive the atrocities and losses they have endured. This suggests that expectations of research may also centre on the fulfilment of justice and retribution. This was very apparent in parts of northern and eastern Sri Lanka, especially in those villages that had endured direct violence, repeated displacement and severe economic hardship. Respondents were at times extremely frank about their experiences.

During a focus-group discussion in one village, the inhabitants noted with precision the timing of attacks – not just the year, month and day, but the exact hour when they began and finished – the forms and effects of the violence, the identities and number of victims and of known perpetrators. They were very vociferous, expressing anger at the injustices they had suffered and refusing to be interrupted until their stories had been told. However, from our point of view this frank exchange posed unexpected ethical dilemmas: the more impassioned or insistent respondents became, the more our concerns grew. After our discussion had ended and while others were dispersing, an old man, who had listened in patient silence throughout, approached us. Referring to an incident in which more than two-hundred villagers had been slaughtered in just over two hours, he described how the soldiers had cut the breasts off the women and hung them on the poles of a fence surrounding the massacre site. I cannot explain why he told us this or why he waited to do so until others had had their say and moved on. What I do know is that our efforts to validate and give closure to his testimony seemed painfully inadequate and that we left the community feeling troubled and deeply humbled. Despite repeated attempts to clarify our role and purpose for being in the village, there remained the nagging anxiety that people may have thought we were human rights monitors with the ability to bring perpetrators of atrocities to justice.[1]

Children often make their own demands of research encounters. Several years ago, a pregnant street girl in Addis Ababa tried to use my research as a vehicle for locating the father who had abandoned her and moved to Germany. In Burma, a young boy who had been wrongfully imprisoned for murder sought redress in law through the testimony he gave to me. His father had killed a neighbour and had implored him to confess to the crime, knowing that as a minor his punishment would be much less severe. Recently, a teenager in Gulu, northern Uganda, who had been abducted by and escaped from the Lord's Resistance Army (LRA) insisted on maintaining personal contact after I had left the country, possibly seeking sponsorship or a means of getting away from the war.

Having consciously discarded the idea of impartiality and adopted the role of political activist, many war researchers today employ a human-rights framework, their studies often being supported by advocacy organisations and their material being applied in lobbying and policy development. The understanding is that there now exist agreed international standards in human behaviour and that scholars have a moral obligation to report violations in accordance with these standards. Some go further, maintaining that it is not ethical to conduct research during conflict unless there is an intention to act on the situation and ameliorate suffering. Undoubtedly such viewpoints are appealing, for they call up a sense of humanity and dignity in research and even invoke the possibility that scholarship may effect societal change for the better.

But from the perspective of anthropology the human-rights paradigm is problematic. For one thing, while it is often promoted as a global standard, it is in fact a normative model that embodies major cultural assumptions. These assumptions clash with the way different societies organise themselves and think about infractions and justice. Ideas about human rights are tied to a worldview in which the individual human being exists as an autonomous entity in itself, and this worldview is specific to Judeo-Christian belief systems. In most other cultures, the individual cannot be isolated from the whole in this way, but forms an integral part of the natural, spiritual and social worlds. Persons are bound to social groups through a complex network of obligations and duties that are associated with their position in those groups: individuals have no claims that are independent, or outside, of these groups and the notion of rights is entirely foreign. Furthermore, the misfortunes of war and the atrocities committed during war may be understood as caused not by the human agency of individual perpetrators, or even the acts of military units, but by upheavals in the social, supernatural or natural worlds.

So, by framing war events in terms of human rights standards, researchers may neglect experiences that are very powerful for affected populations simply because they do not fit in with normative assumptions about infractions. But there is more to it than the mere mismatch of researcher and respondent perceptions, for scholars who conceptualise war in terms of human rights violations sometimes have ideological reasons for blocking the lived experiences of children. A focus on children's rights and protection has brought with it a concern to treat the young as especially deserving victims, as opposed to conscious agents, of political conflict. As a consequence, important topics such as children's moral development, their political consciousness and activism, and hence their motives for enlistment, are neglected in favour of research focusing on impairment to health and other negative war impacts. I address this issue in greater detail below.

Children in War

Researching Children's Political Worlds

While scholarship with children has advanced considerably in recent decades in several fields, war research lags behind in many crucial respects. Most war studies are driven by powerful preconceptions regarding the nature of children and childhood, and of armed conflict and its social, psychological and emotional consequences. Information provided by this literature is largely drawn from adult informants. Scholarship in which researchers define the concepts and issues and adults are used to interpret children's experiences and behaviour is flawed in several important respects. First, it presupposes that the subjective meanings children give to war events do not play a significant part in shaping their reactions to them. Second, it implies that children's insights have no relevance or scientific validity as compared with the expert knowledge and interpretative skills of the researcher. Third, it suggests that children's testimony is unreliable and that children do not have the capacity to give a proper account of their lives. Fourth, it suggests also that children's experiences of war are similar everywhere and that the researcher is in some way privy to these experiences even before interacting with informants. Such research marginalises children in many crucial ways.

Undoubtedly there are contextual constraints to be considered in the repression of children's narratives (see Olson and Hart, chapters 8 and 9 respectively, this volume). In many settings children are thought to lack the maturity to hold and articulate valid views. Attempts to engage children directly in research can lead to some resistance, especially in hierarchical cultures that prescribe a fixed status for all their members on the basis of gender, biological/chronological age and generation. During interviews with staff of orphanages in Burma it was frequently claimed that children 'are too young to remember why they were sent here', or 'too young to understand what happened to them in the past'. Attempts to interview the children in the presence of staff resulted in adults intervening to provide answers and explanations, on the basis that the children 'didn't know' about a particular issue or were not articulate enough to express themselves. But informal interviews with boys and girls alone, in several such institutions, revealed a very different picture. One boy of about 13 described in great detail the day his father died and the day – possibly some months later – when his mother took him by truck to the orphanage. This being the only time he had ever travelled in a vehicle, he recalled the excitement of the journey. Even though he had not seen his mother since, he also recalled her promise that when she had saved enough money she would come to take him home. According to his records, he was 4 years old or less at the time.

It is important to take into account what adults might be losing by giving children a voice in research. It is essential also to consider the implications of possible adverse adult reactions in terms of both children's wellbeing and their integration into society. It needs to be borne in mind too that in many societies a significant proportion of adults are themselves excluded from social, economic and political processes because of their gender, class, ethnic or religious status. Among war-affected populations a particular reluctance to allow children to give testimony may be associated with the difficulties many adults experience in coming to terms with their failure to protect the young from brutality and hardship. Alternatively, suppression of the young may reflect a desire to reinstate adult control and authority in an environment in which children and adolescents may have usurped adult roles as fighters, breadwinners or concubines.

As indicated, researchers may have their own reasons for quelling the voices of children in war. Aside from the ideological considerations already mentioned, there may also be concerns about fulfilling ethical responsibilities towards children. One consideration is the obligation to ensure that no child suffers harm as a result of research. This relates to what some scholars and clinicians term 'secondary traumatisation', or additional distress caused by enquiry into painful memories. Another ethical principle is not telling children about things that they do not yet know and are not ready to know. A concern to protect children from knowledge of violations or from the personal risks of disclosure in a war setting is one of the main deterrents to research processes involving children not merely as respondents but also as researchers.

Nevertheless, by adopting an ethical position in which the protection of children is based on exclusionary processes, the researcher is at risk of infantilising childhood as a life phase that is unfettered by awareness or responsibility, thereby denying the political realities that war-affected populations live with. As Pamela Reynolds (chapter 13) observes in this volume, 'there are no wars where children do not walk'. In fact, large numbers of adolescents and even younger children – mostly boys, but also girls – are directly embroiled in political and armed struggle in both government and rebel forces throughout the world. In one exceptional case in Burma, the Htoo brothers, 12-year-old twins, became the commanders of an insurgent army. Children are drawn into combat through many routes. Abduction and forced recruitment of children has been reported as common in places such as Angola, Sierra Leone, Liberia and northern Uganda (Honwana 1999; Zack-Williams 1999). However, while forced conscription may be rife in many areas, a significant proportion of young people join up voluntarily. Their motives are varied. In Angola, the reasons given for enlistment included political commitment, ethnic loyalties, peer pressure, food and the opportunity to engage in looting. Many children equated violence with power. Economic necessity was a major motivating factor among adolescent boys in Afghanistan (Sellick 1998). In the highly-politicised atmosphere of the Occupied Territories, young Palestinians develop political consciousness from an early age (Barber 2002). Their involvement in the first and second *Intifadas* has been denounced by various Israeli officials as a consequence of manipulation by parents and other elders. However, it seems clear that they have been motivated to engage in battle with the Israeli army due to a strong sense of injustice and by frustration at their social, economic and political marginalisation. Taking action as members of a peer group evidently contributes to feelings of efficacy and empowerment. All of these factors have emboldened the young to assume a role that, in many respects, challenges the values of this patriarchal society (Hart 2002).

This evidence points to the fact that children are often more aware and active politically, and more developed morally and socially, than adults generally assume. It emphasises the validity and merit of conceptualising children as political actors with the capacity to make conscious decisions that are informed by analysis of personal and collective history and circumstances. It highlights the importance of better understanding and researching their political worlds. It also highlights the delicate balance scholars need to achieve between a legitimate concern to ensure that children do not suffer harm as a result of research, and keeping faith with children's views and actual experiences. More than this, though, it indicates the patronising nature of ethical codes that assume all the power – including the power of protection – lies in the hands of the researcher. What is harmful or adverse for children is normally decided by adults, even though children often do not understand, experience or respond to adversities either as adults do or in ways that are entirely predictable, and have many valuable insights into the causes and means of ameliorating their suffering. Indeed, our research in Sri Lanka, which was conducted with all age groups, produced some unexpected and rather surprising results. In many cases teenagers and children in middle childhood were far more articulate about their personal circumstances, the condition of their families and communities and the political options for the future than were adults.

Researching Children's Inner Worlds

As an anthropologist trained to enquire about children's cultural, social, economic and political lives, I find it can be very disquieting when research conversations touch on the inner worlds of children, especially when these worlds involve torture, killing, separation from family and other painful and troubling experiences. As an ethical prerequisite, some might argue that only those trained in psychiatry or psychology, who thereby have the ability to offer therapeutic support, should undertake enquiry into children's inner worlds. I have a certain sympathy with this position, since the ability of the researcher to acknowledge and give meaning to distress, whilst at the same time containing and bringing closure to suffering, clearly does make a significant difference to the outcome of encounters with respondents (Jareg et al. 1989). However, there exists a fairly substantial literature pointing to the inadequacy of psychiatry and psychology in dealing with human suffering of the scale and nature of armed conflict, and to the difficulties derived from their attachment to a specific cultural view (Bracken 1998; Dawes and Donald 1994; Gorden 1988; LeVine 1999; Nsamenang and Dawes 1998; Perren-Klingler 1996; Summerfield 1998). The critiques address both the interpretation and management of distress, and are therefore pertinent also to the research relationship. They highlight the limitations of biomedicine as an explanatory system, of research that focuses on intrapsychic functioning, of talk and drug therapies as modes of treatment, and Western understandings of children and childhood. The relevance of such perspectives to societies that have very different ontologies and social and cultural forms is questionable.

The concept of trauma has now come to dominate much of the psychiatric and psychological research, influencing not only methodology and methods but, more fundamentally, the understanding of children's experiences of conflict. However, I have found that the notion of trauma does not adequately represent children's responses to stressful events and ignores altogether the meanings they attribute to these events. In focus-group discussions conducted recently with boys and girls in northern Uganda who had been abducted and held captive by the LRA, the preoccupation was not with past events – which were by any standards truly horrific – but with practical problems in the present and fear of the future. Having either escaped from the LRA or been captured by the army during combat, these young people were living in a rehabilitation centre in Gulu town prior to returning home. Among the boys, all the teenagers, and all the younger children with sufficient strength and agility, had been trained and made to fight for the LRA. Some had undergone abhorrent induction rites that were intended to guarantee their loyalty and foreclose the possibility of return to their families and communities. A few of the girls had also been forced to fight, although most (particularly those beyond puberty) lived in captivity as the sexual slaves of the LRA leadership. Quite a few of the girls in the latter group had borne children by their captors.

All the young former abductees had witnessed a multitude of brutal acts and had themselves been subjected to extreme hardship and violence. Some had visited terrible atrocities on others, including in few cases being made to torture and kill other child abductees or family members. Several displayed symptoms that are commonly associated with PTSD, such as recurrent nightmares, bedwetting and hypervigilance. Even so, there was no obvious and direct link between these symptoms and past events in the young people's lives and no obvious effect on daily functioning. The young people certainly talked about the past, but were far more focused on their longing to go home. Most were fearful of what they would find on their return – whether family members had died, or would reject them because of the time they had spent in the bush and their involvement in violence. Health, and especially HIV/AIDS, was a major preoccupation for the majority. An overwhelming concern for the young mothers in particular was the difficulty their circumstances posed in terms of returning to the parental home. They were worried about where they would live and how they would earn sufficient income to provide for their offspring. But the overriding anxiety expressed by all, both the boys and the girls, was the possibility of reabduction by the LRA. This was powerfully reinforced by the fact that LRA fighters had been observed hanging around outside the rehabilitation centre and the awareness that the LRA knew they were living there. It was explained to me that reabduction entails greater hardship and danger than abduction for the first time, especially for those who have lived long in the bush and are well trained in combat.

Even if, based on the presentation of symptoms, one chooses to frame these children's responses in terms of PTSD, this diagnosis bears no relation to local understandings of misfortune or local ideas about healing. The young people who are being abducted by the LRA are of Acholi origin (see Mawson, chapter 7, this volume). In this group it is believed that children 'of the bush' who have committed atrocities during combat, children who are 'wild' or behave in a manner that is socially unacceptable, are possessed by the aggrieved spirits of those they have killed. Healing is achieved through the enactment of rituals of purification and atonement that enable those who are possessed to rid themselves of the spirits and gain acceptance back into their families and communities. In other words, healing in this context is a social and spiritual act and involves not only divesting oneself of troublesome symptoms of distress but also retribution and reintegration within family and community. If research is to play a positive role in children's lives, it would seem evident that understanding what really does trouble and can help them is an important ethical directive. Nevertheless, the phenomenological difficulties associated with research into emic viewpoints should not be underestimated, in that the concepts and categories used by scholars may signify very different things from those used by research populations. This is apparent in studies with adults as much as with children. Whilst conducting fieldwork for my doctorate in the central Peruvian highlands, I learned that even a question as seemingly straightforward as, 'How many children do you have?' can be interpreted and answered very differently according to different cultural ideas about personhood, life and death. I thought I was gathering data on actual family size and was therefore rather perplexed when one day a woman who I knew had three children insisted she had five. Only with further enquiry did it become clear that my female informants had been citing the number of children they had given birth to, not distinguishing between the dead and the living.

Conducting research with children raises many additional phenomenological challenges, with significant implications in terms of methods of enquiry. Young children in particular may apply meanings to concepts in common usage that are quite distinct from those devised by adults. In fact, children often employ their own terms as a conscious strategy for distancing themselves from adults, as the influential work by the Opies has shown. Further, social notions of childhood and adulthood, and of the behaviours and attitudes appropriate to each, may radically affect perceptions and reporting. Again in Peru, questions about children's work did not yield very effective answers because only adults are thought to work in the sense of serious productive enterprise. Children's work activities, such as cooking, street vending or gathering firewood, tend to be conceptualised as *cachuelos* (hobbies), since they are believed to contribute to children's learning and entertainment rather than to household survival or maintenance.

Capturing children's inner-world narratives requires methodological innovation. In many contexts children are not accustomed to talking directly with adults, especially in the formal manner of an interview, and research methods based solely or even primarily on verbal communication often have serious limitations (Theis 1996: 72). Some methods are more effective at creating confidence and trust than others and, if integrated carefully within a sequence of different methods, can be very helpful in building an informal, unthreatening atmosphere. Methods that involve a tangible product, a drawing, map, or whatever, shift the attention away from the respondent, making the communication between adult researcher and child researched less threatening. In literate societies, effective use can be made of written methods, such as time sheets and diaries. These can offer privacy to children who are reluctant to share their ideas and concerns openly. Of course, as mentioned, the disadvantage of research in which respondents produce tangible objects is the possibility that these may be used as concrete evidence against them.

Working with subjective interpretations of experience generally entails entering a world of euphemism and cultural metaphor. These mechanisms allow open discussion of things that would otherwise remain concealed, and thereby render relatively impersonal matters that are in practice intensely private. In many cases euphemisms and metaphors are products of social proscriptions concerning discussion of sensitive issues, but in war they may have the added value of marking respect for survivors of atrocities, or ensuring secrecy. In discussions with girls and their families in Burma's East Shan State, the rag trade provided a metaphor for brothel prostitution, the young sex workers being described as seamstresses. This may have been motivated by the compulsion to protect those affected from social stigma, although there was great pride in the filial loyalty demonstrated by these girls who worked hard and under very difficult conditions in order to remit sizeable sums to their families. Another explanation could have been the need to safeguard them against identification by the military, which had begun to arrest, detain and allegedly execute anyone returning from Thai brothels who tested HIV positive. Whatever the reason, embedded within this metaphor was a complex array of experiences and a rich language of both suffering and resilience. Despite the apparent constraints imposed by its use, we were able to learn a great deal about the traffic in hill-tribe girls, the risks they ran, their doubts and fears, the pride of families who had received remitted income and the anguish of those whose daughters had disappeared. Above all, we learnt that it is precisely in such metaphors that children's experiences of war are frequently locked.

Conclusion

Research in war is fraught with problems of many orders. Some of the difficulties are very evidently practical and ethical, while others are due more to disciplinary predilections. Anthropological theory, and ethnographic method and evidence, can and should play a major part in the development of a stronger field of research in the context of war. Yet, as argued, anthropology has neglected this topic. The discipline also has a rather poor record in terms of research with children. It has been inclined to disregard childhood as an area worthy of research in its own right, treating it more as a period of linguistic and cognitive formation, training for competent adulthood, or cultural assimilation. Hence, anthropological study of childhood has commonly focused on rites of passage, the learning of gender roles and other means by which societies integrate and socialise their young. Rarely have young people acted as principal informants in this work and seldom have they been considered in their roles as carers of younger siblings or incapacitated adults, educators of peers, freedom fighters, community advocates or volunteers, workers or political activists. The young are portrayed, in other words, as the receivers of – rather than contributors to – adult culture. The idea that they might play a transformative role in the production and reproduction of cultures is altogether foreign. And only very recently have scholars within the discipline begun systematically to investigate war-affected and displaced children.

Some might argue that without the possibility of full engagement in participant observation, ethnographic research in war is not really feasible, that the findings are unlikely to be valid, or that the risks to all involved are simply too great. There is undoubtedly some authority in this view and it is incumbent upon researchers continually to revisit accepted ethical codes and guidelines and question their role, their impact on respondents and the reliability of their data. However, I would maintain that even with the difficulties, enquiry into human misfortunes like war is an important precursor to the development of theories of societal transformation, value formation, social and cultural reproduction and the like. There is also the possibility that research in war may serve a witness function and thereby directly ameliorate suffering. Some people, especially some of the workers in international non-governmental organisations, were opposed to my doing research in Burma. They argued that the presence of foreigners in the country implied tacit acceptance and approval of the SLORC regime. They pointed to the fact that visitors would often be photographed with government officials and that these photographs were published in local newspapers as a means of legitimising SLORC rule. Others, including many of the Burmese I met, argued that civilians were not so easily deceived by their rulers. They maintained that the presence of outsiders was an important gesture of solidarity with the citizenry as well as a protection against further violations. Such debates have no easy resolution and may ultimately depend on the specifics of each research exercise.

One thing that is apparent is the need for greater attention to the ethnography of children in war. Such ethnography has a vital part to play in understanding how armed conflict affects the gendered social and political roles of the young, their development and their political and ideological alignments. Most of the research on children in war emphasises the negative impacts, the psychological and emotional distress, the physical devastation, the loss of hope, powerlessness and so on. This kind of research certainly has its place. But such stark portrayals can also belie the complex realities confronted by children in war and the strategies – at times highly subtle – they devise to ameliorate their circumstances (see Swaine and de Berry, chapters 4 and 3 respectively, this volume). At great personal risk, some of the children in Cambodia defied the Khmer Rouge by running away from indoctrination centres and hiding in their homes. In order to escape the attention of the authorities, many pretended to be deaf, mute or foolish, on the understanding that if they were too 'smart' they risked torture or execution (Meas and Healy 1995: 30). Ethnography should track strategies such as these as a means of learning more about children's cognitive and social competencies in the context of war.

Research of this nature must clearly address legitimate ethical concerns about child protection. However, ethical codes should not assume a one-way power relation in which the adult researcher is all knowing and wise and has complete control of the process. The agency of child respondents must be taken into account and their insight and knowledge of their situation fully respected. Furthermore, even though it is important to develop agreed standards in relation to ethnographic enquiry, especially with regard to research methods and ethics, these will inevitably be transformed by context. While the researcher may aspire to certain terms and conditions, war will always involve compromises in ethnography and it is impossible to ensure these in practice.

Note

1. Matters were complicated by the fact that at the time of research the Sri Lankan Monitoring Commission had recently been formed. This body, whose presence in the area had been broadcast through the media, was charged with monitoring adherence to the ceasefire agreement and recording and reporting on violations.

References

Allen, T. 1989. 'Violence and Moral Knowledge: Observing Social Trauma in Sudan and Uganda.' *Cambridge Anthropology* 13 (2): 45–66.

Barber, B.K. 2002. 'Politics, Politics and More Politics: Youth Life Experience in the Gaza Strip.' In D. Bowen and E. Early, eds, *Everyday Life in the Muslim Middle East.* 2nd edn. Bloomington: Indiana University Press.

Boyden, J. and Gibbs, S. 1997. *Children of War: Responses to Psycho-Social Distress in Cambodia.* Switzerland: United Nations Research Institute for Social Development (UNRISD).

Boyden, J. with Kaiser, T. and Springett, S. 2002. 'Consultation with and Participation by Beneficiary and Affected Populations in Planning, Managing, Monitoring and Evaluating Humanitarian Aid: the case of Sri Lanka.' www.intrac.org/INTRAC%20Sri%20Lanka%20Study.PDF.

Bracken, P. 1998. 'Hidden Agendas: Deconstructing Post Traumatic Stress Disorder.' In P. Bracken and C. Petty, eds, *Rethinking the Trauma of War*. London and New York: Save the Children, Free Association Books.

Colson, E. 1989. 'Overview.' *Annual Review of Anthropology* 18: 1–16.

Davis, J. 1992. 'The Anthropology of Suffering.' *Journal of Refugee Studies* 5 (2): 149–61.

Dawes, A. and Donald, D. 1994. 'Understanding the Psychological Consequences of Adversity.' In A. Dawes and D. Donald, eds, *Childhood and Adversity; Psychological Perspectives from South African Research*. Capetown and Johannesburg: David Philip.

Gorden, D. 1988. 'Two Tenacious Assumptions of Western Medicine.' In M. Lock and D. Gordon, eds, *Biomedicine Examined*. Dordrecht: Kluwer.

Hart, J. 2002. 'Participation of Conflict-Affected Children in Humanitarian Action: learning from the Occupied Palestinian Territories.' Draft Report for Canadian International Development Agency.

Honwana, A. 1999. 'Untold War Stories: Young Women and War in Mozambique.' Paper presented at the conference 'Children and Youth as Emerging Categories in Africa', 5–6 November, Leuven, Belgium.

Jareg et al. 1989. 'Some Guidelines to Listening and Talking with Children who are Psychologically Distressed.' Paper. Oslo: Redd Barna.

LeVine, P. 1999. 'Assessing "Detachment" Patterns and Contextual Trauma Across Cultures (Trauma Detachment Grid).' Seminar delivered at the Refugee Studies Programme. University of Oxford, 3 June.

Marston, J. 1994. 'Metaphors of the Khmer Rouge.' In J. Ledgerwood, M. Ebihara and C. Mortland, eds, *Cambodian Culture since 1975: Homeland and Exile*. Ithaca: Cornell University Press.

Meas, N. with Healy, J. 1995. *Towards Restoring Life in Cambodian Villages*. Phnom Penh: JSRC.

Nordstrom, C. 1997. *A Different Kind of War Story*. Philadelphia: University of Pennsylvania Press.

Nsamenang, B. and Dawes, A. 1998. 'Developmental Psychology as Political Psychology in Sub-Saharan Africa: The Challenge of Africanisation.' *Applied Psychology: An International Review* 47 (1): 73–87.

Perren-Klinger, G. 1996. 'Human Reactions to Traumatic Experience: from Pathogenetic to Salutogenetic Thinking.' In G. Perren-Klinger, ed., *Trauma: from Individual Helplessness to Group Resources*. Berne-Stuttgart-Vienna: Paul Haupt Publishers.

Reynolds-White, S. 1998. *Questioning Misfortune*. Cambridge: Cambridge University Press.

Summerfield, D. 1998. 'The Social Experience of War and Some Issues for the Humanitarian Field.' In P. Bracken and C. Petty, eds, *Rethinking the Trauma of War*. London-New York: Save the Children, Free Association Books.

Sellick, P. 1998. 'The Impact of Conflict on Children in Afghanistan.' Unpublished report for Rädda Barnen, Save the Children Fund U.K. and UNICEF, May.

Taylor, A. 1994. 'Poverty in Cambodia.' Unpublished report. Phnom Penh: UNICEF.

Theis, J. 1996. 'Children and Participatory Appraisals: Experiences from Vietnam.' *PLA Notes*, 25, February.

Uimonen, P. 1994. 'Responses to Revolutionary Change: a Study of Social Memory in a Khmer Village.' MA thesis. Department of Anthropology, Stockholm University.

Zack-Williams, A. 1999. 'Child Soldiers in the Civil War in Sierra Leone.' Paper presented at Development Studies Association Conference, Bath University.

Postscript

13

'Where Wings Take Dream': on Children in the Work of War and the War of Work[1]

Pamela Reynolds

Many shifts occur in the nature of war and the character of childhood. The patterns of change in both require vigilance and critical attention. With regard to war, forms that have been established to define and confine conflict easily fall away; thus the twentieth century witnessed a proliferation of 'nontraditional' wars. With regard to shifts in the conceptions of childhood, a similar level of vigilance is called for as fixed ideas of childhood can obscure children's experiences. Such an idealised view was expressed by G. W. Bush, the forty-third president of the United States, when, talking about the importance of families, he said, 'families is [sic] where our nation takes hope, where wings take dream' (quoted by Mitchell 2000). Children depend on an ethical attitude that is the basis of sociality and, where conflict erodes it (as it always does), they become targets and participants in war.

A consideration of the manner in which war affects children calls for an analysis of the character of relationships between child and adult, and between child and child, within the atmosphere of tension that accompanies the disruption of the everyday. Veena Das (1998: 174) observes that despite studies of socialisation, '...rarely has the question of how one comes to a shared culture as well as one's own voice in that culture in the context of everyday life been addressed anthropologically'. How much less, then, do we know about how one comes to share in the long-drawn-out wars now engulfing vast territories? We need to study 'the relation between dailiness and the rupture of dailiness' (Byatt 2000) as it affects the young.

I suggest that there are no wars where children do not walk; that childhood is not another country (that is, relationships between adults and children are entwined and children are participants in the social, economic, political and moral conditions of the moment); and that because children move through childhood, its constituents alter: the passage can seem swift and can be foreshortened, for example, through poverty, loss and exploitation or war. (I adopt, for clarity's sake, the definition in the United Nations Convention on the Rights of the Child that childhood lasts until the time a person reaches the age of 18.)

There is little dispute over the desirability of peace (more urgent than that of truth in the view of Emmanuel Levinas, 1999: 136) for all. Given the absence of peace in so many parts of the world, many people hold that the child should be separated from conflict and few argue against this with regard to the young child. Contention arises over the experience of children aged 10 or more. This chapter addresses the young, aged from 10 to 18 years. It is a time when children begin to move from childhood through a period that leads them, in Stanley Cavell's words, to the moment when they have 'to consent' to adulthood (1984: 99–100). He describes it as a choice based on insufficient evidence and as an agreement to join the public world (when agreement is possible given other conditions in society). The entry to adulthood is, he says, at best an entry into a world of possibilities towards which curiosity reaches. It is a time of reversal of rites of passage entailing a shift of responsibility for pain from the world to the young. War undeniably removes the possibility of choice from many of the young, but some engage in it with a consciousness that reflects their views of themselves as integral to sociality and to the limits of sociality. One asks: what, for the young (or for any of us), are the limits of consenting to horror? Of adapting to it? Should we credit the revulsion of youth to horror as conceivably political responses, even as they participate?

In order to begin to research such questions, it may be useful to ask when it is that local worlds lose the sense of powerful moral constraints that organise collective experience (Das and Kleinman 2000: 17). These authors suggest that we trace the 'lineaments of interaction of collective and individual experience'. I am emphasising the view that the young are introduced to, engaged in and contribute to the pattern of sociality and the form that a local community takes whether or not they are engaged in conflict. War does not leave them out. In her account of wars in the former Yugoslavia, Jasmina Tesanovic (1999: 46) says that the two most recent conflicts began with no milk and that, 'The message is: death to the children.'

South Africa's style of oppression under apartheid is well known. It led to a revolt in which thousands of young people participated between 1976 and 1990. There is a broad, popular knowledge of the form that the struggle took, yet it is curious how inadequately the contribution of the young is documented, and it is distressing how little of their needs and desires have been met during the aftermath of the conflict.

During the 1990s, I undertook two studies of the experiences of people who, since their schooldays, had been politically active in standing against the former South African regime. The first study was conducted from 1991 to 1993 with forty-five people who were released from prisons, most from Robben Island, after the release of Nelson Mandela. The second piece of fieldwork (1996 to 2000) was with fourteen young men who, in the 1980s, had been leaders of local activist groups in their stand against the government in a small rural town in the Western Cape: it formed part of an ethnographic study of the Truth and Reconciliation Commission (TRC).

The number of people under the age of 18 who have been directly involved in the conflict is not yet known. No liberation organisation has the figures. Nor do the prison officials. The former government carefully obscured the numbers held in detention and the number who had been harmed. The TRC admitted in its report that it had failed to capture the nature and extent of the role played by the young in helping to achieve a democratic dispensation in South Africa. The report admits that few political activists gave testimony before the Commission. Not knowing how the young fought and with what consequences suggests a lacuna in the description of the recent past in the country. Most of the young who fought within the country have been excluded from pensions granted by the government and by liberation organisations and, at the time of writing, none has received reparations, although some have received interim reparations, from the TRC.

Based on my work in the aftermath of war, it seems to me likely that the young will voluntarily become involved in the kinds of fights that rage in many countries now. In Zimbabwe and South Africa, children between the ages of 12 and 18 participated in the fight for democracy. Some elected to join liberation organisations in exile in order to fight. Many of them were placed in schools in other African countries and given rudimentary military training. Some of the young, aged about 17 years or more, joined armed units. In Zimbabwe, it is said that children were abducted from schools and taken across the borders. For two years, from 1982 to 1984, I worked with *n'anga* (traditional healers) in three areas of Mashonaland studying their concepts of childhood, their training of acolytes and their treatment of children who had become distressed as a consequence of their involvement as *mujibha* and *chimbwido* (messengers) between the guerrillas and the villagers (Reynolds 1996). What is pertinent here is that most of them were aged 12 to 16 at the time and most of them, it seems, had voluntarily assisted the guerrillas. The story of the struggle by the young against the apartheid regime is well known. Less well documented, is how young political activist leaders within South Africa were inducted, how they grew in political consciousness, what ethic of behaviour they developed, over how many years they fought (many did for more than ten years), and what networks they established to ensure continuity in resistance.

Faced with violence, many will eschew a passive role in their own interests or in the interests of others, especially their kin. They are agents in their own life trajectories which, in turn, affects the experiences of those close to them. Besides, their political engagement has force and this is taken into account in the strategy of leaders in some arenas. Their labour, both as combatants and in an array of other tasks, is valued and a variety of means, including coercion, will be used to draw them into wars. I do not mean to underestimate the forces of control that are exerted over the young, nor the power of obligations and duties that are carved into patterns of family relations, social negotiations and political orders that hold the young and inform their decision-making. Nevertheless, it is hard to keep the young from exploring, sharing moral positions, formulating sets of moral tenets and acting in accord with them – whether others see their arguments as right, logically coherent or in the best interests of individuals or groups.

Let us take, as an example, one of the ways in which children will be drawn into wars whether or not they actually shoot or maim people. The International Labour Organisation recently narrowed their call for the abolition of child labour (Convention 122) to the elimination of its 'worst forms' (Convention 138), one of which they identify as child labour in armed conflict. To effect this, the first step is to know how children's labour is used in war. There are two broad fronts to examine. The first is to acknowledge that adults need and use children. When the social order is disturbed, people seek fresh means to organise daily life and, therefore, those engaged in conflict frequently draw the young to them as carriers, messengers, cooks and washers; they use them to bolster their status, keep them company, satisfy their sexual needs, act as their shields and to accompany them in combat. Peacetime roles are blurred, cancelled or reversed. The young may or may not be able to choose whether to participate and how. Soldiers down the ages have claimed to protect the young by including them in their units. The second front is to acknowledge that new forms of war require the reconsideration of myths, fantasies, negotiation formats, conflict resolution models and the categorisation of combatant versus civilian as they affect the situation of the young.

To abolish the use of children as soldiers is to abolish only one use to which they are put during war: girls, in particular, may be left unprotected. It may be thought easy to accept that by their labour the young contribute to maintaining the everyday in the conduct of war, except that we know how difficult it is to measure children's work and how reluctant individuals and institutions are to grant its value and shape policy in accord with that value. To know how adults use children during conflict, we need to ask what kinds of labour they do for whom: at what age; at what cost; within what context; under what conditions; in whose interest; and with what access to protection.

Other questions to ask with regard to any child caught in armed conflict include the following: to whom are children tied and over what time span? How do loyalties shift and under what conditions? These questions suggest the need to investigate the relationships children establish with adults and peers, within and outside the family, because many wars are being fought in areas where children's protection and security was compromised before hostilities began. Many children have already had to rely on their own resources and seek ties with others where they could. It cannot necessarily be assumed that adults are in situations in which they are able to fulfil the tasks of being consistent caretakers or spokespersons for the young (see Reynolds 2000). Times of conflict exacerbate the difficulties of caring for children and, given the duration of many current wars, children's primary relationships may be disrupted for decades. How do wars strip the everyday of the ordinary, releasing attitudes and behaviour into a maelstrom? What does our continuing romanticisation of war contribute to its conduct? What are we still saying about war? How are we still allowing it? What are we documenting about it for the archive?

> Some military ideologies are related to specific notions of masculinity, honour and chivalry ... In the idealised Western imaginary of warfare soldiers in regular armies are associated with strength, aggression, responsibility and the maturity of adulthood [and] ... there is a clear boundary between soldier and civilian, battlefield and home, war-zone and peace-zone. A powerful set of cultural prescriptions develops around the concept and conduct of war. (Carpena-Mendez 2001)

The myth obscures, for example, the involvement of women and the young in war, at the centre or on the periphery. It continues to shape attitudes towards violence in art, history, games, the media and gender stereotyping. And it moulds responses, particularly those of members of international and non governmental organisations, when conflicts end to the detriment of some of the people who had participated.

What forms of healing are we prescribing in the aftermath of war? In accord with whose assumptions and beliefs? Here the questions imply the need to investigate current claims that talking about gross violations is the start of recovery; that truth heals; that Post Traumatic Stress Disorder is widespread among people after conflict and can be cured; that Western psychological and psychiatric models are universally applicable and require intense, systematic therapeutic encounters for healing to occur.

Are we assuming that the pursuit of justice at the end of conflict can only happen after certain kinds of war? If justice is transformed into a purely political calculation, what are the implications for children who were embroiled in the violence? (It could be that one of the effects of international participation in settling conflict will be the quick disbandment of certain groups, such as those composed of young fighters, so rendering them impotent in the claims for redress and reparation.)

In the interests of children in particular, do we name evil for the 'irrevocable harm' (Murdoch 1993: 263) it does?

I am suggesting what a wide terrain our investigation must cover to begin to understand the position of children in war and so begin to know how to limit or cancel their participation. The young are deeply embroiled in the everyday life of society: its production and reproduction, its political ambitions, its fantasies, its ideals and its delusions. Concentration on the role of children in armed conflict should not obscure our analysis of the way in which powerful forces (global and national), including progress in the industry of war, exploit and oppress the young.

Notes

1. Reprinted from *The Journal of the International Institute*, The University of Michigan, Ann Arbor MI 48109, Winter 2000, 9 (2): 2–3.

References

Byatt, A.S. 2000. 'Justice for Willa Cather.' *New York Review of Books* 47 (19): 51–3.

Carpena-Mendez, F. 2001. 'Current Trends of Warfare Affecting Children.' Graduate ms, Berkley: University of California.

Cavell, S. 1984. *Themes Out of School: Effects and Causes*. San Francisco: North Point.

Das, V. 1998. 'Wittgenstein and Anthropology.' *Annual Review of Anthropology* 27: 171–95.

Das, V. and Kleinman, A. 2000. 'Introduction.' In V. Das, A. Kleinman, M. Ramphele and P. Reynolds, eds, Violence and Subjectivity. Berkeley: University of California Press.

Levinas, E. 1999. *Alterity and Transcendence*. M.B. Smith trans. New York: Columbia University Press.

Mitchell, A. 2000. 'The 43rd President: George Walker Bush.' *New York Times*, 14 December.

Murdoch, I. 1993. *Metaphysics as a Guide to Morals*. London: Penguin.

Reynolds, P. 1996. *Traditional Healers and Childhood in Zimbabwe*. Athens: Ohio University Press.

———. 2000. 'The Ground of All Making.' In V. Das, A. Kleinman, M. Ramphele and P. Reynolds, eds, *Violence and Subjectivity*.

Tesanovic, J. 1999. 'The Diary of a Political Idiot. Belgrade, March 1998–June 1999.' *Granta* 67.

Notes on Contributors

Alastair Ager is Professor of Applied Psychology and Director of the Centre for International Health Studies at Queen Margaret University College, Edinburgh. He holds honorary appointments with the Refugee Studies Centre, University of Oxford and The Rivers Centre, Edinburgh NHS Community Trust. With field experience across Malawi, Nigeria, Sri Lanka, Bangladesh, India, Romania, Palestine and Montserrat, he has worked with a wide range of international agencies including UNHCR, UNICEF, WHO and a number of non-governmental organisations, both local and international. He has authored over fifty published works, including the edited volume *Refugees: Perspectives on the Experience of Forced Migration* (Continuum, 1999).

Jo Boyden is a senior research officer at the Refugee Studies Centre, Queen Elizabeth House, University of Oxford. Her initial research interest was the impact of capitalist development on social organisation and structure in a peasant community in the central Peruvian Andes. She was employed for many years as a consultant to a broad range of aid agencies, and focused on the development of research, policy and practical measures for war-affected, displaced, street and working children in South-East and South Asia, the Andean region and parts of Africa. She is currently researching children's experiences of and responses to, armed conflict and forced migration, with special reference to children who assume adult roles and responsibilities in the context of severe adversity.

Joanna de Berry trained in anthropology at Cambridge University and the London School of Economics and Political Science. Her PhD thesis considered issues of post conflict reconstruction at the local level in north-east Uganda. She then moved to research the impact of armed conflict and forced migration on children in South Asia. She worked in India, Pakistan and Afghanistan with UNICEF and as the Children in Crisis Adviser for Save the Children U.S.A. based in Kabul between August 2001 and August 2003. She is currently working with the local authority of Southwark Council, facilitating community development with young people in south London.

Carola Eyber is a psychologist and currently a lecturer at the Centre for International Health Studies at Queen Margaret University College. She has extensive experience of working with refugees in South Africa in the areas of policy development, service provision and research. Over recent years she has focused on researching local strategies for dealing with adversity amongst war-affected communities in Angola and Sri Lanka. Her current research interests include children and young people's perspectives on and experiences of poverty and armed conflict, as well as traditional and spiritual issues in refugee communities.

Thomas Feeny is a freelance child protection consultant with a masters degree in Social Anthropology from the School of Oriental and African Studies, London. As a researcher at the Refugee Studies Centre, University of Oxford, he studied the impact of armed conflict and forced migration on children in South Asia, with particular reference to the Chittagong Hill Tracts area of Bangladesh. He has conducted research for various member organisations of the Save the Children Alliance and UNICEF, among others, while also writing reports and analyses of global child poverty for Christian Children's Fund, U.S.A. He is currently working as Advocacy Officer for The Consortium for Street Children.

Jason Hart is a research officer at the Refugee Studies Centre, University of Oxford. He completed a PhD in Anthropology at Goldsmiths College, University of London in 2000 with a thesis entitled *Contested Belonging: Children and Childhood in a Palestinian Refugee Camp in Jordan*. Since then, he has conducted research on the impact of armed conflict on children in South Asia and the programmatic responses of humanitarian agencies to conflict-affected and displaced children in that region and the Middle East. Jason Hart has also been employed as a consultant researcher by UNICEF, Save the Children, Care International, Plan International and the Canadian International Development Agency (CIDA).

Victor Igreja is a psycho-pedagogue, medical anthropologist and the main war trauma researcher working with AEPATO (a Mozambican NGO) in the former war-zones of central Mozambique. Since 1997 he has been developing a community-based model to respond to the physical and mental health needs of war trauma survivors. Currently he is also working in the Department of Culture, Health and Illness at Leiden University.

Gillian Mann has worked for several years in the field of policy and programmes for children in adversity, as both a practitioner and a researcher. Her interests lie in children's social competencies and relationships at the household, family and community level. Recently, her work has focused on the experiences and perspectives of separated boys and girls in particular, including those children who live without their parents as a result of war, HIV/AIDS, or both. She has just completed an ethnographic study of separated Congolese refugee children living in Dar es Salaam, Tanzania, in which she attempted to empirically investigate many of the questions raised in this paper.

Andrew Mawson has been the Chief of Rights, Protection and Peace Building with UNICEF-Sudan Country Office in Khartoum, since November 2000, managing projects on: abducted children; children associated with fighting forces; abandoned babies and grassroots peace building. Originally an archaeologist, in 1989 he received a PhD from the University of Cambridge for a study of religion and politics among the Agar Dinka of Sudan. In 1989 he joined Amnesty International, researching human rights in a number of eastern and southern African countries. He has also worked for Save the Children U.K. in London as a human rights adviser and on children's issues in the human rights unit of UNAMSIL, the UN peacekeeping mission to Sierra Leone.

Krisjon Rae Olson is a doctoral candidate in the Department of Anthropology at the University of California, Berkeley. Her research on peace processes in the aftermath of war has included fieldwork in the Former Yugoslavia, Bolivia, Peru and Rwanda. Her dissertation addresses the social and ethical implications of a new youth movement, and attendant humanitarian practices, for and by children in the wake of the Guatemalan genocide.

Pamela Reynolds is a professor in the Department of Anthropology at Johns Hopkins University. She has undertaken a number of ethnographic studies of children and youth in southern Africa. In her country of birth, Zimbabwe, she has worked with Zezuru healers and their conceptions of childhood, in particular with the their treatment of the young who had been involved in the War of Liberation; and with Tonga children who labour on their families farms in Omay in the Zambezi Valley. In South Africa, she worked with ex-prisoners who were released from jail, many from Robben Island, after the freeing of Nelson Mandela; and with ex-political activists and their relationships with the Truth and Reconciliation

Commission. Currently, she is studying the situation of children in armed conflict and, with Veena Das, leading a three city ethnographic analysis of children and the everyday in situations of violence.

Jessica Schafer completed her DPhil at Oxford in 1999, which focused on the politics of the reintegration of demobilised soldiers in Mozambique. She has since worked as a post-doctoral researcher at the University of Sussex, researching natural resource management in post-conflict situations, and the history of environmental thought and politics in former Portuguese colonies. She is currently based at the University of Victoria, researching and evaluating capacity building programmes in early childhood development in Africa.

Aisling Swaine has an Msc. in Humanitarian Assistance and a B.A. in Sociology and Information Studies from University College Dublin, Ireland. She has worked with Concern Worldwide in Albania, Kosovo, Burundi and East Timor managing gender and child focused aid and development programmes. Aisling has also completed research on Traditional Justice and Gender Based Violence for the International Rescue Committee in East Timor.

Mats Utas is a senior lecturer in cultural anthropology at Uppsala University, Sweden and Fourah Bay College, Sierra Leone. He obtained his PhD from Uppsala University in June 2003 and his thesis was entitled 'Sweet Battlefields: Youth and the Liberian Civil War'. He is currently working on a research project which focuses on microeconomics and images of wealth and consumption among marginalized youth in urban areas of Sierra Leone.

Harry G. West is Assistant Professor of Anthropology on the Graduate Faculty of Political and Social Science at New School University in New York. He has been conducting research in Mozambique since 1991 and has published numerous articles and book chapters on the relation between the state and the institutions of rural society as well as on sorcery and politics. He is also editor, along with Todd Sanders, of *Transparency and Conspiracy: Ethnographies of Suspicion in the New World Order* (Duke University Press, 2003).

Index